Films for the Colonies

The publisher and the University of California Press Foundation gratefully acknowledge the generous support of the Eric Papenfuse and Catherine Lawrence Endowment Fund in Film and Media Studies.

Films for the Colonies

*Cinema and the Preservation of
the British Empire*

Tom Rice

UNIVERSITY OF CALIFORNIA PRESS

University of California Press, one of the most
distinguished university presses in the United States,
enriches lives around the world by advancing scholarship
in the humanities, social sciences, and natural sciences. Its
activities are supported by the UC Press Foundation and
by philanthropic contributions from individuals and
institutions. For more information, visit www.ucpress.edu.

University of California Press
Oakland, California

© 2019 by Tom Rice

Library of Congress Cataloging-in-Publication Data

Names: Rice, Tom, 1979- author.
Title: Films for the colonies : cinema and the preservation
   of the British Empire / Tom Rice.
Description: Oakland, California : University of
   California Press, [2019] | Includes bibliographical
   references and index. |
Identifiers: LCCN 2019001394 (print) |
   LCCN 2019004370 (ebook) | ISBN 9780520971813
   (Epub) | ISBN 9780520300385 (cloth : alk. paper) |
   ISBN 9780520300392 (pbk. : alk. paper)
Subjects: LCSH: Motion pictures—Great Britain—20th
   century—History. | Great Britain—Colonies—In
   motion pictures. | Great Britain. Colonial Film
   Unit—History. | Motion pictures—Social aspects—
   20th century.
Classification: LCC PN1993.5.G7 (ebook) |
   LCC PN1993.5.G7 R45 2019 (print) |
   DDC 791.430942—dc23
LC record available at https://lccn.loc.gov/2019001394

28 27 26 25 24 23 22 21 20 19
10 9 8 7 6 5 4 3 2 1

Contents

List of Illustrations	vii
Acknowledgments	ix
Accessing Digitized Materials	xiii
Timeline	xv
Introduction	1
1. Beginnings: The Interwar Movement of Nonfiction Film	13
2. Film Rules: The Governing Principles of the Colonial Film Unit	60
3. Mobilizing an Empire: The Colonial Film Unit in a State of War	106
4. Moving Overseas: "Films *for* Africans, *with* Africans, *by* Africans"	149
5. Handover: Local Units through the End of Empire	194
Notes	245
Selected Bibliography	297
Index	317

Illustrations

0.1. "A Peep into the Future," *Colonial Cinema*, December 1954. / 3
1.1. A poster advertising the British Empire Exhibition, 1924. / 21
1.2. An advertisement for "The Empire" series in *Kinematograph Weekly*, February 1927. / 22
1.3a and
1.3b. Titles from *Black Cotton* (1927). / 23
1.4. An advertisement for *One Family* (1930) in *Fortune*, 1930. / 26
1.5. The mobile unit in trouble in Tanganyika. / 38
1.6. Filming as part of the Bantu Education Kinema Experiment. / 40
1.7. Rebuilding the town in *Anti-Plague Operations, Lagos, 1937*. / 49
1.8. William Sellers's mobile cinema van used for Lagos Health Week. / 49
2.1. The front cover of *Colonial Cinema*, June 1951. / 68
2.2. "Leslie Meets Lesaoama," *The Times*, November 1947. / 76
2.3. George Pearson at his desk in Soho Square. / 79
2.4. William Sellers's sample film program, *Colonial Cinema*, December 1951. / 85
2.5. A commentator with the mobile cinema van in Tsame in Trans-Volta Togoland. / 86
2.6. Crowds gather as the cinema van arrives in the Gold Coast, 1954. / 92

2.7. Film show at Dodowa, Gold Coast, 1951. / *95*
2.8. A crowd of 1,200 watching a government mobile film show in Barbados. / *101*
2.9. Crowds gathering at Dodowa, Gold Coast, 1951. / *101*
3.1. A mobile cinema preparing to cross the river Niger. / *109*
3.2. "*Springtime in an English Village*," *Colonial Cinema*, July 1944. / *141*
3.3. On the set of *An African in England*. / *143*
3.4. The Colonial Film Unit filming colonial troops in London, 1946. / *146*
4.1. The Colonial Film Unit filming in West Africa, 1946. / *153*
4.2. Staff at the Colonial Film Unit. / *155*
4.3. and
4.4. The Colonial Film Unit filming in the Gambia, 1948. / *156*
4.5. The agenda for "The Film in Colonial Development" conference held in London, January 1948. / *174*
4.6. The Oni of Ife watching films at the CFU offices in London. / *177*
4.7. Nigerian trainees learning the technical aspects of film production. / *184*
4.8. Nigerian trainees behind the camera. / *187*
4.9. Reporting on the West Indian film training school, *Colonial Cinema*, 1950. / *190*
4.10. The Trinidad Film Unit working on its first film, *Cocoa Rehabilitation* (1951). / *191*
5.1. Discussion around a screening of *Amenu's Child* (1950). / *201*
5.2. Production still from *Mr. Mensah Builds a House* (1955). / *203*
5.3. Filming on *Mr. Mensah Builds a House* (1955). / *204*
5.4. On set with the Gold Coast Film Unit, 1956. / *204*
5.5. Staff at work for the Gold Coast Film Unit, 1956. / *205*
5.6. The cover of *Colonial Cinema*, March 1953. / *217*
5.7. An advertisement for the premiere of *Princess Margaret Visits Jamaica* (1955). / *226*
5.8. R. O. Fenuku bids farewell to George Noble in Ghana, 1958. / *238*

Acknowledgments

Although I did not know it then, my research for this book began in 2007 when I started working as a postdoctoral researcher on a project on colonial film. For three years I watched countless films at the British Film Institute and Imperial War Museum—films on hookworm, newsreels from India, missionary films, war rushes from Burma, educational and instructional shorts for audiences in Britain and the British colonies—and wrote on more than two hundred of these films for the project's website (www.colonialfilm.org.uk). I would like to acknowledge and thank the Arts and Humanities Research Council who funded the project.

As well as gaining access to a (largely) fascinating collection of films and materials through the project, I had the opportunity to workshop ideas, and to work with and learn from some fantastic people. I am particularly indebted to the project directors, Colin MacCabe and Lee Grieveson, an inspiring and hugely entertaining double act, who have continued to support my work, challenge my ideas, and make me laugh. Lee's influence runs throughout the work, as an astute reader, editor, advisor, and distraction. Most of all, he has been a good friend.

The project would not have been as interesting or enjoyable without my fellow postdoctoral researchers, Francis Gooding, Richard Osborne, and Annamaria Motrescu, all of whom helped me in various ways. I am very grateful for the generous support and continued encouragement of Emma Sandon, who advised on the project. Staff at the BFI and IWM were unfailingly helpful, even when they had plenty of other things to be doing (aside from trying to find me desk space or arrange viewings). Even after the project finished, they have continued to answer questions, provide materials (including digitizing the entire run of the Colonial Film Unit's in-house journal, *Colonial Cinema*, which helped my research immeasurably), and generally go above and beyond. I cannot name them all here, but special thanks to Patrick Russell and Nigel Algar at the BFI and to Kay Gladstone at IWM. I have learned a huge amount from them all. It was always an absolute pleasure to work with Kay at the IWM, while Patrick's sharp insights on all things nonfiction have continued to shape the book.

The book is reliant on extensive archival research. Away from the BFI and IWM, I am hugely grateful to James Kearney and the AP Archive for generously providing me with access to many additional films. Thanks also to the brilliant Karl Magee at the Grierson Archive at University of Stirling, to the Bristol Museum and BECTU for supplying interview materials, and to those at the British Library, National Library of Scotland, SOAS, Institute of Commonwealth Studies, and National Archives who have helped me on-site with my (many) requests. I am also grateful to those who have answered research questions from a distance, such as Jonathan Stubbs with information on Cyprus and Liam Buckley on the Gambia. Many other archives have provided information and materials remotely, including Rosa Wong Sang at the National Archives of Trinidad and Tobago and Stephanie Schembri at the National Archives of Malta.

The research and ideas within the book have accumulated over many years, through conferences, email exchanges, and discussions. My colleagues at St. Andrews all get top marks, but I am especially grateful to those friends who have occupied the office next to me over the past seven years—Josh Yumibe, Brian Jacobson, and Lucy Donaldson—for their friendship, good humor, and willingness to listen to my ideas without glazing over. Brian has also read various parts of this work and always asks the right questions. I am also very grateful to Karen Drysdale, Mike Arrowsmith, Michael Cowan, Leshu Torchin, and Robert Burgoyne, who have helped in various ways, and to our brilliant students at St. Andrews. Thanks are also due to those who have invited me to speak at conferences around the world, including Ravi Vasudevan, Madhava Prasad, Vinzenz Hediger, and Ian Aitken. Among the many friends and colleagues who have patiently listened to my work or generously shared materials, I would like to thank Scott Anthony, Martin Stollery, James Burns, Jae Maingard, John Izod, and Jennifer Blaylock. I would also like to acknowledge the pioneering work of Rosaleen

Smyth, David Giltrow, and Peggy Giltrow, who have not only undertaken superb work on the Colonial Film Unit but also helped to ensure that many of the films and materials are available to researchers today.

This book would not have been written without the generous support of the Leverhulme Trust, and indeed the book was largely written during my research fellowship. During the fellowship, I traveled to Ghana and Jamaica and am enormously grateful to all who helped me on these trips. I spent a very productive period at the Ghana National Archives and at the Information Services Department, where I also located some of the images for the book. In Jamaica, I carried out research in the National Archives, the National Library, and at the University of the West Indies, working through government reports, unpublished autobiographies, and a fascinating batch of films produced by the Jamaica Film Unit in the 1950s. Problems with the headphones meant that I had to play the final film through loudspeakers (twice) for all in the library to hear—not ideal, as the film happened to be an all-too-detailed instructional film on the perils of venereal disease. To those in the library that day, I apologize and present this book by way of an explanation. I am extremely grateful to all who helped me during these trips, in particular Rachel Moseley-Wood and Suzanne Francis-Brown.

I have also conducted a number of interviews with those connected with the Colonial Film Unit, who have been uniformly generous and an absolute pleasure to speak to. In particular I would like to thank Sean Graham, Sydney Samuelson, Bill Williams, John Jochimsen, and Dennis Bowden (who also provided me with some extremely useful materials). I am also very happy to acknowledge those who helped with the images, particularly the IWM, National Archives, BFI, and Information Services Department, Ghana.

The book has evolved over time and incorporates and reworks some material that I have previously published in journals and edited collections. In particular, chapter 2 includes work originally published as "'Are You Proud to be British?' Mobile Film Shows, Local Voices and the Demise of the British Empire in Africa," *Historical Journal of Film, Radio and Television* 36, no. 3 (2016): 331–51. Parts of chapter 1 appear as "One Family: The Movement of Educational Film in Britain and Its Empire," in *The Institutionalization of Educational Cinema: North America and Europe in the 1910s and 1920s*, edited by Joel Frykholm and Marina Dahlquist (Bloomington: Indiana University Press, 2019). I am grateful to the editors and readers who have helped improve and direct my work over the course of this project. More recently, the book has been shaped, and significantly improved, by the brilliant team at University of California Press. My thanks to Paul Tyler, Madison Wetzell, Emilia Thiuri, Cynthia Savage (for her work on the index) and, in particular, Raina Polivka for making the whole process not only painless but also thoroughly enjoyable. I owe a huge debt of gratitude to my readers, step forward Priya Jaikumar and Peter Bloom, scholars whose work I have long admired and who offered encouragement and constructive criticism in equal measure. Their suggestions (and Lee's) were always close at hand as I reworked the manuscript and the book is markedly stronger for their input.

Finally, I would like to thank my friends and family. I won't name them all (although I probably could) but, as always, I am indebted to my Mum and Dad. Alex, Chessie, Lizzie (and all at Nananter), Carl, and Caryl deserve more than name-checks, but this will have to do. Most of all, this book is for my favorite people: Suzie, Lottie, and Ernest. With thanks, love, and the promise of many more adventures.

Accessing Digitized Materials

To find links to a wide range of online, digitized materials, including films, archival documents, and articles that are directly referenced in this book, visit https://films-for-the-colonies.wp.st-andrews.ac.uk.

Timeline

1924   Opening of the British Empire Exhibition, Wembley.

1926   William Sellers moves to Nigeria as a sanitary inspector.

The formation of the Empire Marketing Board (John Grierson would head its film unit from 1927).

1929   William Sellers makes his first health films in Nigeria.

Julian Huxley travels to East Africa, examining African audiences' responses to film.

1933   The closure of the Empire Marketing Board.

1935   William Sellers receives funding to set up a Health Propaganda Unit in Nigeria.

The Bantu Educational Kinema Experiment (BEKE) begins its first tour of East Africa, producing and exhibiting thirty-five films over the next two years.

1939   What would become the Colonial Film Unit (CFU) is established in October, shortly after Britain declares war on Germany.

1940   The CFU completes its first film, *Mr. English at Home*.

1941   William Sellers publishes his doctrine for the CFU, "Films for Primitive Peoples," in *Documentary News Letter*.

The CFU launches the Raw Stock Scheme (first sending equipment out in early 1942).

- 1942 In November the CFU publishes the first issue of its monthly magazine (later quarterly), *Colonial Cinema*.
- 1945 After the end of the Second World War, the CFU becomes part of the Central Office of Information (COI).
- 1946 The CFU sends film units overseas, the first to West Africa in January.

  Establishment of the Malayan Film Unit.
- 1948 The British Film Institute hosts the one-day conference, "The Film in Colonial Development," in January.

  The CFU launches its first overseas training school, which starts in Accra, Gold Coast, in September.
- 1949 The Gold Coast Film Unit and the Nigerian Film Unit are formed.
- 1950 The West Indies film training school starts in Jamaica, leading to local units (most notably the Jamaica Film Unit) across the region.

  The CFU is scaled down significantly with its budget and staff severely cut. This includes the closure of its "Home Unit" in London.
- 1952 The Gold Coast Film Unit produces a full-length feature film, *The Boy Kumasenu*.

  Anthropologist Peter Morton-Williams travels to Nigeria to undertake a major survey on African audiences for the CFU.
- 1954 *Colonial Cinema* ceases production.

  The Overseas Film and Television Centre is set up, taking on much of the CFU's postproduction and advisory work from London.
- 1955 The CFU closes its doors for the last time.
- 1957 The Gold Coast (Ghana) and Malaya (Malaysia) secure independence from the British Empire.
- 1962 Local units record independence in Jamaica, Trinidad and Tobago, and Uganda, as further countries celebrate independence during the decade.

Introduction

On May 31st, 1955, I stood with Hugh Davison to close the doors for the last time on empty rooms that had ceased to care.[1]

In describing the closure of the Colonial Film Unit (CFU) in 1955, George Pearson presents the unit as the victim of seismic political shifts; a unit disbanded and broken up like the empire it had served; a unit now out of step, unwanted, and soon to be forgotten. For 80-year-old Pearson, a celebrated pioneer of British silent cinema who had spent the previous fifteen years making films that sought to promote, preserve, and redefine the British Empire for colonial audiences, this seemingly represented a point of no return; the work of the CFU now to be discarded or deemed superfluous as moves toward mass decolonization gathered pace.

From its establishment at the outbreak of war in 1939 to its disbandment on the cusp of political independence, the CFU had deployed particular technologies, practices, ideas, and forms to foster imperialism and to sustain the British Empire. The CFU represents a significant state effort to use film and media to shape Britain's global empire, as it spoke directly to colonial audiences, producing and exhibiting films specifically for the colonies. Its work here was extensive and varied. The CFU produced more than two hundred short films, which were widely exhibited throughout the British Empire. These films, often short instructional pictures showing Africans visiting London, weaving methods in the Gold Coast, or the perils of tuberculosis, employed specific filmic practices based on reductive assumptions about the cognitive capabilities of African audiences, which often precluded the use of close-ups, cross-cutting, short scenes, and excessive movement within the frame. In this way, the CFU projected a colonial ideology through its film form that both justified its own existence and foregrounded the intellectual primacy of the British colonizer. Film was imagined here as an integral part of the colonizing process, speaking directly to colonial audiences often beyond the reach of existing government propaganda. To this end, the CFU established networks for the distribution and exhibition of film across the colonies (most notably by mobile cinema vans), one part of an emerging media infrastructure within the colonies.

The CFU ran training schools, conducted audience surveys, and published a quarterly magazine (*Colonial Cinema,* 1942–54), which sought to direct and disseminate the pedagogical use of film across a disparate, increasingly fractured empire. The unit evolved and responded to political shifts, as cinema was deployed in the service of an imperialism that was both territorial and economic. Initially established to mobilize colonial support for war, the CFU later prioritized welfare and development within the postwar colonies and finally prepared the ground for independence. Indeed, as independence moved ever closer in the postwar era, the CFU helped set up a series of local units—most notably in West Africa and the Caribbean—many of which would continue beyond independence. These units, a complex hybrid of liberal imperialism and local personnel and traditions, would both shape postcolonial cinemas and help to manage and mediate the moves from colonial to independent state.

In this way, the closure of the CFU in 1955 should not be considered an "end," as the work of the CFU helped promote ongoing economic "partnership" and also formalized practices and institutions that would extend well beyond independence. George Pearson hinted at this in the final edition of *Colonial Cinema* in December 1954. Pearson addressed those students—which he said numbered more than a hundred from thirty overseas territories—who had attended instruction with him at the CFU's offices in Soho Square, London. "The good work must go on," he wrote. "From your own people you must find new disciples." This message was visualized on the magazine's front cover, which showed an African looking through a camera. The editorial suggested that this might be "very aptly" entitled "A Peep into the Future" (see Figure 0.1).[2]

Looking through the lens of the Colonial Film Unit provides a fresh historical perspective on both the emergence of global film cultures and the last decades of the British Empire; a history told not simply through

FIGURE O.1. "A Peep into the Future," the front cover of the final issue of *Colonial Cinema*, December 1954.

the films and their exhibition, but also through the policies, administration, and shifting priorities of government filmmaking. Film records, responds to, and negotiates what Paul Gilroy has described as "the slow, fractious blood-soaked decomposition of the British Empire."[3] One of the many ironies here might be that an institution created to administer and maintain an empire through film should also serve as an exemplary study of the empire's dissolution. However, while at first glance the CFU's own decline ran parallel to the empire it served, the CFU also worked to redefine imperial power to colonial audiences. To this end, the British state produced (invariably cheap) media for colonial audiences to help transact a shift from empire to one of development and "commonwealth," from territorial to economic imperialism. In doing so they used media as a form of biopolitics to foster the utility of a laboring population. These government fantasies, which played through traveling units on new imperial networks, projected models of industry and citizenship that helped to establish new social and, in particular, economic relationships between London and the colonies. Whether showing visiting Africans learning from British workers in a car factory in Coventry in 1948 or the visit of Princess Margaret to Jamaica in 1955, these films both preserved and articulated these new relationships to colonial audiences.

This book (and the media discussed within it) is then not simply reporting on the decline of the British Empire, but also recognizing its endurance, highlighting how the CFU helped to preserve, "remake," and—through the units it worked to establish—enact new models of empire that often continue to this day. Building on the recent scholarship of media historian Lee Grieveson, the book highlights the ways in which the CFU's organizational model, content (regarding hygiene, conduct, and economic practices), and mode of delivery (mobile exhibition) helped to transform formally controlled colonies into intra-imperial trade blocks. The CFU created and adapted an imperial network similar to other networks of trade—one routed through the imperial center in London—and, as Brian Larkin shows in the context of Nigeria, facilitated the trafficking of people, products (including film), and ideas over a vast territorial space.[4] The CFU was hardly alone here but rather intersected with other prominent state, media, and administrative organizations, which were producing and projecting information across the world through new forms of media, such as the British Broadcasting Corporation (BBC), British Council, and UNESCO, as one prominent (and critically overlooked) part of twentieth-century imperial administration. These citizen-building organizations often operated in tandem. However, they deviated significantly in their understanding both of what a decline in territorial power would mean to a geopolitically powerful nation-state such as Britain and of how best to respond to these shifts through media. The CFU became an interlocutor within this debate.

The CFU itself remains something of a critical pariah, often consigned to the footnotes, unloved and unwanted as Pearson acknowledged, and invariably ridiculed by other "professional" documentary filmmakers. In challenging this view, this first book-length study of the CFU provides a revisionist history of British and global cinema. While there is no shortage of critical writing on John Grierson and the celebrated British Documentary Movement, this book reveals another path that runs counter to, but intersects with, the more familiar British documentary history. This instructional, educational, "useful" cinema, run by administrators, teachers, and civil servants, forms an integral aspect of British cinema, one that is too often obfuscated by a focus on prestige documentary and the feature film. Indeed, this cinema, deployed as one part of government administration, remains somewhat marginalized within a film history that privileges a narrative form of documentary and bases value judgments primarily on aesthetics. Such a history celebrates filmmakers like John Grierson often at the expense of department officials and subject experts, who apply their expertise to film. While Grierson features across these pages—and indeed recent scholarship, such as Zoe Druick and Deane Williams's *The Grierson Effect,* has helpfully foregrounded Grierson's "engagement with colonial and nationalist formations across the globe"—the central figure within this book is William Sellers, the producer for the Colonial Film Unit. Sellers initially worked as a sanitary inspector in Nigeria, and what we see with the CFU is an organization working with, and run by, disciplinary experts whether in health, education, or agriculture.[5] Furthermore, in recasting the CFU not only as a British institution but, in the vein of cinema historian Priya Jaikumar, as a node in the nexus between empire and colonies, the book positions the colonies at the center rather than the margins of British cinema history.[6]

As a corrective to traditional documentary and British film histories, this book examines the emergence of government filmmaking, nontheatrical exhibition, and wider film culture across the globe, from Ghana to Jamaica, from Malta to Malaya. The work, of course, engages directly with scholarship on colonial cinema, in particular that emerging from the Colonial Film project (on which I worked), a collaboration with the British Film Institute and Imperial War Museum that made many of these colonial films freely available online.[7] Yet for cinema and media historians, the book also contributes more broadly to the recent wave of scholarship on what Charles R. Acland and Haidee Wasson labeled "useful" cinema, a term that can incorporate, as this book does, work on nontheatrical exhibition, educational, industrial, and instructional film but moves beyond a specific focus on production or exhibition to consider a broader "approach toward a medium on the part of institutions and institutional agents."[8] My focus is on this wider deployment of cinema, and indeed its *usefulness,* for an empire in decline. The CFU often inexpertly (albeit through an army of experts) formulated ways to shore up imperial power, not only through film, but through other means, such as its organization of the film space, through talks and demonstrations or through its training programs. In exploring the CFU's institutional genealogy, the book uncovers the longer history of this pedagogical cinema for the colonies, which stretches from the earliest health films screened by mobile units in Nigeria and Kenya in the late 1920s to the work of local government film units into the 1960s, recording and circulating the carefully staged moments of independence whether in Barbados or Uganda.

One of the aspects that makes the CFU so compelling as a case study is that it often appears remarkably unremarkable, at points defined by dogmatic repetition (in their films, writing, and actions), by petty disputes and endless negotiation. This is a story as much of failure as success, of countless unmade films, broken technology, and unreliable commentators, of idealism giving way to pragmatism, of plans discussed ad nauseum in the corridors of London that were then ignored or overlooked in the villages of Nigeria. What is more, the films themselves are often most interesting for what they do not show, for what lies conspicuously absent outside the frame. As one example of many, the Crown Film Unit's 1950 survey of the empire, *Spotlight on the Colonies,* makes absolutely no mention of recently independent India. The commentary does acknowledge that "the colonies have long had their difficulties," but presents only "natural" problems, such as disease and drought, and unsurprisingly makes no mention of the social unrest or mismanagement attributed to the rise of nationalist movements.[9] Although this is not a CFU film—it uses CFU footage but was produced primarily for British audiences by Crown, the in-house government unit—it reminds us that these films are often works of obstruction, smoke screens that reveal as much through what they conceal.

This expansive history, examining the role of film in the governance of the British Empire, is told through an array of archival materials, incorporating previously unaccessed films, images, audio files, and written materials. These include films from the CFU, its local offshoots and related units, official CFU and government papers, personal interviews with filmmakers, newspapers and journals, audience reports, unpublished autobiographies, and personal papers. Many of these materials are housed in London—most notably at the National Archives, the British Film Institute, the Imperial War Museum, and the Associated Press archives—a testament to the ways in which these government films and papers circulated through, and rested at, the imperial center. Records from the center are essential to this history, but they tell only part of the story. In exploring other archives, in former colonized spaces, such as Jamaica and Ghana, I attempt to uncover missing voices and perspectives. For ease and consistency—especially when working and quoting directly from archival sources—I have adopted the place names of the time (for example, I refer to the Gold Coast until 1957 and Ghana after this date).

The scope of this study is broad, encompassing parts of Africa (particularly West Africa), Asia (especially Malaya), the West Indies, and

Europe. Other imperial territories, notably the unique space of India and the white settler dominions, were beyond the remit of the CFU and so remain on the edges of this study. The book does, however, supplement existing studies of other governmental units—such as historian James Burns's work on the Central African Film Unit and Ian Aitken's recent study of postwar government filmmaking in Hong Kong—to build a fuller picture of the place and function of film across the British Empire.[10] Similarly, the book's focus on governmental uses of cinema foregrounds forms of documentary and educational cinema. Commercial, fiction cinema is not central to my history, even if it at times informed and shaped governmental discourses about empire.

These archival records not only allow us to reexamine the colonial past but also to understand its shaping of the "postcolonial" present. While this book addresses a particular historical period up to the 1960s, this history resonates as strongly as ever today. The corrosive effects of colonialism continue to shape postcolonial states, both internally (for example, through violent conflicts borne out of the redrawn borders that often artificially divided ethnic groups) and on an international stage (for example, through the exploitation of natural resources, and unequal economic relationships needed to sustain accelerated globalization). In revisiting these earliest films for colonial audiences, we see how the CFU sought to conceal or reframe the destructive impact of colonialism by promoting modernization projects, welfare schemes, and more broadly the biopolitical shaping of colonial labor to perpetuate an ongoing form of economic imperialism. Indeed, while the CFU might be largely forgotten today—and in many cases its films have decomposed—this pedagogic media helped to maintain often-enduring imperial power structures through the creation and circulation of film.

It is, therefore, essential to revisit and confront this history, to bring it into view, particularly as the end of empire remains such a contested and unresolved moment in British history. Two recent incidents exemplify this. First, in 2013 the British government paid compensation to Kenyan survivors, whom they now acknowledged had suffered "torture and other forms of ill-treatment" at the hands of the British colonial administration in the Mau Mau uprising in British Kenya in the 1950s. While again bringing into focus the devastating, violent impact of colonialism in the former colonies, it also reveals the historic processes of denial and myth-making, in which this media was often complicit. In the legal process for this case, "migrated archives"—Foreign and Commonwealth Office materials that had been concealed and thought lost—were brought into view and revealed both the extent of this systemic abuse and also, given that many other files remain "lost," the partial histories contained within the official record.[11] I noted earlier that the official record is only ever a partial one. This is one concrete example of that. Second, the recent "Rhodes Must Fall" campaign, which originally targeted a statue of Cecil Rhodes at the University of Cape Town, exposes both the unresolved legacies of the colonial era and the enduring power of its imagery. In seeking to challenge and remove symbols of Britain's imperial past as part of a move to "decolonize" education, the campaign presented these visuals as evidence of the wider imperial structures that remain in place.[12] While these campaigns might invite a reexamination of Britain's imperial past, paradoxically they run the risk of removing these contentious histories from view. The empire continues to pervade modern British life—defining the nation's very recent history and dictating what the nation is today—but it does so from the shadows, largely exorcised from national memory. Indeed, it remains barely a footnote in a school curriculum that favors "victory" narratives of war, of underdogs fighting for freedom, of social progression and national heritage.

Britain's failure to acknowledge and think through its loss of empire also continues to shape its outlook and position on the global stage. This is played out through Britain's recent involvement in foreign, neocolonial wars, replayed in territories like Iraq that were already fought over a century earlier in previous moments of imperialism. These wars are fought for a control of space, for the movement of materials and resources, and to perpetuate a modern economic imperialism. The wars are also, of course, fought to retain Britain's geopolitical role and remain tied up in discourses around Britain's place and role within the world. While postcolonial states have often struggled with these complex legacies, at times through civil war and through the looting of resources by corporations and dictators, Britain too continues to be shaped by its imperial past. The issues of the day, such as immigration, are direct products of the late colonial period, a modern nation formed in this moment, and are buttressed by evolving forms of populist nationalism that are themselves founded on ideas of racial and ethnic difference. More specifically, the legacies of empire infiltrate the recent discussions around Brexit. The "patriotic" calls to "reclaim" British sovereignty were fueled by an imperial nostalgia, by a desire to turn the clock back, whether imagining trade links with Commonwealth countries—reportedly dubbed Empire 2.0 by some government officials—or posturing as a global superpower.[13] This response is nothing new. At times of social and economic crisis, we often see what Paul Gilroy characterizes as a "postcolonial melancholia," a desire to return to past "glories."[14] Of course, this demands a voluntary amnesia and a level of historical illiteracy, privileging a particular memory of empire—tea-drinking, railway-building, cricket-playing, and keeping calm and carrying on—which was partly constructed and perpetuated in the films and media examined in this book.

Crucially, this national failure to confront the end of empire begins in the period of this study as the CFU seeks to mediate and conceal this loss, to retain a level of (particularly economic) influence across these territories. While these films were at first about governing the empire, over time they often mutated into a more elaborate game of hide and seek, concealing its dissolution. This concealing—through visualizing—is foundational for the current complex conjuncture of "Great Britain" as it fragments and withdraws from Europe. What we see through the CFU films is a government attempt to stage-manage the "end," to remove violence and injustices, to replace pleasure with responsibility, to ignore what is lost in a bid to celebrate what is gained; a new "partnership" and a continuity beyond independence.

Similarly, film historians have too often neglected to examine the colonial antecedents in modern cinema cultures across the world. Whether appropriating colonial structures or directly rejecting them, these national cinemas did not begin at independence, but are products of this late colonial period. When outlining the work of the mobile cinema vans during the war, the public relations officer in the Gold Coast explained that more than boosting morale during the war, "probably their greater claim to fame is that they have introduced the cinema to every part of the Gold Coast."[15] The point here is that the work of the Colonial Film Unit, some of the earliest organized forays into film by British and colonial governments, shapes both state media today and attitudes and responses to the most pressing contemporary issues.

. . .

The book's narrative begins in interwar Britain, but it is important to acknowledge very briefly here the longer history that informs the initiation, and later institutionalization, of film practices within the colonies. In short, film has always served as both a record and agent of empire, bringing the colonies to Britain and projecting British primacy and ideals back to the colonies.[16] I contend that from the outset, film *is* colonial film, and histories of British cinema are equally histories of colonial (and world) cinema. The earliest films from the late Victorian period visualized imperial power and established the hierarchical structures (in their framing and camera position) between the colonizers and the colonized that continue throughout the period of this study. Film privileged the colonizer, those figures with power and authority and access to the camera, projecting their point of view and highlighting their primacy over the objects they depict.

These early films also highlight the early movement of film across trade routes and through the latest imperial networks. This movement of film transformed the ways in which colonial rule was administered, connecting and transporting the rulers of the empire into hitherto unreached colonial lands. What we see then in the late Victorian period is not only that film can represent the empire—through historical moments, attitudes, and places—and conceal or contain particular voices and histories, but also that even then it served as a tool for colonialism, moving goods, people, and ideas throughout the empire. Whether sponsored by state, religious, or commercial interests, film was part of the colonizing process, taking the camera and technology into distant lands and using film to reach these foreign audiences.

These early films do not, however, attempt to address directly the non-European audiences within the colonies or to reach beyond the urban centers. It was not until the 1920s that nonfiction film—whether "documentary" film in Britain, educational film for schools, or instructional films specifically for colonial audiences—started to be worked through and institutionalized by the British state. This development is examined in chapter 1, which explores the earliest attempts to use films to inform, educate, and inculcate colonial citizens. In tracing the prehistory of the CFU, the chapter reveals the origins of filmmaking in Africa. It foregrounds the role of film in colonial administration and, in particular, examines William Sellers's work with the health department in Nigeria. Sellers's work here begins at a crucial moment when the health of colonial subjects is seen to undergird, and is equated to, the fiscal health of the empire.

William Sellers takes center stage in chapter 2. While the book is largely organized chronologically, chapter 2 more broadly explores the ideologies and operating practices of the CFU throughout its fifteen-year history. This history is told largely through the writings of Sellers, whose influential theories on colonial spectatorship were based on, and reinforced, racial and cultural assumptions about African audiences. In proposing his "specialised technique," Sellers sought to define and create a distinctly "colonial" cinema. The chapter also explores Sellers's innovative attempts to organize and standardize film exhibition across the empire, imagining cinema in the colonies as a means of producing and managing modern colonial citizens. In examining the CFU's attempts to standardize and control the deployment of film across the colonies, the chapter reveals the wider challenges for the CFU, whether uncovering pockets of local resistance or, most notably, the rise of an often unregulated local voice—the commentator or interpreter traveling with the film—within this cinema.

The third chapter considers the CFU during the Second World War, a moment when the CFU's future and function was as uncertain as the empire it represented. A war that brought together an empire, its people and products, would ultimately tear it apart, exposing the ideological principles on which the empire was founded. The fictions of colonialism, projected and protected by the CFU, were now somewhat punctured and exposed by this fight for "freedom." Throughout this period, the CFU becomes something of a battleground, fought over by the Ministry of Information and the Colonial Office, by government administrators in London and information officers within the colonies, and at stake here is the future direction of the British Empire. The chapter analyzes CFU films (and the often volatile discourses around them), whether produced in the UK or the colonies, whether addressing war or imagining a life beyond, and highlights the wider media infrastructures forming across the empire at this moment. It positions the CFU within the context of this wider media, including filmstrips and BBC radio broadcasts, and alongside other film producers, including the celebrated Crown Film Unit and the considerably less celebrated British Council, as the CFU sought to mobilize an imperial army and workforce for war.

The final two chapters examine the seismic social, political, and economic changes, which are played out both on, and through, film after the war. When Winston Churchill spoke in the House of Commons on 18 June 1940 of what he described as the "Battle of Britain," he warned that upon this impending battle "depends our own life and the long continuity of our institutions and our Empire." Concluding his address, he famously exclaimed that "if the British Commonwealth and Empire lasts for a thousand years men will still say, 'This was their finest hour'."[17] Of course, despite withstanding the German invasion and ultimately securing victory in war, the empire would barely make it out of the decade, broken up and splintered as new anthems, flags, and constitutions were created over the next quarter century.

In the aftermath of war, with a Labour administration propagating new models of economic partnership, amidst public and political debate over the function, morality, and *value* of a postwar empire, the CFU moved increasingly into the colonies, promoting welfare and development programs. Chapter 4 examines this postwar movement—of film equipment and personnel—from London to the colonies. In January 1948, the British Film Institute (BFI) hosted a conference entitled "The Film in Colonial Development" in which its European participants outlined the need to "teach the people of the Colonies to run the show themselves."[18] At this same moment, the CFU set up its first ten-month training school in Accra (there would be subsequent schools in Jamaica and Cyprus), training a (first) generation of local filmmakers. These schools, closely examined here, would provide the personnel and equipment for the local units that began to emerge from the end of the decade.

The local units, most notably in Nigeria, the Gold Coast, Jamaica, and Trinidad, are the subject of chapter 5. In analyzing their films and practices, the chapter reveals the different media responses across the colonies. For example, while the Nigerian Film Unit largely endorsed the Sellers doctrine, the neighboring Gold Coast Film Unit more closely followed a Griersonian model, producing ambitious and entertaining fictionalized tales promoting maternity care, government housing schemes, or taxation policy. In negotiating central and local influences, these units navigate and embody moves toward self-government. Looking closely at films of independence ceremonies shows how this particular moment (the move from colonial to independent state) was articulated on film. In analyzing the continuities, as well as the ruptures, that mark the very moment of the postcolonial, we can start to examine the legacies and influences of colonial film on the cinema cultures of today.

The CFU that emerges through these pages represents, in part, a microcosm of empire, indicative of the British government's attempts to contain and manage a social, economic, and political body splintering under the pressure of world events. It is also a significant part of British and global cinema, illuminating the development of nonfiction, "useful" cinema and, more broadly, of state media across the mid-twentieth century. For now, the story returns to the beginning, to the first movements of William Sellers and John Grierson, to the development of cinema of, and for, the British Empire.

CHAPTER 1

Beginnings: The Interwar Movement of Nonfiction Film

On 14 April 1926, William Sellers set sail from Liverpool to Lagos to start work as a Grade II sanitary inspector in Nigeria. Born and raised in Bury, Manchester, 28-year-old Sellers would immediately find himself confronting a severe outbreak of plague. "Before I had time to unpack my boxes," Sellers explained, "I was handed a hypodermic syringe and many bottles and anti-plague vaccine." He inoculated more than six hundred people on his first day, but soon recognized that more needed to be done to explain the causes, methods, and measures required to control the spread of plague. For this, Sellers turned first to lantern slides and, by 1929, to film: "I recruited an enthusiastic team of Africans and then, using exhibits, films, film-strips, wall stencil posters and other visual aids, the life history of plague, and the reasons how as well as why, were clearly explained."[1]

Sellers recounted these early days in Nigeria almost thirty years later in April 1955 at his presidential address at the Royal Sanitary Institute's annual Health Congress in Bournemouth, England. By this stage Sellers had enjoyed a long and successful career in the colonial service, formalizing his initial forays into film by establishing the Health Propaganda Unit in Nigeria in 1935, and then in October 1939 taking up the role of producer at the newly established Colonial Film Unit in Soho Square, London. Over a thirty-year career, which was recognized with honors from the King and Queen, Sellers had witnessed and, through film, helped administer a rapidly changing empire, across war, civil unrest, and impending political independence. His speech at the Bournemouth Health Congress marked a point of reflection both for 57-year-old William Sellers and the empire he had served.[2] A month later, with the moves toward political independence gathering inexorable momentum, the CFU closed its doors for the final time.

Sellers's career in colonial service runs parallel to that of a much more celebrated figure in British cinema history—John Grierson. Born six months after Sellers, Grierson is now widely championed as the father of "documentary" film (a term he coined in a film review from February 1926).[3] It was during Sellers's first year in Nigeria that Grierson began working for the Empire Marketing Board, the elaborate public relations operation set up in May 1926 to promote imperial trade and garner public support for the Conservative Party's largely unpopular economic tariff system. Through the EMB and subsequently the GPO Film Unit (1933–40) Grierson brought together a group of left-leaning filmmakers (comprising the so-called "British Documentary Movement") and then in 1939, as Sellers was setting up the Colonial Film Unit to project government propaganda initially across Britain's African colonies, Grierson moved overseas to orchestrate wartime propaganda efforts in another territory, establishing the National Film Board of Canada.[4] Both represent efforts at this precise moment to institutionalize film and make it useful for an imperial project that urgently required loyal imperial workers and sought to foster intra-imperial trade.

At the same moment that Grierson began using film to promote imperial trade in Britain, and Sellers to instruct audiences in the colonies, Mary Field, a former teacher, started working on films for schoolchildren. In 1926, she took on the newly created role of educational manager at British Instructional Films (BIF), the leading producer of educational films in the UK. Field was soon editing the celebrated Secrets of Nature (and later Secrets of Life) natural history film series and then during the war set up Children's Entertainment Films (1944–50), educating schoolchildren more broadly in "good citizenship." Having received an MA with a distinction in Imperial History, Field's work was characterized by her interest in the British Empire, bringing the empire alive to children in Britain. Into the 1950s, she would serve as an advisor for Commonwealth countries and for the UNESCO center of films for children. She retired against the backdrop of widespread decolonization in 1960.[5]

These three figures, whose careers would intersect, represent three significant, related strands of nonfiction cinema—documentary film, educational film, and the "specialized" film for colonial audiences—that take shape and formalize in this interwar period. Each strand is defined by, and exists primarily to promote and preserve, the British Empire, whether illustrative or instructive in its approach, and whether playing in British classrooms or through traveling mobile health units in Nigeria. Indeed, the early history of British nonfiction film—told here primarily through failed schemes and instantly forgettable, commercially unsuccessful films—is intrinsically tied to the empire it served. Through the example of a single film, *Black Cotton* (1927), which during the 1920s became a foundational film for all three strands, the chapter explores the beginnings of film for colonial audiences, tracing its genealogy across British nonfiction film through to the establishment of the Colonial Film Unit in 1939.

These three strands of nonfiction share a common goal as each form was used to promote and develop economic productivity across the British Empire. The first, and most familiar, strand concerns documentary cinema. In short, the genesis of documentary film and public relations within Britain was borne out of a desire to promote and propagate imperial economic interests and, in showing the production and movement of products, a revised model of economic partnership between Britain and her empire.[6] Documentary cinema can thus be understood as a product of interwar British imperial politics. To provide some context here, the end of the Great War had marked the territorial apogee of the British Empire, a moment when Britain could claim to govern almost a quarter of the globe. The challenge of maintaining and indeed monetizing this splintering mass of people, lands, and ideologies prompted British and colonial governments increasingly to consider the possibilities of cinema. This was often reactive, an anxious response to the more innovative and effective political cinemas in Russia, to the greater state organization of film in education in Italy, France, and Germany, and, most of all, to the rise of American commercial cinema, which the British state now recognized as a threatening form of cultural imperialism.

By the middle of the 1920s, these discussions were reaching the highest echelons of power. The prime minister, Stanley Baldwin, noted in 1925 the "danger to which we in this country and our Empire subject ourselves if we allow that method of propaganda [film] to be entirely in the hands of foreign countries." For Baldwin the problem was one of advertising, seeing film as a way of restoring "trade and national prosperity." "On the production side I have no fears," he wrote in 1927, ". . . on the selling side we must modernize our methods and make use of the great developments which have taken place recently in the art of advertising."[7] This message was taken up by the Empire Marketing Board (1926–33) and the Conservative Party, which used mobile cinema vans and trains to transport support for British industry and imperial trade across the country.[8]

For his part, John Grierson recognized film's ability to travel (like the products it depicted) across the highways of empire, arguing: "The film can travel as no individual, or troupe or expedition can hope to do, even in this age of whirlwind communication." Grierson was focusing here, as the 1926 Imperial Conference had, on the "particular economy of cinema," by which "the ends of the earth are brought to a cutting bench in Wardour Street" and "the unconverted spiritual and temporal are brought within the range of a director's megaphone."[9] The form that documentary cinema took would differ markedly from the specialized technique employed within the colonies, but there are clear points of comparison here, as both focus on imperial productivity and use modes of mobile exhibition.

Indeed, while the pedagogical possibilities of film were widely acknowledged by the end of the 1920s, the form and place that this cinema would occupy was far less clear. Today Grierson's work has been largely characterized by a more liberal, poetic form of documentary cinema, exemplified by his own *Drifters* (1929), but Grierson and his contemporaries worked extensively with other forms of nonfiction film. It is worth noting that the canonical films of the British Documentary Movement, such as *Drifters* and Basil Wright's *Song of Ceylon* (1934), make up a misleadingly tiny proportion of British nonfiction output in this period. While *Song of Ceylon* is now widely celebrated, there is invariably very little mention of the four short instructional films produced simultaneously from this material for the Ceylon Tea Propaganda Board, which were available nontheatrically through the Empire Film Library.[10] There are a plethora of instructional, nonfiction films, often critically invisible in histories of British documentary, which were imagined as part of British education. This is the second way in which nonfiction film develops in this period, as a pedagogical tool in the classroom and in other nontheatrical settings. This form is very quickly, and somewhat arbitrarily, divorced from documentary film. In the foreword to his seminal 1936 book *Documentary Film,* Paul Rotha explained that he had initially intended to consider cinema as a "factor in modern education," but decided that the "educational movement should be considered separately from the documentary movement." Rotha's construction of these two distinct categories—the "so-called general illustration film" and the "direct teaching, or instructional" film—and his statement that he placed a "higher value" on the former, illustrates a hierarchy in nonfiction cinema, which has largely relegated the classroom or instructional film to a critical wasteland.[11]

However, this form of pedagogy, which was often initiated by amateur film enthusiasts and teachers, was repeatedly occupied with geography, economics, and in particular, the British Empire. It provides a notable precursor to the films produced for the colonies, particularly in its use of amateurs and disciplinary experts, and in positioning film as one part of a wider lesson alongside supplementary materials and lecturers.[12] To take one example, Norman F. Spurr, who joined the newly formed Institute of Amateur Cinematographers in 1933, made a series of silent 16mm educational films in the latter half of the 1930s for organizations including the Cinema Christian Council and the British Camp Fire Girls, while also producing instructional medical films, with catchy titles like *The Both Mechanical Respirator* (1938) and *Modern Aseptic Operating Technique* (1939). A decade later Spurr would become an integral figure with the Colonial Film Unit, producing instructional films across Africa and training colonial filmmakers.[13]

By the late 1920s discussions around educational film in Britain increasingly considered the role of film in the colonies. The eminent geographer James Fairgrieve, who published his influential book *Geography in School* in 1926 and would chair a British Film Institute (BFI) committee on the production of geography films in the 1930s, connected the discussion on film in British classrooms to the "larger educational problem" regarding the teaching of "the native races of the Empire." Fairgrieve complained in 1932 about the existing films shown within the empire—"For good or ill, they [native races] are being educated by films. Many films that they see are positively bad; most of the others are unintelligible or uninteresting"—and now outlined the broader political value of film in "the education of the masses." He suggested that the educational film "might help to save political trouble" within the colonies, supporting his oft-quoted earlier assertion that "the function of geography in school is to train future citizens to imagine accurately the conditions of the great world stage."[14] Fairgrieve's language resonates with Grierson, who emphasized the potential of film in teaching "civics," in effect creating citizens and showing how communities should operate. The use of film within fundamental education would become a critical focus after the war for the Colonial Film Unit and for UNESCO's first director of mass communications, John Grierson, even if their notions of how these films should look and work often differed.

Rosaleen Smyth has recently shown how Grierson, with characteristic opportunism, later aligned the work of the British Documentary Movement to the more "simple" instructional film. In his last interview, Grierson claimed that "the greatest thing of all to me has been the use of film for simple purposes," extolling its value for "health and medicine at the most primitive and primary levels" and within "less privileged countries."[15] Grierson can rival Mick Jagger in the paternity stakes, variously described as the father of documentary, the father of educational film, and the father of television documentary, as each of these narratives preserves and subtly reworks the legacy of the British Documentary Movement to respond to the rising concerns of the time.[16] While attributing this strand of cinema ("simple instructional") to the documentary movement helpfully acknowledges the other, numerous overlooked aspects of its work, it further shades the foundational contributions of those amateurs, subject experts, and government officials who used film within the colonies.

It is this development of film as an instructional tool within the colonies, directly speaking to, and shaping, colonial citizens, that marks the third strand here and the principal focus of this chapter. These discussions again escalate in the second half of the 1920s. The Imperial Education Conference of 1927 discussed the "use of the cinema as an aid to increasing knowledge" not only of the empire in Britain but, equally significantly, of Britain across the empire. In the same year, the Colonial Office Conference considered film's place within the colonies, particularly regarding "health and economic development."[17] These "health and economic" motivations were invariably connected, and they fueled early film work in the colonies. Shortly before William Sellers began making health films in Nigeria, Dr. Arthur Paterson, the deputy director of medical services in Kenya, used film to combat hookworm in East Africa. In noting the success of Paterson's films—in outlining causes and remedies, showcasing the work of doctors, and, in their public exhibition, breaking down resistance—Julian Huxley explained that "the white settlers report an increase in the efficiency of their labourers."[18] A healthy workforce is a productive workforce. At the same moment in 1926, Leslie Notcutt began making films, as historian Glenn Reynolds shows, to "maintain a contented, migrant labor force" on his sisal plantations in East Africa.[19] From the outset, these earliest initiatives can be understood as a form of imperial biopolitics, with film used to develop and sustain a colonial workforce.

For the most part, the early history of filmmaking in, and for, African audiences involves individual government workers, whether educationalists, scientists, or sanitary inspectors like William Sellers. Sellers was a health official using film, an expert initially self-taught in film who took training courses at Kodak's Medical and Scientific Department during three leaves (1933, 1935, 1937) in the UK.[20] Immigration records list Sellers's occupation, when traveling back to Nigeria in the 1930s, as a "sanitary inspector" and even in 1940 when in charge of the CFU, he was listed as a "Civil Servant."[21] This background as a health official dictates his approach to film. When the CFU conducted its first audience survey in 1943, it asked colonial administrators—rather than filmmakers—for their feedback. One of Sellers's initial innovations, the Raw Stock Scheme, which provided film stock for the colonies, was specifically intended to allow "experts," whether on hygiene or agriculture, to make films that "adhere to the instructions given from time to time in *Colonial Cinema*."[22] This background, whether in government, education, or science, shapes the cinema that follows, both in form—more akin to Rotha's "direct teaching"—and in its use, not in isolation, but as one part of a wider government campaign. This is a cinema of expertise.

When the first coordinated experiment to present nonfiction films to African audiences took place in 1929, the same year that Sellers began using films in Nigeria, it was overseen not by a filmmaker but by a noted zoologist, Dr. Julian Huxley. This disciplinary expertise—whether from zoology, health, agriculture, or geography—came to inform the approach that film would take in the colonies. In this initial instance, Huxley was asked by Joseph Oldham, the secretary of the London Missionary Council, working on behalf of the Colonial Advisory Committee on Native Education, to test the levels of comprehension among African audiences.[23] We see immediately the multiple players invested in the development of film in Africa—state, education, trade, science, and church groups—and, more specifically, in the use of film in developing and shaping colonial populations.

Huxley traveled to East Africa with three films provided by the Empire Marketing Board. I will next trace the journey of the "simplest" of these films, *Cotton Growing in Nigeria* (more often and hereafter referred to as *Black Cotton*). *Black Cotton* would travel during the 1920s from Africa to exhibition halls in London, to cinemas, schools, and, at the end of the decade, to Africa once more. It is a journey that illustrates the shared roots between documentary and educational film and between films for British and colonial audiences. At a point when state, commerce, and church were trying to develop the use of nonfiction film within Britain and its colonies, the example of *Black Cotton* reveals the still-amorphous nature of nonfiction film as the form, function, and place of film across the British Empire is worked through and, ultimately, institutionalized.

THE EXHIBITION OF EMPIRE:
BLACK COTTON IN BRITAIN, 1923–30

The journey of *Black Cotton* begins in February 1923, when the governments of Nigeria and the Gold Coast commissioned the London-based Greville Brothers to make films for the West African Pavilion at the forthcoming British Empire Exhibition (see Figure 1.1). The exhibition was, as its official guide acknowledged, a "stock taking of the whole resources of the empire," intended to "foster inter-imperial trade and open fresh markets for Dominion and home products." Housed across 216 acres of parkland in Wembley and welcoming 27 million visitors across its two seasons in 1924–25, the exhibition also sought to reimagine Britain's imperial identity, to shift the rhetoric from one of conquest and exploitation to one of duty and development.[24] In promoting a new economic model of empire, these films provide an integral precursor to the documentary cinema of the Empire Marketing Board.

The initial screening venue for this cotton footage, which played to more than ten thousand paying customers in 1924, helped determine a dominant look and function for colonial nonfiction film. The films often depicted an industrial process, defining individual colonies by products and industries and its inhabitants by vocation or ethnic type. This is evident in *Black Cotton* as the film charts its industrial process from the collection of cotton in the fields through to the wearing of the completed dresses and emphasizes the "native workers" throughout. The film, like the exhibition at which it first played, highlights the colonial workforce and the need for investment in new transport infrastructure and machinery. Yet the pedagogical aims for this footage would shift as it was put to use for different audiences and in different spaces. The London-based journal *West Africa* noted a broader value for audiences viewing these films at Wembley, claiming that "it is beyond doubt" that these films would "give to 99 people out of every 100 at Wembley who know nothing of West Africa their master impression of the country."[25] Sir Edward Davson, a leading light on numerous imperial trade committees, speculated before the exhibition even opened its doors that these geographical films could serve in the "development of Empire trade and the encouragement of emigration to the Dominions." Presag-

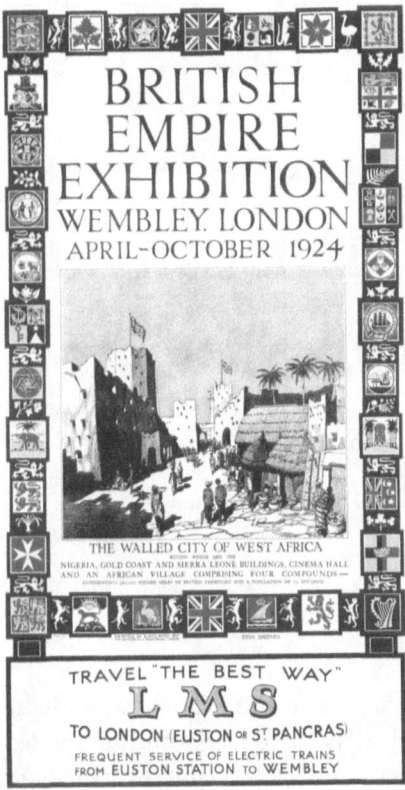

FIGURE 1.1. A poster advertising the British Empire Exhibition in 1924. The free cinema hall in "The Walled City of West Africa" showed films from Nigeria and the Gold Coast every afternoon and evening. Image courtesy of Mary Evans Picture Library / Onslow Auctions Ltd.

ing the work of the EMB, these ideas were taken forward by Graham Ball, a film expert attached to the Department of Overseas Trade, who proposed a series of fifty-two short films under the title "Scenes in the British Empire," which he hoped would play in four hundred theaters before eventually moving to schools and even overseas.[26]

The plans for the series reveal a desire to use film, initially within a cinema setting, to teach British audiences about the colonies and to promote imperial trade and emigration. In his attempts to bridge the commercial and the educational, the directly instructional with the broader promotional—in effect to avoid the categorizations that Rotha would later impose—Ball chose to work with British Instructional Films (BIF). Founded by arch-imperialist Harry Bruce Woolfe in 1919, BIF had accrued a reputation for its coverage of overseas imperial tours, historical military films, and its Secrets of Nature series, which would spawn more than a hundred films by the end of the decade. During its

FIGURE 1.2. An advertisement for "The Empire" series in *Kinematograph Weekly*, 17 February 1927, 12.

fourteen-year existence, BIF established itself as the foremost producer of "educational" film, but it had also, as the Imperial Institute noted when praising its "superior" productions, "succeeded most happily in introducing little scenes of native life, recreations, native types and customs into nearly all of their films."[27] Its films endorse this subtly recoded vision of empire in the 1920s, as they foreground the social and industrial development of the colonies, while still emphasizing British primacy and the critical import of imperial loyalty. This is evident in *Black Cotton*, which was released in cinemas in February 1927, as part of this so-called "Empire series" (see Figure 1.2). Released theatrically in three sets, each between six and twelve films, the Empire series purported to show the "peoples, homes and habits" of the British Empire.[28]

BIF now brought together footage from the Empire Exhibition, from the Empire Cruise and the Prince of Wales's 1925 tour of Africa, stitching together the empire and mapping its spaces and materials for British audiences. It achieved this most notably through the use of intertitles, which in following the structure of the Wembley Exhibition reiterated this notion of individual, and vastly different, colonies and dominions united within the imperial family. Whether describing Singapore Harbor as "the Clapham Junction of the East" or explaining that the island

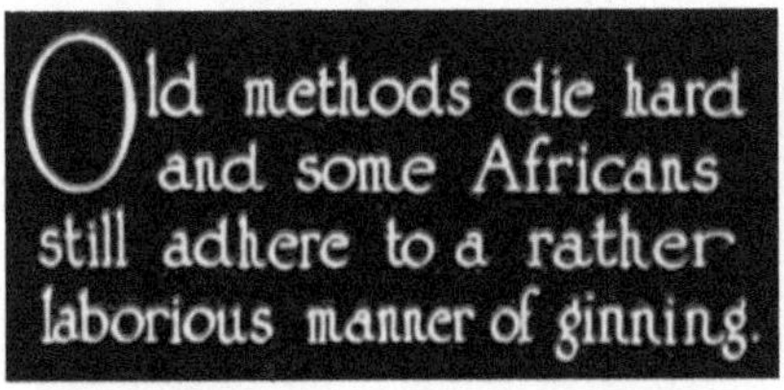

> Old methods die hard and some Africans still adhere to a rather laborious manner of ginning.

> Great new areas of production await opening up as soon as the Railways now in course of construction are completed.

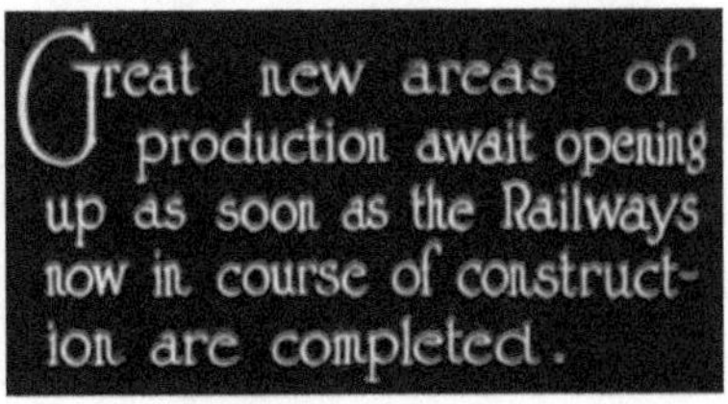

FIGURES 1.3a AND 1.3b. Titles from *Black Cotton* (1927) emphasizing British primacy and development.

of Zanzibar "is the size of a small English county," the intertitles served to relate the events on screen to nonspecialist British viewers.[29] This mode permeates the British representation of colonial subjects far beyond the 1920s. Historian Jo Fox notes the colonial voyeurism inherent in John Grierson's STV series, *This Wonderful World* (1957–65), which took viewers on a "global tour" as Grierson stood over a desktop globe and brought together films and clips from documentaries around the world. Fox notes the ways in which Grierson's links and commentary served to connect these international images to the people and places of Scotland.[30] In the case of *Black Cotton*, the titles emphasize British primacy, contrasting the modern British methods and machinery with the traditional, "primitive" methods of the locals, and highlight the developments introduced by the British (see Figures 1.3a and 1.3b). Adapting these educational images for a commercial audience presented its own problems, as *West Africa* noted in its review of *Black Cotton*. While praising the "very interesting and instructive" pictures, the paper lamented the inclusion of the "usual idiotic" intertitles.[31]

Black Cotton also becomes imbricated here in broader debates about British cinema's role in promoting imperial interests. These debates would directly inform the formation of the EMB and the imperial bent to documentary and educational cinema in Britain. Upon the release of *Black Cotton* in 1927, *Kinematograph Weekly* responded to the lack of support for "this type of film" by urging "all showmen to support these splendid British subjects, which are great stuff and should supplant much of the utter drivel now seen in 'Shorts.'"[32] A couple of years earlier, when a letter in the *Times* had asked why the "admirable cinematograph displays" at Wembley were not commercially available, the writer questioned "how sincere the British film producers and those engaged in the industry are in their claims for sympathy against American encroachments."[33]

The publicity surrounding the Empire series engaged with and fueled these escalating anxieties around American cultural imperialism, and also responded to the paucity of British films within the colonies and dominions. A *Times* report in 1926 complained that the distribution of British films "in our own Dominions is lamentable in the extreme." It cited the example of *Britain's Birthright*, a BIF film made with the Royal Navy, which depicted its 38,000-mile Empire Cruise of 1923–24. *Britain's Birthright* shares much in common with the Empire series, in its format (depicting and connecting individual places around the empire), its mode of titles, and most directly in sharing footage. In this instance, the *Times* complained that the film was "refused by all the Dominions" and only shown by private enterprise.[34] *Britain's Birthright* is a noteworthy example because the film was, in effect, intended to replicate and surpass the work of the Empire Cruise. The cruise had sought to showcase British technological power and connect the colonies back to Britain, work that it was argued could now be performed more successfully by film.

By this stage, the axiom "Trade follows the flag" was increasingly usurped by "Trade follows the film."[35] The two terms ("flag" and "film") were often entwined, as film paraded the flag around the world (titles in *Britain's Birthright* explained that the ship will "show the flag"). The flag remained an essential visual motif on screen—*Britain's Birthright* is framed by its raising and lowering—and served as a visual shorthand for British rule across the globe. In complaining that "the American flag gets more than its fair share of publicity," *Kinematograph Weekly* argued that "Every schoolboy and girl should see [*Britain's Birthright*] since the flag needs 'showing' nearly as much in England as it does in the Colonies."[36] Grierson acknowledged these stakes a few years later in 1931, recognizing film not only as a way to bring the colonies to Britain but also as a means of ruling and displaying authority from afar, allowing British values to infiltrate the colonies. "The major part of national publicity does nowadays rest in the hands of a country's cinema industry. In the old days we sent our Navy round the world to show the flag," but today, Grierson concluded, "a film goes further and faster than a fleet."[37] Of course, the problem here was that the *British* films were not traveling as freely and widely.

The ultimate failure to find a commercial audience for nonfiction subjects, like *Black Cotton* and *Britain's Birthright,* had two immediate impacts. First, it helped to redefine what documentary film would look like in Britain and secondly it increasingly pushed these short, instructional films toward an emerging noncommercial, educational market. On the first point, the Crown agents argued that these commercial failures proved "that purely propaganda or educational films are not the type to succeed commercially," instead suggesting that the background of local customs should be combined with fiction.[38] This is a model that BIF would pursue with what we might generously label "mixed" results.

The most notable, and damning, example of this educational and fictional hybrid is *One Family* (1930), which was suggested by Rudyard Kipling, directed by Walter Creighton (who had previously organized the Wembley Tattoo at the 1924 Empire Exhibition), and sponsored by the Empire Marketing Board. In *One Family* (1930) we follow a young boy who, bored by his classroom geography lesson, falls asleep on his desk and starts to daydream. In a bid to learn more about the empire—and, crucially, to find more interesting ways to learn about the empire—the boy heads to Buckingham Palace with a London policeman. From there, he sources ingredients for the King's Christmas Pudding, extracting products from the colonies and dominions that he brings back to London as he embarks, through the medium of film, on a tour of the British Empire. This representation of empire—one that foregrounded London as the heart of the empire, and the colonies and dominions as producers for Britain—promotes a model of economic imperialism and, in its form, combines elements of the general promotional or illustrative film with the directly pedagogical. The film is structured around a series of short instructional films, for example showing the production and export of fruit from South Africa, raisins from Australia, and butter from New Zealand, attempting to incorporate the dominant form of colonial nonfiction film (the short geography film about a colony and its products of which *Black Cotton* is a prime example) within a semi-fictionalized, prestige production.

This curious mix of short films and traditional pageantry ultimately created a pudding of its own, a film that was critically and commercially reviled to an almost legendary level. EMB filmmaker Harry Watt described it as "abysmally vomit making"—not a line used on the poster—while even as late as 1950, *One Family* would be discussed in the House of Commons "as the greatest flop you ever saw in your life." While the film's production subsumed most of the EMB's film budget for two years, its box office reportedly failed to cover the costs of the band hired for the film's premiere.[39] The film does have its modernist touches—particularly in the editing and use of asynchronous sound in the classroom scene—but it is telling how critics now saw this film as outdated. Director Arthur Elton noted the "very old fashioned" adoption of "society ladies playing Britannia, and the Empire Cake, Buckingham Palace and so forth," while

FIGURE 1.4. An advertisement for *One Family* (1930) in *Fortune* 4 (1930): 110.

John Grierson suggested that its reliance on symbols belonged to the Victorian era (see Figure 1.4).[40] The *Manchester Guardian* complained that "we have waited for a march past of the British Empire on the screen, and now that we get it we find it allied to a Christmas shopping tour conducted by a little boy with ungracious manners and a squeaky voice."[41]

The failure of *One Family* marks a significant moment within this history of British nonfiction cinema. Aligned with the concurrent critical success of John Grierson's Soviet-inspired *Drifters,* it helped consolidate Grierson's reputation and position at the head of the Empire Marketing Board Film Unit and ensure that it was the documentary aesthetics of *Drifters*—as opposed to the more antiquated hybrid form of *One Family*—that would now be championed as the celebrated, prestige form for state-sponsored imperial filmmaking. The short instructional film would still occupy a significant space in educational and nontheatrical frameworks, but a space that has often been neglected or, based on aesthetic judgments, seen as ancillary.[42]

By 1927 *Black Cotton* was increasingly housed within an emerging educational market. The film had already featured in a BIF demonstration in London in 1926 on the future of educational film, introduced by imperial historian Sir Charles Lucas, while the *Christian Science Monitor* discussed its value as an aid to classroom teaching, enabling Nigeria to become "a definite conception, a 'real life place' as the child describes it."[43] BIF would make *Black Cotton* available "for educational purposes" in July 1927 at the precise moment that the Imperial Institute, an established center for imperial education, opened its own cinema. This cinema would show imperial films (including *Black Cotton*) four times a day to children.[44] Described by its director as a "permanent Wembley," the institute displayed the "products of each and every part" of the empire, and the cinema, funded by the EMB, continued to define and organize the colonies through their trade value to Britain.[45] By 1928 *Black Cotton* was also advertised for nontheatrical hire through British Instructional's newly established Education Department. The BIF catalogue contained sixty geography films, the largest section by far, and as with the Empire Exhibition continued to divide these by country. The catalogue entry for *Black Cotton* (now listed as *Cotton Growing in Nigeria*) showed how these individual examples were mapped and related back to Britain. In showing an industrial process through to the point of export, "the interdependence of one nation upon another is realised."[46] Throughout this period, we can see how the form and structure within this emerging educational film market was tied directly to notions of imperial productivity, foregrounding the economic value of the colonies to Britain.

THE SCRAMBLE FOR AFRICAN SCREENS:
BLACK COTTON IN AFRICA, 1929

The journey of *Black Cotton* helps to unpack the emergence of documentary and educational film in interwar Britain. Its travels back to

Africa in 1929—the same year that Sellers started making health films in Nigeria—also reveal the start of a more concerted interest in developing and using films for colonial, and in particular African, audiences.

Black Cotton was one of three films chosen as part of Julian Huxley's experiment in East Africa; the other two were also BIF films, and both were from the Secrets of Life series: *Fathoms Deep beneath the Sea* (1922) and *The Life of a Plant* (1926). The films were chosen because they were perceived to represent different levels of difficulty, evidence that the experiment was predicated on assumptions about African cognitive capabilities. For example, *Fathoms Deep beneath the Sea* is more complex than *Black Cotton* because it uses underwater technology and shows creatures unfamiliar to most of its audience, while *The Life of a Plant* is deemed even more complicated because it uses microscopic close-ups and a speeding-up device that "could only be appreciated by an intelligent and novel use of the imagination."[47] The selection of the films is thus based on assumptions about subject matter and, especially, film techniques that would shape the work of the Colonial Film Unit. What's more, presenting *Black Cotton* alongside the Secrets of Nature films foregrounds the African workers as subjects of scientific study, metaphorically under the microscope.

The experiment, and indeed the selected films, were a further product of the wider discussions and anxieties around the corrosive influences of film on colonial populations. These anxieties, which had been articulated through the commercial failure of *Black Cotton*, were now shaping policy. The most striking intervention occurred at the Imperial Conference of October 1926. Intended to reinvigorate the British film industry by enforcing a "quota" of British films on British screens, the Cinematograph Act of 1927 was also, as Priya Jaikumar has shown, "equally shaped by imperial aspirations" in extending these initiatives throughout the empire.[48]

BIF had its own part to play here as it looked to extend its pedagogy overseas. It signed deals in 1928 to ensure that its existing productions could be exhibited in Australia, New Zealand, and South Africa. In 1930, when a Colonial Films Committee was established to "promote the better distribution of British films in the colonies" and to supply films of an "educational value to the native races," reports noted that BIF already "send instructional and interest films to places so far distant as the West Indies, Nigeria and the Gold Coast, the Malay States, India and New Zealand for exhibition in places other than those of entertainment."[49] The committee further proposed the production of a series of films—sixteen health, twelve agricultural, eight educational, and four general interest—for the West Indies, with a similar program for Africa and another for the Far East.⁵⁰ The selection of three BIF films—although all are labeled as Empire Marketing Board films in the official reports—foregrounds a professional, commercial response to these discussions even as individual government workers such as William Sellers began their own experiments with film.

The Cinematograph Act manifests this escalating desire to promote "British" film subjects, to challenge producers and exhibitors to present the empire on screen, and to regain control of its representation. Within India and the Dominions this was often perceived as a losing battle, or at least the influence of Hollywood in these markets was more firmly established. When James Parr, the New Zealand high commissioner, spoke at the House of Commons in 1930 on "the Americanization of the Dominions by film," he argued that "nothing has eclipsed in seriousness the menace that affected the whole Empire of having young people brought up with American ideas," and despaired that they received their education from "this place called Hollywood."⁵¹ Yet in other colonies, most notably in Africa and the Caribbean—and even more so in rural areas—there was still an opportunity to shape what, and how, audiences watched. Sir Hesketh Bell, a former governor of Uganda, Northern Nigeria, and the Bahamas, outlined this view in 1926 and again in 1930 when mourning the "mischievous influence" of film. Bell suggested that in "our African tropical territories" there is still time to "safeguard . . . our protected subjects."⁵² This view was reiterated in an influential 1932 report, *The Film in National Life,* which suggested that despite the "incalculable" damage done to the prestige of Europeans in India and the Far East, "*there is yet time,* to see that the same shall not be repeated in our Tropical African Empire."⁵³

The response to this threat in Africa was often reductive, with Bell demanding a tightening of censorship laws to prevent showing "before the eyes of hundreds of thousands of unsophisticated natives travesties of the lives and habits of white people."⁵⁴ Echoing language that would be used by William Sellers and the Colonial Film Unit, Bell spoke of the impact on the mental and moral development of "primitive people" and suggested a different set of requirements for this audience, "who have little sense of proportion and who, in the great majority of cases, are unable to distinguish between the truth and a travesty of it." Bell further suggested that producers might make two versions of the same story, with the one for "tropical exhibition" replacing "objectionable" scenes with "innocuous" ones.⁵⁵ The *Times* printed responses to Bell's letter from religious figures in Africa, which for the most part supported this notion of a "different mentality" for European and African audiences. "The censor must be a man with a knowledge of the mental processes of the African," wrote a bishop in Southern Rhodesia, "for what might be quite innocuous to a European audience may be suggestive to the African."[56]

Huxley's early experiment appeared against this backdrop. While widely referenced today, it was extremely limited in scope. Indeed, the films only screened in two "native" schools, in Kenya and Uganda (partly again because of a shortage of projecting facilities), and Huxley's reports recognize the danger of drawing conclusions from these screenings. When writing about the second screening in a cinema hall in Uganda, Huxley estimated that more than three quarters of the several hundred boys and girls in attendance were seeing film for the first time. "During the first minute or so of the cotton film, they were very quiet. Partly I think the whole thing was new and for the moment incomprehensible. Partly," he concluded with disarming honesty, "the opening of the film is rather dull."[57]

Yet, despite his warnings, Huxley's observations set the tone for future thinking on colonial audiences in a number of ways. For example, Huxley determined that audiences wanted local films, relatable to their own lives. Once the audience saw "natives" working on the screen, Huxley suggested they grew "wildly excited." "They applauded, stomped with their feet, laughed, shouted, explained to each other," he continued, "the noise was particularly deafening when anyone was seen on the film doing a hard job of work." This emphasis on hard work, on industrial labor, and on the creation of *productive* citizens fits dominant interwar imperial thinking. Huxley also employed methods that the CFU would replicate, inviting the children from the government schools to write essays about the films. "We found that the people of Nigeria are now civilized," one wrote after viewing *Black Cotton*, while schoolchildren in Uganda noted, in contrast to their own situation, how the cotton was used in the local trade and not only shipped overseas. Huxley suggested that the film appealed because it "represented people like themselves, engaged in familiar occupations," highlighting the importance of making films that directly represented and responded to African audiences.[58]

Huxley's screenings also highlighted some of the challenges in using film within African education—for example, in the difficulties with equipment and in a reliance on local commentators or translators to relay the intended message—but it was a significant initiative in propelling colonial audiences into educational film discourse. Huxley's report emphasized the impact film had on local audiences, as he argued, in familiar colonial rhetoric, that Africans watched film with "almost childlike delight," that film could attract a crowd in ways that a lecture could not, and that visual displays leave a stronger impression than that which is heard.[59]

Most strikingly, Huxley "was very enthusiastic regarding the potential of African audiences to comprehend sophisticated film techniques." He noted that "native boys and girls are capable of grasping difficult subjects such as speeded-up films" and concluded that "African audiences should be treated no differently from any other group." In this instance, Huxley was whistling in the wind, his view largely ignored or directly opposed by others like William Sellers.[60] Already by 1932, a dominant rhetoric that seemingly responded to, but challenged, the findings of Huxley appeared in *The Film in National Life*. "Illustrations of the life history of the mosquito or of the devastating effects of the hookworm, which might be understood by more or less civilised people who have some notions about microbes or microscopes," wrote Hesketh Bell, "would be quite bewildering to unsophisticated natives who have not the faintest idea of modern science."[61]

In his endorsement of cinema, Huxley recognized the ways in which cinema could support the activities of government departments. Huxley's view was determined by the work of Dr. Paterson, a "very strong monsoon" who in his role as the deputy director of medical services showed him how film had been used to gain the confidence of local groups, to show the merits of building concrete houses, and to build latrines to prevent hookworm (a familiar theme in colonial film). In many respects, Huxley was witnessing and imagining the kind of work William Sellers was also doing in Nigeria and reiterated that this work "must of necessity" be carried out by local departments and experts. Huxley recognized the value of film here in colonial administration. "This will become a very important use of the cinema," he concluded, "the recording of special activities of Government Departments for demonstration and propaganda purposes."[62]

PROPOSALS FOR "PRIMITIVE PEOPLE," 1930-34

At the same moment that Huxley was conducting his experiments in Africa, Leo Amery, the secretary of state for the colonies, set up the Colonial Films Committee, which included Hesketh Bell, Bruce Woolfe, and Walter Creighton. Amery's successor, the Labour politician Lord Passfield, then wrote to all colonial governors in 1930, urging them to pay the "closest attention" to the use of film especially "with primitive people."[63] Passfield encouraged government officials to film in the colonies—a precursor to the CFU's Raw Stock Scheme—and wrote to the Gold Coast government asking it to notify him "when any officer is coming on leave whom you would wish to receive instruction."[64] On the back of this encouragement, historian Glenn Reynolds notes five proposals between 1930 and 1934, which constitute significant precursors to the Colonial Film Unit and advance particular priorities and assumptions about this cinema and its audiences.[65] Yet, what ultimately unites these proposals is their failure to secure funding. At the height of economic depression, talk was cheap.

The proposals came from professional filmmakers, educationalists, colonial officials, and doctors, traversing the still-nebulous boundaries between documentary and instructional film and between commercial and nontheatrical film. Geoffrey Barkas, an experienced and well-respected filmmaker who had worked in Nigeria for British Instructional Films, was unsuccessful in his scheme to set up a government bureau that would distribute films in East Africa.[66] Next up was James Russell Orr, a former director of education in Kenya, who had served as secretary of the Commission on Educational and Cultural Films in 1929 and was writing up its report at this time (which would be published in 1932 as *The Film in National Life*). Orr had the credentials in colonial education and his proposal, which he submitted to the Colonial Office in 1931, involved a chain of cinema houses throughout the empire for "the advancement of adults and children of native races."[67] He drew up plans and costings for the buildings and outlined the proposed programs, which included familiar films from BIF's Empire series. He proposed films on sanitation, hygiene, and first aid, in collaboration with medical departments, and foregrounded films promoting trade ("how the colony co-operates in production with the great industrial centres of the world"), social development ("what British administration has done for native races"), and the specially tailored general entertainment film ("suitable for the mentality of backward races, as approved by the standing committee in London"). Orr's proposal was intended as a commercial venture and pulled together the rising concerns (in providing a form of proactive censorship) and dominant ideologies (film specially tailored for "backward" races). He also recognized film as a means of political control. Speaking the following year at a meeting of the Educational Council on "The Film in Empire Education," Orr argued that "in a rapidly changing world, one of the main functions of the film should be to steady opinion."[68]

The Colonial Office ruled out various locations for the scheme, including Kenya, Zanzibar, and Somaliland, which it described "as the last place in which to try an experiment" and instead suggested sending the proposal on to the governments of Uganda and Tanganyika. This was little more than passing the buck. Film was hardly a priority for colonial governments under increasing financial pressure, and ultimately the project failed to secure funding.[69] These ideas did not disappear, however. *The Film in National Life,* which Orr worked on, reported the workings of the Colonial Films Committee and stressed the need for "some form of central administration" to arrange the distribution and development of film within colonial territories, imagining in 1932 a form of Colonial Film Unit.[70]

Orr had outlined his proposal when giving a talk for the Africa society at the Royal Society of the Arts (RSA) in April 1931. Attending that day was Roland Vernon, a veteran of the Colonial Office who had most recently served on its Films Committee.[71] Vernon was invited to respond to Orr's talk and did so in familiar terms, first noting that the Colonial Office was "exceedingly dissatisfied with the practical monopoly of the Kinema by America" and "instead of the purely sensational American films" sought a larger proportion of commercial British films in the colonies. Vernon's personal interest, however, was in the educational film. After lamenting the "extraordinary want of imagination" in this area, he explained (while sitting in the lavish surroundings of the RSA) that he had tried to "put myself in the position of a comparatively uncultured African savage" and emphasized the need for "oral instruction" to complement the work of the film. Vernon saw a particular role for teachers here, imagining a time when the projector would be as much a part of the school apparatus as a blackboard. A few months later, Vernon would submit his own proposal to explore the use of film "among more primitive races" in Malaya. Once again, it was unsuccessful.[72]

While these failed proposals might seem incidental, they served to work through the place, form, and function of film for colonial audiences, effectively preparing the ground for the Colonial Film Unit. For example, Beresford Gale, "an American Negro," proposed a traveling cinema show in West Africa, using a mobile lorry that would be equipped in London. In what already read like a familiar list, he suggested touring a "selected group of films including sanitation scenes, comedies, school life in England" and others that will help audiences "visualize the manifest blessings of modern life" now "commonplace" in the West. Beresford Gale further outlined to the Colonial Office the value of the mobile cinema in colonial government. "It has been conclusively demonstrated, time without number," he wrote, "that governing an intelligent class of people, wherever situated, is far easier than governing the benighted and ignorant." Education was imagined here as means of political control, whereby "intelligence" is demonstrated by those who understand and support the colonial authorities.[73]

With the establishment of the British Film Institute in 1933, there was a new center to coordinate these schemes. Indeed, within a year the BFI established a designated "Dominions, India and Colonies panel," although this London-based panel stressed that any successful proposal required "the full support of the territorial governments." The panel provided advice and practical assistance to schools and educational departments across the empire and, presaging the CFU's Raw Stock Scheme, invited colonial officials and amateur enthusiasts to submit footage taken in colonial territories that might be used in educational films.[74] The committee preempted some of the organizational work of the Colonial Film Unit, and set up a subcommittee, often chaired by Bruce Woolfe, which looked at proposals and reviewed the existing work within Africa. One of the panelists, G.T. Hankin, reported in 1934 on a recent trip to South Africa where he had presented a selection of films—including Secrets of Nature and EMB films—at an educational conference attended by "over a quarter of the teaching strength of the Dominion." While outlining how film was, and might be, used in education for Europeans, he admitted: "Neither I, nor anybody else that I met, has any clear idea of what ought to be done concerning Films and Native Races." "Every variety of view was expressed," he explained. "Some said that natives couldn't understand films, some said they could. Some said that films would be of great value in teaching hygiene and giving some idea of Western civilisation. Some seemed to doubt it." Hankin did note, with more certainty, that the economic situation made the point moot. "A general complaint was that Native Education was so starved already financially that it was futile to think of travelling projectors and films or even of 16mm. silent projectors with spoken commentary."[75]

Despite this, the committee directly invited a proposal in 1934 from Dr. A.R. Paterson, one of the pioneers of instructional film in Africa. Paterson's proposal defined, and sought to develop, the colonial citizen as economically productive. In suggesting a series of films for East African natives, which were designed to "make the native peoples happier, healthier and more useful," he intriguingly placed the most emphasis on "useful." Paterson's notion of the productive citizen was defined by their relationship to Europeans, as he argued that an African might never be healthy or happy unless he could provide the European, American, and Eastern manufacturers "with those products of heavy industry and with such hardware and textiles as he cannot produce for himself." The proposal received support from the panel and the Colonial Office but this was still not enough to secure funding.[76]

Throughout this period, we see significant figures in colonial administration submitting proposals that imagine the work of the Colonial Film Unit. Another example came in 1936 from S. A. Hammond, an education commissioner in the West Indies, who proposed a "Colonial Film Unit" that would administer a library of films for the colonies, produce films on health and agriculture, and encourage and assist in local production. Hammond spoke of the role of film in preparing Africans for "citizenship of the Empire" and thanked leading figures of the British Documentary Movement—Donald Taylor and John and Marion Grierson—for helping with his proposal. The proposal was again rejected on financial grounds, suggesting once more that the lack of support and infrastructure for a colonial cinema in interwar Britain was a product of the broader economic situation; the perilous state of the nation's finances exacerbated by the need to prop up and monetize its sprawling empire. In this instance, the BFI's "Dominions, India and Colonies Panel" explained that the project "had to prove itself more desirable and more urgent than numerous other schemes" and cited the ongoing work of the BFI, GB Instructional's filming expedition to the West Indies, and, most significantly, the Bantu Educational Kinema Experiment (BEKE).[77]

THE BANTU EDUCATIONAL KINEMA EXPERIMENT, 1935–37

The BEKE represents the largest, most organized, and widely discussed colonial film experiment of this interwar period. Between March 1935 and May 1937, it produced thirty-five films, with titles ranging from *Hookworm* to *Healthy Babies* and from *Tax* to *Tea,* and through its traveling mobile cinema van exhibited these pictures across Tanganyika, Nyasaland, Northern Rhodesia, Kenya, and Uganda. The project has received a wealth of critical work, but what is immediately striking here is that the largest film project for colonial audiences in this period should be funded not by British or colonial governments, but rather by American philanthropy and African commercial interests.[78] Indeed the project was initially rejected by the BFI's Dominions, India and Colonies panel, after Roland Vernon, its Colonial Office representative, dismissed it as "altogether too ambitious an undertaking for an experimental exercise."[79]

Instead the proposal secured $55,000 from the Carnegie Corporation and smaller grants from Northern Rhodesia's Roan Antelope Mines and Mufulira Copper Mines. Led by the American Congregational missionary John Merle Davis, it was "essentially a missionary undertaking," and what's more (as its funding from mining corporations suggests), it sought to investigate and support worker productivity.[80] Extending the work that individuals like Leslie Notcutt and Dr. Paterson had carried out in East Africa, the project was initially imagined in response to the rapid cultural change caused by mass labor migration to Northern Rhodesia's Copperbelt. Film might provide the "connective social tissue," a means to address, homogenize, and monitor disparate worker groups.[81]

The project also sought to learn more about the use of film in African education, with Davis identifying three aims that would especially appeal to those, like Sellers, with an interest here. The first, Davis explained, was to uncover "the African's preference for films," the second to determine "the technique of film production best suited to the mentality of different types of Africans—the educated, the partially detribalised native, the primitive villager"—and the third to examine "the technique of displaying films to Africans—how far they wish to participate in the performance." The BEKE responded to long-held anxieties—for example, its films looked to counter the dangerous, pervading influence of Hollywood on colonial screens—and confronted questions on African audiences, which the Colonial Film Unit would take up soon afterwards.

The personnel involved also reveal a model for this instructional cinema that foregrounded the work of subject experts and film enthusiasts rather than professional filmmakers. The two men charged with running the project were Leslie A. Notcutt, a plantation manager who now served as field director, and Geoffrey Latham, a former director of native education in Northern Rhodesia. Notcutt brought amateur film experience, having used film in his work on an East African sisal plantation, while Latham provided the educational credentials.[82] Indeed the advisory board contained considerably more experience in education, health, agriculture, and African affairs than it did in film (three representatives from the BFI and one from Gaumont-British Instructional [GBI]) and included familiar names from earlier schemes and initiatives including James Fairgrieve, Roland Vernon, and G. T. Hankin. Furthermore, Notcutt acknowledged the influence of Huxley's earlier experiment on their project. Having read Huxley's report, he "was interested to find his belief that films could be used in their [local African] education confirmed."[83]

In their detailed report on the BEKE, published as *The African and the Cinema* in 1937, Notcutt and Latham outlined three phases to their project. The first saw the production of thirteen films, which were widely exhibited, as the unit covered more than nine thousand miles by road, rail, and lake between 4 September 1935 and 13 February 1936. They began filming a second batch of short subjects in August 1936 with a loan from the Tanganyika government. These productions focused predominantly on agricultural and health subjects, teaching new farming methods and promoting Western medicine, and included *African Peasant Farms, Tropical Hookworm,* and *The Veterinary Training of African Natives,* the three surviving films housed at the BFI.[84] Further financial shortages delayed production on a final group of films until January 1937. This third batch was "made to the order of the Kenya, Uganda, and Tanganyika Governments" and was "entirely concerned" with agriculture and animal husbandry.[85]

It is the first batch that most helpfully informs the subsequent work of the Colonial Film Unit. These initial films covered a wide range of genres and subjects, beginning with *Post Office Savings Bank,* which adopted the widely used Mr. Wise and Mr. Foolish format. *First Farce,* the last film in this initial series, tested the African audience's perceived preference for slapstick, while other titles were classified "instructional" (for example, *Soil Erosion* and *Hides*) or presented morality tales within a fictional framework (*Gumu*). Further films addressed topical issues (such as *Tax,* which received a "certain amount of criticism and was not often shown") or responded more specifically to this generational conflict between the old and the new (*The Chief*). The filmmakers suggested that the topics shared a common theme, which they summed up as "progress vs African methods."[86]

Formally, the early films largely follow, and indeed endorse, a method of filmmaking that was gaining increasing orthodoxy and which catered to the supposed different cognitive abilities of the African viewer. Latham noted in 1936 that there were "very few" existing films that were suitable for African audiences and outlined the "special requirements of more or less primitive communities as yet unaccustomed to the moving picture and living in an environment very different from our own." While Latham may have been suggesting that this special requirement was a result of limited viewing experience and cultural differences (rather than mental or physiological differences), he was raising the kinds of questions

FIGURE 1.5. The mobile unit in trouble in Tanganyika, in *The African and the Cinema: An Account of the Work of the Bantu Educational Cinema Experiment during the Period March 1935 to May 1937*, ed. L. A. Notcutt and G. C. Latham (London: Edinburgh House Press, 1937), 112.a

that William Sellers was also addressing in Nigeria. "The presentation must be simple and logical," Latham wrote, "more time must be given to most of the shots than is usually desired." Indeed, some of the initial feedback to the first set of films perpetuated this, claiming that the "action and speech were too quick."[87] While Sellers would extend and more clearly define a specialized technique, Notcutt and Latham continued to argue that African audiences required specific films. Writing in *Sight and Sound*, Latham stated that films should deal with African life and familiar settings and those that depict European life "should be specifically taken, or at any rate re-edited, for exhibition to Natives."[88]

The BEKE was equally significant in presenting a model for mobile film exhibition (see Figure 1.5). In its initial six-month tour, the unit gave ninety-five performances, attended by approximately 80,000 Africans, 1,300 Europeans, and a large number of Indians. As with Sellers, the film space was carefully organized and managed, while the show was often preceded by music and ended with an "interest" film shot in England by BEKE cameraman Captain Coley, which featured shots of London (titles included *White People,* parts one, two, and three). The show finished with a picture of the King and a performance of the national anthem.[89]

These clear manifestations, and indeed celebrations, of colonial power were hardly unusual. Simon Potter notes the British "branding" of its BBC Empire Service at this moment, where transmission would end with the national anthem, the chimes of Big Ben, and an announcement proclaiming, "This is London calling." The Empire Service, which was set up in 1932, provides a useful reminder that film was merely one part of this imperial propaganda. However, while the Empire Service used the new medium of radio to project Britain to the colonies and, in effect, to rule from afar—the first King's Christmas message, written by Rudyard Kipling, was broadcast shortly after the service began in 1932—its target audience was initially serving "British Whites." These were expatriates with access to the technology who were familiar and well versed with British life rather than the unconverted or unreached local audiences that the BEKE and the CFU would primarily target.[90]

Reports repeatedly emphasized that the BEKE was making films "in Africa for the Africans with Africans acting in them" and its British directors, somewhat paradoxically, projected it as an African cinema (see Figure 1.6).[91] Rosaleen Smyth has argued that the BEKE organizers were "emphatic about the 'Africanness' of their films," soliciting advice from elite Africans during filming, offering a prize to African students at Makerere College for the best screenplay, and training Africans "in all aspects of production and exhibition." This was, the organizers argued, what audiences wanted.[92] The unit sought black input—and indeed asked Paul Robeson to sit on the advisory board (he declined)—but did receive criticism, as James Burns shows, both for its British interpretations of African life and for its form of proactive censorship that sought to protect "the natives' respect and homage for the white race," as Marcus Garvey described it, by preventing Africans from seeing "white films" that displayed the actors "as they really are."[93] Yet while the paternalism of the missionaries and the Colonial Office may have subjugated any meaningful African involvement, the BEKE did illustrate the perceived preference, recognized need, and tentative moves toward a local cinema produced by, and for, Africans.

For now, however, these moves were on hold. While Davis, Latham, and Notcutt argued for the BEKE's continuation, this was reliant on funding from the colonial governments. The Northern Rhodesian government "agreed unconditionally to co-operate," but other territories were less forthcoming, with Kenya and Nyasaland most damningly

FIGURE 1.6. Filming as part of the Bantu Education Kinema Experiment, in *The African and the Cinema: An Account of the Work of the Bantu Educational Cinema Experiment during the Period March 1935 to May 1937*, ed. L. A. Notcutt and G. C. Latham (London: Edinburgh House Press, 1937), 129.

deeming the films too amateurish.[94] The secretary of state for the colonies, William Ormsby-Gore, sent copies of *The African and the Cinema* to other governments across Africa, asking for their comments. The acting director of education in the Gold Coast wrote a two-page response, explaining "that extensive and very valuable use could be made of the cinema in the Gold Coast and that the time is now ripe for its introduction as part of the educational system." He envisaged an organization like the BBC and warned against using amateurs, which "would in all probability result in indifferent films," in favor of "thoroughly experienced, professional directors." While the Education Department sought government support to produce and exhibit films "not merely in schools but among the general public," there is little evidence of further action here.⁹⁵

Having been at the whim of colonial governments—chasing money and changing plans along the way—Notcutt and Latham now sought a long-term scheme that would put "the production of films for backward races on a permanent footing." The *Times* deemed this a scheme "emphatically worth careful study," explaining that it "envisages the formation of a central organisation in London," supported by and serving all colonies, with "local film production units in each territory."⁹⁶ Significantly Latham's own individual proposal, which Reynolds discusses, responded to the shifting political situation, suggesting that more scenes of European life—"making peoples of the world known to one another"—would "do much to counteract the hate propaganda of nationalist governments."⁹⁷ Latham was not only calling for what would become the Colonial Film Unit, but was also now recognizing the political motivation behind its establishment. He would continue his calls over the next few years. In a letter to the *Times,* written in April 1939, he urged the "Imperial Government to establish a Colonial Film Unit, to take the field without delay, starting, perhaps, in East or West Africa." "The cost would not be great," he concluded, and the benefits "incalculable."⁹⁸

The work of the BEKE was also noted beyond Africa. Against the backdrop of prolonged, wide-scale labor riots in Jamaica—in May and June 1938 strikes by dock laborers erupted into violent protests across plantations and towns—the governor of Jamaica contacted the BEKE organizers in 1938. At this point, the recently established Jamaica Welfare Ltd had begun touring two mobile film units across the island. Jamaica Welfare Ltd was funded through a small portion of the profits of the United Fruit Company, the American corporation that controlled and drove the Jamaican banana industry. With funding from American capital interests, the motivation for this mobile cinema partly replicated the BEKE as it directly responded to economic unrest and the movement of rural workers. At a moment of labor migration, mass unemployment, and, for others, pitiful wages, the traveling unit sought to control worker unrest through education to promote and enact community development.⁹⁹ One of the lecturers, writing to Martin Rennalls, who would subsequently become the first head of the Jamaica Film Unit, described the aims of the show in familiar terms—to shape the colonial worker by privileging "hard work" as part of the nation-building process. "That hard work is enabling and not a curse," he wrote, "that efficiency will receive reward even if long delayed at times, that building a nation means each individual, being and doing his best at all times."[100] While reports described the cost as "tremendous," they again countered that the benefits to the "general knowledge and the general sharpening of the individual child's perception, cannot be estimated."[101]

Again, we see an overlap here with the development of educational film in Britain. In 1936, Bruce Woolfe, now heading Gaumont-British Instructional (GBI), sent Frank Bundy and two cameramen on a six-month tour of the West Indies as the first part of an intended film series that would show "the whole Empire as it is for the benefit of school children in various parts of the British possessions."[102] Bundy's completed films, which included *Jamaican Harvest* (1938), came with additional teaching notes about the local industries and were approved by the Royal Empire Society. Alistair Weigall, the chairman of council for the society, in discussing its work with GBI, noted the "urgent need" to present the story of the empire to children, so that "as they grow older they have a reasoned foundation for their political faith."[103] In a decade when political and ideological divisions intensified to a crushing nadir and, particularly in the case of Jamaica, worker unrest and anti-imperialist feeling grew more pronounced, this educational cinema in Britain and abroad had a strong political function, shaping and homogenizing the "political faith" of schoolchildren and local workers in an attempt to maintain the empire for a next generation.[104]

The early reports on Jamaica Welfare Ltd. indicate the ways in which film functioned as part of a wider pedagogical event. The commentators "answered questions from the audiences" while audience participation was encouraged, whether through prizes for student essays or through local performances connected to the film shows. There was also already a clear demand for more local films. These films, it was reasoned, would address agricultural and health issues and could once more define the value of the colonial worker by showing "the workings of local industry."[105] In response, Leslie Notcutt submitted an application to the Jamaican government for a local production unit in April 1938, which James Burns notes was rejected primarily because of the poor reputation of the BEKE.[106] Reviewing Notcutt's proposal in May 1939, Christopher Eastwood described the BEKE as "not all together a very successful experiment," and quoted from the "illuminating" Kenyan report that labeled the films as "such inferior quality." Eastwood added that the BEKE "was certainly an expensive experiment, largely I think because it did not employ the right personnel," and concluded that any money would be better spent "teaching some enthusiastic local person [an officer in the Jamaican government] how to take decent films."[107]

Yet, the calls made by Notcutt and Latham for a central, permanent Colonial Film Unit continued to gather support. Oliver Bell, a member of the BEKE advisory board writing to the *Times* in his role as director of the BFI, offered a particularly frustrated, urgent response. After describing the present situation in the colonies as "deplorable," Bell complained that "the natives were looking to America rather than to England as a source of their cultural inspiration." Among his suggestions was the formation of a small unit "whereby medical, agricultural, or other officers could obtain as an instrument in their work the most powerful organ of instruction that exists in the world to-day."[108]

With the increasing likelihood of war, other familiar figures returned to the fray, recognizing an opportune moment to use film within the colonies. J. Russell Orr wrote to the Ministry of Information (MOI) in October 1939 with a scheme involving mobile exhibition across Kenya. In using a familiar set of subjects—such as hygiene and soil erosion—Orr claimed that it would "considerably expedite the government's object of eventually turning the African into a self-governing and responsible citizen." At the outset of war, Orr again emphasized film's potential in shaping audience behavior and conduct, prioritizing ideologically supportive and financially self-sufficient colonial citizens. Orr's proposed costings proved too much for the Colonial Office, which was not convinced that charging to see a film about malaria (and, in particular, building new fixed-site venues) would be sustainable.[109]

In the summer of 1939 Geoffrey Latham presented a further unsuccessful proposal, which would invite commercial companies to produce films in the colonies. At the same moment he screened examples of his work to MOI officials, as one of the applicants to head what would become the Colonial Film Unit.[110] Despite now sitting on the BFI's Dominions, India and Colonies panel, Latham's experiences with the BEKE evidently counted against him. Christopher Eastwood wrote dismissively at the end of 1939 of the "rather grandiose schemes" put forward at the end of the BEKE report. "They are now dead," he wrote, "but I hope that we shall soon work out in conjunction with the Ministry of Information, plans of a rather less ambitious nature for circulating libraries of films for both East and West Africa."[111] It is then perhaps no surprise that the MOI would look beyond Latham when appointing a figure to oversee their film operations in Africa, turning instead to a health official who, over the previous decade, had produced films and established a local cinema unit across Nigeria. His name was William Sellers.

THE FILM AS LIFE SUPPORT: WILLIAM SELLERS IN NIGERIA, 1926–39

Christopher Eastwood praised the "quite excellent" work of William Sellers in Nigeria when recommending him to the BBC to broadcast on colonial affairs in June 1939. The praise came, however, with an illuminating caveat. "He is, I think of quite humble origin," Eastwood explained, "and his accent may not be all that it should be."[112] Eastwood's observation, while revealing more about the expectations of the time, also suggests that Sellers was not what we might think of as an archetypal colonial officer. Growing up in Bury with an accent that deviated from the home counties and sounded, to Sellers's chagrin, like a "Lancashire cab driver," Sellers was a practical, skilled man. His father (also William) was a hand sawyer, and as a teenager the younger William Sellers listed his trade as a fitter when working for the Bury and District Munitions War Committee.[113] Standing at five feet six and only 126 lbs, Sellers enlisted with the Royal Engineers in 1916 and would serve as a sapper in France at the end of the war.[114] His early film work in Nigeria was characterized by a practical, hands-on approach. His boss in the medical services would praise his "genius for technical work," which was evident when he adapted a government lorry into a mobile cinema and subsequently designed and oversaw the first purpose-built mobile cinema van in Nigeria.[115]

Sellers was still living in Bury when he first moved out to Nigeria at the height of the bubonic plague in 1926.[116] Over the next thirteen years—until returning to the UK in May 1939—he would undertake a succession of eighteen-month tours.[117] In his own writing Sellers noted the constant challenges in this early work, reporting the "wide confusion" among locals as bodies of plague victims were "dumped in dark corners or thrown into lagoons with no hope of tracing contacts." Other government initiatives proved counterproductive, such as the rat-buying stations where the government paid locals who brought in dead rats. "Imagine my surprise," recalled Sellers, "when one African, who honestly thought he was aiding the cause, came along with nearly 100 live rats feeling quite proud of the fact that he had bred them himself."[118] By 1928, with reported cases of the plague on the rise again, Governor Thompson acknowledged that continuing with the current "costly organisation is out of the question." Instead Thompson now argued that the true remedy was in the "townplanning and drainage schemes," the kind of preventative, welfare measures that Sellers espoused and would showcase on film.[119]

At this point, Sellers appeared somewhat disillusioned. During leave at the end of 1929, he informed the Crown agents that owing to the "inadequate salary and lack of prospects" he would return for only one more tour. The Crown agents were trying unsuccessfully to find candidates to fill sanitary inspector posts in Nigeria, and while quickly dismissing the pay complaints, did accept that "there was some cause for complaint" over the lack of prospects. Sellers was one of thirty-one Grade II sanitary inspectors in Nigeria, but there were only two posts at the higher Grade I level.[120]

The fact that Sellers chose to continue in Nigeria—and indeed would be promoted to Grade 1 sanitary inspector in 1935—likely owed much to his increasing opportunities with film. The Medical Health Service, and more specifically Sellers, began showing films from England in Lagos in 1929, and he was also now working on his own health films. This gained momentum and institutional support in 1931 when, as one of a range of health schemes in Nigeria, the Colonial Development Advisory Committee approved £6,000 for "sanitary improvements." This sum included equipment for producing and projecting 16mm films and was "handed over" to Sellers. Clearly this was still a tentative move—something of a one-man show—as Sellers was expected to work on this in his "spare time," yet through this funding, film became one part of the government's wider sanitary schemes. When the first two cine-Kodaks were bought in June 1932 to make "health propaganda films," money was also spent on school medical clinics, health posters, and model sanitary structures for demonstrations. These posters and demonstrations also feature in Sellers's films, which as early as 1933 were playing both in Nigeria and, on occasion, back in the UK where the original films were processed and stored.[121]

By 1935, Sellers's work was increasingly recognized and championed by his superiors. Dr. Thomson, the acting director of medical services, wrote to the government's chief secretary after watching Sellers's films at the Health and Baby Week in Lagos. Thomson praised the "extreme value" of the show: "The films were witnessed each evening, not by hundreds but literally by thousands and there can be no doubt of the impression made. The audiences comprised every class, old and young, literate and illiterate and their reactions and applause demonstrated beyond any questions their enthusiasm and the depth of the impression made."[122]

With Sellers's work noted in high places, he not only got a promotion but also the chance to head up a newly established Health Propaganda Unit. The unit's formation was a validation of Sellers's existing work, with film production no longer consigned to his "spare time." It also formalized a particular use of film that, aligned with specific government initiatives like Health and Baby Weeks, formed one part of health propaganda. There were comparable moves elsewhere in the empire. James Burns and Nadine Chan have recently highlighted the widespread development of the rural caravan in Malaya, taking locally produced films—the first of which, *Thrift and Extravagance,* was also produced in 1929 by a member of the Medical Department—to rural Malays. The films, it was determined, must "reek of the soil in which it is shown" and often used the Mr. Wise and Mr. Foolish format to teach "good colonial citizenship" and administer what Chan refers to as "the regulation of private economic life." These were not isolated screenings but part of the "overall machinery" of government, supported by lectures, demonstrations, and advice from officials.[123]

Sellers also connected his work with school education. The mobile cinema van often traveled with a model exhibit, showing ideal sanitary structures, and set up in a local school or hall. For this, the unit directly targeted educators, seeking to instruct teachers, headmasters, health workers, and local chiefs, even staying to watch the local teachers repeat the lessons to their students. These afternoon lectures could last three hours—without any films shown—and were supported by government literature (24,000 copies of a booklet entitled "School and Domestic Sanitation for Rural Districts" were distributed free to all schoolteachers). The unit would even visit the homes of these "influential Africans" so that they could encourage and inspire others. Sellers similarly looked to identify and garner the support of respected local figures when organizing the CFU's film shows. In this way, he quickly recognized the need to work with local Africans to ensure that the unit's messages were reinforced and supported not only during their brief visit but also more significantly after the van's departure.[124]

On a small scale, this process, and in particular the establishment of "rural health units," represents an early move toward a decentralized form of colonial administration. The rural units brought together the resident or district officer, medical officers, representatives of the Native Administration, schoolteachers, and "one or two influential townspeople (literate and illiterate of both sexes)," and received material assistance from Sellers's central Health Propaganda Unit. Members of the rural unit would meet monthly to arrange local activities and Sellers would follow their progress through the monthly minutes. By 1938, when six of the rural units were up and running, Sellers determined that the mobile cinema shows were "more fruitful" in towns with rural health units, supporting the notion that films worked best in conjunction with wider government work.[125]

The daytime lectures and displays would be followed by the evening cinema show. Official government reports claimed audiences of up to fifteen thousand at a show and suggested that the appearance of the van could collect a quarter of the town's population within a few minutes. Over a period of three years, the mobile cinema would provide more than four hundred demonstrations across seventeen of the twenty-two Nigerian provinces to an estimated audience in excess of one and a half million. While the scale and reach were used to validate the unit's work, Sellers's experiences with the mobile film unit in Nigeria would also inform his hugely influential theories on colonial audiences and, by extension, the work of the Colonial Film Unit.[126] Brian Larkin has brilliantly examined these film shows and shown how Sellers was already imagining and organizing the film space as a political space. "The spectators at these events were addressed not as consumers but as citizens," Larkin wrote, "and what was exchanged was not money but political education."[127] I will discuss the film show in detail in chapter 2, but a closer look here at the health films produced and shown by Sellers elucidates the ways in which he already imagined and used film to shape the conduct and productivity of modern colonial citizens and to generate their loyalty to the empire.

The first film produced by Sellers in Nigeria directly responded to the crisis that had led him to Nigeria, the bubonic plague. The exact date of *Anti-Plague Operations, Lagos* is complicated by its apparent reworking over time. While most likely initially produced in 1929, government reports list versions of the film—including *Anti-Plague Operations in Lagos 1932*, and others from 1933 and 1937—as additional material was added. These government films were malleable, constantly evolving, reworked by the filmmaker and, in particular, by local commentators at the site of exhibition. In this instance, the initial footage focuses on the immediate, practical responses to the plague in Lagos—the numerous different ways of catching and removing rats. By 1937 the film is more clearly a celebration of what has been done and a record of the progressive work of government. With greater emphasis on town-planning initiatives and the longer-term British responses to the problem, the film now acknowledges the shifting response to, and apparent successful eradication of, the plague.[128] Sellers's films often foreground these preventative methods. *Anti-Malaria Field Work* (ca. 1933) depicts the construction of drainage systems and shows the use of "Paris Green" (arsenic salts) to kill off larvae. In showing bush clearing and the eradication of disease, it celebrates the European conquest of the colonial land.[129]

These early films played in February 1933 to local Nigerian audiences at the Lagos Health Week, and then a few months later in June at the National Baby Week Council in Kingsway Hall in London. While the primary audience was local—although even this is multifarious, including "primitive peoples" and respected teachers, chiefs, and health officials—Sellers's early films traveled and served both to instruct locals in particular methods and to showcase the health work carried out in the colonies. They were used in Tanganyika and South Africa and by the director of medical services in Sierra Leone and were also picked up by the Ministry of Health in England, the Church Missionary Society in London, and the Society for the Care of Infants in New Zealand.[130] In this way, the films could variously serve as instructional films for local audiences but also as an advertisement for the pioneering work of the Health Department and for the wider use of film in colonial administration.

We can see these often-conflicting aims in Sellers's early films, such as *Infant Welfare Work in Nigeria* (ca. 1933), which depicts the work and training (by European women) of African nurses and health visitors. The film outlines the merits of infant health clinics, but rather than performing or replicating the work of the clinics, it directly encourages its audience to support and attend these government centers. "All mothers are welcome at the Infant Welfare Clinics which are held in the afternoons," a title explains before the film concludes with additional details: "Lagos Clinics at Massey Street Dispensary on Monday, Tuesday and Friday. Ebute Metta Clinics at 1, Ondo Street West, Every Tuesday." This is an advertisement, time-sensitive and primarily intended for a very localized audience, which comprised women and, in particular, mothers. The health unit acknowledged this audience—"Lectures were also given to the general public, when women were specially urged to attend"—but, despite this, Sellers would not distinguish by gender or address a female audience when conceptualizing "primitive" African audiences.[131]

The final title in *Infant Welfare Work* illustrates how these films were supplementing other government schemes. This is clearly articulated in the many films of Health and Baby Weeks (there are films from 1933, 1935, and 1937 and the footage reappears in numerous other films, including later versions of *Anti-Plague Operations*). These films use familiar signifiers of colonial authority—fans of the pith helmet will not be disappointed (see Figure 1.7)—and showcase the modernizing work

Interwar Movement of Nonfiction Film | 49

FIGURE 1.7. Rebuilding the town in *Anti-Plague Operations, Lagos, 1937*.

FIGURE 1.8. William Sellers's mobile cinema van used for Lagos Health Week. Screengrab from *Anti-Plague Operations, Lagos, 1937*.

of the colonial powers. Film is an integral part of this modernization agenda and images of the film shows and the mobile van feature prominently and recurrently (see Figure 1.8). Footage from the 1935 event most notably celebrates the technology here; the van is set up, the screen erected, the power supply plugged in, and the music plays on the turntable. Other films contain shots of the power cables overhead and also highlight the mobility of the unit—one film shows the mobile cinema traveling on a small ferry—showcasing the work of the unit but also more broadly the ability of the colonial powers to show film and bring this new technology to the colonies.

The films of Health and Baby Weeks also serve as a record, taking these events and exhibits on tour. They move the various stalls—cot-making, an anti-mosquito section, food exhibition, or gardening exhibits—beyond the restricted space and time of the health week. Yet clearly Sellers's films are not all (and always) directly instructing and shaping colonial citizens but are also showcasing this process, providing only brief glimpses of the instruction and affording as much attention to the appreciative crowds. What we see here is the empire in action. An untitled Sellers film showing the work of the medical teams in rural areas depicts the medical checks, displays the sickly patients to camera, and offers multiple lingering shots of the injections. The film celebrates modern British medicine and the training and support of African medical officers, who look through microscopes under the supervision of a European officer. While the film may be intended for rural Africans, it makes no attempt to explain why these people require injections or to show the successful recovery of those injected. Instead, it highlights to educated Nigerians and to British and overseas audiences the work of colonial health officers. This health education appears, as historian Megan Vaughan argues, "highly ritualistic."[132] The numerous sequences of physical training, the militarized displays of schoolchildren and even the orderly lines of attending, uniformed children celebrate, through the pageantry of the empire, the state's control and organization of its citizens. While film is used as part of this process—to encourage "better" practice—it also provides evidence of its success and of the broader welfare efforts of the British state.

This is most clearly articulated in some of Sellers's story films, such as the two-reeler *Young Nigeria* (ca. 1937). The film shows the state's support for a young woman from pregnancy through to the early years of her son's life. In highlighting the work of the maternity home in Massey Street (shown also in *Infant Welfare Clinics*), the film not only presents an aspirational model of childbirth but also of domestic life. The husband visits his wife and new baby in the maternity home and then goes home to build a cot. He is shown cleaning the space, while the young boy, shown at ages two and six, attends school in his uniform and completes his homework. The state continues to look after him—when he hurts his ankle, he goes to the school clinic—while the film highlights the success and support for this system as the pregnant mother returns to the maternity clinic to have another child at the end of the film. To reinforce the paternal support of the state here, a title asks the mother, "Are you pleased you took my advice?" The mother responds, "I am pleased and very grateful to you." *Progress in the Colonies: An African Hospital* (ca. 1933) shows the state's care for a cyclist who has been knocked down by a truck. He is taken by ambulance to the hospital where he is given an injection and has an x-ray. The film shows both European and African doctors and celebrates, through medicine, the modern colonial state. The film concludes with a shot of the patient smiling.

Sellers's films also connect to the other related strands of health propaganda. The films of Health and Baby Weeks show the model exhibits and linger on the hand-drawn posters, with captions reading "There's health for all clean children," "Health insurance—no age limit," "Health via cleanliness," "Good health makes happy homes," and "Where there's bad health there's misery." These posters are consistent with the notion of happiness extolled in Sellers's films. *Dirt Brings Sickness— Cleanliness Brings Health* (ca. 1935) follows a familiar narrative structure by showing "Before" (bad practice represented by tapeworm, a boy limping with a stick, flies hovering around rubbish) and "After" (good practice represented by a mother washing her child, kids exercising and collecting water from a tank). This structure extends to the stalls at Health and Baby Weeks, which included a "Clean House" and an "Unclean House," and on the posters that contrasted the happy/healthy with the unhappy/sick. In one poster, two healthy boys comment, "Look how unhealthy and miserable they are. But we are always happy because we are healthy." In *Slum Clearance and Town Planning* (ca. 1933), Sellers shows the slum housing from 1930 and then the new houses, schools, shops, and "wider motor roads" introduced thereafter. Modernization is aligned to health here as a title explains that "with those that live under these ideal conditions, health, happiness, prosperity and long life go hand in hand." As with the work of Dr. Paterson in East Africa, happiness and economic prosperity are aligned to health and this health is provided by the colonial state.

Sellers produced *Slum Clearance and Town Planning* with the credited assistance of C. L. Waide, the town planning officer in Lagos. Sellers would show films from other departments and film companies, and while often very different, they would further inform the work of the Colonial Film Unit. *The Oil Palm Industry*, made by Dr. Thomas in collaboration with the Agricultural Department, is an industrial process film that would not be out of place in British Instructional's Empire series. The film emphasizes the *value* of work—foregrounding worker payment—and in its editing flourishes and short shot duration, is notably removed from the film language that Sellers would promote. Sellers included other commercial films, such as the Charlie Chaplin comedy *The Man Hunt*—colonial orthodoxy stated that African audiences loved Chaplin and slapstick—and Ruby Grierson's short documentary *The Heart of an Empire* (1935).

The Man Hunt proved enormously popular, too popular in some cases, with reports that audiences immediately forgot or overlooked any message from the other government productions.[133] Significantly, *The Man Hunt* was an edited version of *The Adventurer* (1917), taking specific sequences that were deemed appropriate. In this way, it already adhered to Sellers's belief that films needed to be specially adapted or created for African audiences. Indeed, one of the early challenges for the CFU was to satisfy audience demand for further Chaplin films. As *Colonial Cinema* explained in 1942, many of his films were deemed inappropriate, often for ideological reasons and the oft-repeated fear of undermining authority and, in particular, racial and gender norms. Sequences that the CFU avoided included "Chaplin or some other character dressing himself up as a woman; scenes which showed the police in a bad light; scenes in which a priest or a clergyman was a figure of fun."[134] There were also cultural changes—snow is not so funny to an "audience who thinks that snow is sand and wonders how it sticks together"—while the CFU warned that comic scenes "would fall very flat in the case of the less sophisticated." In releasing another edited Chaplin film (*Charlie the Rascal*, 1942) it reinforced its position as moral arbiters, creating and curating specialized films.[135]

The Heart of an Empire was not adapted for African audiences and indeed makes no reference to African or West Indian colonies. Much like the earlier Empire Marketing Board films, it maps the empire primarily through its economic links to Britain. In particular, the film indicates how interwar nonfiction film positions London—its history, its pageantry, and the grandeur of its buildings—as the physical and ideological center of the empire.[136] While Sellers determined by the late 1930s that "films produced locally are the only type that are appreciated and understood by illiterate Africans," the CFU's home unit would foreground, through the iconography of London in films like *An African in London* (1941), both Britain's primacy and her acceptance of

Africans within this imperial center.[137] While on leave in the UK, Sellers produced *A Day with an English Baby Boy* (ca. 1937), a possible attempt to relate aspirational British life and methods to the African viewer. It is also a clear precursor to the first film produced by the CFU, *Mr. English at Home* (1940).

Sellers's work in Nigeria would shape the Colonial Film Unit in myriad ways. Most tangibly, a number of the films produced by Sellers in Nigeria—such as *An African Hospital, Barless Incinerator,* and *Machi Gaba*—would be reedited by the CFU and shown across Africa during the war. However, for the most part it is the perceived "failings" of these early films, whether produced or used by Sellers, that would solidify Sellers's approach to film and, in particular, his language when addressing "primitive" African audiences. There are very specific anecdotes from screenings—audiences distracted by a chicken moving on the edge of the frame in *Anti-Plague Operations* and reading the close-up of an "enormous" mosquito in literal terms in Kodak's *The Life History of a Mosquito* (no date known)—which would inform the film practices of the Colonial Film Unit. As such, these early films might appear inconsistent or deviate from the subsequent work of the CFU. Certainly, they reveal a desire to understand and develop a language for "primitive" audiences. For example, *Slum Clearance and Town Planning in Lagos* looks to train its audience—"Look at this Bird's Eye view of Oko Awo, photographed from the Great Mosque in Victoria Street"—but also provides a level of detail that Sellers would avoid in future. He asks the audience to "compare these plans" for new buildings, and it is hard to imagine a local audience desperately interested in seeing a picture of the chairman of the Lagos Executive Development Board. Sellers was quick to recognize these problems, self-critical of an early tendency to present local culture through a British context, and by the late 1930s had largely formulated his influential views on colonial audiences. Sellers now wrote of the "care" required when producing films for Nigerians who are "primitive people and whose strongest emotion is fear." "Films must have a familiar background," he wrote, "the general tempo of the films must be slow throughout and they should contain human interests, be faithful to native habits and customs and state true facts." Sellers further argued that "affairs of the heart" should be avoided and, in a notable break from more celebrated documentary film, so too should "transition by suggestion and camera tricks."[138]

SELLERS IN LONDON: THE START OF THE COLONIAL FILM UNIT, 1939

Sellers handed a detailed report of the Health Propaganda Unit's activities to Christopher Eastwood at the Colonial Office when back in the UK in August 1939. Impressed with what he read, Eastwood circulated it to all African governments. The report not only reflected on the work of Sellers in Nigeria but also, on the cusp of war, looked to the future. It outlined the merits of a central film organization in London, one that would edit and process films from the colonies and connect films and ideas across the empire.[139]

The report from Nigeria explained how this film work could be extended beyond health—for example, to further the efforts of the Agricultural Department—and outlined the many ways in which films might be shown in schools or to "influential people" in "remote places" otherwise cut off from government administration. Its priorities were outlined in its budget, which called for an additional cinema van, projection facilities, and a library of "suitable" commercial films. The report stressed that Sellers should be put in "complete charge" to oversee all production, organize a central film library, arrange the itineraries of the units, and train African staff in the exhibition of film.[140]

Sellers's plans—and in particular, evidence of his achievements—arrived at an opportune moment. On 15 May 1939, the colonial governments received a highly confidential report outlining plans for a Ministry of Information in the event of war. The correspondence quizzed each colonial government about their existing press and publicity channels and initially sought to coordinate activities across the empire.[141] On reviewing these responses, the secretary of state for the colonies, Malcolm MacDonald, outlined to the governors the particular ways in which film might serve the colonial war effort. As a priority, the MOI would send additional projectors and a cinema van to both Nigeria and the Gold Coast.[142] These priorities now neatly dovetailed with Sellers's proposals.

Sellers's report circulated around the Colonial Office and the responses to it acknowledge a more receptive context for government film within the colonies. When one official at the Colonial Office adopted a familiar response, stating that it was a "pity that financial considerations prevent expansion at present," he was widely challenged. Others now suggested that Sellers's proposal was "obviously just up the new C.D.F.'s [Colonial Development Fund] street" and it would be a "tragedy" if it was abandoned. The under-secretary of state for the colonies suggested it would be "good business" to proceed with "this cinema propaganda." "It seems to offer," he wrote, "the possibilities of a short cut to results which otherwise may take a lot of time and a lot of money." In this way, the main stumbling block throughout the previous decade—the unquantifiable *value* of this instructional cinema—was dismissed. With the prospect of war, this now represented "good business."[143]

The discussions, anxieties, and arguments projected over the previous decade by educationalists like Orr and Latham, scientists like Huxley, and health officials like Sellers, now came into sharp focus. The exigencies of war foregrounded particular functions (for example, around population management) and a mode of delivery (the mobile film show) that resonated with Sellers's specific health work in Nigeria. At the same time, Bruce Woolfe and Mary Field were working on a new series of Empire films for British and international audiences that sought to dispel the idea that "the Empire consists mainly of wheat and apples," instead highlighting, on the cusp of war, an empire that was connected and mobilized. Based upon a "new teaching method" and telling these histories through animated diagrams, the films were focused, not on individual colonies or products, but around the oceans.[144] *Atlantic* (1940), which was produced for the British Council, highlights trade routes and concludes by celebrating and mythologizing the British role across the empire, "where the wilderness has been made to blossom. Human beings are free and problems are settled by arbitration."[145] As the music builds to a crescendo, the map of the empire transforms into a question mark and the commentator asks, "What comes next?" This was a question not only for the British Empire, now facing war, but also for nonfiction film, looking not only to generate support for the empire in Britain, but also increasingly to instruct and mobilize citizens across the empire.

The earlier example of *Black Cotton* highlighted the mobility of film—moving products and ideologies across the empire—with these ideas expounded by Grierson and the Empire Marketing Board and motivating the albeit tentative and often aborted plans in the 1930s for film pedagogy in the colonies. Malcolm MacDonald's report now foregrounded the role of cinema vans in reaching citizens across vast spaces, keeping "in touch" with all the important towns and villages. The movement of cinema, a symbol of colonial modernization, was a product of decades of colonial exploration, expansion, and exploitation, manifested (and realized) more recently through the infrastructural development of road networks. In Nigeria, the report explained, there were 21,000 miles of "motorable" roads, of which 8,000 were all-weather (the numbers were 6,500 and 2,119 respectively in the Gold Coast).[146]

In describing how the mobile cinema show would work, MacDonald's report followed many of the "rules" previously outlined by Sellers (and others). Without any detail or discussion, it presupposed Sellers's arguments about audience comprehension, explaining that films would be "carefully graded by the Information Officers according to the different types of native audience." The film was imagined again as one part of the show. The operator would give a talk to the crowd in a local language (and would provide "news" from the war). He would play records through a gramophone, including a speech "of exhortation to his African subjects by the King himself," while the lessons from the film would be followed up afterwards by postcards and pamphlets distributed among the audience. Significantly the report recognized that the scheme required "educated Africans," multilingual figures, to speak at the shows and assist the European officials. The report even listed offices, banks, and educational institutions where suitable candidates might be found.[147] The selection and training of the traveling staff would be "exacting" and, as so often, was presented as an example of the tentative, carefully moderated exchange of power between colonizer and colonized. A government memorandum in the Gold Coast explained: "The Information Department holds its mobile cinema staff in high regard as an example of the high degree of attainment possible when the right Africans are chosen with the right kind of education and given further training under the close personal supervision of the right kind of European."[148] One of the primary functions of the CFU was to train and define the "right" kind of citizens, both as producers and consumers of government propaganda.

In the summer of 1939 as war came closer into view, the Colonial Office reviewed and supported further proposals, most notably from the West Indies. For this, the BFI advocated the employment of a film expert who could train "local personnel" in the production of "simple films of local subjects."[149] Eastwood intervened here, recognizing an opportunity to expand Sellers's role with the MOI. He explained that the "germ" of such a scheme, to produce 16mm educational films, already existed with Sellers at the MOI.[150] Sellers provided some notes on this which, in effect, outlined a proposal for an expanded CFU, one that could move beyond West Africa.

Sellers proposed two types of film, based on their place of production. "Films of England" would be produced entirely in the UK, while "Films of the Colonies" would be shot by "local officials" and then processed and edited in London. While the CFU would, by necessity, present scenes of British life, Sellers championed the work of the local expert. He spoke repeatedly of "how easily, how inexpensively and above all how effectively" films could be produced by "almost any member of staff." For Sellers, film was not the preserve of the professional filmmaker, an outsider visiting and glimpsing at unfamiliar cultures. It was not an elitist form championed by "artists" but an instructional tool, available and useful to those, albeit still "colonizers," with an intimate knowledge of the country, industry, or problems addressed on screen.[151]

In explaining how this would work, Sellers created a need and *place* for an expanded Colonial Film Unit. The need was addressed through his own writings and earlier work in Nigeria, foregrounding a specific language and set of requirements for colonial audiences. The place was marked by a mediated relationship between the center (a London-based CFU) and the periphery (the officers in the colonies). As a model for colonial administration, Sellers explained how the central authority would exercise influence and authority in the colonies. The CFU in London would provide each "regional centre" with camera equipment and a "hand-book of special instructions." It would discuss appropriate subjects with the regional centers and agree on a shooting script, which would be prepared by the London-based CFU and would "contain clear detailed instructions regarding such things as camera angle and distance." The CFU would provide film stock for the regional centers to shoot the films, but they would be processed, titled, and edited back in London. The completed films would be housed in a central library where they would be available for general distribution.[152]

Sellers described this model as "practical, economical and [it] gives each colony an opportunity of taking an active part in the production of films." At the outset of war and with a threadbare budget, there was little chance of the CFU sending production units around the territories, but it also reflected Sellers's own background as a government official making films, privileging local expertise so that the films would be "most suited to the local mentality." Sellers's language highlights the need for local knowledge, but unsurprisingly at a moment when he was trying to establish the Colonial Film Unit, he also espouses a close level of control from London, a centralized model in which all film would flow through the imperial center.[153]

This center was found in Soho Square, the spiritual home of the Documentary Film Unit, where the CFU initially borrowed space, equipment, and technical expertise from the GPO Film Unit. In this way, the paths of documentary, educational, and instructional cinema intersected once more. Indeed, Sellers's first, and most important, appointment for the CFU was working as a writer for the GPO unit (in "the Documentary film world"), when Sellers convinced him to join him as film director early in 1940.[154] George Pearson is best remembered today as a pioneer of British silent cinema, a champion of cinematic "art," celebrated as a pivotal figure in British fiction film. Yet his career highlights the tributaries of fiction, prestige documentary, and education flowing from British cinema and out across the empire.

Pearson began as a schoolteacher, and in order to attain the post of Film Producer at London's Pathé studio in 1912, he had to quit his post as a headmaster. He saw film as an opportunity to speak beyond the classroom walls, "a vehicle for mass instruction, direct or even indirect through entertainment, a teacher's true medium, as yet unused, and scorned as disreputable."[155] By the mid-1920s, in line with the professionalization of public relations, he emphasized the wider potential of cinema in shaping populations and behavior across the world. "The kinema is the greatest, the most tremendously powerful force for the bringing about of that universal brotherhood of the world that mankind has ever known," he wrote in 1924, "and only by living for it, giving oneself to it, housing it, seeing it, and believing in it, can great things from it be achieved."[156] Such an acknowledgment brought with it a threat. By this stage, Pearson was president of the Association of British Film Directors and was directly involved in the discussions to promote British film in the mid-1920s. "The Cinema screen had become a powerful medium for influencing public opinion," he recalled in his autobiography; "the American way of life, so attractively revealed in their films was clearly affecting our British outlook. The British film was being strangled."[157]

Pearson brought a particular perspective to the CFU, an experience and awareness of the roots from which this cinema emerged. As a producer in the 1920s, he had confronted the threats of American cultural imperialism as British images faded from colonial screens. He was an accomplished professional filmmaker but also a teacher, embedded in the world of fiction but with recent experience in documentary. His views on documentary film were informed by his own background in fiction. He identified *Grapes of Wrath* (1940) as a model, emphasizing the importance of emotion, dramatization, and screencraft, of "interpreting" rather than recording. Documentary represented a "fearsome word" that conjures "words *not* pictures," and "non-theatrical" as a byword for "non-entertainment" was a "completely suicidal attribute." It may seem strange that a man who championed film as an art form should take up a position with the CFU and should embrace Sellers's doctrine on film form. Yet, Pearson would bring his commercial sensibilities (an emphasis on story and emotion) to the CFU and was clearly drawn to the wider project. Describing his time with the CFU as "a destined end," Pearson embraced "a teacher's classroom with no boundary walls, a world of film in a vaster field of purpose, the enlightenment of the unenlightened peoples."[158]

Pearson recalled the CFU's "humble beginning" at 21 Soho Square with a staff of four. "I had no conception that the tiny staff would increase tenfold," he later wrote, "nor that the work would continue for over fifteen years to help towards a closer understanding between the Motherland and her Colonial children."[159] That it did continue and expand beyond the war, through cataclysmic changes, new governments, and onto redrawn maps, owes much to the early work of Sellers and Pearson and, in particular, their ideology for colonial cinema that defined and justified a culturally specific form of cinema which was not adequately served by prestige documentary or other existing forms of nonfiction film. This ideology, developed by colonial filmmakers in the interwar years, found its expression through the CFU filmmakers, in their writings and talks, in their teachings both to the "expert" expats and later to a first generation of "local" filmmakers, and most of all through their films. This is most clearly evidenced in the first CFU production, *Mr. English at Home*, a template for the cinema that followed.

CHAPTER 2

Film Rules

The Governing Principles of the Colonial Film Unit

The first Colonial Film Unit production, *Mr. English at Home* (1940), opens with a long shot of a policeman walking along the pavement (from right to left) on an otherwise deserted suburban English street. After he walks off screen, the film cuts to the exterior of one of the houses he passed, then to an upstairs window where a woman is drawing back the curtains. The next shot is inside the house, as the mother fully opens the curtains and wakes her son. For the next few minutes, the film follows the young boy, and through the editing that connects by the opening and closing of doors, orientates his movements as he leaves his bedroom, enters the hallway, and then arrives in the bathroom. In a particularly lengthy single shot, the boy washes and brushes his teeth, before drying himself for what feels like an eternity. He eventually leaves the bathroom, wakes his sister, and returns to his bedroom where he gets dressed into his school uniform. He leaves the room, walks downstairs, and sits for breakfast opposite his father (the titular Mr. English), who is drinking tea and eating egg and toast. Mr. English leaves the table and, after taking the newspaper and kissing his wife goodbye, walks out of the front door. A shot from the exterior of the house shows him closing the door and walking off screen. He is next seen walking toward a bus stop, where he gets on a double-decker bus. After the bus leaves the screen, the shot fades and we see a building site where Mr. English walks from off screen to center frame.[1]

These opening few moments in the life of the Colonial Film Unit, drawing back the curtains and introducing itself to the world, assume a significant place in the history of the unit. The sequence would help to define colonial cinema throughout, and sometimes beyond, the CFU's fifteen-year existence, serving as both a template for its work and a justification for its existence. These first waking moments introduce a specialized form of colonial cinema, propagate a dominant colonial ideology, and foreground themes and representational tropes that would shape the cinema that follows. What may appear an instantly forgettable domestic scene would become a staple of William Sellers's showreel, reused when outlining the aims, function, and operating principles of the unit. This extract featured on BBC TV in January 1948, when Sellers discussed with Roger Manvell the film technique used for African audiences, and was shown by John Maddison, of the Central Office of Information (COI), when speaking on the use of cinema for "primitive peoples" at the Sorbonne in September 1947. A version of Maddison's lecture was subsequently broadcast on the BBC overseas service and applied to other empires when published in *La Revue Internationale de Filmologie*.[2] Even in the last days of the unit in 1953, Sellers showed this sequence as part of his talk to the Royal Society of Arts and again a few months later when presenting in Sicily at a UNESCO event on the use of visual aids in fundamental education.[3] So why was this brief sequence, and this first film, so useful to Sellers and the CFU?

In the first instance, this representation of British life responded to particular colonial priorities within Africa (and indeed from Sellers's own background), for example in foregrounding cleanliness and hygiene. When a Ministry of Information (MOI) official questioned the film's depiction of such a clean home and indeed the display of porcelain basins and chromium bath taps, the unit's director, George Pearson, explained that the home was "carefully chosen" and was "absolutely correct in type and cleanliness." "The underlying lesson is one of order and a clean home," he added.[4] Indeed the film extolls British ideals and order through its depiction of the family and home. The opening sequence centers on the male characters and defines Mrs. English's role in relation to them (waking up her son, handing her husband his hat) as she is introduced, to borrow the title of a proposed unmade 1948 sequel, as "Mrs. English the Homemaker." This emphasis on cleanliness and the management of domestic space is further evident in another somewhat unappealing working title for the sequel, "Mrs. English Cleans and Cooks."[5] The gender roles are also clearly defined through the camera in *Mr. English at Home*, so that when father and son sit centrally framed at the table building a model airplane, mother and daughter knit at a lower level in the corner. The film not only represents a traditional, idealized model of domestic life, but emphasizes the ways in which this can be achieved through hard work. In this way, Sellers uses the sequence to illustrate film's broader value as a colonizing agent.

When showing this sequence, Sellers often recounted individual responses to show that African audiences recognized and embraced these clearly defined roles. He noted, for example, a viewer that praised Mr. English's "high sense of responsibilities" and labeled his wife "a true specimen of a conscientious and dutiful helpmate."[6] More significantly, the audience responses were used to show how the film (and by extension film more broadly) challenged popular perceptions of English life by promoting the much-vaunted ideal of hard work. "I have been 22 years in West Africa," Sellers said in 1948 when discussing this sequence, "and know only too well how our way of life in this country is judged by the very artificial lives we officials and others live in the colonies."[7] The CFU presented the film as a retort to the "damaging" images appearing on commercial screens. It quoted African teachers, who on seeing the film remarked, "Do many English women have to work as hard as that?" and "Do they not have servants?" while another viewer contended that to many Africans it came as a revelation that not all English households had a "complement of servants." The responses to the sequence helped showcase its value by confronting those lingering, prewar anxieties around the representation of white women and British authority on colonial screens.[8]

In this way, the film fulfills the interwar calls for more proactive government film work to counter American screen dominance. "No civilized country can to-day afford," wrote Stephen Tallents in his influential 1932 pamphlet, *The Projection of England*, "either to neglect the project of its national personality or to resign its projection to others."[9] A pivotal figure in the history of the British Documentary Movement, Tallents emphasized the need to project positive British values as a counter to global threats on the nation. The sequence focuses on traditional signifiers of English identity—the policeman in the opening shot, the double-decker bus, drinking tea (which represent order, modernization, and imperial trade)—and reveals its documentary roots by prioritizing the "everyman," selecting a hard-working "lower-middle-class" family as its model.[10] The film's image of the English town—the transport networks, technological infrastructure (the power cables spotted in the first shot), schools, shops, and, of course, the home that Mr. English both enjoys and, in his work, helps construct for others—showcases the models that the CFU would seek to export after the war (for example, in instructional films on house-building or education). Noticeably at the height of war, *Mr. English at Home* conceals all traces of conflict, instead highlighting the aspirational function of the English family and projecting a nation, and way of life, worth defending.[11]

The parallels with the more celebrated work of the documentary movement are unsurprising as at this stage in 1940 the CFU was sharing not only equipment but also a workforce with the General Post Office (GPO) unit in Soho Square. While *Mr. English at Home* was "devised" by Sellers, it was directed by 23-year-old Gordon Hales and photographed by 24-year-old Faulder (Fred) Gamage. Hales had advertised his services in *World Film News* in 1937 "for any wage, however small, all hours, anywhere"—a sentiment that received a strong rebuke from the Association of Cine-Technicians—but having joined GPO went on to enjoy a successful career principally as an editor.[12] Gamage was also trained at GPO and subsequently served as Humphrey Jennings's cinematographer, working on such seminal wartime documentary productions as *Listen to Britain* (1942), *A Diary for Timothy* (1946), and on the postwar Oscar-winning Crown production in Nigeria, *Daybreak in Udi* (1949). *Mr. English at Home* contains traces of the wartime cinema of the Crown Film Unit, particularly in its celebration of British life, but it also clearly outlines the ways in which the CFU would develop its own distinct response to war. In particular, the sequence reveals the CFU's "specialized" film technique, and it is in this way that the opening of *Mr. English at Home* proved most durable and useful for the CFU.

When introducing this sequence in 1953, William Sellers quoted an East African official who stated that the film is "certainly a lesson in the presentation of a subject to illiterate Africans through the medium of cinema." This "lesson" is presented in these opening few moments. The sequence involves minimal camera movement (exemplified by the lengthy, static shot of the boy washing), and largely avoids ellipsis or multiple movements on screen (as seen in the opening shot with the policeman). The "simple" editing seeks to train the spectator—mapping movements on and off screen and through doors—and while using fades, avoids cross-cutting or "trick" devices popular in other forms of documentary. The report from East Africa further noted the value of such a "simple" approach when explaining that "the characters are few and the scenes remain on the screen sufficiently long for the native to appreciate their meaning."[13] In these ways, the sequence became a template for the CFU's work. Years later in June 1947, *Colonial Cinema* described the film as "a classic of its type," adding that it "has never to this day lost its popularity with the unsophisticated film-goer. It is slow in tempo and almost perfect in pictorial continuity."[14]

Sellers used this sequence, in part, to justify the CFU's existence. In showcasing a "specialized technique" for illiterate colonial audiences, Sellers reasoned that existing nonfiction films were not fit for that audience. In effect, Sellers claimed a monopoly over this cinema, establishing the rules for colonial audiences and then controlling its production. This *modus operandi* became its calling card, repeatedly cited in Sellers's institutional dealings, in his calls for further staff, financial support, or control. For example, in 1941 when he was trying to divorce his unit from Crown, he explained: "Films for African audiences require very different material from films for Western audiences. It is therefore very desirable that we should make our own arrangements and thus save a great deal of trouble."[15]

Emphasizing the specific requirements for African audiences would also help protect the CFU from criticism. Members of the Films Division of the MOI (in effect, the traces of the British Documentary Movement) and the Educational Advisory Committee at the Colonial Office were quick to chastise *Mr. English at Home*'s slow, dull, and seemingly regressive form, but Sellers was able to counter with individual reports from audience members and colonial officials.[16] He showed *Mr. English at Home* as part of a program of ten films during his first overseas CFU trip to West Africa in June 1940. He gathered essays on the film from schoolgirls, which he would quote from, and argued that the film was "in a class by itself" and at every demonstration was "voted the most popular by a very substantial margin."[17] Responses to a questionnaire sent to colonial officials in 1943 labeled *Mr. English at Home* the most popular film in Nigeria, Kenya, and the Gold Coast, and there were even reports that the film had found its way to Bangkok where university students "voted it the best film which they had seen as giving them a clear idea of life in a foreign country."[18] These widely circulated responses reinforced the notion of difference, that these films should not be judged by Western audiences or by existing criteria (such as aesthetics), but instead could only be appreciated by African audiences and by their effectiveness and *usefulness* within the colonies, which of course would be determined and reported by the CFU. Defending the CFU approach in the first issue of its in-house magazine, *Colonial Cinema,* an editorial acknowledged: "Some people, seeing their first Colonial

Film Unit production, dismiss it as a simple straight forward silent film. In fact, of course, the films are not so easy as they look."[19]

The opening few minutes of *Mr. English at Home* addressed themes and representational tropes that would reappear across the CFU's work, while the audience responses served to highlight the broader value of film in challenging colonial perceptions, constructing loyal colonial workers, and shaping the relationship between colonizer and colonized. However, such a process was only possible, the CFU argued, through its distinct film form, which in turn promotes a pervading colonial ideology and embodies a colonial logic. In foregrounding difference, in assuming British intellectual primacy, in suggesting African audiences were more susceptible to media and in showing the need to train and develop colonial audiences, this form of cinema became a further means to justify not only the existence of the CFU, but also, throughout a period of war and civil uprising, the continuation of the British Empire.

WHY DID THE CHICKEN CROSS THE SCREEN? DEFINING COLONIAL FILM

In March 1940 during the filming of *Mr. English at Home*, *Documentary News Letter* published an article entitled "Films for Primitive Peoples: A New Technique."[20] The article borrowed heavily from William Sellers's previous writings and argued that his work in Nigeria "proved clearly that films for natives must be regarded as a highly specialised subject." In noting that existing educational films were "of little use," "Films for Primitive Peoples" listed five "essential rules," formulated by Sellers in Nigeria, which "must be followed in making films for primitive populations."[21]

> 1. The general tempo must be slow, and the length of individual scenes must be twice or three times as long as is usually considered necessary for English school audiences.
>
> 2. The content of any given scene must be very simple in its composition, because natives view all objects on the screen with equal interest, unless the important object is clearly emphasised. Close and mid shots are therefore preferable to long shots.
>
> 3. Strict accuracy is vital in portraying native habits and customs. Mistakes at once turn a serious film into a comedy.
>
> 4. No camera tricks of any sort. Continuity must be clearly maintained in all changes of scene, even if it means using three shots where one would normally do for audiences more used to film technique.

5. Films must be made as silent. A master commentary is then written, and is added by a native commentator, or by disc records, through a microphone during each performance. This system is vital, owing to the great variation in local dialects.²²

Sellers published his own credited version of this doctrine eighteen months later in September 1941, once more in the pages of *Documentary News Letter* and again under the title "Films for Primitive Peoples." While Sellers now stated that "it is not possible to lay down hard and fast rules for the making of films for primitive people," he sought to outline, justify, and theorize these previously stated "rules," using his experiences in Nigeria to legitimize his ideas. Sellers repeated the same anecdotal examples—memorable, extreme, and quite possibly apocryphal tales—that became the factual, historical bedrock on which this colonial cinema was built. The story of the audience laughing inappropriately when shown the scene of a badly maimed leper—"Africans also laugh to express sympathy"—was used to highlight cultural differences but also served as a buttress, providing an explanation for potentially contrary audience reactions that undermined the CFU's aims.²³ The tale of audiences viewing a mosquito in close-up and giving thanks that they didn't have them that size in their own country—not used in "Films for Primitive Peoples," but already popularized by Notcutt and Latham and repeated by Sellers in his talks in 1953—was indicative of the "literal" readings adopted by the African viewer, who "believes everything he sees on screen."²⁴ Audiences distracted by the dog or chicken moving on the edge of the frame provided a warning against excessive movement on screen. Of course, these examples, in generating laughter through cultural difference, also served to celebrate the primacy of the British viewer. Contentious claims are passed off as unquestionable fact and isolated responses as indicative of collective requirements. "These early experiments," Sellers explained in 1941, "proved conclusively that if films were to be successful in conveying a story or teaching a lesson to these people they would have to be specially made."²⁵

"Films for Primitive Peoples" creates a clear division between "them" and "us." In support of his personal experience, Sellers makes scientific claims, which are repeated throughout his career. For example, in discussing the different "angle of acceptance" between the human eye and the cinema camera, he argues that "we" (European viewers) are able to imagine the picture beyond the margins of the frame, while "illiterate people" struggle when "using their imagination this way." Sellers used this to explain why associations through editing and montage should be avoided, why familiar local scenes were favored, and why panning shots, "which educated people have always taken for granted," confuse. If an "illiterate" African sees a vertical panning shot, Sellers reasoned, he will "tell you he saw the buildings sink into the ground." Sellers further surmised that "illiterate people have their own way of looking at a picture," so that while "educated" (and, by extension, Europeans) focus on a point in front of the screen, "the eyes of illiterate people are not trained to see non-stereoscopic things in this way," and so instead focus flat on the screen and fixate on any movement.[26]

The theories proposed here assume different cognitive capabilities for the European and African spectator, between colonizer and colonized, reasserting a division and highlighting the intellectual and cultural superiority used to justify colonialism. Writing a couple of years later, the CFU (and most likely Sellers) clarified that the technique "is skilfully related to the psychology of the African," outlining that conventional tricks of the camera (panning or dolly shots) used to "short-circuit time and space" will "certainly create confusion in the minds of illiterate audiences." Similarly shots should be made from a viewpoint that is "normal," while editing must serve to preserve visual continuity. While a "more sophisticated audience have been educated" to connect dimly related images, "their [illiterate] minds are not sufficiently versatile to comprehend these swift and sudden changes."[27] This last line highlights a tension in the CFU's writings, between the physiological capabilities of the "primitive" spectator ("not sufficiently versatile") and the cultural stage of development ("educated"). For the most part, Sellers implies a process of development and cultural conditioning, concluding that "it is reasonable to believe that the African will not be slow in becoming cinema minded" and that it will be possible "step by step" to introduce "some of the less technical tricks" into these films in due course. A decade later, Sellers suggested that in many areas "illiterate" colonial audiences were becoming "cinema minded" and were "capable of understanding much which only a short while ago was strange and confusing to them."[28]

Sellers's use of the prefix "illiterate" to describe the African viewer further infers a stage of education. In response to a question in 1953, Sellers clarified that he deliberately used the term to refer to those people who have had "no access to pictures, either still or moving." In reading the "grammar of the screen," audiences must be led by "easy stages"—a term he often used—as when new inventions have been "thrust upon" the African, "the result has been confusing and bewildering to their very conservative minds."[29] This rhetoric of audience development

FIGURE 2.1. The front cover of *Colonial Cinema*, June 1951.

connects to wider colonial policy, now imagining the education of the African audience as one part of a colonizing process that would eventually lead to self-government. "The object of the Colonial Film Unit," *Colonial Cinema* explained in 1943, "like that of every branch of colonial administration, is to raise the primitive African to a higher standard of culture."[30]

Sellers's ideas traveled far and wide. "Films for Primitive Peoples" was republished elsewhere—including in *Oversea Education* and *Colonial Review*—articulated in a number of talks, on the BBC Home Service and then, over the next decade, spread through the CFU's publications.[31] In 1942, the CFU established its own in-house magazine, *Colonial Cinema*, which, as its first editorial stated, aimed "to provide a convenient means for the exchange of views on the production, distribution and exhibition of films for specialised audiences in the colonies."[32] The magazine would be widely circulated—by 1950, 1,200 copies were distributed each quarter in thirty-five colonial territories, fourteen foreign countries, and eight American states—and it sought to standardize film practice within the colonies (see Figure 2.1). "Our aim is to make *Colonial Cinema* a really useful magazine to the men in the field," the magazine stated in 1945, "and our hope is that they will make it their forum."[33]

Colonial Cinema contains numerous articles and editorials propagating the unit's specialized technique and these served as direct instruction for the CFU's Raw Stock Scheme. Given the difficulties of sending units into the colonies during the war, and the noted preference for local, familiar scenes, Sellers launched the Raw Stock Scheme in 1941 as a way of getting "enthusiastic amateurs," who were usually government officials, to shoot and send material back to the CFU in London. To this end, he initially provided 16mm cameras and a supply of film stock to six colonial territories (five others joined soon afterwards). Dennis Bowden, who joined the CFU the day before his fourteenth birthday in 1943, worked on the raw stock footage in Soho Square. He recalled that the cameras "were basically given to anyone that could point a camera in the right direction" and how he and his colleagues then "cut it silently, put titles on it and sent it back in a diplomatic bag." Bowden outlined the importance of this scheme beyond the war, claiming that "this basically started all the units, I think, in Africa."[34] While certainly not rejecting the professional filmmaker, there remained a lingering suspicion that professional filmmakers, brought in from other units, may be more reticent to embrace the specialized technique and instead produce "first class photography" ideally suited to "more sophisticated people."[35] The professional might look for "artistic perfection" and would not have "sufficient psychological knowledge of the African," while the "informed amateur would be guided rather by the urgency of the lesson to be learnt" and how it could be presented to the "African mind."[36] As such, *Colonial Cinema* contained numerous articles for the "enthusiastic camera-director" that it hoped would improve the quality of the often patchy and unusable material received from Africa. "We believe," the magazine continued, "that a careful study of articles that will appear from time to time will bring about that improvement and maintain enthusiasm." In this way, *Colonial Cinema* became the instructional manual for these enthusiastic amateurs and Sellers's "specialized technique" the method to follow.

Colonial Cinema identified three "essentials" for those making films—"the *matter*, the *method* and *continuity*"—and included detailed shot breakdowns and practical suggestions.[37] It listed subjects for filming (notably agriculture, hygiene, and housing) and emphasized the importance of showing the process as much as the product—to borrow modern parlance, the "journey" rather than simply the end product—whether depicting Africans building a modern house or gradual improvements in cleanliness and comfort brought about by a new chief.[38] It included reports on completed films and shows in the colonies and, to help the "enthusiastic amateur" further, details about training opportunities for those on leave.

The CFU began courses of instruction at its offices at 21 Soho Square during the war, and one of the early attendees was H. E. Lironi, cinema officer in the Information Department of the Gold Coast. Lironi shared much in common with Sellers and was recruited from the sanitary branch of the Health Department in a bid to replicate Sellers's "pioneer" work in Nigeria. Lironi carefully studied Sellers's ideas, set forth in the "excellent instruction book" provided with the mobile cinemas, before coming to London to train with the CFU in 1943. By this stage, Lironi oversaw a staff of sixteen "highly trained Africans"—operating and supporting four mobile units in the Gold Coast—and offered an unwavering endorsement of Sellers's theories. In a report submitted to the Colonial Office in 1943, the Information Office explained that the CFU films were "of a type and quality obtainable from no other source," and that it was "beyond doubt that a large part of the effectiveness of the Gold Coast Unit" could be credited to the "special qualities of the films supplied by the Colonial Film Unit."[39]

Lironi wrote of his experiences while studying with the CFU in *Colonial Cinema* along with O. Waterfield of the Nigerian Education Department. They explained how they trailed CFU filmmakers, attended courses of instruction, and were then invited to apply the lessons learned to their own production. Both imbued the specialized technique and emphasized the particular requirements needed for colonial audiences. Waterfield noted how the vast majority of existing educational films are of no value as "the technique is too advanced for illiterate audiences," while Lironi surmised that "I had not quite understood just how many different things had to be borne in mind in making a film to appeal successfully to illiterate audiences."[40] When the CFU began its overseas training schools later in the decade, it provided not only practical training but also taught students on subjects such as "Propaganda and the Film" and "Films and Their Audiences" (over four sessions).[41]

Sellers's ideas are rearticulated throughout the pages of *Colonial Cinema*. One further example will suffice. A cameraman on loan from another unit (most likely Crown) explained that his initial perception of the CFU was that "technically the films were beneath contempt for any one seriously interested in his profession." This view is one heard often from documentary filmmakers—another Crown filmmaker, Denny Densham, stated that the CFU represented the lowest rung on the professional ladder, buried somewhere below newsreels—but in this case, the cameraman reportedly saw the error of his ways and learned that the work required "a considerable amount of specialised knowledge."[42] To illustrate this point and reinforce Sellers's "rules," *Colonial Cinema* describes a scene from the 1944 production, *Land and Water*, which included a moving branch on the edge of the frame. On seeing the rushes, it was explained to the cameraman, most likely using the anecdote of the chicken, that African viewers were liable to fixate on this movement. The footage was thus discarded. Based on what he was told, rather than what he saw or learned from audiences, the cameraman reasserted: "What is appreciated in a film for Western audiences may be useless for illiterate people, and may be quite misleading."[43]

The specialized technique was questioned within the MOI. Dr. Julian Huxley, displaying views established firsthand on his trip to Africa in 1929, sent a letter to Jack Beddington, the head of the Films Division in 1942, which was inadvertently passed on to Sellers and "upset Mr. Sellers a bit." In response, Huxley hastily explained that it was "not that Mr. Sellers was not doing admirable work, but that this work might be incomplete and that it might not be necessarily the case that straight British documentaries were unintelligible to all African audiences." Huxley's cousin, Gervas Huxley, the director of the Empire Division at the MOI, was also a noted skeptic. It was somewhat diplomatically noted in MOI minutes that the "specialized technique" "did not wholly coincide with the practical experience of Sir Angus Gillan [director of the Empire Division at the British Council] and Mr. Huxley." In the same year, in 1943 the CFU initiated audience research to test its assumptions, sending a questionnaire to colonial officials across the empire from Ceylon to Zanzibar.[44] Yet, this research was founded on the same inherent racial assumptions that underpinned the specialized technique. For example, the survey failed to credit or consider the opinion of the African spectator. When asked how the audience responds if a film does not interest them, the official in Tanganyika explained: "Audiences here [are] not sufficiently sophisticated to be bored."[45]

The vast majority of these twenty-three questions concerned the specialized technique and were clearly framed to support the CFU's assumptions. There were individual questions on the use of color, cartoons, and diagrams, while others asked whether "scenes without any movement (human or otherwise) mean anything to your audience." After receiving examples of typical sequences that make people laugh, *Colonial Cinema* repeated its earlier assertions, now adding that laughter equated to comprehension. "The simple explanation appears to be that Africans do not reserve laughter to express only feelings of pleasure. They will laugh outright at any point in a film which they find novel or which they clearly understand."[46] Ultimately the questionnaire was used to reaffirm the merit of the specialized technique. "The main points of interest arising out of the replies is the confirmation of the success of the Sellers technique," concluded G. A. Girkins of the Colonial Office. "There is no doubt that Colonial Film Unit productions are both intelligible and of interest to illiterate audiences."[47]

While the CFU would often deviate from these "rules" in its productions, they very quickly became gospel. At the start of 1944, a subcommittee of the Advisory Committee on Education in the Colonies published their influential memorandum entitled "Mass Education in the Colonies." Led by Arthur Creech Jones, who would subsequently serve as secretary of state for the colonies, the memorandum outlined postwar welfare plans, calling for measures to expand schooling, increase adult literacy, initiate mass education as a community movement, and coordinate these wider welfare measures to develop "social and civic responsibility." While offering a word of warning (based on a lack of evidence) on film's effectiveness among "backward people," the report outlined the unique appeal and potential reach of film. Significantly, it reaffirmed Sellers's theories as unchallenged fact, stating that "experience has confirmed" that existing films produced in Europe and America are not suitable for "large sections of the colonial peoples." Instead, "a special type of film is necessary," and usefully at a moment when the CFU's future was somewhat uncertain, added that these films should be "produced by individuals with a first-hand knowledge of those they seek to educate." The report borrowed from Sellers's language, explaining that filmmakers need to know about the "sense of humour peculiar to the people" and that short sequences, quick transitions, and "trick shorts" perplex the "more primitive people."[48]

THE CIRCULATION OF IDEAS: FROM AFRICAN AUDIENCES TO BRITISH CHILDREN

Historian James Burns argues that by 1945, "the Sellers style had established a kind of orthodoxy among colonial filmmakers throughout the

Empire."⁴⁹ These ideas would also, as he notes, spread beyond a British context, applied by French and Belgian filmmakers after the war. In 1947, the Film and Photo Bureau was set up to produce and distribute films in the Belgian Congo, and when its head, L. Van Bever, published his own doctrine in a 1952 pamphlet, *Le Cinéma Pour Africains,* he included a chapter on the Colonial Film Unit. Van Bever outlined the need to film "with a special technique, simplified in the extreme," and largely followed the Sellers model.⁵⁰ The wider circulation of Sellers's ideas owed much to John Maddison, the COI official who showed *Mr. English at Home* and spoke at the Sorbonne in September 1947 about Sellers's work. *Colonial Cinema,* remarking on his talk, observed that "it was clear that the Unit's work was not yet sufficiently familiar to social workers in other countries," but Maddison's publication in *La Revue Internationale de Filmologie* helped to position these ideas within international discussions around film language, perception, and more broadly mass communications.⁵¹ In Maddison's conclusion, translated and discussed by Peter Bloom, he again emphasizes the need for particular techniques—such as "special editing, a slow narrative 'tempo' "—but suggests that these are required temporarily as the African viewer "has not yet achieved the same stage of development." At a moment when moves toward self-government were gathering pace, and when the CFU itself was looking to decentralize operations and develop local film units, Maddison presents this development narrative, suggesting that "in time" the need for these "specialized techniques will disappear."⁵²

Maddison's article would be widely quoted, disseminating Sellers's ideas to a non-English-speaking audience. Brian Larkin shows how they were rearticulated by German theorist Siegfried Kracauer in 1952 when he was tasked with summarizing reports produced by the Bureau of Applied Social Research (BASR) on the influence of media in non-Western societies. Larkin highlights Kracauer's familiarity with Sellers's doctrine (via Maddison), particularly around the development of film literacy. People not yet adjusted to cinema "may be utterly confused by flashbacks, close-ups, and transitions which an ordinary moviegoer takes in his stride," Kracauer noted, while in *Theory of Film* he recalls the chicken anecdote, although now as evidence of the "blind spots of the mind," fixating not on the African viewer but rather on what "habit and prejudice prevent us from noticing."⁵³ Another hugely influential theorist, Andre Bazin, would also deploy this anecdote and referred directly to Maddison's work when comparing the "decorative" women confined to the edge of the television frame to "the white chicken who crosses the corner of the screen in some documentary about the tsetse fly, and which the natives of Bantou-Bantou do not fail to notice, to the detriment of their learning about disease prevention and to the great despair of the missionaries."[54] In their application of this theory of film form, the classical theorists largely evade the context of empire, a context that is intrinsic to Sellers's writings. For Sellers the question of "what is cinema?" and what justifies close attention to film form is centered on the explicit and implicit political intent of the films and, more specifically, on the audiences whom cinema is meant to serve. For Sellers, these are theories, at their broadest, about people; theories that underpin colonialism as a whole; theories that shape particular practices to use media to communicate with, and educate, colonial subjects; theories that seek to foster biopolitical, economic development. In short, form cannot be divorced from context here.

However, Sellers's calls for a "specialized technique" were also noted by those addressing other audience groups, most notably children. Mary Field, in her role as head of Rank's Children's Entertainment Films (1944–50), produced a doctrine not dissimilar from Sellers, which sought to cater to, define, and homogenize her own disparate audience. In her 1946 article entitled "Making Films for Children," Field outlined the need for specific camera techniques, expanding on these ideas in her 1952 book on the CEF. Like Sellers, Field argued that the "composition of each shot should be simple" and urged filmmakers to "avoid sudden and unexpected movement or quick changes of scene." She called for "controlled simplicity and clarity" in editing, with a "much slower tempo," arguing that a "child audience likes to be able to look at a scene longer than adults." Indeed, Field reasoned that younger audiences were "rather slower than film-trained adults" at assimilating action—suggesting again a different stage of film literacy—and based her findings on a combination of audience feedback, infrared pictures that tracked where audiences looked on screen, personal experience, and "scientific claims" (for example, when discussing sound, "it seems likely that their ears are sensitive to loud noises").[55]

Field foregrounded questions of film form, arguing that films for younger audiences should be worked out by "action and not by dialogue" and that children go to "look and not listen." She suggested a preference among children for close-ups, warning that children's extreme curiosity lead them to explore every detail on screen so that the composition of the frame must direct the eye to the "essential feature of the scene."[56] When writing about this aspect of Field's work in a 1950 UNESCO report on entertainment films for children, Belgian filmmaker Henri Storck directly referenced William Sellers and his anecdote about the chicken. Storck also referred to Sellers when discussing Field's resistance to excessive camera movement. He explained how in "similar experiments with primitive peoples" the "uneducated African" audience sees a house that has "run away" or "buried itself in the ground." Roger Manvell directly compared Field's and Sellers's work in his 1949 study, *Experiment in the Film*, while James Fairgrieve also suggested that the model adopted for African audiences might best serve British classroom children when arguing in 1946 that "probably the Colonial Film Unit is the most successful in producing films with a tempo slow enough for children."[57]

The opening example of the first CFU film, *Mr. English at Home*, elucidates a further point of comparison between the theories of Field and Sellers. Like Sellers, Field emphasized the importance of familiar, identifiable figures on screen, not glamorous stars but "ordinary, plain, rather pudding faced little boys and girls" in "very ordinary British scenes."[58] As a staunch imperialist, Field recognized how this process of identification could stretch beyond geographical borders, encouraging British audiences "to identify themselves with film children of other nations whom they recognize as human beings like themselves."[59] This is evident in an advertisement for the 1947 CEF film *Basuto Boy*, which presents a heroic and moral African protagonist helping to catch some cattle thieves in Basutoland (Lesotho)(see Figure 2.2). With the heading, "Leslie Meets Lesaoama," the advertisement shows the African protagonist and British viewer face to face and framed within the cinema screen. It imagines a process by which spectator and subject interact and become one, fostering this image of partnership, of working and learning from each other through film. While the advertisement does highlight the physical differences between Lesaoama and his British viewer, these differences also serve to pique the viewer's interest in the empire ("what children like best is seeing how other children live").[60] In effect, much of Field's work for children and Sellers's for African audiences had reciprocal goals. While the CFU brought films of Britain, such as *Mr. English at Home*, to colonial audiences, the CEF often presented the Dominions and colonies to British children. Both saw in film a way to promote British interests on a global stage, to shape colonial citizens, and to manage a political shift from empire to commonwealth.[61]

These instructional films for African audiences and entertainment films for British children also often responded to familiar, shared anxieties. Having argued that most films produced for adults were "positively

FIGURE 2.2. An advertisement for the Children's Entertainment Film, *Basuto Boy* (1947), in the *Times*, 28 November 1947, 6.

harmful for children," Field outlined the potentially corrosive influence of American culture on children. She provocatively claimed that British children now expected to hear Americans on screen and needed to be "trained" to accept English voices.[62] Talking years later in 1958 at the Royal Commonwealth Society, Field outlined the pervading influence of American culture on children, arguing: "We have either to join in the battle for men's minds or we have to see ourselves and everything we stand for defeated." Field used the example of Zorro hats that were selling at a rate of 400,000 a month in America and questioned why Commonwealth characters were not popularized in the same way. She suggested, with tongue presumably partially in cheek, that you could have Livingstone bubble gum and a "Mr. Nehru charm bracelet." Field's more serious point here—one that had shaped British nonfiction in the 1920s—was that other nations were quicker to recognize the wider potential of film in shaping the "minds of young people." At the height of the Cold War, she cited a "beautiful" Russian film of an Indian fairy story playing in Delhi and "charming" Chinese productions "all ready to go down into Malaya." The stakes were clear for Field, with film not only essential in combatting threatening "foreign" ideologies but also in projecting a single, unifying "Commonwealth point of view."[63]

These theories of film form were also then an attempt to unify and develop disparate groups. Field imagined a longer-term plan to create literate film viewers, "training intelligent adult film audiences before whom the film industry might put its best and most intelligent products."[64] Much of this audience training was, of course, inherently conservative and designed to protect and preserve social and gender "norms" in much the same way as the CFU. For example, Field notes how a "cardinal rule" stated that all living rooms should be furnished with books, a writing desk, and an area for needlework, rather than containing three-piece suites and radios. Similarly all fathers "should be tall, slim and handsome," all mothers "Young, slender, pretty and well-dressed, but not too glamorous or fashionable" and, alas, only bad men would be "fat, middle aged or bald."[65] The exhibition of these films, at Rank's Saturday morning cinema clubs, would also serve as a way of standardizing behavior. Often viewed as a form of glorified crèche, these hugely popular cinema clubs included club membership, a club badge worn at all events, and a club song sung by the rowdy audience each week that, in one incarnation, contained the lines "As members of the G.B. Club we all intend to be . . . Good citizens when we grow up and champions of the free." The CFU shows were also imagined as part of the colonizing process and ended with a club song of their own— the national anthem.[66]

These points of comparison between the films for colonial audiences and children—in the theories, motivations, and their function in perpetuating colonialism—might suggest, as James Fairgrieve inferred, that these films could be used for both audiences. Indeed, the CFU did explore the possibility of making its material available for Children's Entertainment Films in 1948, but as early as 1942 Sellers had asked for the authority to reject requests to use CFU films "because of their simple technique" to instruct children in schools. He believed that it was "unfair that films made for Africans should be shown to western audiences, even of children, without alteration," refusing to extricate his theories from the colonial audiences that they were created for.[67] George Pearson, erstwhile director at the CFU and the most resolute proponent of Sellers's specialized technique, also strongly refuted the popular criticism that "our work is nothing more than making films for children." "Films for children must be built within the ambit of their stored memories of child life," he wrote. "How vast the difference between such minds and those of the adults we serve—adults who cannot read or write, primitive in customs and environment, heirs of an age-long tradition of folklore, fetish and strange superstition."[68] Yet, this desire to apply Sellers's theories, and films, to British children is testament to the endurance of a colonial rhetoric that sought to imagine the colonial subject as child (and England as the "mother" country).

George Pearson warrants closer attention here, because as senior director, he had his fingerprints all over the CFU's films—on-site at film shoots, providing storyboards, and training new recruits (see Figure 2.3). Pearson was far more involved than Sellers in the day-to-day filmmaking and was the pivotal figure in applying Sellers's theories to film. Young filmmakers at the CFU all speak fondly of Pearson as a "father figure." John Jochimsen recalled "George with his old typewriter and a fag sticking out the corner of his mouth," describing him as a "lovely man and we all learned a lot from him."[69] Yet, most of what Pearson learned about African audiences came from Sellers. Pearson explained in 1942 that his firsthand knowledge of the "African native is confined to the American negroes (USA) and the West Indian natives of Jamaica," and so it was from Sellers, as he explained in his autobiography, that "I learned the story of the backward peoples he knew." It was not just the story but also the language and rhetoric. He repeated familiar anecdotes and phrases, explaining in 1942 that "films that are fully intelligible to the European may be utterly confusing to the native mind" and listed ten "main principles," which Sellers circulated. Sellers suggested that these summed up the unit's work in a "nutshell" and helpfully, given his respected place within the industry, Pearson's "faith" in the unit's work also provided further legitimacy for the CFU at this early stage.[70]

Pearson, who was 65 years old when he started his fifteen-year association with the CFU, also brought with him his own reference points. First, he put a greater emphasis on storytelling—indicative of his background as a filmmaker and of Sellers's as a health official—as he called for a "cinema of story." In looking to imbue story into the instructional film, Pearson sought to respond to an inherent human interest in narrative. "Is there any request older," he asked, "than the child's: 'Tell me a story, Mother'?" Secondly, Pearson looked back to early cinema, highlighting the technological supremacy of the European colonizer by comparing the experience of the modern "illiterate" African to the early

FIGURE 2.3. George Pearson at his desk in Soho Square. Published in George Pearson, *Flashback: The Autobiography of a British Filmmaker* (London: George Allen and Unwin, 1957), 193.

Western cinemagoer. He spoke of the African audience's response to the "magic," "mystery," and "wonder" of the moving image. "Imagine the confusion of thought at such a kaleidoscope of pictures passing before unsophisticated eyes," Pearson wrote. Pearson did suggest that "in time" cinematic language "may be appreciated," but such a construction preserved the hierarchy between colonizer and colonized and justified the CFU's (and by extension British government's) role in educating and developing its African subjects.[71]

This comparison with early cinema was picked up by other CFU filmmakers, most notably Norman Spurr, who titled his 1950 speech to the British Kinematograph Society, "Films for Africans—1910 or 1950?"[72] Spurr had extensive experience working in Africa, for the public relations office in Nigeria and most recently for the CFU in Uganda, and suggested that the experience of film for "illiterate peasants" might be "nearer that of 1910 than 1950, for they see films rarely and there are no sound films."[73] Spurr again referenced Sellers—the kind of audience he was interested in were the illiterate peasants "who notice and remark upon the passing of a chance chicken across the corner of a screen"—and was generous in his praise of the pioneering work of Sellers and Pearson, whom he described elsewhere as a man of "remarkable insight and genius." Spurr outlined how his own experiences largely supported the existing "rules," and like Pearson emphasized the value of the story film in diffusing government messages, referring to this as "coating the pill."[74]

However, Spurr was notably more skeptical of the existing theories, lamenting that they "depend upon information gained at first hand over twelve years ago." While his inclination was to follow Sellers and Pearson's technique "until such time as they are proved false or outmoded," he concluded that it was the theories themselves that were "nearer 1910 than 1950" and, thus by extension, ripe for challenge.[75]

"PUPILS TEACHING TEACHERS": THE CHALLENGE TO COLONIAL ORTHODOXY

This challenge did arrive in 1950, and from a former student of the CFU, J. B. Odunton. Joseph Odunton had studied in the Gold Coast and toured the country as a commentator with a mobile cinema van during the war. After receiving a scholarship to study at Oxford in 1943, he moved to England and, on completing his studies in 1946, the Colonial Office Welfare Department recommended that Odunton should "take a course of instruction with the C.F.U." The CFU's minutes provided regular updates on Odunton's "promising" progress and noted that Lironi had "suitable work" waiting for him on his return to the Gold Coast in 1947. The disproportionate attention paid to Odunton's training indicates the political value that the CFU attached to his work, a point reinforced at a CFU meeting in January 1947. "It was agreed that the C.F.U. should keep in touch with him," the minutes noted, "and that any endeavor be made to associate him with C.F.U. work." Sellers referred directly to Odunton in 1948 at "The Film in Colonial Development" conference, when responding to a student from the Gold Coast who suggested Africans should be used to write the film scripts. "Our experience of training Mr. Odunton has been a very happy one indeed," Sellers explained. "He has imagination above the average, can think in terms of pictures and is keen to the work he is going to do."[76]

By 1950, Odunton was working for the recently established Gold Coast Film Unit and now took clear aim at his former teachers in a piece entitled "One Step Ahead" in the June 1950 issue of *Colonial Cinema*. "What a lot has been written about the illiterate African and films," he wrote. "How little solid sense, how many debatable theories, and how much high-falutin nonsense!" The gloves stayed off for the rest of the article, as he criticized the "fragmentary and unscientific" research, which he suggested was based on the "personal opinions of self-appointed experts." Odunton now called for a new approach—"abandon the current stereotyped methods and adopt new techniques"—and refuted the assumption that the "uneducated African does not understand films." The London-based weekly *West Africa*, reporting on this under the heading "Pupils Teaching Teachers," presented this as "an attack on the whole theory of the Colonial Film Unit."[77]

In his criticism of the CFU's "rules," which were "sanctified and given the name of 'specialised technique'," Odunton dismissed the preference for a "rudimentary and simple plot," the "painfully obvious" moral, and the "patronizing commentaries." His current employers, the Gold Coast Film Unit, itself an offshoot of the CFU, was presented as an alternative model here, a challenge to the status quo. Its head, Sean Graham, viewed himself as a disciple of John Grierson, "who believed in changing the world through film" and positioned himself almost as the antithesis to Sellers. "I am a film-maker first," Graham explained in 1955, pulling apart the CFU's symbiotic world as he argued that "educationists should not enter into film-production and vice versa." As a champion of documentary, Graham was fundamentally skeptical of the instructional film—"I would go further and say that a good many instructional films should never have been made at all, since film, like every other publicity medium, has its limitations, and detailed instruction is one of them"—and argued that the "brutal kind of audience research" needed to test these theories "has never to my knowledge been carried out."[78]

As such, Graham argued that audiences in the Gold Coast had been "underrated." "The word 'illiterate' should not be used with contempt; no more than the word 'primitive' can be regarded as an expression of abuse," he wrote. "Illiterates are neither child-like nor simple; they are responsible, intelligent men and women." Graham argued that too much had been made of their illiteracy and, in an area that would soon achieve independence, dismissed the early cinema comparison. "They get bored as easily as any other audience," he wrote, "and have by long ceased to marvel at the mechanics of film projection."[79]

At this same moment, the GCFU's first feature production, *Amenu's Child* (1950), was traveling across West Africa (and would soon play at European film festivals). *West Africa* described this as a "bold experiment," and a fundamental challenge to the ideology of the CFU, noting that the film "pays no regard to the principles evolved by the Colonial

Film Unit." It cited an "imaginative sequence, brilliantly photographed and edited," which uses techniques that by CFU theory should make the film "incomprehensible to audiences for whom it is intended." *West Africa* was delighted to report on the film's success in a later issue.[80] It was not simply the specifics of the "rules" that were being challenged here but rather the assumption that a set of rules was required; in other words, that colonial audiences needed to be treated differently.

Odunton's criticisms elicited direct responses from both George Pearson and Norman Spurr. Pearson, who had personally overseen Odunton's initial training in London, was evidently affronted by these claims, particularly the labeling of "self-appointed experts," which Pearson repeated three times, suggesting that Odunton had now joined these ranks. He criticized Odunton for "stating dogmatically a completely vague solution," refuted his "wild and unsupported charges," and concluded by suggesting that Odunton is, in fact, "one step behind." Pearson was particularly irked at Odunton's call for story films.[81] "We want to appeal to the emotions of our audiences, rather than their reason," Odunton explained in language familiar to British documentarians, "for what is art if it fails to appeal to the feelings?"[82] Sean Graham also viewed himself "as a storyteller," in contrast to Sellers and Lionel Snazelle, the head of the neighboring Nigerian Film Unit, whom he said were "educators really." "If so many of the films made for and about technologically backward people have failed in their power of impact," Graham wrote in 1952, "it has been because the missionary, the teacher and the 'uplift' influence have tended to oust the story-teller."[83]

There is a clear tension here, as Sellers implored the emerging local units to resist the lure of more glamorous or celebrated film forms. A report on the West Indian training school in 1950 insisted that any attempt "to aspire to the heights of a Hollywood production must be instantly checked." The aim instead was simplicity. "There is no glamour in documentary film production," it explained, "no film premieres with radiant film stars, glittering cars, and publicity stunts." Martin Rennalls, one of the trainees at the school, recalled trying to impart some drama into a film on road safety and being told this was "too much Hollywood style." A few years later when Rennalls, returning from the Berlin film festival, sought to secure 35mm production facilities for the Jamaica Film Unit, Sellers "strongly disagreed," fearing a loss of support for the core 16mm, instructional work of the unit.[84]

Yet, both Pearson and Spurr strongly favored the use of narrative and, as Pearson explained in his response to Odunton, had "advocated [this] with constant reiteration." Pearson emphasized that storytelling was "not new" and that "this is no discovery of Mr. Odunton's," while Spurr had written elsewhere that he believed the best method of presentation was by the "narrative-teaching film."[85] Spurr was, however, clearly more receptive to Odunton's criticisms and recognized the need for feedback and audience research, seeing "far too much opinion, too little fact." He concluded one article on film exhibition in Nigeria by stating, "We think we are right, but there is always the unhappy possibility that we may be wrong."[86]

While Spurr speculated on possible new approaches to storytelling, he crucially recognized that these questions of form were obfuscating a more significant consideration of "the user." He concluded his 1950 talk by backtracking on his original question (1910 or 1950?) as it "implies concern with means rather than concern with ends." He warned against worshipping "the false gods of technique," instead suggesting that any technique is permissible if it conveys its message to the audience.[87] Spurr conducted experiments on Disney films, on the use of color, and on technical processes such as the magnetic stripe. He introduced diagrams, made films to accompany filmstrips, and conducted research on audiences, sound, and commentary.[88] In all this work, he was motivated by the audience, imagining the mobile cinema van as a "weapon in mass education."[89] He warned against judging success on head counts and attendance records or on a few anecdotal audience reports, and argued that production should always be tied to exhibition, that films should never be made in a "vacuum," but "planned to assist and be *part* of department propaganda."[90] Spurr, like Sellers, worked within larger government departments in Nigeria, Uganda, and Tanganyika, and this shaped how he produced and used film, in contrast to Pearson and other professional London-based CFU filmmakers, who often fixated on the "rules," producing films as self-contained texts for their imagined audience.

Spurr recognized the limitations of fixating on production and of seeing these "rules" as a means of control. This focus on the text is perhaps understandable. The films are often what remains, the most tangible evidence of colonial cinema both for colonial governments then and historians of the empire today. Yet, the films were not isolated texts, dutifully viewed and read on message, but one part of a wider social and political event. When Arthur Champion, who was quoted by Sellers for his praise of *Mr. English at Home,* described this film as a "model," he went on to explain that "the best film ever produced will not be a success with an unsophisticated native audience unless the commentary is clear, well-timed and in a form intelligible to primitive minds." Champion's praise of *Mr. English at Home* came with a huge caveat, which Sellers chose to overlook. Champion argued that the films will only work if "given a suitable introduction or running commentary in the native language. Compared with this, the technical standard of the film is of secondary importance."[91] The film was transformed at the point of exhibition, in particular through this live performance by a local commentator and through its position as part of a wider political event. This presented a particular challenge for the CFU and colonial governments who sought to regulate and control not simply the images that they sent out, but also the ways in which these films were presented.

COMMENTARY ON THE EMPIRE: RISING VOICES

The CFU was initially set up to distribute and exhibit films around the colonies. Production was secondary here, servicing the needs of the mobile show. This is easily forgotten as most of the attention and criticism directed at William Sellers's writing has fixated on his doctrine on film form. However, Sellers's headline-grabbing views on production are always accompanied by detailed plans for their exhibition. What's more, while the CFU stage-managed the production of its films, which were intended to project the modern colonial state, to instruct and define citizens, and to legitimize the work of the colonial government, Sellers's articles intriguingly recognize the specific ways in which the live event itself could more directly achieve these goals.

Sellers imagined these film shows, as both Charles Ambler and Brian Larkin convincingly argue, as political events, as opportunities to gather and address disparate, dislocated citizens, regardless of the films shown.[92] In "Films for Primitive Peoples," Sellers situates film as one part of the show and gives equal prominence to the spoken word. He writes of the mobile units giving "talks and film demonstrations" and of inviting crowds along as "we have something interesting to talk to them about and show them." In a subsequent article Sellers outlines a model film show, emphasizing the appropriate "balance between films and talks" and intersecting four short films with four separate talks (see Figure 2.4).[93] A further sample program from the Gold Coast in 1943 offers more detail, explaining that an opening speech would discuss "the reason for the van's presence, the care of Britain for Colonial peoples," and various aspects of the British and African war effort. These

Programme Balance

In arranging a programme careful attention should be given to the balance between films and talks. The talks should be made short and crisp; they should be straight to the point and devoid of all padding.

Experience has shown the most effective length of a demonstration (to be approximately 75 minutes.

The following outline of a programme is given as a guide:

(1) Music	4 mins.
(2) Introductory talk	3 "
(3) Film	8 "
(4) Talk	4 "
(5) Film	20 "
(6) Talk by influential local	5 "
(7) Film	15 "
(8) Talk	4 "
(9) Short entertainment film	8 "
(10) God Save the King	1 "
	72 mins.

FIGURE 2.4. William Sellers's sample film program, *Colonial Cinema*, December 1951, 81.

themes of imperial solidarity were again prioritized at the end of the show: "Remember what you have seen—The Empire is strong, all are members and are safe and free within it."[94] Another opening talk, reprinted in *Colonial Cinema* in 1947, addressed the development of cinema "and what it means to you." The talk largely followed established colonial rhetoric—"it is little wonder you called it [the cinema] *magic*"—celebrating the British mastery of modern technology.[95]

This example reveals the prominent role of the local commentator in addressing the assembled audience and, moreover, the ways in which this local voice was politicized as part of the government show (see Figure 2.5). In "Films for Primitive Peoples," Sellers explains how the interpreter should grab the attention of the audience by asking "a question to which the obvious answer is yes." Sellers suggested that such a question in 1941 might be, "Are you proud to be British?" The commentator repeats the question three times, finally with the microphone at full volume. "This time," Sellers wrote, "almost every member of the audience will reply and their answer comes back in a roar. This is followed by complete silence everywhere" and the film can begin.[96] The chosen question ("Are you proud to be British?") hints at the ways in which Sellers and the CFU imagined these film shows as political events, as a means of monitoring, addressing, and homogenizing varied groups

FIGURE 2.5. A commentator with the mobile cinema van in Tsame in Trans-Volta Togoland explains the voting procedures for the forthcoming election, 1954. Photograph from the National Archive (UK), INF 10/129/37.

of colonial subjects. This is equally apparent in the model film program, which concluded with the British national anthem, another important part of this citizenship process. Reports in East Africa suggested that some government officials took most pride in discovering that the crowd had learned to stand to attention at the end of the show and sing "God Save the King," while in Jamaica the mobile cinema operator reported in 1940 that "the discipline of the National Anthem has been enforced at the beginning as well as the conclusion of our shows."[97]

The microphone is as powerful a tool here as the projector, and while the film cameras often remained—at least until the 1950s—in the hands of the colonizer, the microphone was more often accessible to locals. Audience members would be invited to take part in singing or elocution contests. Proposing the latter in Jamaica in 1948, the district officer and cinema lecturer explained that "the unit's microphone will be used to advantage by those taking part and [they] will be trained in elocution." In this instance, the microphone was intended as a civilizing tool, a way of training, molding, and rewarding "Britishness."[98] Handing over the microphone had a particular value and appeal to the British authorities who now looked to use local voices to speak on their behalf. Arthur Champion, who oversaw the mobile cinema operations in Kenya, argued that African audiences "believe much more readily what is told them by other Africans," adding that "their jokes went down better than ours."[99] In her recent work on nontheatrical film in Malaya, Nadine Chan shows how the commentary and lectures in 1930s Malaya were exclusively performed by locals, who acted as "mediators of the imperial project—'natural allies' who did the work of normalizing the politics of empire within vernacular life."[100] The local commentator, or "influential local" invited to speak within the show, provided a legitimacy to the colonial administration and very publicly displayed the government's reported moves toward self-government. These political moves, which promoted local agency and purportedly empowered local figures, at times appear as window-dressing for the colonial administration. When it was suggested to William Sellers at the end of 1942 that "one or two" Africans might be employed by the CFU, Sellers resisted the idea on the basis that a suitably qualified African would be "too out of touch with conditions among the more illiterate sections of the community for whom the films were principally designed."[101] In this example, a compromise was proposed—a single figure, part-time and in an advisory role—although the CFU was certainly quick to publicize the appointment of the chosen figure, Fela Sowande, at any opportunity.

As the CFU looked to these shows to project its modern empire, these local voices became ever more important and simultaneously increasingly difficult to control. Sellers acknowledged this potential problem when stressing that "it is as well to ascertain the views of the person invited and give them guidance when necessary," while reports in *Colonial Cinema* outlined the need for "close liaison" between a "highly intelligent commentator" and the European officer. However, language divisions coupled with the paucity of traveling European personnel made such close supervision virtually impossible to administer. One report explained that the European would need to "understand enough of the language to pick up ideas . . . and check the commentator," while an account from Kenya highlighted that "the overall supervision of all cinema vans is the responsibility of one European officer."[102]

While Sellers's filmmaking technique is indicative of the CFU's attempts to organize, formalize, and centralize film production, the centralized administration of film exhibition was both harder to achieve and less clearly prioritized. A 1949 UNESCO report on the use of mobile cinema vans recognized that there were no "fixed standards" across the empire and noted that the quality of training for cinema operators in the British colonies "depend[s] more upon facilities and plans arranged locally than upon any system of instruction determined from London."[103] One of Sellers's first tasks with the MOI was to prepare a "Handbook of Instructions for Mobile Cinema and Travelling Projector Vans," which was sent to the African colonies in advance of his first CFU trip to West Africa. Sellers had planned to run a training course there but bringing staff together in one place proved impossible, immediately highlighting that standardizing the equipment was considerably easier than standardizing its operation.[104]

Given these difficulties, the CFU often chose to watch *not* the commentator, but the commentary. Norman Spurr writes at length and with a reductive precision about how the commentator translated the script into local languages. "The original commentary of approximately 870 words was reduced to 539," he explained, "and this when translated came down to 467 words."[105] One piece of training for commentators involved translating English commentaries, "which, on being re-translated into English, are compared with the originals."[106] Such a scientific approach underestimates the role that the commentator performed, a role that made it difficult to regulate colonial film at the point of production. Sydney Samuelson and Sean Graham, filmmakers in Nigeria and the Gold Coast respectively, both noted the divergence between the government text and the words spoken by the commentator, while Arthur Champion, writing in 1947 about his experiences as a government film worker in Kenya, noted the inevitable tendency of the busy commentator "to employ the imagination where knowledge or memory failed."[107] Indeed beyond film, the Kenya Information Office suggested that during the war it was impossible to let African artists broadcast without lengthy rehearsal, as it would "have little idea what they are going to say next." "The necessity for censorship made giving this kind of performance impossible," the report noted, "and so we had to fall back upon Gramophone records." Even if there was no deliberate, political motivation for their deviation, the nature and magnitude of the commentator's role suggest that such close analysis of the script was misdirected. The Gold Coast report indirectly acknowledged these problems when concluding that the commentator "must be absolutely trustworthy and imbued with something of the missionary zeal."[108]

Such close attention to the script more closely supports William Sellers's notion of an "interpreter," charged with "translating" government scripts. Yet, Sellers's writings also reveal the inherent problems in such an approach. "The success of film demonstrations depends on showmanship and stage-management. *This cannot be too strongly emphasized,*" he argued. "The officer in charge should combine the best qualities of the teacher, the orator and the showman." The reference points are useful here, as Sellers presents his "interpreter" as a showman, a figure drawn from the traditions of early Western cinema and local oral literature; a figure that should engage, respond to, and inspire an audience. Reports of unsuccessful film shows across the empire support this assertion. Arthur Champion's complaint about Ahamed, the commentator in Kenya with the mobile unit in 1941, is one of many examples. "I feel sure he regards his lethargic and often inaudible speech as more dignified," Champion wrote. "This may possibly be so, but his words are too often ignored and drowned in a buzz of conversation."[109]

Sellers recognized the interactive role of this showman and even performed this role himself on occasion. When C. F. Strickland gave a talk in 1940 on instructional films in India, he invited Sellers to provide a commentary over *Machi Gabi*, a film Sellers produced in Northern Nigeria in the 1930s and which was later reedited by the CFU. Sellers did so "as my interpreters would give it in the vernacular," directing audience responses, talking extensively, and explaining that the commentators would even make noises to make the "picture live." He argued that encouraging the audience to articulate their (correct) responses to the film engineered a wider acceptance of the film's lesson, while also ensuring that the crowd was quieter and more attentive at other moments.[110] This approach is evident in poet and writer Montagu Slater's account of a "first" film show in a bush town in Eastern Nigeria. Speaking on the Home Service, Slater vividly described (or imagined) the locals' responses to the arriving CFU van. His account romanticizes the event and perpetuates differences through the "wonder" of cinema, with latecomers "gazing" at the screen. "If they couldn't quite believe the pictures, I couldn't quite believe the audience," Slater concludes. "I don't think I'd ever seen hunger for knowledge on quite such a big scale as in that bush cinema. They want the cinema to tell them how—how a motor car works, how diseases are cured, how things come to be as they are." Yet beyond this largely familiar rhetoric, Slater provides further details on how the show worked: the crowd brought together by the music of George Formby on the loudspeaker; the organization of the audience (this time by a local policeman) with children seated at the front, men and women sitting separately, and elders prominently positioned next to Slater; the bringing together of different groups and the crowd's excitement at a close-up. Once more, the commentator, taking the microphone by the side of the stage, involves the crowd in the film, talking to them and firing questions. On seeing a newsreel item featuring elephants, Slater explains that the commentator says in Ibo, " 'This is an elephant. Say it after me. Elephant'. Everybody says 'Elephant'. The children are squealing with delight. Even the men press in closer."[111]

The commentator becomes a part of the film, entwined with the images on screen. Filmmaker Martin Rennalls provides a more literal example of this, when describing an early Jamaica Film Unit production, *Delay Means Death* (1951). Rennalls explained how the film's "good patient" was played by the projectionist of the Bureau of Health's mobile cinema unit. In the film, this character suffers from tuberculosis but, on dutifully following the advice of the Health Services, makes a full recovery. Rennalls claimed that the audience's "belief" in the film was enhanced when they recognized the projectionist from the film. "They gathered around him and expressed their sympathy for his having been ill and their joy in his recovery."[112]

The role of the commentator was scrapped in Jamaica in the 1950s, replaced by subject specialists—"field officers" from the appropriate department. This shift responds to the "failings" of previous colonial film shows and suggested that the commentator's role (speaking on numerous subjects) was so vast as to be beyond the capabilities of one person.[113] Anthropologist Liam M. Buckley noted a similarly motivated government backlash against the local commentators presenting filmstrips in the Gambia in the 1950s. The colonial secretary of the Gambia proposed culling the position of "interpreter/announcer" in 1956, complaining that invariably the local figures were barely trained and were unaccounted for during their travels.[114] By the early 1950s as emerging local units sought inexpensive, locally produced visual media, the CFU increasingly promoted the merits of the filmstrip. The CFU's proposed film school in London in 1954 was divided into two parts—Motion Picture and Filmstrips.[115] Ostensibly the filmstrip would appear the ideal media for the Sellers's doctrine, offering a complete reduction of editing and movement within the frame. Yet its success in delivering government doctrine was dependent on its operator and commentator. Writing in 1952, George Pearson argued that "the quality of the commentary determines the quality of the strip," adding that "in film strips the all-important factor is the spoken word."[116]

While recognizing the merits of moderating the commentary script, Norman Spurr warned that film cannot be a "teacher on its own."[117]

"The expert should always be in attendance to answer questions, stimulate discussion, encourage endeavour," Spurr argued, "then the film becomes an instrument capable of injecting new ideas into the very blood stream of the people."[118] In an earlier piece, Spurr described the local commentator as "the most vital link between the film and the audience." "It is upon the commentator's shoulders," he added, "that there falls the duty of explaining obscure points, clearing up misunderstandings, and generally being responsible for the proper impact of the film; and all this without direct European supervision." The commentator transformed the film, but more than this, he shaped the event, setting up screenings, providing lectures, music, and direction. He answered questions, countered unrest, and of course translated and talked over the film. In this way, the pivotal role in colonial cinema was not the film director, as was so frequently the case in Western cinema, but rather this local commentator.[119] While clearly integral to the imagined performance, the agency of this local commentator has been largely overlooked, not only within contemporary histories of African cinema, but also by the CFU authorities that sought to regulate and administer film throughout the empire.

THE SHOW OF STRENGTH: POWER AND RESISTANCE AT THE MOBILE FILM SHOW

Evidently it was not simply the flickering images on screen that projected visions of the modern colonial state. The wider event—from the appearance of the cinema van to the gathering of the crowd and the accompanying talks and displays—could also project, and more than this, enact, immersing these citizens within the colonial state. The film show offered a way of maintaining order, reaffirming support, and administering colonial authority. To this end, Sellers viewed cinema as a symbol of colonial progress, placing particular emphasis on the (standardized) technology used, positively celebrating and anthropomorphizing the machinery at the expense of those operating it. This celebration of the equipment was connected to what Charles Ambler refers to as "the modernising agenda of the cinema spectacle."[120] The maintenance and correct display of the technology was essential because this technology (regardless of the film shown) projected the modern colonial state, highlighting British modernity and technological primacy. To reinforce this point, Sellers recommended giving local elders and chiefs a tour of the equipment before the show, suggesting that, in representing an image of the modern colonial state, the film was often

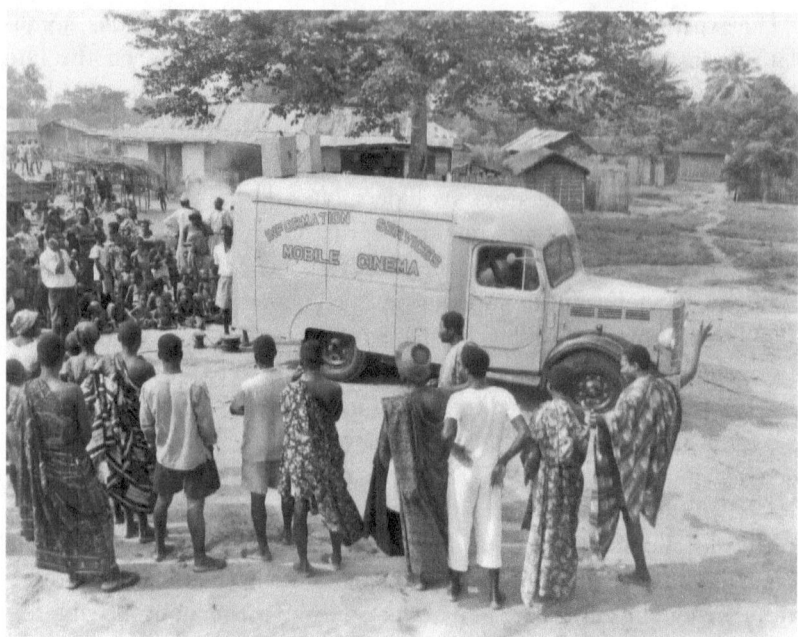

FIGURE 2.6. Crowds gather as the cinema van arrives in the Gold Coast, 1954. Courtesy of Information Services Department, Ghana.

less important than the ability to show film. The very presence of the cinema van served as a celebration of colonial "progress," reaching villages across newly constructed road networks (see Figure 2.6). George Pearson described these travel networks as the "arteries along which the life-blood of the world pulsates," arguing that "where communication ends life stagnates." Reports on these vans recalled earlier, romanticized accounts of colonial exploration and conquest. A report from Tanganyika in 1946 explained: "The van has crossed crocodile-infested rivers on ferries made up of planks resting on native canoes. It has travelled hundreds of miles by railway, and at the moment of writing is taking a three-day trip by lake steamer southward from the rail terminus." The report explained that the van would next be slung onto a "raft made of petrol tins" before undertaking a hundred-mile road journey, "always heading for villages where the cinema has seldom or never been seen before." A later report from Tanganyika concluded with the line "Join the Mobile Cinema and see Darkest Africa."[121]

Reports noted the excitement generated by the arrival of the cinema van—one report from the Gold Coast claimed that the van's arrival during a funeral prompted villagers to "flock to the performance 'leaving the dead to bury themselves'"—while Sellers noted how its arrival helped the government reach large crowds "in the space of a few minutes." Film functioned as a way of "contacting directly and at one time," as a report from Sukumaland noted, "several classes" that were dislocated from government and usually "untouched by normal methods."[122] Alec Dickson, the mass education officer in the Gold Coast, argued in 1950 that ultimately this was the primary use of the mobile cinema—to draw crowds. Dickson concluded that its sporadic appearances offered no discernible educational value and that "squirting pictures at them [large audiences] in the dark" was useless as a vehicle for mass education. Dickson did not present the films as the root of the problem here—he commended the professional and imaginative work of Sean Graham and the Gold Coast Film Unit, which meant that audiences were no longer confined to what Dickson described as *"Mr-Clever-Who-Banks-His-Savings* and the like"—but instead suggested the whole manner of presentation required overhaul. In challenging the pairing of film and commentator, he called for "a complete framework of teacher, discussion and some central over-riding aim."[123] This was, in many respects, what Norman Spurr and others envisaged, with the arrival of the van across the empire bringing crowds not only to the images on screen but also to other forms of government propaganda. Spurr quoted a district officer, who on attending one of his screenings was "particularly pleased with the way the film put an audience in a receptive frame of mind, or, to borrow a phrase from the advertising world, 'it broke down sales resistance'."[124] The film was intended here as one attractive part of colonial administration, of this live, political event.

This process becomes clearer when reading some of the accounts of film shows. A 1945 report on a "typical" mobile cinema visit in a Fanti village describes a cinema van arriving in the village with a Post Office savings bank van, which was accompanied by a policeman. The presence of both the savings van and policeman bestowed legitimacy on the film show, while the film show helped to organize the crowds for the accompanying government presentation. The report explained that after the film show (presumably featuring the sort of film Dickson hated) the chief would summon a general meeting near the savings bank. He would then open a new account before "one by one" the masses followed. The local commentator again provided the link between image and practice, the people and the government. "When the music stops, a speech is made by the interpreter on the urgent need for the people to practise saving," the report notes, adding that "the interpreter of the cinema van speaks on behalf of the two units."[125]

This model structure, especially promoted in West Africa, was part of a more concerted effort to use film exhibition to integrate local authorities within the colonial state. During the 1930s, Sellers presented film shows at the emir's palace in Kano, bringing together the "indigenous traditional elite" and using the visible presence of respected local figures to legitimize the work of the British administration.[126] Writing later in 1951, Sellers again noted the importance of addressing "all local influential people" before screenings both to "pass on" the unit's message after its departure and to enact public support for the visiting colonial authorities.[127] These dignitaries would then be displayed at the show, sitting in a few specially assigned chairs thirty yards from the screen. The seating plans helped to reaffirm traditional colonial hierarchies. In this way, the gathering became a microcosm of the empire, a way of organizing and ordering the colonial space (see Figure 2.7).[128] The public outdoor space was especially important here. In response to dwindling audiences in Jamaica, The Central Film Service recommended in 1955 that mobile film shows should be held in village squares rather than at indoor sites. Not only would this allow farmers to stop and view the shows on their way home, but this neutral public space represented something of a " 'no man's land,' where people of different religious dominations, social status and persuasions could gather without personal embarrassment."[129]

The organization of the film space was part of a broader effort to regulate colonial space, often operating with no European presence on the ground. This is neatly visualized in a 1943 report from the Gold Coast, which explained that a lamp had been fitted to the screen "to reduce any slight tendency to friction in audiences." "Isolated trouble makers," the report notes, "are thus exposed to the general gaze and come under the censure, unmistakably expressed, of the main body of the audience."[130] What we see here is both a reliance on self-regulation within this colonial space and a literal attempt to use the cinema screen to light up audience behavior and political dissidence; in effect, the film is watching the audience.

The adoption of the lamp responds to a perceived fear, and awareness, of potential unrest against the government. These fears become more pronounced in areas and moments when nationalist fervor intensified. We can glimpse this, indirectly, in Sellers's writing. In 1941 Sellers posited that the rhetorical question used to grab the crowd's attention should be "Are you proud to be British?," but by 1951 when he

FIGURE 2.7. Local dignitaries seated for the film show at Dodowa, Gold Coast, 1951. Courtesy of Information Services Department, Ghana.

revisited this model in the pages of *Colonial Cinema,* the suggested question had intriguingly changed to "Are you all well?" The subtle change provides a neat illustration of the shifting political situation within Africa in the last decade of colonial rule; a realization on the part of this government unit that the original question no longer appeared rhetorical within an increasingly volatile political environment.[131]

By the early 1950s there were more frequent examples of audiences challenging or rejecting the intended government message. In Malaya at the height of "the Emergency"—what was in effect a decade-long war between colonial authorities and so-called "Communist Terrorists"— the government cancelled screenings of *1955: The Year in Malaya.* While intended as a piece of anti-communist propaganda, the colonial government balked when newspapers reported cinemagoers applauding the on-screen appearance of communist leader Chin Peng.[132] The film was often read in unimagined ways or deemed inappropriate for culturally specific audiences. The governor of Malta suggested that it would be "little short of a disaster" to show *A Queen Is Crowned,* the most patriotic of British pictures and biggest UK box office hit of 1953, "especially at a time when there are signs that certain elements wish to attack the British connection, even by going to the length of disparaging the Monarchy."[133] However, any form of censorship also ran the risk of eliciting more comment and attention. The Colonial Office proposed cuts to a short government film, *Hello West Indies* (1943), after it was "generally agreed that a scene involving mixed dancing which concluded the film was unsuitable for presentation, at any rate in the West Indian colour-bar Colonies." Once reports of its inclusion leaked out, the Colonial Office backed down, not wishing to perpetuate the story and recognizing that "any alteration at this stage would cause unnecessary comment."[134]

There was also criticism in Jamaica after the mobile unit showed a film on George Washington to schoolchildren in 1940, which took as its themes for the last two reels, "Winning Independence" and "Building the Nation." The verdict was that showing Washington's fight against the oppressor was "most injudicious."[135] Evidently the content of traveling shows could prove counterproductive in particular areas. The Public Relations Office in the Gold Coast received a complaint about a mobile screening to miners in Tarkwa in February 1947. "During a newsreel, a picture was shown of the colliery disaster in England (or Scotland) in which about 16 people were killed," explained Hugh Thomas, the secretary of the Gold Coast Chamber of Mines, "and the dead were being brought away on stretchers by the rescue squad." The chamber noted, not unreasonably, that such a scene was "hardly likely to do any good" or encourage the "recruitment of underground labour of which there is a great shortage." The situation was not helped by the fact that the mine on screen so closely resembled the one visited by the unit—an example where the identification between Britain and Africa was not helpful—although the public relations officer defensively added that his department "could hardly have been expected to foresee that." On this occasion the dispute led to the withdrawal of the mobile cinema in the mining areas.[136]

Political tensions also prompted governments to abandon mobile film tours, with the units in Cyprus halted in 1955 "owing to the unsettled conditions."[137] Mobile vans were, of course, often seen as a way to counter these "unsettled conditions." For example, in Malta in 1962, the Civil Defence Mobile Cinema Van (with the "words 'Civil Defence' splashed all over the van") was repurposed by the director of information to show local news in Maltese across towns and villages in the buildup to independence.[138] However, the shows themselves could also become sites of contestation. While there is a danger of overstating this, of seeking political resistance in these shows when most passed without comment, James Burns shows how local figures literally obstructed the government apparatus in Nyasaland and Northern Rhodesia, blocking the mobile vans from reaching their destination and standing in front of the projector. Burns concluded that by 1963, "the criterion for a successful film show in Nyasaland had become one unmarred by violence."[139] John Izod recalls delaying the start of his mobile film shows in the Central African Federation in 1963 until audience members had finished listening to the radio broadcasts from Tanzania. These radio broadcasts effectively offered guerilla propaganda from a recently independent state and this delay, while receiving oppositional media messages, provides a significant counterpoint, if not a direct challenge, to the work of the film show.[140] Charles Ambler also shows how the exhibition site was reimagined within a changing political environment. "As Kenya moved toward violent rebellion," he writes, "the idea of thousands of people assembled after dark for outdoor cinema shows suggested not the pageantry of the local state but a potentially dangerous assemblage of rebels and malcontents."[141]

In some areas, indifference subsumed the novelty. Attendance at the government mobile film shows crumbled in Jamaica under competition from commercial mobile units that exhibited feature-length "entertainment" films. Film historian Terri Francis correlated the emergence of mobile cinema in Jamaica with the worker riots of the late 1930s. The traveling units had prioritized areas where rioting had occurred and, in this way, functioned as a "surveillance mechanism and a device of distraction in areas where folks were potentially ready for political ferment and insurgent collectivity." Early exhibitor reports in Jamaica actually contained a section entitled "Discipline," with exhibitors emphasizing that the shows were "directly teaching discipline and order in the communities." The reports claimed that "A public opinion is gradually being formed against unruly elements," but by 1953 Roger Marier stated in a UNESCO report that resistance had increased, primarily because audiences were bored and expected entertainment films. While the mobile units initially tried to respond by incorporating more "diversional" (entertainment) films, this merely accentuated the perceived "dullness" of the other instructional films. "Discussion is difficult," Marier concluded, "and audiences have a tendency to disappear."[142] These frustrations were keenly felt by the local commentators in Jamaica, who complained that they were forced to show the same films repeatedly—to give a taste here, one of the films on the circuit in 1946 was Mary Field's British Council film, *The Life History of the Onion* (1943)—which the lecturers felt had "little direct educational and less entertainment value for Jamaica. It is almost with 'fear and trembling' that Lecturers present such films to audiences no longer quiescent but coherent in their demand for more suitable films."[143]

Of course, our understanding of these film shows often comes from the commentators themselves, who not only delivered government messages but also, to varying degrees, received and relayed audience responses. A report from the Gold Coast explained that commentators would "make a point of questioning individual members of the audience on the morning following a performance," while Sellers urged that, "wherever possible," observers (and this often fell on the commentator) should be present to "listen for any interesting remarks."[144] Charles Ambler suggested that staff in Kenya used the tours for "intelligence gathering and surveillance," so that the tours were "as much about gauging political sentiments in this rural area as they were about documenting the efficacy of the films shown."[145] Yet, there is little evidence of the CFU initiating or collating political responses. The CFU addressed neither the politics of the audience nor the reactions to the live event, and when they did conduct audience research, it continued to focus primarily on the film text.

WATCHING THE FILM SHOW: AUDIENCE RESEARCH IN 1952

In January 1952 Peter Morton-Williams, a social anthropologist at University College London, began a six-month tour of Nigeria. In the planning since at least 1947, this CFU research trip was intended to put Sellers's "specialized technique" to the test. The research was predicated on established assumptions. For example, one of the primary questions centered on "vision." "It should not be taken for granted that unsophisticated peoples see things as Europeans do," *Colonial Cinema* determined when first discussing this proposed scheme, adding that the research should establish whether "these characteristics are racial or a product of environment." On the subject of "mental reactions," the research would examine the extent to which "audiences can become accustomed to more advanced technical conventions," while "psychological reactions" would study the different associations of ideas, self-identification, and, once more, causes of laughter, which "often seems to mean emotions other than simple amusement."[146]

In seeking scientific data, Morton-Williams also needed to standardize how these films were watched. Once again, this proved difficult, and while the CFU was able to control the technical details and operations (what films they showed, where, to whom), the "important" role of "interpreter-commentator" was outside the CFU's jurisdiction.[147] The

Colonial Office did suggest a candidate for the role (Mr. Maliki), but failed to secure his secondment from his role as a clerk with the local government. The Colonial Office now acknowledged that it was not possible to have a single commentator who was fully conversant with the customs, languages, and dialects of the vastly different areas, and so sought instead a "permanent link" who could oversee a team of itinerant commentators.[148] This interest in codifying exhibition practices was not a priority in itself but rather necessary to validate the scientific results and attain accurate data on film production and form. Furthermore, the CFU's intervention here highlighted again the tensions between the center and periphery, between a policy administered from London and the specific requirements within the colonies.[149] The public relations officer in Nigeria questioned the need for such a scheme, pointedly stating that his Cinema Section already carried out audience research "to a larger degree than is generally realized," and that traveling staff members "regularly send back reports on audience reaction."[150] Again any monitoring here was occurring locally and was not centrally administered or acknowledged by the CFU.

The research responds to, and reflects on, the CFU's perceived failings over the previous decade, identifying three particular shortcomings (which Norman Spurr had also noted). First, it noted the CFU's propensity to define success by attendance figures. K. W. Blackburne, director of information services, now stressed: "It is not the size of the audience which matters but what the film does to that audience." Secondly and connected to this, "Educational film should not be given in vacuo [sic]" but should be one part of government work. Thirdly, Blackburne questioned the value of seeking the opinions of Europeans and "educated Africans" and now sought the opinions of the local viewers on the ground "who are not accustomed to films and whose reactions are all important if the film is to serve a useful purpose."[151]

Yet, while appearing more progressive in its treatment of audiences—which it now defined by their social and tribal groups, rather than simply as "African"—Morton-Williams's study fell into many of these same traps. His research study still focused on the film text rather than the performance and presented films individually ("in vacuo"). This erroneous model, overlooking the wider show, shaped his findings. To take one example here, Morton-Williams offers a comparison of the Gold Coast Film Unit's *Amenu's Child* (1950) with the Nigerian Film Unit's *Smallpox* (1950). He argued that *Smallpox* was more effective as the ideas "were very clearly and simply expressed in action" with an "unobtrusive and uncomplicated background." In contrast, *Amenu's Child* was "overcrowded with ideas" and with "obtrusive" background incidents. Morton-Williams's comments seemingly support Sellers's "rules," but they also overlook how *Amenu's Child* was meant to be presented (as one part of government propaganda with government representatives on hand) and the familiarity of its intended audience within the Gold Coast with the images on screen.[152]

This audience study was ultimately motivated once more by production, by a desire to develop film technique, yet the final report represents perhaps the clearest surviving record of the aims and failings of the colonial film show. Consigned to the appendix are the individual screening reports, which in contrast to Sellers's vision for model film shows reveal the "external variables" that shaped audience responses. These reports expose the technological failings which often ensured that the shows were cut short or presented in unimagined ways.[153] These failings were often attributed to human error. Morton-Williams notes how a screening of *Development—Awgu* (1949) was projected at the slower rate of 16fps. This prompted two responses, both of which worked against its intended pedagogical function. Initially the audience laughed, but later complaints were made in a Group Council Meeting in Awgu. "As everyone was shown moving very slowly," the report explained, "it looked as if they were lazier than other people, and they felt they had been shamed and were angry."[154]

The preeminence of the film text was also undermined by a failure to organize the exhibition site (see Figures 2.8 and 2.9). At a screening in Dashit, the film was stopped at times while the "audience rearranged themselves" after clamoring too close to the screen. Other screening reports noted groups of men "standing all together behind the projector" or "crowded very close to the screen," restricting their view and ensuring that they were "unable to see adequately anything intricate."[155] The Central African Film Unit insisted on using color within its films, but the nature of outdoor mobile exhibition meant that the details within the film were often obscured. Morton-Williams appears to acknowledge this when later concluding that color was of "very little importance" within these films.[156] Indeed, given the exhibition context, the details and intricacies within the frame, so closely monitored by Sellers and colonial filmmakers, were often of far less importance than those producing or reviewing the films from London cared to believe.

The screening reports also highlight the myriad roles performed by the African commentator, yet the failure to address this directly within

Governing Principles of the CFU | 101

FIGURE 2.8. A crowd of 1,200 watching from all sides at a government mobile film show in Barbados. Published in Colonial Office, *Barbados: Review of 1954–55* (London: HMSO, 1955), 56.

FIGURE 2.9. Crowds gathering at Dodowa, Gold Coast, 1951. Courtesy of Information Services Department, Ghana.

the main body of the report attests to a critical lack of attention and supervision. For example, the reports reveal the CFU's continuing attempts to monitor the commentary at script level. When describing a screening in Egan of *Smallpox,* Peter Morton-Williams noted that "the film had been discussed thoroughly with the commentator two days before it was shown." He outlines in detail the changes made, largely for cultural reasons, to the script. The failings of this approach are evident at a screening of *Mixed Farming* (1948). "The typed commentary was not faithfully translated by the village schoolmaster who commented during the first screening," the report notes. "He described instead what he saw on screen."[157] Morton-Williams often notes in brackets the minor omissions or mistakes of the commentator, while also noting their failings in delivery. At one screening he bemoans that the commentator, "who tended to speak slowly," was unable to keep pace. The commentator's failings here are connected to the control of the audience ("some of the children were becoming inattentive").[158]

The reports also illuminate the preeminence of the commentator in delivering the film's message. The failure of audiences to understand *The Two Farmers* (1948) was partly credited to the commentator's apparent confusion, while a screening of *Wives of Nendi* (1949) was undermined by the delivery of the commentator.[159] Significantly the reports also present the commentator as this direct conduit between the film and the audience. The end of *Smallpox* was met "with a prayer from the commentator that they might never have smallpox in their village." This provoked "a general buzz of conversation and exclamation."[160] The commentator effectively does what the film text cannot, making it relevant and connecting it to the local audience as it travels. The reports show the commentator directly addressing his audiences ("many of you schoolboys don't wash your hands") and the audiences similarly engaging with the commentator ("One or two called out: 'Thank You!' to the commentator when the film ended").[161] The commentator offers call and responses, asks questions of the audience, outlines the intended message of the film, and directs where the audience looks on screen. He even manages to generate comedy when watching a film on venereal disease, evidence once more of his integral role in redefining the text for local audiences.[162]

The commentator's direct involvement as part of the film text is apparent when looking more closely at the thirty-four films shown during this scheme. Of these thirty-four films, twenty-six contained an English commentary or soundtrack and only six were silent. For these twenty-six films, the text was reworked in intriguing ways. The commentator would often appear as part of the film text, replacing the original commentary and played directly through the loud speakers. The local commentator thus became a part of the film text, in a way that the CFU, reviewing the films from London, failed to acknowledge. On further occasions, the local commentator would speak alongside or over the original commentary. Peter Morton-Williams suggested that the original commentary retained a value here as viewers "enjoyed hearing people on the screen speak" even if they could not understand them. Speech, he argued, "is so important a part of behavior, and tones of voice are significant."[163] The tones of voice here denoted a traditional form of colonial authority. When *Colonial Cinema* discussed the English soundtrack applied to these films, it noted that "Mr. Lionel Marson of the British Broadcasting Corporation, who has spoken many of the commentaries, must now be quite familiar."[164] This BBC voice represented a traditional authority from London, which alongside language and music was integral to the ways in which these shows were imagined as part of the colonizing process. The local commentator now replaced, spoke over, or competed with this authoritarian voice. This potentially provided a disjuncture between colonizer and colonized on screen and represented the rise of a new voice within African cinema, one that in its formal adoption began a process of reclaiming authority from the colonizers.

REFLECTIONS ON THE SPECIALIZED TECHNIQUE

Peter Morton-Williams's research for the CFU sought to test the assumptions by which the unit had operated. While noting a preference for simplicity on screen, the report now dismissed the need for a specialized technique, arguing that "it seems quite evident that the physiological aspect of the problem can be ignored." What's more, it refuted the oft-repeated assumptions that audiences were baffled by editing techniques or by rapid changes that "compressed time," concluding: "In general, all the apparatus of cinema was taken for granted [by the African audiences]."[165] By the time the report was published in 1953, the CFU had largely ceased production—although it was still involved in training, editing, and processing films—and the report's ultimate rejection of the specialized technique might sound like a death knell for the CFU and for the technique and ideals upon which it was founded.

By this stage even Sellers was critical of the CFU's previous efforts. Reflecting on its work in 1953, Sellers suggested that while "the technical and pictorial quality" of the CFU films was "of a high standard," few could be classed as "successful and right for purpose." Sellers's somewhat surprising admission did not reflect a change of attitude toward the specialized technique but rather the shifting position of the CFU (and the empire it served), which was by 1953 scaled down, cash strapped, and increasingly devolved. Sellers acknowledged particular failings, at both production and exhibition stages, which had stymied the CFU's work, arguing that European technicians had a tendency to relate a subject to their own culture, while language barriers placed a huge onus on local commentators. By foregrounding these problems, the CFU sought to underline its wider achievements and secure its future within a remodeled empire. It now looked to work with, and for, the emerging local units it had helped establish, overcoming these cultural and language problems by training and supporting local production. "If successful films were to be made *for* the people and *with* the people," Sellers asserted, "they must be made *by* the people."[166]

Sellers's criticisms in 1953 speak of a disconnect between a film's production and its exhibition. For all its emphasis on tailoring film production to African audiences, on training local filmmakers and monitoring individual films, the CFU was slower to recognize the importance of local figures in presenting, and redefining, the film text to colonial audiences. This was partly an issue of control—the film could be edited and checked from London and was thus *manageable,* whereas the dissemination and reception of the film was far harder to monitor. Sean Graham, with characteristic candor, criticized the predilection for quantity over quality when visiting the local units in Jamaica and Trinidad in 1955. "Not so much value for money, as footage for money," he wrote. "This [film production] looks good in annual reports, and feeds the local mobile cinemas. Quality—that is, efficiency—of the films is rarely critically examined."[167] Sellers and the CFU absolutely did recognize the value of the mobile film show, the ways in which this could function politically in shaping productive citizens and in nation-building, and were often innovative in how they imagined this. Yet the CFU determined the criteria for its own success and, given the difficulties of monitoring the usefulness of the film, focused predominantly on the text itself. The examples repeatedly shown in Sellers's showreel, of *Mr. English at Home* and later films that depicted mobile units at work or the training school in Africa, served to represent both an unchallenged, stage-managed vision of empire and the necessary work of the CFU within this model.

The CFU would not always follow the rules articulated in its first production, *Mr. English at Home,* but these persistent theories on film form continued to serve not only as the basis for the CFU's work but as a justification for its existence. They were not simply a doctrine for filmmaking but for colonialism, predicated as they were on hierarchies of difference between colonizer and colonized. As such, these rules, and the films to which that they were applied, were used to preserve, sustain, and in their promise of audience development, helped to gradually remold the British Empire. The CFU would grow, develop, and later splinter into local units, and in next tracing the evolution of the CFU (and of cinema's deployment by an empire under extreme duress), we return to 1939 and the outbreak of war.

CHAPTER 3

Mobilizing an Empire

The Colonial Film Unit in a State of War

While the interwar period saw the escalation of discourses, experiments, and rejected proposals that would shape the form and function of the Colonial Film Unit, it was the advent of a horrific, relentless, and truly global war that provided the catalyst for the CFU and ultimately dictated both its future and that of the empire it served. Here was an imperial war, as historian Ashley Jackson has argued, "fought in imperial theatres by imperial forces for imperial reasons," a war sustained by imperial products and economics.[1] The eventual "victory" marked the empire's greatest triumph and its inexorable point of decline, at once a validation for its existence and evidence of its obsolescence. This was a war that temporarily propped up, while bringing into sharp focus, the crumbling foundations on which the empire now stood, from the paradox of fighting for freedom *and* for the maintenance of colonial rule to the diminished British prestige and myths of white superiority exposed in military defeats, most notably in the East. As historian Keith Jeffery surmised, "the ultimate cost of defending the British Empire during the second world war was the Empire itself."[2]

What role then did film play in the colonies at this moment of crisis, in defending but also reimagining the British Empire? Much has been written about the Ministry of Information, the wartime government propaganda and publicity department in which the CFU was housed and, in particular, about the more celebrated documentary work of the Crown Film Unit, but what is often overlooked is the part that the

Colonial Film Unit played in both mobilizing and sustaining an imperial army. Here we have a small group of filmmakers and civil servants, operating out of a basement in Soho Square, seemingly one more voice within the often-sparring MOI, negotiating and formulating the state measures and policies for intra-imperial cooperation. Yet, while unloved, and much maligned, the CFU provides a fresh, distinctive voice within this transnational fight against fascism, as through film it speaks directly to colonial audiences. This is a voice that reaches across an empire at war, that exposes the difficulties and contradictions within this imperial fight, articulating and massaging an ideology worth fighting for, one that sought to nuance the distinctions between colonialism and fascism and ultimately project a new model for a postwar British Empire.

The films produced and projected during the war were often dictated by the broader, shifting goals of the state, to generate loyalty to the empire, to connect and unify colonial citizens with Britain, to stitch together the imperial theaters through film, and to highlight common, shared experiences. These films reveal both the ideological and practical demands of war. For example, the abundance of films depicting life in Britain can be attributed both to practical restrictions—a paucity of cameramen and units working in the colonies—and ideological preferences, in presenting the colonial populace at the heart of the empire. In the same vein, the instructional cinema, pioneered by Sellers in the 1930s, was now subjugated and redirected by the demands of war. In its task of mobilizing war support, the CFU was not simply working to enlist imperial troops but often more importantly to facilitate the movement of labor and to support production in the colonies. It not only produced films, but also created an infrastructure to move and exhibit other films of Britain—through local Information Offices—and became a part of the wider fantasy factory within the MOI, projecting and enacting a global military power that was, at the outset, largely aspirational.

Before examining its output on film, this chapter first investigates the institutional operations of the CFU, not only as a producer, distributor, and exhibitor but also as an organization looking to cement its place (like the empire it represented) within a world order shaken up by war. The CFU was buttressed between the MOI and the Colonial Office, between London and the colonies it served. Navigating the corridors of Whitehall and the colonies, the CFU sought to locate a place for film as part of a wartime propaganda that included other emerging forms of media, like filmstrips and radio broadcasting, all used to foster imperialism. The CFU would develop across war, not only articulating what the empire was, but also, if victory was secured, what it would become.

THE FIGHT FOR A FUTURE: THE CFU, THE BRITISH COUNCIL, AND THE MINISTRY OF INFORMATION

While plans for the Ministry of Information pre-dated the war by four years, these did not appear to address what would become the Colonial Film Unit. The CFU's own histories may date its beginnings to October 1939, but the MOI's initial plans in this regard, like much else, were somewhat piecemeal. James Chapman eloquently outlines the widespread criticisms from public, press, poets, and parliamentarians that beset the early days of the MOI—the impression of "blundering bureaucracy and amateurish incompetence."[3] Certainly the CFU did not arrive fully formed at the outset of war, but rather in the summer of 1939 the MOI approved the acquisition of mobile cinema vans for various African colonies (see Figure 3.1). These units would, the MOI reasoned, show "films displaying the material strength of Britain and her general prosperity" and, with this continued emphasis on economic productivity, would rely on those films already produced from the collaboration between the British Council and TIDA (Travel and Industrial Development Association).[4] In November, the Colonial Office offered the services of William Sellers, who a month later took up a three-month secondment from the Nigerian government with the MOI's Films Division, primarily to prepare the mobile cinema vans and units for Africa.[5]

Sellers was now answering to A.G. Highet, a Scot with a barely concealed dislike for the work (and workers) of the British Documentary Movement, and immediately sought to differentiate his work from that of the Crown Film Unit whose facilities he shared. Within a couple of months, the MOI said that the mobile units had "already proved of such value" that it was of the "utmost importance" that Sellers should stay for an additional eighteen months until the MOI had established the "necessary machinery" to function "without his guidance." Sellers quickly created a role for himself within the Films Division, adding the production and distribution of film "for native audiences" to his job description, while the popularization of his "specialized technique" served to define and necessitate the work of such a specialist unit within the Films Division.[6]

Even the term "Colonial Film Unit" seems to be one adopted by Sellers to demarcate his work from the larger, more widely known Crown

FIGURE 3.1. A mobile cinema, owned by the Nigeria government, preparing to cross the river Niger between Asaba and Onitsha, Southern Nigeria. Courtesy of Imperial War Museum.

Film Unit. As Jo Fox explains, the reputation of Grierson and his "Documentary boys" within the walls of the MOI reached a nadir in the early 1940s, and the Crown Film Unit was often viewed with reflected suspicion and distaste by "civil servants" within the MOI.[7] There is a convenient dichotomy here between the liberal filmmakers and the civil servants, the poetic documentaries and the instructional shorts, films for Western audiences and those for "primitive" colonial audiences, and there was, it would appear, little love lost between Crown and the CFU. Certainly Crown filmmakers were frequently damning of the CFU's work. As one example of many, Arthur Elton rebuked the suggestion in 1942 that filmmaker Ray Elton ("a man of this calibre") could work for the CFU: "I cannot help thinking that the Colonial Film Unit photography can be undertaken by men with rather less technical knowledge and reputation."[8] The practical Sellers was no more impressed by the workings of Crown, and repeatedly argued that ordering and operating through Crown slowed production down. Throughout 1941 Sellers sought to divorce from Crown—getting letters of support from leading figures in the Colonial Office—and argued that it would be "more economical and satisfactory" to work independently. He objected to being charged for expensive facilities that his films would not use, and maintained that this quest for independence was not about "prestige" but about efficiency. E. L. Mercier, deputy director of the Films Division, supported Sellers on this, but others remained unconvinced, suggesting that, given Sellers had already secured the site in Soho Square vacated by Crown, this was "much ado about nothing."[9]

Yet clearly for Sellers this was about securing a future for this "highly specialised" work. By May 1941 Sellers claimed that the Colonial Office had agreed that it was "not practical" to adapt existing films and that "it was definitely decided that films for Africans must be specially produced, and I feel strongly that it should be mentioned that the work is of a highly specialised kind."[10] "I should like to make it clear," he wrote in a letter to Mercier, "that the idea that films for Africans are something in the nature of amateurish versions of films for Europeans is wholly erroneous." By this point Sellers had begun referring to his team as the "Colonial Film Unit" at every opportunity. When Mercier challenged him on this, he explained that "it seemed desirable that films for backward colonies should be distinguished from the Crown Film Unit productions, which are, of course, primarily for western audiences." Sellers listed seven reasons for adopting the label, concluding that this would serve to "avoid delays, endless confusion and explanations as to our identity and work." This final point was clearly motivating Sellers. "The Crown Film Unit means one thing," he explained, "the Colonial Film Unit something quite different, and I feel it is important that films for backward colonies should have their own label."[11] This was approved in July 1941, with support from the Colonial Office and the Empire Division, and a few months later, Sellers would try once more to sever the final ties with Crown. "I do not know why this would be such an awful prospect," he wrote; "the Colonial Film Unit is, in fact, quite separate from the Crown Film Unit in everything except accounts." He described the present situation as an "intolerable waste of time," complaining of highly paid experts having to act as clerks and cited the example of George Pearson cancelling shooting because he was furnishing returns to Crown. In making his argument, Sellers emphasized the different operating practices of the two units and offered a thinly veiled attack on Crown: "That unit is dealing with films which may be spread over months. Our films are completed quickly."[12] In so doing, he further pulled apart these related strands of British nonfiction cinema, deepening this chasm between films for British and colonial audiences, between the prestige documentary and instructional film, between the work of the "poetic" filmmaker and the amateur expert.

Sellers was determined to build up his unit and throughout the war there were repeated calls and demands for further administrative support, equipment, and in particular, technical staff. Sellers took every opportunity to ask for more staff—for example, when asked to serve on the BBC's Transcription Committee in 1942, he wrote to Jack Beddington, the head of the Films Division, and explained that all this additional work would require extra assistance.[13] While the barely concealed tension between the Colonial Office and the MOI often stymied action, Sellers sought to maneuver from both sides. Early in 1942, the Colonial Office helped push largely successfully for a major expansion of the CFU, which would allow the unit to double its output to a hundred films a year and crucially, with an eye to the future, include "nonpropaganda films." It would also allow for the establishment of its monthly (later quarterly) bulletin, *Colonial Cinema,* provide courses of instruction for visiting officers from the colonies, and as every project had tried before, examine libraries to see if there were existing films that could be made "suitable for backward peoples." For all this work Sellers suggested that he would need at least six new staff.[14]

Significantly the motivation here was no longer the immediate war, but rather the imagined future. For the Colonial Office, this was a chance "to build up for peacetime." Mercier warned that "war propaganda films" would be useless in peace and that "the elaborate organization for display will come to an abrupt stop." He also questioned the value of "soaking native audiences" in war propaganda that emphasized the might of Britain when "the news has nothing to show for it but setbacks."[15] While the plans for an expanded CFU were approved in 1942—with an additional annual expenditure of more than £24,000—the MOI would still insist that films related to the war effort took priority over those for welfare purposes.[16] This expansion offers a tentative look forward, imagining a world and an empire beyond the current conflict, but many within the Colonial Office believed that a more progressive approach would only be possible if the Colonial Office took full responsibility for the CFU.

One of the more vocal proponents here was E. R. Edmett, who had the often unenviable task of liaising between the Colonial Office and the MOI. Edmett's vision for film was more poetic than practical, perhaps more Grierson than Sellers. "The Colonial peoples want sympathy not films on soil erosion, humanity not lectures on how to kill bugs," he wrote. "Can we not discard this pose of intellectual superiority and get down to learning from people as well as teaching them?" Edmett argued that what was needed was "direct human contact" between governor and governed and saw film as the perfect vehicle for this. "I cannot help feeling it is not the colonial peoples that need education," he added, "but ourselves, and the running of the Colonial Film Unit by this office would be an inestimable element in our education."[17] Edmett described the Colonial Office as the "stepfather of the Colonial Film Unit"—he saw the "real parent" as the Social Services Department that had been set up in the Colonial Office in 1939—while W.S. Morgan, working in public relations at the Colonial Office, presented the CFU in similar terms as a "foster child of the M.O.I., probably needing new parents" at the end of the war.[18]

The Colonial Office had presented a detailed proposal for a Central Film Organisation in 1940, which it sporadically revisited, and suggested that the CFU could provide the "nucleus" for this unit. However, Edmett rued the one element lacking within the Colonial Office—a "decision"—and complained that "after two years of cogitation, the project for Colonial films remains an embryo draft," neglected and misunderstood by the MOI. He maintained that Sellers's "loyalty belongs to the Colonial Office and the colonies" and that "like any other normal human being" Sellers wanted to "escape into a more creative field than war propaganda." Morgan was equally keen to note that the CFU's "loyalty is undoubtedly to the Colonial Office" and, like a scorned lover, explained that the CFU had never been happy with the MOI and that the MOI could never satisfy its long-term needs. Morgan now called for greater intervention from the Colonial Office—"a careful and persistent pressure"—to ensure that the CFU's longer-term educational program was not obfuscated "by the propaganda interest of the Ministry."[19]

Ultimately the "pressure" from the Colonial Office, whether careful or otherwise, provided further tension—between the MOI and the Colonial Office, between present demands and future plans—with members of the Colonial Office attending meetings and commenting on proposed films. Indeed, the CFU's position remained in a constant state of flux, blown by the oscillating fortunes and priorities of war, by petty internal politics, and by the frequent changes in leadership across the MOI. Sellers now found himself in regular meetings with members of the Films Division and the Empire Division at the MOI, the British Council, and the Colonial Office, trying to satisfy, or at least tolerate, groups and individuals often with wildly different and intractable views. A not-untypical account of a meeting in January 1943, written by C.A. Grossmith of the Colonial Office, noted that "the atmosphere was so heated in the quarrel between the Films Division and the Colonial Film Unit that I don't think that any decision on the film was reached." The film in question was "English War-time Family," a sequel of sorts to *Mr. English at Home* that, the writer noted, the Films Division "heartily condemn[s] on advice given to them by certain individuals. The Colonial Film Unit, on evidence from Africa, regard it as a first rate film." In this way the tensions within the aptly named Films Division can again be traced back to the CFU's very first picture. Grossmith was sympathetic to Sellers, arguing that he was put in a "totally unfair" position. "If his work is as inefficient as the Films Division would make out," he argued, "he ought to be got rid of, but many of us think that he is doing some very good work." At the same meeting Jack Beddington, the head of Films Division, expressed "extreme dissatisfaction" at the nascent *Colonial Cinema*, on the rather damning grounds that it was "unnecessary" and "badly written." It was agreed that the text each month would now have to be approved by Films Division. This is rather typical of the tug-of-war internal politics and it is unsurprising that Sellers agitated to move the CFU to the Colonial Office.[20]

There was little letup for Sellers and the CFU from the MOI's Empire Division. Gervas Huxley, its director, wrote to Noel Sabine at the Colonial Office in May 1943 candidly explaining that he was "increasingly unhappy" with the CFU's work. Huxley was already a noted skeptic of Sellers's specialized technique and of the operating practices of the CFU, challenging, for example, what he saw as a CFU preference for quantity over quality.[21] The tipping point for Huxley, however, was a recent "Bicycle" film that he described as "really lamentable." "[It] seemed to show," he continued, "a basic misunderstanding, not only of our proper purposes, but also of what would be likely to bring home to Africans—and especially uneducated Africans—what we want to tell them through our films." The completed film never saw the light of day—viewed by the committee and, along with *This Is India*, "agreed to be unsuitable"—but what remains is a description in *Colonial Cinema* from its production. The film's objective, we learn, was "to bring home to Africans the necessity of attending to running repairs and making periodic adjustments to cycles." Written around a familiar colonial format, the film depicts James Wise looking after his cycle while Thomas Foolish neglects his and ends the film by "coming to grief in a ditch." Evidently a light comedy about a bike was not what Huxley had in mind for war propaganda—let's hope he didn't see *Sam the Cyclist*, which showed an "old-style comic" in

England performing bicycle tricks on stage—and Huxley was equally unimpressed by the list of forthcoming subjects, which focused predominantly on scenes of British life. Huxley argued that these films were clearly the domain of the British Council and could not be said to have "even a remote connection with our O.P.C. [Oversea Policy Committee] objectives." Huxley directly quoted from these objectives, which focused both on the immediate goals of war ("to help maintain their confidence in the victory . . . and to secure their maximum contribution to the war effort"), to the broader imperatives of empire ("to maintain the West Africans' loyalty to the British connexion [sic]"), and now to the longer-term postwar welfare plans ("to take a fuller share in the government of their countries"). Huxley clearly felt that the CFU should be supporting the work of the Colonial Office and MOI, reiterating that the CFU "should be tied definitely to our propaganda aims."[22]

These aims, which both responded to the immediate present and imagined a more distant future, had evolved from the initial discussions on colonial participation in the war. The *Crown Colonist* called in 1939 for solutions to the "Colonial Question when peace is restored" and argued that "the Colonial peoples should be told clearly and simply (and as far as possible in their own languages) that we are fighting for their freedom, to develop on their own lines, as well as for our own."[23] The Colonial Office would acknowledge the dangers of adopting phrases that might, in turn, be used against the British, but the term "freedom" certainly permeated these initial responses. The secretary of state for the colonies argued that the "spontaneous" support of the colonies for the British war effort was because the British "respect their individuality and desire their existence as distinct people to be preserved, and are determined to develop and maintain their freedom."[24] In this way, the calls to war across the empire resounded with the promises of a different future and largely warned against, in the words of the Information Department in the Gold Coast, the "jingoistic nonsense about the British Empire being a heaven on earth." The Gold Coast Information Service instead adopted the line that while the empire was "by no means perfect, there can be no two opinions about its being infinitely better than anything that Hitler could put in its place."[25]

The MOI articulated its response in its first empire publicity campaign, which was launched in 1940 and intensified after the fall of France, highlighting that Britain was a "partner in a worldwide and immensely powerful family of nations." Partly reactive, to counter criticisms of the "imperial idea," the campaign also sought, as Minister of

Information Duff Copper explained, "to encourage people to look not only at the present strength of the British Commonwealth, but also at its immense capabilities for the future welfare of the human race."[26] These motives were manifest in the Colonial Development and Welfare Act of 1940. Historian Stephen Constantine has argued that the introduction of this act, with its purported desire to improve social conditions within the colonies, was "essentially a defensive operation, to provide a new justification which would legitimise the perpetuation of colonial rule."[27] A postwar incarnation of this act would partly fund the expanded CFU after the war and, from the outset, the CFU sought to deliver these "defensive" motives. The CFU was established to help preserve the empire and perpetuate colonial role, but in order to preserve and sustain an empire, it had to offer the promise of a new model of "commonwealth."

As war dragged on, as the empire began to crumble in Southeast Asia, and as criticisms of the British system of "imperialism" grew louder, there was an ever-stronger need to articulate and redraft the reasons for supporting the British war effort.[28] Elspeth Huxley, the renowned writer (and wife of Gervas Huxley), outlined the importance of film in challenging perceptions, when reviewing a proposal for an East African Film Unit in 1942. "Events in the Far East have, unfortunately, created throughout America, and indeed here, a very low opinion of the nature of British rule," she wrote, "that it is all take and no give, a matter of sahibs and dividends, not of helping the people to stand of their own feet." While acknowledging that this may contain some truth, she emphasized that "the other side needs desperately badly to be put." Huxley wanted to show the "constructive work" in Africa, rather than British rulers "just sitting down collecting taxes and making themselves comfortable."[29] By 1942, there is a notable shift in rhetoric, with discussions of development and partnership (in place of trusteeship) and heightened emphasis on training, which now presented the empire, in the words of one MOI pamphlet, as a "laboratory ... in the science of community-building."[30] Rosaleen Smyth credits a change in the "tone" of propaganda to the decisive turn in the Allies' favor, while historian Kate Morris argues that by 1943 the empire was "morally rearmed" with its mission of "partnership" and that this theme would come to shape colonial propaganda beyond the war. This moral rearmament was required to tackle new postwar threats to the empire, which included, as one official noted in 1944, "Soviet ideology and/or American material prosperity."[31]

The CFU was shaped by these shifting pressures, its work responding to the changing needs of empire, and its structure and operating practices similarly redrawn as war progressed. The CFU was now asked not only to project but also embody a new model of empire. Sellers agreed, with some reticence, to look for two Africans to join his unit in London in 1943 and to gain training in film work. The discussions around their hiring reveal inherent tensions in these early, tentative moves toward increased African involvement in colonial administration. On the one hand, the CFU was conscious of appearances and eager to make moves toward integration—"it is important that they should not feel underpaid compared with others in the unit"—but on the other, this was founded on assumptions about a unified "African" perspective and exacerbated racial division and segregation. A note explaining the motivation for seeking two rather than a single African worker, stated that "it is preferable if he can have a fellow African with whom he can discuss suggestions."[32]

By the end of the war, the CFU was also expanding its number of junior staff, recognizing the superior opportunities it could provide for trainees and the overarching benefit for the CFU as it looked to build up young specialist crews to film in the colonies. The three trainees at the end of the war would all carve out very successful careers in the industry—Dennis Bowden, John Jochimsen, and *Thunderbirds* creator Gerry Anderson ("who seems to have a special flair for cutting"). They worked alongside other trainees including the noted cinematographers Bob Paynter (responsible for Michael Jackson's *Thriller* among many others), the Oscar-winning Billy Williams, and the first British Film Commissioner, Sir Sydney Samuelson.[33] As war drew to a close, the CFU also saw an increase in those from the colonies asking for instruction, with six trainees in the latter part of 1945, including a Scottish missionary, officers from Northern Rhodesia and from the Colonial Office, and soon after, "the first African applicant." *Colonial Cinema* explained that "each one trained means an increase of filming activity overseas."[34]

The experiences of the CFU at war—the relentless, shifting pressures and demands that shaped its work—were often shared by another organization that increasingly overlapped with the CFU. The British Council Film Department was formed, like the CFU, in October 1939, taking over the work of TIDA (Travel and Industrial Development Association) and produced films that projected British life to overseas audiences. William Sellers was aware of their work from an early stage and served as a consultant on their 1939 film *Royal Review*, which would play across the colonies and was described by Arthur Champion as "quite the most suitable and telling picture" to play on the mobile circuit in Kenya. Sellers, who was asked to consider the film in relation to "the mentality and outlook of the colonial peoples," evidently found much to criticize, although the Council took comfort from the fact that his concerns primarily addressed the very limited audience of West Africa.[35] British Council films would become a staple of the touring mobile film vans. The Council provided and ran, for example, the film library in Jamaica, while its newsreel *British News* was widely circulated from the summer of 1940, providing regular updates on the colonial war effort.[36]

The MOI amazingly appeared to have an even lower opinion of the British Council than it did the CFU, and its criticisms highlight the demands and conflicting views on those producing films for the colonies. Upon viewing four British Council films late in 1941, the Colonial Section of the MOI's Empire Division stated that "however innocuous the Council's conception of British culture may be in peacetime, it is thoroughly dangerous to disseminate it during our present life and death struggle for very existence." The report presented a clear dichotomy between the MOI, which was trying to persuade the world that Britain is "fully mobilised for totalitarian warfare," and the British Council, which "persists in flooding the market with films showing life proceeding around the village green or local inn interspersed with technicolor pictures of exotic flowers blooming in Kew Gardens."[37] Exhibitor reports in the colonies showed some "scepticism" toward such depictions, with a report from Jamaica in 1944 stating that audiences of *London 1942* felt "duped," having previously believed that London was "more battered and scarred than suggested by the film."[38] For its part, the council acknowledged in its annual catalogue that "these level-headed studies of British subjects bear little trace of war's excitement," but in so doing, it envisaged a life (for both Britain and itself) beyond the current conflict. "They show the enduring fabric of freedom and progress," the Council Film Committee's chairman Phillip Guedalla wrote, "which lives and works long after the war-makers have been forgotten." The MOI were evidently unconvinced and actually sought to stop the dispatch of these four films from Britain, claiming that they serve as "living proof of Goebbels' statement that the British are frivolous." It further suggested that they would have a "bewildering effect" and somewhat dramatically claimed that the films could go far "toward bringing the neutral countries in on the German side and allied countries and the Empire to cynicism." Brendan Bracken, the minister of information, concluded that the council's film department was "simply a drain upon the constantly dwindling resources of the industry."[39]

These criticisms fueled the MOI's own discussions with the CFU and would impact on the CFU's work. The MOI would increasingly cluster the British Council and CFU together. This is hardly surprising as the British Council began producing films specifically for the colonies, while the CFU's lack of material from overseas meant an overreliance on the kind of footage of Britain favored by the British Council. Sir Angus Gillan, a two-time Olympic gold medalist who now served as director of the Empire Division at the British Council, explained that while the MOI addressed "how Britain was waging the war," the British Council was responsible for showing colonial audiences "what Britain was fighting for" and "purely educational films," the kinds of work that the CFU also claimed.[40] Further distinctions were based on levels of literacy ("illiterate," "semi-literate," and "literate") and while the British Council argued that it was not primarily focused on the CFU's "illiterate" audience, it acknowledged that the boundaries between illiterate and semi-illiterate were increasingly blurred.[41] In addition, the British Council was unconvinced of the need to differentiate between these audiences. Sir Angus Gillan argued that illiterate audiences were "very quick" at picking up a new technique and suggested that adhering to Sellers's technique would lead to "rather a dull lot of purely educational films."[42]

The British Council and CFU began meeting regularly in 1943 to view and discuss each other's films. Noel Sabine of the Colonial Office believed that the CFU's slate of "technical and inventive films" (and more broadly films showing British life, such as a proposed picture on an agricultural school in North Riding) could be met by the British Council.[43] Sellers was also invited (not by the British Council) to comment on prospective Council films and agreed that the British Council would be consulted on CFU "home" productions both to avoid possible overlap and to determine which unit was best placed to produce the film.[44] However, Sellers was understandably eager to ensure that the British Council would not replace or fulfill the work of the CFU. He reiterated in meetings that adapting Council films for "less sophisticated audiences had not proved to be a practical proposition" and maintained that only the CFU and its specialized technique was suitable for most colonial audiences.[45]

The first of the British Council's designated "films for the colonies" was *Local Government* (1943), which showed the election of John Blunt, a farmer, to a local council in England.[46] The film encapsulates the stakes, challenges, and downright frustrations of producing films for the colonies. The Council was first asked to produce the film at a meeting in April 1942. A Colonial Office report listed twelve further stages—working through various drafts and receiving the opinion of everyone from the Ministry of Health to Geographical Departments across the colonies—until by July 1943 the Colonial Office conceded that the film "has probably gone too far to withdraw."[47] Indeed, it is hard to imagine that there were many people left at the Colonial Office or MOI, or indeed in the English-speaking world, who did not pass a critical opinion on the proposal, script, or completed film. The comments on the proposals from overseas—labeled "either lukewarm of negative"—suggested that the film would be unsuitable in most areas and reveal the uncertainties and anxieties crippling the distribution of propaganda within the colonies at a time of war.[48]

Local Government opens with shots of the Houses of Parliament followed by the procession of the King. This focus on the traditional architecture and pageantry of the imperial center is entirely typical of preexisting films for the colonies—supplemented by the British Voice of God narration—but the film, consistent with moves within the CFU, then moves out of London to a smaller town. Its focus is now on a farmer—another version of the hard-working Mr. English—and showcases British welfare and support, showing a hospital, school, police, parks, and other amenities as a way of illustrating the work of the local council. While *Local Government* does not adhere to the specialized technique—it is verbose and with more editing and movement in the frame—in its subject matter and representation, the film could easily sit within the canon of the CFU. This depiction of England again received criticism from overseas. One official from the Mediterranean colonies complained that "I have no doubt that the picture will include shots of one of the palatial town halls on which money has been squandered in recent years," while W. S. Morgan argued that the "palatial" style may be appropriate when the British Council is trying to "sell" Britain overseas, but there was no counterpart to these services in the colonies.[49] These concerns were also expressed in local screening reports. The officer in Nicosia, Cyprus, responded to a screening of *Second Freedom* in January 1946 by stating: "Films of this type do more harm than good—presenting England as a Utopia where maternity homes, model schools, specialized training, employment under ideal conditions, are within everyone's reach. Why not show food queues, the tiny meat and fat rations, housing shortage and other uncomfortable facts?" The report saw a danger in idealizing Britain, adding that "The audience, believing the film gives a true picture of conditions in England, is dissatisfied with the absence of similar amenities in Cyprus."[50] The MOI was perhaps sensitive to these criticisms. A 1942 report on the MOI catalogue in *Documentary News Letter* criticized the "parochialism" of its films. "Too many films assume that Britain is the centre of the world, and London the centre of Britain," it wrote. "Too many imply that civilization rests in our own little blitzed cabbage patch."[51]

A further widely quoted comment outlined the importance of tone within *Local Government*. "The emphasis should be 'you will all be interested to see how these things are done in England'," it wrote, "and not this is the way things are done in England and should be done in your country."[52] Sir Angus Gillan clearly agreed on this final point and sought a shift here in line with wider changes in colonial policy. Describing the work of the British Council in April 1942, Gillan explained that "our main policy is to prepare the peoples of the colonies for complete self-government" and to this end saw a demand for films "showing the way local administration was run in England and how the British people govern themselves." Gillan added that it was "important to make native peoples realise that local government is the same problem in their countries as it is in England."[53] *Local Government* represents an early, tentative acknowledgment of these moves toward self-government—still made by and depicting Britain—and over the next decade this on-screen model would move overseas in films such as the COI's Indian-set *District Officer* (1945), the CFU's 1949 film *Community Development in Awgu Division,* and the Gold Coast Film Unit's tax collection comedy (a most "colonial" genre) *Progress in Kojokrom* (1953).[54]

The CFU, like the empire it served, was reconceived through war, shaped and fought over by the many organizations invested in the colonies. In his often-fractious dealings with the MOI, British Council, and Colonial Office, Sellers imagined and prepared a place for the CFU beyond the present conflict. His efforts were noted. Brendan Bracken, the minister of information, described the CFU in the House of Commons in 1944 as a "small development, which I hope will grow," and argued that after the war the CFU will, "under the benevolent eye of the Colonial Office, greatly increase its activities. It is highly desirable," he concluded, "that the British Empire should be given more news of what is happening."[55] However, increasingly it was not news that the CFU would look to provide, but rather instruction—instruction on how to be British, on economic productivity—and when the secretary of state for the colonies was asked about the CFU's future in October 1945, he now noted the unit's films on educational and social subjects. "It is my intention to maintain and expand these arrangements," he explained, "to ensure a vigorous presentation of the British case in the colonies."[56] In effect, the battle had only just begun.

MEDIA INFRASTRUCTURE: FILMSTRIPS, RADIO, AND THE WORK OF INFORMATION OFFICERS

While Sellers and the CFU produced material in London, and circulated directives and advice, the task of taking the messages and films to audiences in the colonies rested with regional information officers. This relationship between the information officers and the CFU was part of a wider negotiation of power between London and the colonies, as the colonies adopted and adapted centralized media. Indeed, any expansion of the CFU was dependent on the more significant growth of information offices across the empire, catalyzed by war, and directly liaising with the CFU (for example, the responses to the CFU's first questionnaire in 1943 came from these officers). The work of these officers was often shaped by local war conditions, as was the case when a severe petrol shortage hindered the work of the mobile film unit in Mauritius.[57] Yet these information officers were not only presenting film but were also taking the messages of war across the colonies through posters, pamphlets, books, press reports, talks, radio broadcasts, public events, and filmstrips. In this way, the work of the Information Offices uncovers both the specificity of film as a medium and its position within an emerging media infrastructure.

In her work on the press and propaganda in wartime Kenya, Fay Gadsden argued that the aims of the Kenya Information Office were "to counteract enemy propaganda, publicize information about the war, strengthen loyalty to Britain and create confidence in the ultimate victory of the Allies."[58] While this sounds like a fairly generic set of aims, the colony's particular response was further shaped by its own priorities during war. This is evident in the leaflets sent out by the Kenya Information Office to explain the causes of war. Written in Swahili, the leaflets responded to the direct Italian threat on the Kenyan border, but when this direct threat faded, so too did the public appetite for war propaganda. The Information Office now looked beyond the war, as the CFU would agitate to do, to "implement wider economic and social policies."[59] The nature of its response was also shaped by local attitudes to the different media forms. While reports now noted that the "novelty" of its broadcasting had worn off, significantly film did not appear to be a "novelty." The mobile cinema unit was arguably the most successful component of the Kenya Information Office, championed in contrast to its broadcasting and printed media as an "unqualified success."[60]

This single mobile unit, provided by the MOI in 1940, was run by the "tireless" Arthur Champion, a retired provincial commissioner, who wrote extensive reports at the end of each six- or seven-week tour. Through experience, Champion nuanced and developed the approach of the CFU.[61] A *Mombasa Times* article in March 1941 explained that "care has to be taken to assess the mental calibre of the audience" and, like Sellers, Champion categorized his audiences based on their perceived mental capabilities (when he gave a show to Indians and Arabs, he wrote, "it was a pleasant change to address a more intelligent audience").[62] Similarly he argued that broadcasting was less successful than film because it was "beyond the mental grasp of at least 90% of the audience." His organization of the film show resonated with Sellers (whether on the program or the use of local authorities) with some tweaks based on local expectations ("women and children on one side and males on the other of a central line").[63]

Reflecting on his work in 1948, Champion explained that "the primary objective was undoubtedly to establish confidence (without too much obvious propaganda) in our successful conduct of the war and our ability to win it," but he talks of later "developing the cinema into a mobile welfare unit."[64] This shift happens relatively early within the war, as the immediate threat to Kenya fades. By the start of 1941 Champion's reports include notes on subjects such as soil erosion, cattle farming, and water conservation which he observed as he traveled, and soon Champion was incorporating his own welfare and agricultural films, including those "illustrating the evil effects of soil erosion," into his traveling program.[65] His film of the KAR training camp in Uganda would play alongside a CFU-produced film of the campaign in Somaliland and Abyssinia, an amalgamation of materials (from the CFU and Information Offices) that helped redefine and rework the narrative of war. Champion was adapting CFU material for his local audiences and producing films of school and maternity homes, which he claimed by 1942 "prove quite as popular as the political films, and if properly employed, should have a far-reaching effect on social development." Champion was already looking beyond war and was now making the kinds of films that the CFU would soon look to prioritize.[66]

The Information Office hoped to extend and formalize its local production work, arguing that films for the mobile units were "probably best made in Africa," and informed the Colonial Office of its plans for a film production unit in Kenya in 1942. Significantly, the Information Office saw film as one part of its work—it also proposed "still pictures" of "improved agriculture, animal husbandry, forestry, careers for Africans"—and looked to link together "the written, the oral and the visual propaganda" so that, for example, audiences would listen to African broadcasts, which would then be explained with the help of a map.[67] By the end of the war, the Kenya Information Office was producing a steady stream of films—including *Jonathan Builds a Dam* (1944), *Kenya Daisies* (1944, at the request of the Pyrethrum board), and a film on the benefits of paying local rates—which were often edited and processed by the CFU. It produced a mixed program—including a slapstick film showing how an African wife can help her husband "if she's educated and puts her knowledge into practice"—and already worked with local government departments in developing these films.[68]

This was then a more complex relationship. The Information Offices were not simply relaying but also producing and developing media, shaping the CFU and future film practices. The relationship here was not simply between center and periphery, between London and the individual colony, but also between colonies. Information officers held conferences, sharing local experiences and bringing collective issues to London. The first of these was held in Nairobi in May 1941 and included officers from Uganda, Tanganyika, Northern and Southern Rhodesia, Zanzibar, Nyasaland, Aden, and Belgian Congo. Introducing the four-day conference, the governor of Kenya explained that while the war remained the immediate priority, it was "important to keep an eye on the future and so far as war time needs and stresses permit to build up an organisation and technique which can be adapted to the arts of peace." The call mirrored Sellers's own longer-term hopes for the CFU in London. The governor presented the information officer's role as one that has "come to stay," envisaging that the changes brought about by war would extend to peace. The conference considered the operations across Africa—with discussions of mobile vans in Uganda, Zanzibar, and Egypt—before concluding that cinema represents "one of the most powerful means of direct propaganda" and that new units were "deserving of the strongest encouragement."[69]

In 1943 there were further conferences for West African officers in Achimota, Gold Coast, and for Central and East African officers in Nairobi. The conferences formulated regionally specific approaches to propaganda—the Achimota conference outlined that "particular attention should be paid to West African women, in view of the important position they hold in African society"—and also brought forward local problems. The Nigerian information officer pointed out that relations with the press in Nigeria "were not satisfactory" as the press gave preference to "local racial issues and to ill-informed and mischievous criticism" of the government.[70] The conferences marked an attempt to organize power from the colonies, sharing ideas and discussing possible innovations, which were then followed up by information officers who corresponded directly with the MOI in London.

One of the innovations concerned the MOI's plans to develop filmstrips, an important, and critically neglected, form of visual media that clarified, complemented, and sometimes complicated the use and function of film in the colonies. The assistant information officer in Sierra Leone wrote to H. V. Usill in the MOI's Colonial Section soon after the conference, extolling the filmstrip as an "excellent and practicable way of contacting the illiterates in the Protectorate." He recognized particular benefits here—low cost, simple operation, easy (and economical) to transport, and adaptable (thorough the commentary) for local use. "The scheme seems ideal for immediate application in Sierra Leone," he wrote, recognizing a practical value not served by film and radio broadcasts: "I need hardly say that this utopian state [of film projectors and radio broadcasts in all schools] looks about 1000 years away at the present rate of development. What we want is something that we can do *now*." The outlined merits of the filmstrip inadvertently emphasized the perceived failings of the traveling film.[71] Yet others remained unconvinced and defended the particular qualities of film. W. S. Morgan at the Colonial Office noted that the mobile film could attract an audience of "anything up to 150,000 a year." "It is excellent jam for the pill," he continued, "because it has entertainment as well as instructional value; and it seems to be agreed that the moving picture means more to the illiterate African than the still picture." Morgan concluded that the filmstrip would remain in the classroom and would never "compete with the moving film."[72]

Morgan's view was not shared by all. When Usill argued that filmstrip projectors may be "more suitable for propaganda purposes than normal cinema projectors," he used Sellers's own theories on "unsophisticated" audiences. "There are a number of people in most of the colonies," Usill wrote, "to whom the normal cinema technique makes little appeal, even the slow tempo type of film as evolved by Mr Sellers." An MOI document sent to the colonies in 1943 added that filmstrips "are particularly useful for unsophisticated audiences who sometimes find the rapid movement of cinefilm difficult to follow."[73] A later report in the Gambia suggests a process of development here, presenting the filmstrip as a "most valuable initial step in educating illiterate primitive people to appreciate cinematograph films."[74] This argument was often challenged by another racial generalization, using the oft-quoted example of an African viewing a picture upside down to suggest that movement, rather than stillness, was more readily understood.

While reports often sought to promote one form of "visual propaganda" over the other, such a narrow approach ignores the ways that these media often worked alongside each other. The public relations officer in the Gambia described how "The Royal Family" filmstrip served to validate the government's work, not only through its images but, as with the mobile film show, through the organization of the event. Weekly shows in villages were "extremely popular" and speeches of thanks were given by the chiefs to everybody concerned including the MOI. The filmstrip was another form of attraction here, and given its adaptability, useful not just for "general propaganda" but to disseminate "local advice or information."[75] The filmstrip might be used to work through ideas raised on film and certainly the MOI's catalogue of film strips highlights close overlaps with existing colonial film. The strips were divided by specific colonies, and again often focus on economic productivity as in "Tea from the Empire." They use formats also adopted by the CFU ("A Day in the Life of a Bus Conductor in Kenya," "A Day in the Life of an African School Teacher"), and topical titles that could have come direct from the CFU ("The Bicycle at War," "An English Village at War," "The BBC at War"). Most notably the MOI filmstrips increasingly addressed the wider themes of health, education, and welfare that would dominate the postwar CFU output (such as "Achimota College," "African Doctors in Training," "Housing in West Africa").[76] These filmstrips were also locally produced and offered the coverage of the colonies that was so often lacking in the CFU's wartime films.[77]

However, these filmstrips did not represent a new local media but instead exposed familiar tensions between London and the colonies. While a number of colonies were very keen to produce their own strips and even requested cameras to produce "local propaganda on specific subjects," the MOI insisted that all strips were produced in the UK.[78] There were well-worn reasons preventing a local filmstrip service—inexorable wartime delays (a 1943 letter complained that "precisely nothing has been done"), a shortage of suitable staff and funding from

London—but the information officers continued to complain that London was inadequate and "too slow" and pushed for a local service.[79] A further problem of producing this media in London was neatly encapsulated in the response of director Barbara Fell when she was asked to produce a specific filmstrip for Uganda: "I could not know less, for instance, about the subject of tape-worms."[80]

The discussions surrounding the filmstrip also brought forth internal tensions within the MOI. While the CFU acknowledged that the filmstrip could be a "useful addition" to the mobile van, their bosses at the Films Division told them "not to undertake any film strip work whatever."[81] By the end of the war, the MOI sent filmstrips to at least twenty-nine colonies—including Granada, Mauritius, and Malta—and the CFU increasingly sought to involve itself in this work. Later the CFU would train workers in filmstrip production, and into the 1950s the local units would produce filmstrips alongside their films (such as the Jamaica Film Unit's first production, *Farmer Brown Learns Good Dairying*, which was produced in both media).[82] In 1951 Sellers would publish a doctrine on filmstrip production in *Colonial Cinema*, in which he noted that if the strip was well prepared it could "hold its own sandwiched in a programme of cinema films." Sellers imagined the filmstrip as part of the wider film show, as he had witnessed in the West Indies, but he also highlighted what he saw as the key difference between film and filmstrip. For film, he argued that the commentary supports the visuals, whereas with the filmstrip the commentary takes precedence and the visuals support the commentary. In this way, the filmstrip might equally be understood in relation to other talks and broadcasts.[83]

Film was thus one small, though increasingly valued, part of the Information Offices' work. What we start to see here is the formation of a media infrastructure within the colonies, and integral to this was the development of radio broadcasting and the work of the BBC. Through the war, the BBC began to establish its place within the colonies and often in ways that mirrored, and directly aligned, with the CFU. In his recent work on colonial media, Peter Bloom quotes a 1936 Colonial Office report that recognized the BBC Empire Service as a potential "instrument of advanced administration . . . for the enlightenment and education of the more backward sections of the population and for their instruction."[84] These goals were suspended for much of the war, but recent scholarship on wartime broadcasting in Africa highlights the development of an infrastructure for both radio and mobile film. Historian Fred Pratt shows how the onset of war brought forward improved broadcasting facilities in the Gold Coast—in this case a 1.4kw transmitter in Accra, 30 wireless sets for communal listening, and 114 radio sets for stationed servicemen—which one local editorial hoped would help unite the people and educate "the illiterate community who are so quickly misled by pseudo scholars in matters affecting the war."[85] These developments were not matched in Nigeria, where newspaper reports in 1940 complained that radio broadcasts struggled to reach beyond Lagos. The *Daily Service* commented on "the dynamic little sister colony to the West of us [which] just moves along at top speed, leaving Nigeria to grope along about a century behind." Government reports also recognized the value of radio as an outlet for "counter-propaganda" to "ferret out the mischief makers who have been making trouble in the provinces" in Nigeria, while the *Eastern Nigerian Guardian*, in lamenting the advances in Accra, saw this technology as "a connecting link between the Governor and the Governed."[86]

As Brian Larkin reminds us, radio began its life in Nigeria as a "public technology," much like the mobile film show. In this way, it was part of a process of "mediating urban space," of gathering and organizing large audiences around new technology (the loudspeaker), of extending colonial authority, and of fostering a larger imperial network, one that connected the local to Britain.[87] In Pratt's example of the Gold Coast, the transmitter relayed a combination of BBC broadcasts and local programming, which by 1945 accounted for about 20 percent of its daily output. These early moves toward local media were again restricted by money, expertise, and the exigencies of war but did include fifteen-minute daily broadcasts in five local languages. Pratt suggests that those in charge believed that this local broadcasting required a "fundamentally different approach," incorporating, as information officer James Wilson noted, "fables, customs, music and village ballads."[88] As with cinema, local voices were again essential here. Wilson argued that although the loud speaker was a " 'white man's box', it spoke the black man's language and sang his songs," while Wendell P. Holbrook argued that radio propagandists recognized that war propaganda would only work when "endorsed and carefully presented by Africans themselves," who would call for war donations, stimulate recruitment, and later recount heroic tales of African soldiers at war.[89] Wilson noted the enormous reach of the radio and cinema in speaking to illiterate audiences. "Indeed, the cinema and the radio," he speculated in 1944, "may be inventions which will contribute as much to the advancement of West Africa as the invention of the printed press contributed to the advancement of the people of Europe."[90]

The BBC's engagement with the empire illustrates the wider challenges of disseminating propaganda to, and about, the colonies during war. For the most part, its radio shows were intended to project the empire to the "white British world," focusing on the UK, Europe, the dominions and, increasingly, the United States. It recognized that popular interest in the empire at home was limited—Noel Sabine at the Colonial Office remarked that on hearing the word "empire" "the automatic reaction is to switch off"—and this led to a policy of "infiltration," in which features and aspects of the empire were incorporated into regular programming.[91]

The experiences of the BBC shed further light on the CFU's own response, as the BBC's broadcasting was straightjacketed by a fear of upsetting or provoking controversy among colonial audiences. The BBC was notably anxious over how to address audiences across the empire. A broadcasting handbook in 1944 stated: "Avoid darky jokes and references. Never use 'native' unless it is unavoidable." Like the CFU, it sought to downplay class hierarchies by finding a "new language of imperial authority" told in the "common idiom" not immediately associated with the "prosperous Englishman."[92] The MOI was also anxious about the increasing popularity of US radio across the empire (revisiting fears around Hollywood's cultural imperialism) and, in response, suggested more entertainment in the BBC's overseas transmissions. Practical restrictions further shaped the BBC's output, such as the paucity of material from overseas that meant a reliance on available talks and speakers in the UK. This also defined the output of the Empire Transcription Scheme, which made discs of programs available free of charge for African and other colonial audiences. Its topics ranged from "What Britain Is Fighting For" to "How England Is Governed," which sought to show how "the paying of taxes and other inconveniences are not limited to other Colonial peoples." Like the early work of the CFU, the broadcasts often showed London to the colonies and sought to tie the empire back to Britain, while the royal family functioned as *the* symbol of imperial unity across this media.[93]

The BBC's output also acknowledged an ideological shift from an earlier form of imperialism. For example, a program of Kipling planned for Empire Day in 1942 was scrapped and labeled "most undesirable . . . in fact, mad" in discussion with the High Commission of India. The traditional jingoism of empire—the tales of *One Family*—was now replaced by a program focusing on imperial responsibilities. Historian Simon Potter concluded that while broadcasting may not have "decisively transformed the empire's war effort, it is clear that the war played a major role in reshaping collaborative links among the British world's public broadcasting authorities."⁹⁴ A similar claim can be made for the CFU. Film may not have changed the war in the colonies, but the war certainly reshaped the use of film across the colonies.

As we will see, it does this in many ways, as personnel, equipment, and models are repurposed to tackle the critical challenges within the postwar empire. Information officer James Wilson noted how by 1944, a life after war was more readily imagined in which the local information services "might be put to good use in teaching the adult population social welfare, better education and good practice in health."⁹⁵ Indeed, there are numerous examples of information officers who spent time with the CFU in London and later shaped government film work in their countries. To take an example from further south, W.D. Gale, the Southern Rhodesia information officer, was a pivotal figure in the establishment of the Central African Film Unit alongside Harry Franklin, his Northern Rhodesian counterpart, who also contributed to *Colonial Cinema*. The officers would bring forward local reflections on wider colonial policy. As James Burns argues, Gale added the "popular prejudices of white Rhodesia" to the existing theories of Sellers, a somewhat toxic mix.⁹⁶ While we might assume that the infrastructure served to further the aims of colonial governments—to carry the fight beyond war—Wendell P. Holbrook reminds us that this was not always the case. The Information Office in the Gold Coast had used "radicals" as speakers during the war to incorporate them within the state and legitimize the government's motives, but Holbrook argues that this wartime "model" was subsequently adapted and appropriated by those who led "anti-colonialist mass political action."⁹⁷

The Information Offices adopted and adapted the films, technologies, and ideas of the CFU and, furthermore, reported back, providing a local perspective on the imperial models projected from London. As John Wilson acknowledged, the CFU was "indissolubly linked with Colonial Information Departments." For the most part the information officers strongly endorsed and legitimized the work of the CFU, recognizing that an expanded CFU was in their "best interests." However, the function and future of the CFU, like the empire it served, remained unstable, fought over, and at times condemned by those working in the colonies.⁹⁸ Early in 1943 H.V. Usill sent the West African information officers extracts from the minutes of a recent MOI meeting that had listed CFU "policy." Usill was "disturbed" by the four points, which all focused on the merits of showing images of Britain to colonial audiences. Wilson, a longtime champion of the CFU, took particular offense. While extolling the merits of the "slow technique," he questioned the very existence and purpose of the CFU if it relied on "images from the remote country, Britain." Wilson suggested that the films from Britain, regardless of technique, could only appeal to the tiny majority (around 5 percent) who have some education. "Given this new aim," he concluded, "I really can see little reason for the continued existence of the Colonial Film Unit."[99]

While the Colonial Office admonished Usill for stirring up the situation and not behaving "properly," this tension over media control was never fully resolved. A few months later at the Achimota conference, the information officers offered their somewhat qualified support for the CFU. While agreeing that "the technique developed by the Colonial Film Unit is excellent for its purpose, and should not be changed," the officers maintained that "no effort should be spared to implement the avowed policy of securing African material." The conference reiterated, and formalized, long-held concerns that the CFU was too focused on the "projection of the English scene."[100] Indeed, the films produced by the CFU were often defined, categorized, and criticized in two ways—by location (between those films produced in "Africa" or "Britain") and by event (war).[101] Even within these categories, the films are often most notable for their absences, for what is missing or unseen, and these absences are often profoundly political.

RAW STOCK AND ABSENT IMAGES: REPRESENTING AFRICA AT WAR

The West African conference had pointedly noted that only seven of the twenty-eight CFU films listed in the opening issue of *Colonial Cinema* in November 1942 contained any pictures of Africans and that the proportion shot in West Africa was "almost negligible."[102] Those films that did contain footage from Africa came from familiar sources. There was a reedited film from Sellers's time in Nigeria (*Progress in the Colonies*), which was followed over the next year by further additions from his back catalogue (including *Machi Gabi* and *Barless Incinerator*), compilation films from war office newsreel material (*African Troops on Active Service*), and footage from Uganda shot by Captain Roberts, the deputy police commissioner (*Uganda Police*).[103] There was also footage from Arthur Champion (*Early Training of African Troops*), whose work was held up by the CFU as evidence that the Raw Stock Scheme could now produce the "desired quality." At a meeting in 1943 Sellers lavishly praised two of Champion's color films, *Seven Acres* and *Native Welfare*, which were currently being edited by the CFU. Gervas Huxley made a point of requesting that "in the editing the partnership theme should be developed," further highlighting the pressures to fit wider MOI imperatives and the multiple voices heard in every CFU film. Sellers was very eager that a suitable fuss should be made over Champion's material—a telegram sent to the governor of Kenya, a letter from the CFU asking Champion for more material of the "same human-interest appeal," and a special showing for the Colonial Office.[104]

In many cases, the material that came in from Africa was somewhat less inspiring. When the CFU minutes noted that "Wild Rubber" (subsequently renamed *We Want Rubber*) "was bad from a propaganda point of view," W. S. Morgan of the Colonial Office intervened. Morgan readily admitted that the photography was "not of professional standard," but saw the wider benefits of showing a rubber estate "owned and run entirely by Africans." Most of all, Morgan felt it prudent to support the film in light of the information officers' recent criticisms. "It would seem strange," he wrote, "if we were to reject offhand one of their first efforts under the raw stock scheme."[105]

The scheme initially identified a handful of suitable amateur filmmakers, and so this was not as far-reaching or democratizing as the official reports might suggest. The MOI had provided a number of African colonies with a 16mm camera—Kenya, Tanganyika, Uganda, Gambia, Sierra Leone, Gold Coast, and Nigeria—and identified eight operators including Arthur Champion, Harry Franklin, H. Lironi, and O. Waterfield (who trained with the CFU), Captain Roberts in Uganda, and Major Kingston Davies who had filmed in East Africa before the war. While acknowledging that there must be many other suitable candidates, the CFU explained that "their work as yet is unknown to the unit."[106] Some of these did step forward, although most were already embedded within government operations. For example, the popular and widely viewed CFU film *Plainsmen of Barotseland* (1944) was shot by Louis Nell, who traveled with the mobile cinema unit as the films officer for the Northern Rhodesian Information Office. Nell would go on to enjoy a long and successful career as joint head of the Central African Film Unit. Like Arthur Champion in Kenya, Nell identified a need for local productions, arguing that his African audiences struggled to relate to the experiences of foreign characters and to a "war they did not understand." He made

16mm recruitment films for the veterinary and police departments—the latter "a crime doesn't pay" picture called *Keepers of the Peace*—and, while his films did not directly follow Sellers's specialized technique, thematically they followed other CFU productions. *Plainsmen of Barotseland* depicts royalty and traditional ceremonial practices, while also now outlining and promoting modern Western developments. In one sequence a veterinary officer demonstrates how "modern scientific methods" will protect local animals, a European is shown inspecting cattle, while trained, skilled African workers administer medicine. The tentative moves toward a British model of self-government are further represented in the figure of the chief, depicted not in traditional ceremonial robes but rather in a suit and shirt and who was, as Nell noted in his memoirs, particularly interested in film and Western culture.[107]

The CFU was concerned then not only with the technical capabilities of the filmmakers, but equally with the ways in which they represented Africans on screen. When the CFU agreed in 1943 that it needed a couple of filmmakers in East and West Africa, the name of Leon Schauder was suggested. Schauder was a South African who had lived in Britain before the war and had produced films in Africa for Gaumont-British Instructional's "Focus on the Empire" series. Perhaps given his South African background, the CFU was concerned that even if Schauder had the requisite technical skills, "it was by no means certain he had the right attitude towards Africans to enable him to take good films from a propaganda point of view." It cited the example of Captain Feilmann in West Africa, who had served with the Army Film and Photographic Unit, and warned that "apparent contempt for the native population made obvious through pictures ruined a film's value."[108] Feilmann's filmed subjects included a staged piece on the work of the 5th West African Field ambulance units (bringing the patient to the British doctor), an archetypal British sports day put on for Africans (and featuring a "mammies race"), shots of manual and transportation work, and a sequence showing the production of goods for Britain. This final item was used in the sixth edition of the CFU's monthly newsreel, *The British Empire at War*, under the title "Gold Coast: Soap from Cocoa," and also featured in an issue of *Gaumont British News*. The footage follows the conventions of industrial process films, in showing the manufacture of soap within the Gold Coast. It shows Africans transporting sacks and local women cultivating the beans, and when presented in newsreels was contextualized as an indication of the Gold Coast's loyalty to the empire and its continued support for the war. Yet, the nature of this support was more problematic and the dominant representation of Africans transporting material, manufacturing goods, and performing manual labor was often deemed counterproductive in the efforts to mobilize and generate support among African audiences.[109]

Colonial Cinema noted that the raw stock footage in London was often "edited in the evening to the sound of dropping bombs."[110] Yet, while the war provided the backdrop and soundtrack to these films from Africa, it was often notably absent from the films, prompting audiences to demand more footage of the African war effort. "Everybody asks why they cannot see more of their own soldiers in action, at the infantry training school and during other phases of their everyday army life," wrote one district commissioner in the Gold Coast. He further suggested that audiences were dwindling and that "films of suburban English life" were "neither understood nor much appreciated."[111] The CFU was acutely aware of this criticism and did produce a few films that focused predominantly on the African war effort. Perhaps the most widely seen was *Africa's Fighting Men*, a compilation film produced from library material that had already featured across the first eight issues of *British Empire at War*. In total there would be thirty-nine issues of *British Empire at War*, each issue stitching together footage of parades and other activities from across the empire, routing the colonies through London as part of a narrative of imperial collaboration and solidarity. *Africa's Fighting Men* similarly unpicked items from the newsreels and now foregrounded "the contribution the African colonies are making to the fighting forces of the Empire." In doing so it sought to encourage further African support for the war, and, beyond this, promote a message of continued imperial interdependency.[112]

These messages are most explicitly revealed through the commentary, which acknowledges the African contributions to the war effort in two ways: "by the production of raw materials and by assigning men for the armed forces." It suggests that their efforts had been widely recognized, but this view was repeatedly challenged by the notable lack of footage of African troops from overseas theaters. Instead the commentary foregrounds the role and support of the British in preparing the African men for war and defines the "Africans" by generic racial characteristics. "They are at their best when fighting in the bush," the commentator asserts, further noting that "the great strength and endurance of the African is an invaluable asset in work like this." In its attempt to position the Africans as a self-sacrificing part of the wider imperial cause—"brave, loyal men who are ready for any sacrifice"—the commentary presents the Africans as "typical of the colonial troops from every part of the Empire." The images largely reinforce these messages, a collective shown training across the first five newsreel items within this compilation film.

Within this context, the missing action footage appears indicative of the often invisible and unrecognized contributions of the African soldiers. "Show us films of actual fighting face to face," wrote an African teacher from Chalimbana, "bombing towns, sinking ships, so that we may understand war: not manufacturing aeroplanes, repairing guns, inspecting troops etc., which are mostly unintelligible and quite uninteresting to us Africans."[113] *Colonial Cinema* noted the "regrettable shortage" of footage, attention, and recognition of the increasingly pivotal military activities of the African soldiers in 1945, suggesting that "the outstanding events in the European theatre of war have overshadowed the campaign in the Far East, where so many African soldiers are fighting valiantly in the Allied armies." *Colonial Cinema* hoped that with "no counter-attraction," there would now be "a constant stream of material to make the films for which Africa is anxiously waiting."[114]

This is not to say that there was no merit in showing African army life. The Gold Coast Cinema Officer argued that when the cinema unit traveled with a recruiting party, "the result was a marked increase in the number of recruits." He explained that "the rumour had gone around that the army food was neither good nor plentiful. The films shown completely killed the rumour."[115] Yet, for others these sequences were "ill chosen" and counterproductive. Captain Dickson of the East Africa Command Mobile Propaganda Unit, which toured Northern Nyasaland in late 1943 and early 1944, argued that the scenes of Askari transporting gun carriage wheels over the river (the third item within *Africa's Fighting Men*) "revives the most hideous memories of the Carrier Corps in the E.A. campaign of 1914–1918 and confirms Africans' worst suspicions regarding present-day service conditions." He was also critical of the opening item, showing jungle training in Ceylon, suggesting that the footage of Askari "naked but for shorts and boots, and wielding machetes," led Africans at home to assume that "they don't even give you proper uniform in the K.A.R. now." Curiously, given his criticisms of the regressive representation, Dickson reserved some of his ire for the film style itself, writing that "practically 100% of films sent out by the Ministry of Information proved quite impossible for Africans [to understand]" as they followed European film conventions. This is perhaps unsurprising as this war footage was rarely filmed with the CFU and "illiterate" African audiences in mind.[116]

These criticisms could also be applied to another CFU war compilation film, *Basuto Troops on Active Service,* a 1945 film that, in bringing together two previously released films, now moves beyond its earlier call to arms to a more flagrant celebration of imperial cooperation. Stylistically, the two sequences within the film appear vastly different. The first showing Basuto firemen in the Middle East is carefully staged and features numerous shots edited together in order to highlight the speed and urgency with which the Basuto firemen operate, while the second item of Basuto troops in Italy contains lengthier shots of the Africans tending to the mules. While ostensibly offering a familiarly subservient image of the African troops, the film also extolls the merits of British instruction. For example, it highlights the uniforms and, in the words of *Colonial Cinema,* the "smartness and efficiency" of the firemen, using costume as a signifier of the perceived social developments under British supervision. Then, in the second segment, there is a display of social interaction and imperial collaboration as Europeans sit and smoke with Basuto troops in an informal context. Finally, the film depicts skilled Africans, such as the African vet who tends to a horse, while a European man holds it. The war footage begins here to fit a postwar agenda, to project gradual development for the Africans under British supervision.

The CFU's projection of the African war effort invites a brief comparison with the situation in India, where the much-derided government newsreel *Indian News Parade* offered a weekly vision of the imperial war effort to Indian audiences in five languages.[117] The newsreel was widely and expressively condemned by both the nationalist Indian press and much of the cinema-going public as it peddled government fantasies divorced from the ever-changing political realities on the ground. Earlier issues are largely united by their support of the war effort. They depict the work and, in particular, the welfare of Indian troops overseas and show these troops receiving training and recognition, usually within official formal ceremonies. The newsreel advocates imperial cooperation under the British flag, its sutured form furthering this goal; shows Indian civilians supporting the war effort; and carefully positions India within a colonial hierarchy (for example when depicting West African troops in Burma). As with the CFU's war films, the newsreel is as striking for what it does not show. Perhaps the most prominent example concerns the Bengal famine, the initial absence of which is profoundly political. The subsequent carefully staged account of the famine presents the British and Indians working together to combat this "natural" disaster, prioritizing the humanitarian efforts of the British and, as Indian independence becomes imminent, highlighting the role of the Commonwealth in responding to the food "shortage." Historian Sanjoy Bhattacharya shows how local publicity officials often "felt uncomfortable" about the mass screenings of these episodes within areas most affected by the shortages, as the films, with their jocular and jingoistic commentary, presented a triumphant account of British aid that was far removed from the experiences of millions of Indians.[118] The point here is that the newsreel, put together from various international sources, often struggled to address the rapidly changing situation—not only in the context of the war but equally in the context of the empire—adapting local visions of the war effort that meandered somewhere between the superfluous and the spectacularly counterproductive.

The CFU was always looking beyond war and wanted to pursue the kinds of instructional pictures that had first motivated Sellers. By 1943, this appeared possible and the CFU and Colonial Office discussed plans for a health film on venereal disease, a favorite subject of colonial filmmakers. They outlined the three morals for the film—"V.D. is a scourge and a pernicious disease. Its effects can be disastrous. IT CAN BE CURED"—and asked H.V. Scott, a former director of education in Kenya now in Britain with the Colonial Office, to develop a "simple story."[119] Scott's story followed the Mr. Wise and Mr. Foolish format, although, as with the British Council's *Local Government,* suggested changes came from all sides. A Colonial Office representative argued that, given the difficulties of getting treatment in villages, Mr. Wise should be seen leaving hospital a "cured and happy man," while Elspeth Huxley warned that showing the city as inherently dangerous might undermine government moves to encourage people to work at the docks. Huxley's solution, lacking somewhat in drama, was to introduce another friend who does not go to the brothel but "perhaps solaced himself by a jolly evening in the local salvation army club (if there is one), or a highly respectable dance at the local dance-hall!"[120] The pre-production reveals again the challenges of producing a film to stretch across the colonies. It was already determined that in some areas the film should be "not for general exhibition but for exhibition to Government officials," instructing the instructors rather than reaching the "illiterate" Africans directly. There were further concerns over the film's exhibition in areas where "facilities for treatment was lacking," although on this point the Colonial Office argued that the film might serve to "stimulate" change and accelerate improved medical facilities within the colonies.[121]

Despite being the CFU's top priority in 1943, the VD film was never made, or rather it was made many times but not by the CFU during the war. After learning that there was a recent VD film produced in South Africa, *The Two Brothers,* the CFU agreed to edit this instead.[122] The decision reveals the realities of the CFU's work at war, in particular the difficulties of filming in the colonies and its tendency to reuse or rework existing material. It also highlights the remarkably consistent, dominant colonial narratives that permeate this cinema. The CFU often emphasized the need to be culturally specific, and indeed Harry Franklin, who had a copy of the film, posited the view "that the African here [Northern Rhodesia] would regard the film as a comedy, and not as an object lesson."[123] Yet, there is a generic framework to these colonial films, with structures, characters, and motifs that often appear remarkably intransigent. The topic would be revisited again, most notably a decade later by the Jamaica Film Unit's *It Can Happen to You* (1956), which although experimenting with technique and focusing more closely on the treatment of the disease, would again follow the Mr. Wise and Mr. Foolish format to tell the story of two brothers—Joseph, whose motto was "eat drink and be merry for tomorrow we die," and Charlie, who "was just the opposite."

PROJECTION OF ENGLAND: REPRESENTING COLONIALS IN WARTIME BRITAIN

Given the difficulties of filming in the colonies, the CFU relied heavily on films showing the "British way and purpose." There were films explaining British institutions, such as *These Are London Firemen* (1942) and *This Is a Special Constable* (1941), and those addressing the war effort in Britain, some of which featured colonial personnel. *This Is a Barrage Balloon* (1941) depicted a Nigerian, J.S.D. Gordonu, attached to a barrage balloon unit in Britain, while *West Indians with the R.A.F. in Britain* (1944) shows the secretary of state for the colonies inspecting a large group of West Indian recruits. Filmed at the request of the Colonial Office with "an eye" on the West Indian audience, *West Indians with the R.A.F. in Britain* reportedly "attracted larger audiences" than any other recent release on the mobile circuit in Jamaica. Its appeal lay in its familiarity, with some audiences "concerned chiefly with identifying those from their locality who have volunteered. When they do their enthusiasm knows no bounds." The report further suggested that the film would be particularly useful "prior to a recruiting campaign," although this is less clearly a priority by the time of the film's exhibition in 1945. The majority of films in Britain instead prioritized the wider economic contributions of colonial workers to the British war effort and, beyond this, the imperial cooperation, economic partnership, and movement between Britain and the colonies that would shape the postwar empire.

Timbermen from Honduras (1943), which shows the influx of West Indian timber workers to Britain early in the war, emphasizes Britain's debt to, and care for, the colonial workers: "the mother country is grateful for this help and gives close attention to the health of the men."[124] The film is a reassuring depiction of a welcoming and inviting Britain— "Fortunately everyone was very friendly when they arrived and the men from the West Indies soon felt at home in Britain"; "They have friends with a cheery greeting for them in every street"—and highlights the ways in which the British and colonial visitors have learned from each other. Theirs is a common cause as the conclusion spells out, showing that some of these men have chosen to "train and stand shoulder to shoulder with the Home Guard of Britain, that great civilian army of war workers, who know what they want, and are all out to get it—victory."

The Home Guard was the subject of another CFU film and one with a very personal connection to William Sellers, as it featured his own battalion, the 12th Essex Home Guard (in which he was signals officer). The film militarizes the traditional English village scene, positing the "ordinary" workers in their military uniforms within this familiar rural scene. The men march and stand to attention, they perform exercises (camouflaged and dressed as bushes in what appears to be a glorified game of hide and seek), and even carry out a controlled explosion, showing the threat, destruction, and enforced protection of this rural idyll. The film shows the "everyman" supporting the war effort, and the organization of civilian life in war.[125] This is also evident in *Boy Scouts,* which was made in close collaboration with the Boy Scouts Association and was intended to bolster the Scout movement across the empire. Indeed, there were numerous other films showing scout movements overseas—a well-established model of citizen-building—including *Boy Scouts in Uganda, Boy Scout Rally, Accra,* and *Visit of Chief Scout to Kenya* as well as newsreel items showing Boy Scout activities in Nigeria and Tanganyika.[126]

While the CFU produced many "projection of England" pictures, it differs from the British Council in more explicitly relating this image to the colonies and, indeed, often situating African "visitors" within this scene. These "projection" films invariably open with the same establishing shot over green fields and feature recurring signifiers of British identity—the village school, the church, the rolling fields, and farms—as we see in *Education in England: A Village School* (1945). *A Village School* depicts the workings of an English rural school and foregrounds a pedagogical approach, rather than elaborate resources or infrastructure, which the film suggests can be applied to Africa. This is not an affluent school; children and staff make the materials they use, the senior boys do the necessary odd jobs, while emphasis is on practical work. The commentary makes explicit the connections with African education—the classes are divided by age "just as the children in an African school are"—and foregrounds the value of school for agricultural work (the boys will make "better farmers because they have been to school"). The school is evidently understaffed—teachers run multiple classes at the same time—but with a politician's spin this is presented as beneficial to the schoolchildren, as "it teaches them to work by themselves." As *Colonial Cinema* explained, the school serves as a model of "what can be achieved with a small staff," while the lessons within the film, such as the emphasis on practical work and on subjects like agriculture, are "vital to educational progress in the colonies." A report from Sierra Leone noted the merits of showing British men and women performing manual labor, as many of these films did, not only as a relatable lesson for colonial audiences but also to challenge perceptions, and "disabuse their minds of the idea that the British are a race of rulers and overlords who, lily-like, neither toil nor spin."[127]

A Village School was intended as a lesson to teachers and parents in Africa as much as children. Some of the customs and activities also highlight common ground. The film normalizes traditional gender boundaries. It opens by explaining that "the men are busy in the field and the women in their homes," while boys are shown creating maps as the girls carry out needlework. At the film's conclusion two girls chastise a boy who takes eggs from a bird's nest and convince him to return them. The creation of "self-reliant" and self-policing citizens, who as the commentator notes "learnt to take their place in the world with confidence and responsibility, knowing how to behave towards other people and other creatures," is, of course, another metaphor for the empire. This metaphor is played out in the abundance of films about children and education, which showcase continued British support for the colonies as they "grow up" and move toward self-governance.

African children are more directly inserted into this projection of England in the 1944 CFU film *Springtime in an English Village*. The film initially depicts an almost identical, quintessentially English landscape, apparently unaffected by war—fields, animals, the village school—before assimilating an African girl into this image of England. It does this through another staple of traditional rural England: the May Queen ceremony (see Figure 3.2). In celebrating the wartime integration of Africans within the British Empire, the film carefully mediates the heritage that has traditionally defined Britain to the colonies and a social mobility that now acknowledges and embraces colonial involvement (albeit on British terms). The film shows the girl's selection by her fellow students, while the choreographed performance of the May Queen ceremony—leaving the church, receiving the applause of the white establishment, and then receiving a kiss from a young British woman—illustrates her acceptance within Britain. In this way, the film furthers the CFU's citizenship process as through this ceremony, the African schoolgirls effectively *become* British. The final shot—a staged tableau of the crowned girl surrounded by English children—positions the African girl at the center of this image of England and is maintained for a few seconds, ensuring that the African audiences depart with this image of African integration. This is presented as a typical and unremarkable scene, eliciting no undue attention from the surrounding villagers, although the very fact that it was filmed suggests the opposite. Indeed, the CFU had read about the crowning of an African May Queen, a newsworthy event, and re-created the girl's selection and ceremony for the camera after recognizing that "a story like this was too good to miss."[128]

While the film eschews any reference to war, the event is both a product of, and a defiant response to, the global conflict. The chosen girl and her sister were daughters of an African seaman serving with the Merchant Navy, relocated during the war to the village of Stanion in Northamptonshire, while *Colonial Cinema* explained the absence of war on screen by stating that "the war has not been allowed to interfere with many of the old English customs, particularly those which affect the happiness of the children."[129] While offering the kind of traditional representation of rural England, loved by the British Council but widely derided and questioned within the MOI, the CFU articulated this as evidence of stoic continuity and defiance, of racial integration and development. These themes recur in other "home" productions, such as *An African in England: An English Village* (1945).

FIGURE 3.2. A discussion of *Springtime in an English Village* in *Colonial Cinema*, July 1944, 27.

An African in England again provides a tour of the rural countryside and acknowledges, in a line that could likely be heard in the corridors of the British Council, that "the English countryside is always greatly admired by visitors from other countries." The film opens by moving from the city to the countryside (as with *Local Government*), a move that acknowledges the CFU's desire to relate and connect to its rural African viewers. The film is, in some respects, a sequel to the CFU's 1941 film *An African in London* in which a Nigerian is shown the landmarks of London. This earlier film had been the subject of protests from the West African Students' Union (WASU) in London, after the Guyanese actor, Robert Adams, was cast in the title role, a particularly stark illustration of the absence of Africans within this wartime cinema. While *An African in London* had celebrated the primacy of the imperial center, *An African in England* follows a visitor, Kofi (played by WASU member, O.B. Alakija, a student from London's St. Martin's College of Art), who arrives by bus and is offered a tour of the village by a retired farmer. The widely adopted "tour" format allowed the viewer to see Britain through the eyes of the traveler, and as a report in the *Essex Chronicle* noted, Kofi "asks exactly the kind of questions the people of his native village far away on the Gold Coast would ask, because what he wants to know is what they also want to know."[130]

The treatment explained that the film sought to "give as representative a picture of English village life as possible," and to this end Sellers chose the village of Finchingfield, which he explained "is about the most beautiful of Essex villages and the most representative. It has preserved its old-world character against all the changes of time."[131] Again we have this emphasis on the old-world character, which is represented through the architecture (such as the thatched roof), the countryside and institutions (school, post office, church), and the recreation (cricket on the green, English tea). The film shows the post office, the council gardener, the bakery that "baked for the whole village" and the local library, and notes that many of these services are paid for by local taxes. It recognizes skilled, practical jobs, shows familiar gendered activities (a sewing class in the village hall), notes "the neatness and tidiness of the street," and highlights cooperation in agriculture and health, most notably as the film introduces the village nurse. In this way, the village serves as a microcosm of the nation, of the kinds of cooperative developments in services, health, and agriculture that the CFU would look to promote within the postwar colonies.

Yet while *An African in England* seeks to translate British customs and practices to Africa, it also foregrounds the wartime message of "partnership." The commentator concludes that the British people are "just as eager to learn about African village life," while the original treatment described the final image of the farmer and his wife listening to Kofi talk about his homeland as "this friendly scene of mutual interest."[132] As with *Springtime in an English Village*, Kofi is welcomed and, more importantly, seen to be welcomed, through a seemingly endless display of handshaking. The treatment for the film explained that one of its aims was "to touch on the increasing interest being taken in colonial affairs by the people of this country," to project continued British support and appreciation for the colonies at a moment when questions

FIGURE 3.3. On the set of *An African in England*. George Pearson is seated with the script. Published in George Pearson, *Flashback: The Autobiography of a British Filmmaker* (London: George Allen and Unwin, 1957), 192.

over the economic viability and longer-term future of the empire grew ever louder.[133] In this way, the CFU films sought to challenge the perception of British indifference within the colonies—a perception exacerbated by the paucity of films acknowledging the military contributions of colonial troops—by positioning colonial workers and "visitors" within what clearly remained the imperial center (see Figure 3.3).

An African in England also seeks to export practices, services, and values to Africa. Toward the end of Kofi's tour, he visits the village hall where they are setting up a cinema show for the evening. The sequence, which was filmed at Pinewood Studios, speaks to those watching in Africa, to address and reflect on the function of the mobile cinema show. Kofi asks about the evening's film program and learns that the subjects deal with the lives of the people in the village, which will "help them to make better homes, grow better crops, keep better health and generally improve conditions." In this way, the film explains the work of the CFU to the audience, what it hopes they will take from *this* film and, beyond this, what the CFU hopes to become after the war. Filmed in the last days of war, this self-reflexive sequence looks forward and acknowledges the priorities of the CFU as it prepares to move out to the colonies, to make instructional films, promoting social welfare and development. As *Colonial Cinema* explained in 1946, the unit may have been initiated as a "weapon of war," but it now had a "far more important future before it as a weapon for peace."[134]

MARCHING ON: *VICTORY PARADE* AND THE "END" OF WAR

Before the CFU could make these instructional films, it had a more immediate event to record: the end of the war. Over the next year, the CFU would exploit this "victory" narrative, tied as it was to a rhetoric of imperial cooperation and mutual loyalty. One of the earliest films from the summer of 1945 was *Freed War Prisoners Return to Africa*. The film emphasized British appreciation and support for the African soldiers, highlighted the excellent care afforded to African soldiers when brought back to Britain, and, with an emphasis on their welfare, showed them eating, playing football, receiving new clothes, and touring historic British landmarks ("these excursions cost them nothing"). As *Colonial Cinema* explained in September 1945, these films served to foster an imperial pride now useful beyond the war ("Their homeland and the whole Empire may well be proud of the part they played in defeating the enemy").[135] These films of returning soldiers also served to compress the empire, to connect Britain to Africa. Films of victory celebrations and returning troops arrived in London as part of the Raw Stock Scheme from Cyprus, Fiji, Sierra Leone, and the Gambia.[136] The very first film produced by the CFU unit sent to West Africa after the war was *Welcome Home* (1946), which showed troops from the 8th Battalion, the Gold Coast Regiment, returning from Burma. It was not only the soldiers moving now, but the cameras as well, traveling across Africa to capture, respond to, and seek to shape an empire emerging from war.

The CFU certainly recognized the value of war, a currency it hoped to convert into postwar goodwill. This is most evident in the films produced to mark the victory celebrations in London on 8 June 1946. Here was an event that the Colonial Office asked the CFU to film—suggesting it spend "four or five weeks" filming the arriving colonial contingents and "their activities in Britain"—as men and women from all parts of the British Empire marched through London to celebrate and acknowledge their part in "winning" the war and, in so doing, providing life-support to an ailing empire.[137] While marching forward, the parade afforded a lingering glance back, not only in what it celebrated but also in how, as the format of the event—a military parade before the King at the "heart of the Empire"—revived a colonial relationship in which the empire was brought together and contained within the imperial center, and in which differences were concealed within a choreographed pageant. Reporting on the parading colonial men and women, the *Times* saw "their khaki and the swing of their arms [as] the symbols of their common allegiance and discipline. Every type of crown government was represented, many stages of civilization and independence, years of training, education and example."[138]

The CFU's film of the parade was a chance to show the colonies what the empire might look like now that the war was over. What we see is an attempt to transfer the values deployed in war into a new postwar empire, catalyzing a celebration of a united imperial war effort into a call for continued imperial cooperation in peace. "The men and women of the Commonwealth march side by side in victory as they toiled together in war," the commentator announces. "United in the mother country, they look forward to their common progress in calmer days to come." *Colonial Cinema* articulated its hopes for the CFU in very similar terms. "But with the wreck of war dispersing and some of the ghosts being laid," it wrote, "we can look forward with confidence and good hope to a future of constructive mutual effort."[139]

The empire depicted in *Victory Parade* may appear remarkably similar to prewar incarnations, as the film positions the "visiting" colonial troops within a traditional image of "the mother country." The troops attend a tea party at the Colonial Office in London (see Figure 3.4), they visit the "Empire memorial to the great Queen Victoria" and see Buckingham Palace, "the home of his majesty the King." They appear alongside dignitaries as the film highlights the hospitality shown toward them ("of course the colonial visitors were invited to go along"). This show-and-tell recalls an earlier sense of wonder and deference, highlighting British primacy and making a claim on future loyalty ("for most of them this was their first visit to Britain, but it is one they will remember all their lives"). *Victory Parade*, in part, records and reveals the politics of the events it depicts, but the commentary and editing privilege some moments that suggest change. For example, while *Victory Parade* still presents the Africans as performers, it also shows among the appreciative crowd for the KAR band in Edinburgh a few Africans who "are studying at the University." The film nods here toward the wider

FIGURE 3.4. The Colonial Film Unit filming colonial troops in London. The troops were attending a reception with the secretary of state for the colonies as part of the victory parade celebrations in 1946. Courtesy of Imperial War Museum.

presence of a new generation of educated colonials within Britain, although postwar CFU productions would also emphasize that they were visitors, learning from Britain before taking this knowledge back to their own country.

The public relations officer in the Gold Coast spoke of how film provides a "steady stream of irrefutable factual information" and conveys "factual proof in a form which the African illiterate understands."[140] This spectacularly naïve view ignores the choices made at each turn by the CFU, which were acutely political, showing events that were performed for the camera (for example, with the emphasis on cheering crowds) and edited and stitched together for colonial audiences. This becomes clearer when viewing the many other versions of the victory celebrations, which included films by Castleton-Knight Productions, Chelsea Colour Films, and British Movietone News. What is striking about these other versions is the almost complete absence of colonial troops; an absence that is again acutely political. For example, the British Movietone News version focuses extensively on the dignitaries, shows the "pride of place" assumed by the Americans, highlights that the "biggest cheer" came for "our own" men, and offers only the briefest of mentions of the Commonwealth troops: "then from the empire, men from India, Australia, New Zealand and South Africa." The colonial troops are consigned to the cutting-room floor.[141]

This did not go unnoticed. The *Daily Comet*, a nationalist paper in Nigeria owned by future president Nnamdi Azikiwe, commented on the omission of colonial units from versions screened in England and other parts of the world, a move that "arouses not so much resentment in us as contempt." "The invitation of these gallant men who had fought to preserve imperialism to London," the *Comet* argued, "proves after all to be an act dictated by mere expediency." Indeed, the CFU decided to re-record the commentary for *Victory Parade* to ensure that "individual colonial contingents" were identified and mentioned for specific colonial audiences.[142]

The CFU's *Victory Parade* would play widely across Africa—even in a prison in Freetown, Sierra Leone, where the film met with "great applause"—and according to *Colonial Cinema*, "Colonial audiences were delighted to see their compatriots so well covered."[143] Yet even here, the CFU acknowledged that "the technical exigencies of cutting" had limited the amount of coverage afforded to some territories and so actually produced four additional films for East Africa, West Africa, the Middle East, and the Far East. In providing "the maximum possible coverage to the contingents," these additional films created fresh histories, privileging each colony's place within the empire.[144]

It was evidently imagined that these films, like the parade they depicted, would promote unity and imperial pride, but paradoxically there is evidence that this idealized vision served rather to highlight the inequality often experienced back "home." T.K. Impahim, a soldier from the Gold Coast, claimed that his experiences in London for the celebrations shaped his attitude toward his own country. "I had stayed in England and I had experienced the treatment the English people gives us in our own country and over here," he wrote. "There was tremendous difference." Impahim argued that in England he was on "equal terms with my fellow soldiers," but when he returned to the Gold Coast, he was "discriminated against by this very white man." These experiences, he suggested, encouraged him to "join together and fight for independence because if we get our independence, we will be in a position to change so many things."[145]

Impahim's comments, along with those of the *Daily Comet*, highlight that the fight did not end in 1945 and that battles over the future of the empire were often fought through, and over, images. Indeed, Paul Gilroy's assertion that "colonialism is always war" reminds us that while the CFU emerged in response to one particular global threat, its work in defending, managing, and visualizing a modern empire would continue well beyond the dates of armistice.[146]

CHAPTER 4

Moving Overseas

"Films for Africans, with Africans, by Africans"

In the first week of January 1946, William Sellers led a party of four out to the Gold Coast to start a new chapter in the history of the CFU. Described by *Colonial Cinema* as "by far the most significant development" in the unit's short history, this five-month trip marked a first step in the CFU's attempt to make—as George Pearson described them— "films *for* Africans, *with* Africans, *by* Africans." It would be followed later in the year by two further expeditions to Nigeria and East Africa so that by the end of the decade the CFU had sent twelve units to work in eight territories across the continent.[1] These units mark the early development of cinema in parts of Africa; a significant, often overlooked, moment in the formation of postcolonial cinemas.

The units also represent and embody a new model of empire under the postwar Labour government. Their movement into the colonies was part of the decentralization of colonial administration, taking operations (and finances) out of the center and into the colonies; a move crystallized later in the decade with the establishment of local training schools and production units. The work that these units undertook on film similarly endorsed the government's new African policy, which promoted community development and welfare programs. This is hardly surprising as by 1947 funding for the CFU's overseas "educational" work came through a grant from the Colonial Development and Welfare Act. Returning to Sellers's roots, the CFU now foregrounded practical instruction, producing "really useful films" that, according to

Sellers, helped "to develop self-reliance and to break tradition-bound ground so that the seeds of progress in health, industry and agriculture could be planted."[2]

Films like *Better Homes* (1948) and *Why Not You?* (1950) sought to instruct rural African audiences in modern agricultural and building methods. These films were teaching not only how to build houses but, more broadly, how to build a nation, based on "British" values (such as hard work), structures, and institutional practices. These films, and the work of the overseas units, reveal the reconfigured goals of the CFU after the war. With the empire redrawn, most notably with Indian independence in 1947, with new international organizations such as UNESCO staking a claim to coordinate instructional and educational film across the globe and with the rising political threat of Communism across the British Empire, imperialism mutated into globalization for the CFU. The CFU begins, somewhat tentatively, to prepare for an "end" by promoting continued British influence across the colonies in the form of social, economic, and political structures that would survive beyond independence.

Films like *Weaving in Togoland* (1946) and *Nigerian Cocoa Farmer* (1948) highlighted industrial "progress" and cooperative efforts, looking to inspire support for wider government initiatives. "It is the aim of the Colonial Film Unit to give the African native that outlook and vision which will urge him to break the bonds of illiteracy," explained George Pearson in 1947. "In this way he can become a good citizen, which will eventually lead to the final goal of self-government."[3] These first moves toward self-government, by becoming what the CFU defined as "a good citizen," are also recorded by the CFU, for example when showing constitutional developments within East Africa in *Towards True Democracy* (1947) and *Nairobi* (1950), presenting government welfare schemes in *Community Development in Awgu Division, Nigeria* (1949), or focusing on the development of universities across the postwar empire in *West African University* (1948), *University College of the Gold Coast* (1948), *Foundation Day at Ibadan University College* (1948), and *University College of the West Indies* (1951).

As the CFU moved overseas, its home unit became increasingly marginalized, financed separately and now accounting for no more than 20 percent of the CFU's output. Yet, in depicting a series of conferences, tours, and public exhibitions, the home unit's films show how the Colonial Office imagined Britain's changing relationship with Africa and, more significantly, sought to articulate these changes to an African audience. The films depict African sportsmen (*Nigerian Footballers in England,* 1949), musicians (*Colonial Cinemagazine* 9, 1947), and leaders (*African Conference in London,* 1948). They celebrate British interest in the empire (*Colonial Month,* 1949), and show social and political events that sought to challenge popular perceptions of Africa within Britain. The events depicted may espouse increasing autonomy within African political life, yet this is rarely reflected in their largely traditional formal structure, which still defined London through its landmarks, institutions, and repeated references to the royal family as the ideological center from which the empire could be controlled and contained. These contradictions, evident across the CFU films and also, for example, in the organization of its film training schools, acknowledge the escalating moves toward decolonization while simultaneously resisting the pace of change.

FILMING IN AFRICA: THE CFU, CROWN, AND THE TASK OF NATION-BUILDING

The departure of the first unit to Africa in January 1946 was recorded by the CFU and included in its newsreel, *Colonial Cinemagazine 4*. As a film intended for African audiences in 1946, it indicated the value and political expediency of this shift in colonial (and CFU) policy. The CFU was not only looking to film in Africa, but also to show that it was filming in Africa. The commentary begins by countering earlier criticisms of the unit, explaining that "during the war it was impossible for the Colonial Film Unit to send out people to make films in the colonies about colonial people." The film offers little in the way of action and is confined to three spaces; the room in which they inspect and select equipment; outside the Ministry of Information (MOI) building at Senate House where the head of the Films Division, Jack Beddington, says goodbye to each of the men; and the airport from which they depart for Accra. The sequence at the airport, in which Sellers appears like the royal figures so often depicted waving at the door, shows an empire further compressed and conquered through British technology. "More than 3,000 miles of sea and land lie between England and the Gold Coast," the commentator states, "yet this powerful aircraft would take them there in less than three days."

The film concludes with a familiar shot of the airplane taking off, as the British commentator explains the wider purpose of this trip. "With the departure of this unit, the peacetime work of making films in the colonies begins. The films will show to colonial audiences many things to interest them and will help the people to improve their farms and industries, their health and education and the conditions under which they live." While the mode of address does not suggest that this is directly speaking to local audiences, the next item in the newsreel offers a hint of what is to follow. Filmed shortly after the unit's arrival, the item shows the manufacture of leather—a "thriving craft" undertaken exclusively here by Africans—which assumes an "ever more important place in West African industry." The item represents local craft and industry but serves not only to show local labor but also the work of the British beyond the frame. Appearing under the title "The Unit starts filming: Leather workers in Accra," the item again foregrounds the act of filming and this new direction in colonial film policy.

This first expedition marked a new opportunity for the CFU, "full of hope for the future" in the words of *Colonial Cinema,* and was used to reframe a colonial relationship that was now defined by partnership. *Colonial Cinema* noted the "tremendous spirit of co-operation" displayed by locals on that first trip, and the "kindly welcome, simple hospitality and unfailing co-operation," while one of the unit commented that "almost all the friends we made were among the Africans, with whom we were constantly at work" (see Figure 4.1).[4] While many of the CFU filmmakers spoke fondly and enthusiastically of the individual Africans helping them, this was still clearly a relationship based on existing structures of power. Filmmaker Bob Paynter recalls staying in a bungalow in Accra during the first trip with "three or four slaves as it were to help."[5] Even when traveling in the bush, the filmmakers had locals to carry out their laundry and a cook, who was singled out for praise on the first East African trip in 1947, for having "a nice sense of seasoning, and a very light hand with puddings and pastries." Billy Williams, recalling this trip to East Africa, describes a curious scene with waiters dressed all in white: "It was all very formal in the middle of the bush as if we were in a restaurant."[6] The filmmakers further noted the benefits—particularly an abundance of tinned food denied in rationed Britain—comparing their experiences of Africa favorably to the postwar British landscape they had left behind.[7]

From the very beginning, the CFU's work in Africa was blighted by illness, failing technology, and internal conflicts. Almost as soon as the first contingent arrived in Accra, Peter Sargent, the director-cameraman, contracted "some obscure tropical disease" and spent the first month in hospital where he "completely shed his skin."[8] His assistant, Bob

"Films *for*, *with*, and *by* Africans" | 153

FIGURE 4.1. The Colonial Film Unit filming in West Africa in 1946.

Paynter, would later contract malaria. There were further problems with the equipment. The sole camera broke down, while early film tests were "veiled and flat" as the crew sought to adapt the filters and lenses. The unit also had to operate without any feedback because all airmail was held up for six weeks, while transportation difficulties and the vagaries of the weather would become a recurring feature of these overseas trips, often destroying filming schedules (most notably in East Africa in 1947).[9] There were further challenges here. For example, filmmakers wrote at length about the specific requirements when filming Africans, repeating tales of "superstitious" locals fearful or suspicious of the camera or of opportunist actors taking advantage of a European failure to distinguish between Africans by queueing for their pay on multiple occasions. While most reports labeled the Africans "natural actors," such impressions were again presupposed on racial generalizations ("the native does not suffer from an inhibition" and "as actors, the people have their limitations, probably due to their low level of sophistication").[10] For all these problems, a note from Nigeria concluded that the "difficulties of the Colonial Film Unit are mainly petty and personal." The note complained that the traveling units were largely independent from normal colonial disciplinary sanctions. Sellers had to fly to Nigeria early in 1947 to try and resolve a dispute, which resulted in the dismissal of "an unsatisfactory cameraman" recruited from South Africa, while Grierson was asked to "apply a rocket" to the unit in East Africa late in 1949.[11]

After the first units traveled to Africa—to the Gold Coast in 1946 and then to Nigeria and East Africa in 1946–47—the CFU sought to expand its overseas operations. A staff of twenty-three in 1946 (eighteen overseas and five at home) became thirty-nine (twenty-nine overseas and ten at home) by 1948, aided now by funding from the Colonial Development and Welfare Act (see Figure 4.2). An initial grant of £26,400 to cover overseas filming in 1947 was followed by £133,568 over the next three years.[12] With this additional funding, the CFU doubled its units for the 1947/48 season, sending four units to seven territories (Nigeria, Kenya and Uganda, Tanganyika and Zanzibar, Sierra Leone and the Gambia) but still used the same number of European technicians (reduced from five to two in each unit). One upshot of this was that these units now actively sought "suitable Africans" to help them, looking not only to produce films but also to train local filmmakers. In the case of the "less prosperous colonies" of Sierra Leone and the Gambia, where the CFU noted "the raw stock scheme has made little progress," part of its work was to train Africans to continue this work after the unit's departure. By 1946, eleven colonies had cameras and film stock from the CFU, but "so far no colonial has done any actual production under the raw stock scheme."[13]

The CFU now had a 16mm department that would report on incoming material at each monthly staff meeting. The reports reveal the same subjects filmed repeatedly (in particular, scenes of pageantry and displays) and provide feedback on the quality and suitability of the material. A typical note on material from the Gambia highlighted the CFU's continued preoccupation with technique and the ways in which it sought to train from a distance: "General standard of photography is good, but the films tend to be monotonous through lack of knowledge of film making technique. The cameraman has been advised as to improved methods." The reports further reveal the challenges of using raw stock footage to produce instructional or narrative films, rather than simply depicting news events or local color. After the CFU received 600 feet of footage from Mauritius for a film on malaria, it wrote "exposure and quality good, but as a film on malaria [it] is meaningless, in fact it is a moving camera record of scenery and pools of water." The decision to

FIGURE 4.2. Staff at the Colonial Film Unit. Image provided by Dennis Bowden, who also helped identify those pictured.

FROM LEFT TO RIGHT:

FRONT ROW: Alan Lancaster, Dennis Bowden, Peter Nash, Pat Hastings

SECOND ROW: Vic Gover, George Pearson, William Sellers, Alan Izod(?), Hugh Bradshaw

THIRD ROW: Bill Woodhead, Helen Main, ?, Dorothy Sparks, ?, George Sewell, Bill Williams, Joan Stebbines, Marjorie Dawson, Mabel Kelly, Hal Morey

BACK ROW: Len Birchett, Bill Williams Jr., ?, Lionel Snazelle, Fela Sowande, Hugh Begbie(?), Peter Sargent, Mrs. Wilson(?)

send a 16mm unit to the Gambia and Sierra Leone was an attempt to improve the material coming through the scheme and after determining that its trip had left behind "competent colonial operators," the CFU proposed similar expeditions to other so-called minor territories such as Aden, Mauritius, and the Seychelles (see Figures 4.3 and 4.4).[14]

This longer-term planning, centered on the training and development of local film units, was an integral feature of the CFU's Colonial Development and Welfare funding. In 1947 the CFU outlined an eight-year program, which incorporated into the CFU new territories including the West Indies, Western Pacific, and Mediterranean. The ultimate goal here was to establish local self-sufficient film units so that by 1954 the CFU's own production could be conducted by a single traveling unit.[15] While the Treasury repeatedly requested their "terminal dates" when

FIGURES 4.3. AND 4.4. The Colonial Film Unit filming in the Gambia, 1948. Courtesy of the National Archives in the Gambia (with thanks to Liam Buckley).

the colonies would take over this film work, the Colonial Office argued that any long-term program was "unrealistic" and that Malaya, now in a state of Emergency, "was an example in point" of the difficulties of long-term planning. This would prove a continual stumbling block for the CFU, with budgets confirmed at the last moment, short-term hires secured, and plans subject to the winds of political fortune.[16]

The CFU was not the only government unit traveling to Africa at this time. Indeed, while the Gold Coast government welcomed this initial CFU trip, it added a significant caveat. "I consider that we should make it clear from the start," wrote Alan Campbell, the public relations officer in the colony in November 1945, "that as regards the subject matter covered by a film and the accompanying commentary we trust that consideration will be given to our wishes." This concern was motivated by "certain disappointments" over MOI material that had recently been shot locally by John Page and edited in England.[17] This included *Achimota* (1945), which had a commentary written by Julian Huxley and was roundly condemned by H. L. Gurney, the colonial secretary to the Gold Coast in a letter to Noel Sabine at the Colonial Office. "This is such a deplorable production that, if you have not seen it, I hope that you will suggest to the Ministry that it should be withdrawn," Gurney wrote. "If you have seen it, you will no doubt have already done so." Gurney pulled apart every aspect of the film, from the "preliminary advertisement of Julian Huxley" to the section on agriculture ("a complete fake and obviously so"). He asked Sabine if they could "have a shot at reconstructing the picture" from all the unused material, but was told that Sellers had dismissed this as a waste of time as "Page did not shoot good material."[18] What we see here is an extension of earlier tensions between the British documentarians, represented by Crown (and Huxley), and the instructional cinema of Sellers and the CFU.

These tensions are exacerbated in another of Page's Crown productions, *Fight for Life* (1946), a film condemned by the Nigerian nationalist paper, the *Comet*, for its depiction of unclothed Africans. "This is the stuff that imperialism revels in," the *Comet* wrote. "The African must be presented to the world at his worst not best."[19] The director of veterinary services in the Gold Coast, J. L. Stewart, took particular offense at the film, complaining to Gurney that "this wishful thinking, over optimistic type of propaganda is thoroughly bad." He argued that instead of painting an "inaccurately rosy picture," it was better to show the difficulties and the "strenuous and competent efforts" to counter them. Stewart's criticism could equally be leveled at the CFU films, which also often sought to conceal and foster a simple transformative narrative. In this instance, Stewart complained that the film "gives the impression that those concerned have turned a wilderness into a land flowing with milk and honey," and further argued that such attempts to "fool the British public" were "stupid" when in reality scientists were not performing these "amazing metamorphoses" but were "overcoming constant setbacks and slow progress." On seeing a draft script in 1944, Campbell had suggested that the way to explain difficulties or failings in the colonies was not to ignore them but to present them as products of the extra responsibility given to the Africans.[20]

Stewart also complained about the "Hollywoodisation of myself in the commentary" (again written by Julian Huxley) which "cast ridicule" on the "fully qualified" specialists working in the colonies. "I personally take considerable exception to being referred to as Capt. 'Jock' Stewart which reads more like an all-in-wrestler than a scientific director," he wrote, "and to be described as a legendary figure owing to my size and vigorous personality is sheer distortion of fact." The film was recalled and the offending lines cut, while the public relations officer in the Gold Coast asked that all films be vetted in the Gold Coast before screening, a request rejected by Noel Sabine on the grounds that there were already plenty with knowledge of West Africa in London who could advise. This exchange further exposed the persistent tensions between London and the colony—"Mr. Sabine's attitude is, I am afraid, only too typical of the Whitehall mind"—while also highlighting this question of expertise. For all his complaints, Campbell did not envisage a problem with Sellers, "a most helpful, understanding person who has served in the Health Department in West Africa." The suggestion here was that Sellers and the CFU understood and worked within the government departments, while the Crown unit was met with considerably more suspicion.[21]

The reactions to Page's films reveal an ideological disconnect between London and the colonies, which was again evident in 1949 when the Kenyan government refused to show a film of the Northern Frontier in Kenya for "political reasons," despite its earlier approval by the Colonial Office.[22] The reaction attests to an escalating sensitivity over colonial representation, which was played out over seemingly mundane incidents, such as the filming of dancing in Sukumuland in 1949. While the COI (Central Office of Information) argued that showing this traditional culture "would make a film of high cultural and artistic nature," the Colonial Office worried that such a subject "would be criticized by Colonial students and others in this country as an attempt to portray Colonial people as backward and primitive, a point on which colonial opinion is ultra-sensitive." The COI view highlighted Crown's roots in British documentary (creating a "cultural and artistic" film), while the Colonial Office's concern was a direct hangover from John Page's work in the Gold Coast. The Colonial Film Committee expressed a desire at this moment in 1949 to amend Page's film *Here Is the Gold Coast* "in view of frequent criticism of the film by colonial students and others in this country."[23]

These discussions caused a form of paralysis within the COI, resulting in an overreliance on the same familiar examples and language within colonial documentary. As such the films often appear remarkably unremarkable, a point noted by John Hyde, who sat on the Colonial Film Committee and now worked in the administration of the CFU. Hyde complained in a letter to John Grierson: "Insipid pictures depicting dully-shot scenery, natives driving cattle about and women crushing maize have been done to screaming point," adding that an intended film on Uganda "may well be another flowery, superficial picture showing Makerere College, a few maternity homes and a V.D. centre." While Crown was enjoying critical success at this moment with the release of the Oscar-winning *Daybreak in Udi,* Hyde argued that the anxieties of the Colonial Office perpetuated colonial fantasies. "The next twenty years will see staggering developments—and perhaps a lot of bloodshed," he continued. "The political and racial problems are dramatic but the C.O. are touchy to the point of neurosis." Hyde sought to deflate what in modern terms would be labeled political correctness—"the one thing I loathe is the soggy attitude which produces empty Women's Institute films about the African who can do no wrong"—burrowing further to the right as he complained about the "apologetic Labour MP who crosses the word Empire out of his vocabulary" and "the sandal wearers of the Fabian Colonial bureau." Hyde's motivations were economic, arguing that the colonies should be presented as a "hard business proposition." In noting the enormous, untapped mineral deposits, he argued that "European enterprise" was the only solution to "bringing up" the African.[24]

John Page's West African productions highlight the global extension of interwar tensions between the Colonial Office and British documentarians, between the Sellers and Griersonian models, but they also evidence the often-overlooked movement of British documentary filmmakers, ideologies, and practices into the colonies after the war. The Griersonian tradition—with its purported humanistic, liberal, pedagogical agenda—found a fresh outlet within the postwar colonies as part of the "nation-building" process. Indeed Grierson himself was embedded in this. In the aftermath of war, Grierson was recruited by Julian Huxley, the first director of UNESCO, as UNESCO's director of mass communication and public information. The role envisaged film as fundamental education and sought to create an "international clearinghouse" for national film-producing groups. In this work, Grierson was supported by fellow figures from the British Documentary Movement, such as Basil Wright, who was tasked with planning a series of films on national subjects, produced by individual national units, which would then be distributed and shared internationally. This aligned with Wright's own international outlook, as he sought to avoid the "selfish and useless outpouring of unilateral propaganda" by forging "the closest relationships between producing groups in all countries." Wright called for an exchange of ideas and personnel, coordinating the works of emerging local units and supporting international conferences.²⁵ One of these conferences, sponsored by UNESCO, was "The Film in Colonial Development" held at the BFI in January 1948. The speakers included George Pearson and Grierson, who endorsed the escalating moves toward local film production.²⁶

Shortly after the conference, Grierson would take up his next role as head of the COI's Films Division, where his responsibilities included the Colonial Film Unit. During his brief two-year tenure, Grierson attempted to oversee the reorganization of the CFU, which it was proposed would also incorporate Crown's "informational" films about the colonies. While the proposals outlined in some detail the existing failings of the "cumberous, unstable and inefficient" CFU, it now attempted to reunite these two, often competing factions under the supervision of a Colonial Film Committee. The proposals still acknowledged the "distinction" between films *for* and *about* the colonies, noting the very different skills and personnel required, but suggested that in time the "great difference" between the required techniques would diminish and the "ultimate aim" in each area would be a unit capable of carrying out all official work. While Sellers would remain in charge of all existing CFU work, the man intended to head the expanded Colonial Film Unit was a noted documentarian and brother-in-law of Grierson, John Taylor, who had most recently overseen Crown's production of the Oscar-winning *Daybreak in Udi*.²⁷

The paths of Grierson (and the documentarians) and Sellers (and the "administrators") may have intersected, but their approaches remained significantly different. In his recent work on colonial documentary, Ian Aitken suggests that the Griersonian approach fared much better in larger territories such as Canada, Australia, and New Zealand, but further argued that this underlying tension between these approaches influenced the development of filmmaking in Malaysia, Singapore, and Hong Kong.²⁸ In the example of Malaya, members of the Crown Film Unit (Ralph Elton and cameraman Denny Densham) had filmed the first official landing party at the end of the war before traveling over the next year, with a nucleus of four Englishmen and six Malayans, throughout Malaya and shooting 250,000 feet of film. The unit was not only recording the history of a country rebuilding after war—the social rebirth of a nation—but was also shaping this future, providing equipment, personnel, and expertise for the Malayan Film Unit (MFU), which formed in 1946 on their departure.²⁹ The Crown filmmakers traveled with and trained local personnel and discussed plans for the formal establishment of a local unit in correspondence with, among others, Basil Wright. The unit would, it was imagined, utilize Malayan staff, overseen by a "single knowledgeable" (European) man.³⁰ A further celebrated figure from the British Documentary Movement, Edgar Anstey, also visited to discuss the "future of documentary films in Malaya," calling for a locally manned Malayan Film Unit with training and support from "British documentary filmmakers."³¹

By the time of Crown's departure in October 1946, the trainee Malay and Chinese filmmakers who had traveled with the unit, most notably Lee Meow Seong, Osman bin Shamsuddin, and O. W. Kheng Law, had all been absorbed into the MFU and by 1953, Kheng Law was one of 30 Chinese working for the MFU alongside 70 Malays, 22 Indians, 9 Eurasians, and 4 Europeans.³² However, by this point the MFU was increasingly shaped by the politically conservative, instructional cinema, propagated by William Sellers and the CFU, which now rather overpowered the Griersonian idealism. In 1949 the CFU had planned to go in and "save the Malayan Film Unit," setting aside £550 in its budget to investigate the function and prospects of the unit and offering an expert to advise on its reorganization. As Aitken shows, this was an underhanded maneuver, and a serious break from protocol on the part of the Colonial Office, who were attempting to "keep Grierson out" and to push the Sellers and Colonial Office model into Malaya.³³

To an extent, as we will see, the opposite happens in the Gold Coast in the 1950s where the Griersonian influences come to the fore in the local unit, but both examples remind us that the tensions between the MOI and Colonial Office, between Crown and the CFU, between the professional filmmakers and government "experts," do not relent at the end of war. The debates over the form and function of film continued, but while previously they were, at least ostensibly, motivated by the war effort, now they were applied to the task of nation-building across the postwar globe.

"SELF-RELIANCE AND CO-OPERATION": REIMAGINING AFRICA ON SCREEN

The CFU's first expedition in 1946 had originally intended to visit the Gold Coast and Nigeria, producing two films in each. The secretary of state for the colonies wrote to both colonies in October 1945 requesting "advice and help locally" and proposing possible subjects for filming. The suggested topics, negotiated between the CFU in London and local government departments, were broadly categorized by themes that supported and promoted the economic productivity of the colonial workforce ("mixed farming," "economics," "social," "medical and health") and followed existing narrative structures (contrasts, a day in the life, the wise and foolish protagonists). On the health front, the Gold Coast government was most enthusiastic about a film on tuberculosis, but had little interest in one on leprosy since this was not a major problem in the colony. It supported a film on training schools but emphasized that the trained teacher should be seen to return to their village "to show the practical application of his training." There were also plans for a film entitled "A Day in the Life of an African Nurse," which would show the "important part that women are beginning to take in public life" and on mixed farming and cooperative farming (to be made in Nigeria). "An African Village School" would serve as a companion piece to *Education in England: A Village School*. While the plan here was to concretize, and make explicit, the links inferred within the wartime home unit production, the CFU in London admitted that it had little idea of "where such a school exists," as it still idealized the colonies from afar.[34] Indeed while the CFU sought to highlight common ground, all traveling units were simultaneously tasked with producing material for "contrast" items, which foregrounded British primacy, as the units negotiated what Sellers saw as the "twofold theme of self-reliance and co-operation."[35]

In the end, this first tour never made it to Nigeria.[36] Instead, the unit prioritized two major films in the Gold Coast, the one on TB (*Fight Tuberculosis in the Home*) and another on the weaving industry in Avatime (*Weaving in Togoland*). These choices are indicative of what would follow, seeking both to instruct directly in modern (British) methods and also to project a broader model of colonial partnership, one that simultaneously promoted social welfare and economic productivity (a healthy, productive workforce). These initial choices reveal a unit that was both looking back—to Sellers's earlier work in Nigeria and his background in public health—and peering forward toward self-governance by promoting mass education work and the modernization of traditional industries within Africa.

Rosaleen Smyth has written extensively, and with characteristic expertise, on these postwar films but they warrant some additional comment here.[37] In the case of *Fight Tuberculosis in the Home,* the film integrates Sellers's and Pearson's sensibilities. As a "simple story in pictures" that addresses its subject "in the simplest possible way," the film largely follows the Sellers technique and mirrors his first film in Nigeria, *Anti-Plague Operations,* in showing the spread of disease in an overcrowded, unclean, and poorly ventilated urban house.[38] It does, however, present this lesson through a narrative, "a rather unpleasant subject," as Pearson noted, "made intensely interesting by carrying the implied lessons through a human story of a happy native family menaced by the disease."[39] The film combines this narrative of a son and a laborer both contracting the disease in an overcrowded house, with clear instruction (how to prevent the spread of disease and then what can be done to help those suffering). In so doing, the film projects a message of mediated African development and training under European supervision. After an African technician investigates the son's sample through a microscope, the European doctor comes to check it, and later when an African sanitary inspector helps clear up the living quarters and finds other accommodation for the laborers, the European doctor arrives to recap on the measures taken.

The film showcases a model of collaboration with government units, in this case the medical department, both on and off screen and was described by Pearson as a "pioneer in its kind," which was "profitably used in West African campaigns."[40] This model is perhaps best seen in another film from the Gold Coast, *Swollen Shoot* (1946), which was directed and photographed for the Department of Agriculture by H. E. Lironi, the cinema officer in the Gold Coast who had trained with the CFU during the war.[41] The CFU collaborated on the script and edited this Kodachrome film, which toured extensively in rural areas through mobile cinema vans. The message is again presented in story form, reasoning that "human interest would add to its effectiveness," as it depicts the good, attentive farmer who goes to the agricultural officer for advice, and his dismissive counterpart, who eventually does the "wise thing." The film directly instructs its viewers (a high proportion of the running time is spent showing to camera and comparing diseased and normal plants) and, as so often, attempts to justify this government intervention in economic terms, concluding with the farmer happily receiving payment for his crop. *Swollen Shoot* was widely cited as an example of film's effectiveness within government campaigns and was said to be "so helpful" that a sequel entitled "Cut to Cure" was planned.[42] However, historian Francis K. Danquah shows the "formidable friction" that the issue provoked between government personnel and cocoa growers, exacerbated as the government used "legal and physical coercion" to cut down the trees (and in effect the farmers' income). The film attempts to alleviate this, for example by removing European involvement from the screen, yet this remained a hugely valuable industry for the British and, despite the efforts of the film, rural support for nationalist movements and in particular the United Gold Coast Convention (UGCC), the Gold Coast's first nationalist party, mobilized around this issue.[43]

The other major film produced during the CFU's initial expedition to West Africa, *Weaving in Togoland,* shows the modernization of a local African industry. As *Colonial Cinema* explained, the film was "never intended to be an instructional film on weaving," but instead to "capture the spirit of self-help." While a number of CFU films sought to instruct directly, *Colonial Cinema* reasoned that if *Weaving in Togoland* encourages "the people to make some effort to improve themselves in any way, then its purpose will have been fulfilled."[44] The film fits very clearly within the CFU's postwar plans, showcasing African development through the well-worn example of Achimota College. Introduced here as "one of the most important schools in Africa," Achimota represents the affluent, prestigious center from which a team of Africans learn their skills before imparting their expertise back in the traditional African villages.[45] The film shows Africans teaching Africans and crucially outlines how industrial modernization benefits the whole community and has "entirely revolutionised the life of the people." A report from the unit emphasized that "through co-operative working, prosperity has come to stay," as the film highlights these wider economic benefits through health ("a healthier and more virile population is growing up") and living conditions, represented by new schools and houses. The film concludes with shots of locals dancing ("look at the people . . . in every way better off") and explains how this all came about "because a wise chief got clever teachers to tell them of new ways of working far better than the old."

The economic benefits of industrial modernization are further shown in *Better Pottery,* another CFU film from its "rural industries" series. The film contrasts the "old and clumsy" traditional methods with those employed by Awusu, who is introduced through his house. "As you can see from the look of his house," the commentator explains, "he's a prosperous man, prosperous because he makes better pots, more quickly." The commentator never leaves this point—"More pots means more money. No wonder Awusu is a prosperous man"—yet crucially the film again ends by outlining the wider benefits for the community: "He can provide more employment at better wages which will mean better living for his workmen who are being well rewarded for their labour." These films are remarkably consistent, not only in form, but also in their narrative structure, themes, and message, promoting imperial co-operation, gradual development (under British leadership) and building on the earliest prewar films for the colonies, an economic interdependency between Britain and the colonies.

For the most part, the CFU films served a dual function during this period, instructing in particular methods (how to prevent disease, how to build a house) and, more broadly, inspiring support for modern government. A report from one of the filmmakers in East Africa in 1947 explained somewhat earnestly that the films should "make it clear that apparently 'repressive' measures are actually designed for the ultimate benefit of the population as a whole."[46] A film such as *Better Homes* (1948) from East Africa ostensibly serves as an instructional film, but it also shows how house-building contributes to social development. The commentator suggests that better homes provide a "brighter outlook for those who live in them," while better gardens make for a "happier family." This, in turn, helps to make "the whole village a more contented and better housed community." Such building and development—of the house, the community, and the nation—is achieved through partnership as the Africans build the houses themselves while retaining a level of British supervision. This British influence is evident both through the British narrator, who outlines the building specifications and examines the existing local houses ("he has not made the best use of the material at hand. His house needs rebuilding"), and also on screen by the European official, in jacket and tie, who advises on house-building and returns at the end of the film to inspect the work.[47]

There are, however, notable distinctions between the films produced in East and West Africa. Sellers reported back from his 1948 trip to East Africa that mobile cinema staff and government officials had emphasized that "the average East African audience could not understand fully the more advanced film such as is now acceptable by West African audiences." These attitudes shaped the cinema produced. Sellers explained that it was found to be difficult in East Africa to "sustain interest" in a subject over three or even two reels, resulting in a preference for short, 16mm instructional films that addressed local issues "in the simplest possible way."[48] These entrenched racial hierarchies further dictated the development and roles of local personnel. In emphasizing the difficulties of finding "trained experts" to join the traveling demonstration teams in Uganda at this time, officials chose members for their "personality and their ability to 'put over' ideas to the public."[49] These attitudes also prompted the CFU to abandon plans for a film training school in East Africa in 1949, instead sending ten technicians under the control of a senior director, H.L. Bradshaw, to East Africa. In each of Uganda, Kenya, Tanganyika, and later Zanzibar, a 16mm technician was brought in to support the Information Department, with a central editorial section established in Nairobi. The plan was that the imported film specialist would recruit African assistants, ultimately training them to "make educational films themselves for their own people," so that they could then, with the European staff, "form the nucleus of a permanent film production unit."[50]

The prejudices toward East Africa are equally apparent in the films. Norman Spurr, who noted the lower level of literacy, "sophistication and general knowledge" in East Africa and who had warned in 1948 that an East African training school might "be overloaded beyond the capacity of African trainees," traveled to Uganda with the CFU in 1949 to become the colony's territorial films officer. His film *Why Not You?*, the first part of an unlikely trilogy showing the making of building blocks (the next two in the series were intended to show their uses and finally the building of a house), relies on repetition to instruct its audience, displaying the process of block-making on three occasions. Furthermore, the makeup of the units in East Africa—a single man seconded to the Public Relations Office—shaped the type of cinema produced and encouraged this cinema of expertise. *Why Not You?* contains very few titles and is evidently intended, as Rosaleen Smyth argues, as a visual aid, presented alongside other media and embedded within wider government campaigns.[51]

Spurr explained how this worked in Uganda through the example of *Pamba* (1950), a "narrative-teaching film" that follows, as Spurr noted, the "hoary old formula of the good versus the bad" by showing the correct (translated as modern, British) way and the bad methods of cotton planting. Spurr collaborated closely with a local agricultural officer and with the welfare section of the Public Relations Office, which sent demonstration teams across the countryside. These teams "interspersing their teaching with entertainment, and in their plays combining the two," worked for months in the same area to establish and consolidate government policy.[52] A member of the health department in Uganda similarly noted the importance of "showing the film on successive nights at the same place" and of using other media such as filmstrips to emphasize and talk through particular moments from the film. He argued that sending a film around without other forms of health propaganda and dissociated from the work of health inspectors was "an almost complete waste of time."[53]

Spurr's films embrace and display these collaborations across media and departments. For example, *Pamba* features the comic character of Kapare, "a victim of his own stubbornness, conceit or disobedience," or in the words of George Pearson "a nit-wit character, a kind of African

Monsieur Hulot, whose mistakes brought gales of laughter from the people." Kapere already appeared in government comic strips and touring plays where he might feature in the same performance as "a bad farmer, a drunkard, a reckless cyclist and a man with a dirty home."[54] We see this in Spurr's *A Challenge to Ignorance* (1950), a record of the demonstration teams' work in Uganda. The film shows a wide range of performances—music, a Mr. Wise and Mr. Foolish play showing the "proper" way to plant cotton, demonstrations on soil erosion, banana growing, and bicycle safety—and highlights how the government units used different media and organized the local space "to bring all the people together." The film shows almost exclusively Africans on screen, both performing and watching, with the exception of the British welfare officer (always alone in the frame) who watches and advises on particular problems. This model of colonial supervision is also evident in the film itself, which while depicting African government work is directed by Spurr and with a British Voice of God narration.

These postwar CFU films sought to project a shifting colonial partnership, one that the CFU might more concretely visualize by filming political developments across Africa. On his first tour, Sellers discussed plans for a film on local council and hoped to send a unit to the Gold Coast in the summer of 1946 to record a "landmark in colonial history," the opening of the Legislative Council. Ultimately the governor refused to allow access to the interiors, labeling the procedure "undignified." The CFU considered it "impractical" to send a unit across the globe to film men shaking hands outside a building, although it did make it inside for the opening of the Nigerian Legislative Council the following year.[55] In *Towards True Democracy*, this political moment is contextualized within a historical narrative that celebrates the perceived developments introduced by the British, in much the same way as the interwar Empire series did for British audiences. These developments are presented through a commentary that contrasts modern Africa with a precolonial model— "Not very long ago instead of fine docks and harbours, good roads and bridges, there was a malaria-ridden swamp"—and through lengthy aerial shots that highlight the British architecture, buildings, and transportation developments within modern Lagos. The influence stretches beyond the material—"Here too are people taught to be good citizens"—presenting education as a step toward self-government ("Africans are taught to be good doctors and nurses for themselves"). Crucially this is a gradual process and a chance to "learn and gain experience" so that when independence comes, "they will be all the wiser."

The opening of the council was far from universally celebrated, boycotted by three elected nationalist members (including Nnamdi Azikiwe, who would become the first president of independent Nigeria). Their protest is largely ignored as film allows the colonial authority (the governor) to pass judgment, stating that the Africans are "as yet inexperienced in positions of authority" and that to transfer power to "untried hands" would produce a "sham democracy." The commentator determines that "African and European people work side by side towards a common goal," yet even if there is a "common goal," the time frames for this remain wildly divergent. As late as 1949, when George Pearson explained that the CFU's "long-term aim" was the "cultural uplift that achieves a higher standard of living, ends illiteracy and leads eventually to self-government," he suggested this "is a matter of many years, probably generations." He spoke of a purpose "steadily pursued," yet within a decade the Gold Coast Film Unit and Malayan Film Unit would be filming independence ceremonies in their new nations.[56] In Nigeria, the Nigerian Film Unit would record a range of constitutional changes from town council elections in 1950, to elections for regional legislatures in 1952, and self-government for Western Nigeria in 1958. Through these films, the CFU sought to highlight British support but also to contain and control the pace of these moves toward self-government.

While the CFU sought to perpetuate this narrative of colonial development—both through its films and its publicized activities—there is as much to learn from its failures, from the aborted schemes and unmade films. For example, the Colonial Office and West African governments strongly supported a plan in 1947 to make two animated films, which if successful "would be the forerunners of a series of cartoons for unsophisticated audiences." For this, the COI commissioned Geoffrey and Mina Johnson, who had previously made animated instructional films for Information Films of India. The pair traveled for months, first in the Gold Coast and then Nigeria, undertaking tours and meetings with members of the agricultural department and medical services, making rough sketches, taking still photos and a "certain amount of cinefilm" to obtain "local colour" for reference back in the UK. They were supported by £7000 from the CFU's Colonial Development and Welfare funding.[57]

From the outset, the scheme raised questions about the suitability of animation for African audiences. There was a concern that the cartoon was "perhaps even more liable" to cause offense than an "ordinary" film and Lironi's own fear, after viewing some of the sketches, was that "overexaggeration of some African facial and physical characteristics may be construed as ridicule." The visual form of animation ran the risk of reinforcing stereotypes, and all the more so as the Johnsons had to work with the Sellers technique, which they were evidently well-versed in.[58] The acting governor of Sierra Leone argued that "the drawing would have to be particularly simple and clear and the tempo would have to be kept much slower than in the case of films prepared for educated audiences," as the ideological assumptions on which the Sellers technique was founded were now applied to the animated form. The Johnsons noted this, agreeing that film content should be restricted to "cause and effect and that quasi-scientific films with diagrams would not get across to the illiterate."[59]

Sellers was very closely involved and suggested the subject for both films. The Johnsons felt that soil erosion "lends itself to treatment in cartoon film technique," for example in very quickly and clearly showing the effect on the land over many years. Sellers was even more invested in the other subject: malaria. The Johnsons noted that "there is probably nobody with more experience of health propaganda in West Africa than Mr. Sellers," while Pearson would describe health education as "definitely the first directive of the Film Unit."[60] Disney had recently made a cartoon of its own on malaria, *The Winged Scourge* (1943), as part of a series of health films intended primarily for South American audiences. The film features the seven dwarfs, who undertake preventative measures—spraying ponds, covering cracks, putting up screens, and destroying the mosquito-breeding grounds—to the tune of "Whistle While We Work." Walt Disney noted the huge success of the film and argued that the widely recognized dwarfs exercised more authority than the "learned doctors" in the remotest areas. However, Sellers now proposed the CFU's own film on the subject, determining that the Disney version "would confuse illiterate African villagers."[61]

Sellers's response may attest both to the CFU's commitment to its specialized technique and his wariness of American cultural imperialism. In this context, it is striking that the Disney films served to protect and further American imperialist ambitions. Walt Disney explained that their health films were intended to help "wherever our troops were stationed" and supplemented other materials—Dr. Seuss provided a 1943 pamphlet on malaria for the US Army—some of which did reach British Africa.[62] Indeed, these Disney cartoons played across the empire, and when its cartoon on hookworm was shown in the West Province, Uganda, Norman Spurr examined its reception. Spurr reinforced some existing colonial preconceptions, for example in suggesting that audiences credited those moments that use "traditional cartoon comedy" to "European magic."

However, for the most part Spurr challenged Sellers's view and suggested that because the disease, symptoms, and remedies were not regionally specific, the film traveled freely.[63] This view was supported by further screenings in the Gold Coast in 1953. "The fact is neither the characters nor the background in the film have nationality," wrote one of the social welfare officers conducting the tour in the Gold Coast, further adding that the "unlimited flexibility" of the cartoon leaves "nothing to the imagination" and helps clarify the intended message. Both reports stressed the need to follow up on the lessons within the film, through talks, displays, and filmstrips: "In isolation their dangers are manifest. Used as a complement to other forms of teaching, their potentialities are profound."[64]

When first considering possible subjects, the Johnsons explained that they wanted to adapt a West African folk story, perhaps on the subject of cooperation. They argued that this familiar story would serve to introduce the cartoon film to illiterate audiences and to combine propaganda and entertainment.[65] This question of entertainment looms large here. Walt Disney argued that the informative materials "should ride along on entertainment as much as possible" and that the "fun factor" was essential in getting the message across.[66] Those who have watched a number of CFU films will detect a somewhat different approach from the CFU. Indeed, this issue is regularly brought up in monthly meetings, with representatives from both the Colonial Office and COI "constantly receiving requests" for more entertainment films in the traveling programs. The CFU explained that it only included a "very small proportion of purely entertainment films," one point on which the COI representative was quick to agree. The "constant inquiries for comedy films" did prompt the CFU to produce a "simple comedy" in 1946, *Deck Chair*, in which a man makes several unsuccessful attempts to put up a deck chair. The CFU also looked at including a few COI films—such as films on boxing and firefighting—as a way of "leavening" the programs although, with never a truer word spoken, the minutes reported that the term "entertainment films" was rather misleading in this context: "the films were in fact interest films judged suitable for African audiences."[67]

The Johnson cartoons were "subject to continual delays and misfortunes" and by 1950 the CFU had scrapped the second film on soil erosion. It still hoped to complete the film on malaria, but by the end of 1950 the CFU had ceased all production, and more than half of its staff had been made redundant.[68] While this dramatic shift was often framed as the next planned stage of colonial decentralization, this was a messy, contested, and volatile breakup, especially in East Africa. The filmmakers' initial departure to East Africa had elicited much positive press coverage, albeit coverage that reaffirmed dominant stereotypes and that was predicated on difference. The *Daily Mail* reported under the headline "Talkies Rival Tom-Toms" that the unit would bring films to the "wildest bush country, where the beating of the drums is the only entertainment." Yet barely a year after sending ten technicians to East Africa, the CFU had shut down its operations.[69]

The unit's year in East Africa was characterized by escalating tension between the filmmakers and their bosses in London. At a Conference of Information Officers in Nairobi in June 1949, the delegates put on record their unanimous "lack of confidence in the London Administration of the Colonial Film Unit," urging the transfer of the CFU to the Colonial Office.[70] In return, H.M.K. Howson, the films officer of the COI (the CFU's current home), lamented the poor standard of the unit's work in East Africa and their "low reputation" at home and overseas, while a COI representative complained that he had asked for the accounts on six occasions, but had had no response.[71] This animosity erupted at the news of the unit's closure in March 1950. The East African delegates now threatened legal action and seven of them signed a lengthy petition, complaining that they had suffered "innumerable setbacks by not having a well-organized and intelligent backing from England." They explained that, having accepted their brief "in good faith" as a three-year project, they had decided to experiment in the first year, to familiarize themselves with the culture and to establish the "ideal method of making films for African audiences." By the end of the first year, the delegates claimed to have 40–50 productions at various stages of completion, and to have trained twelve Africans who had produced two films of their own.[72] Senior director Geoffrey Innes expanded on these achievements in an article in *East Africa Standard*. He noted the "terrific reception" of one of the films, *Eunoto,* when he showed it to the Masai. "Eight members of the audience were in convulsions and had to be carried out," he said, adding that "it is a great pity that we have to close down now before we see the fruits of our labour" (he added that most of these fruits were still in London, interminably delayed). The Kenyan government was said to be "very disturbed" about this "somewhat indiscreet" interview. A further letter in the *Manchester Guardian* questioned the wisdom of starting this scheme "if it was so early to be abandoned." "One can hear the ghostly voice of the Unit enquiring," the anonymous writer concluded, " 'I wonder what I was begun for if I was so soon to be done for.' "[73]

The final 35mm film produced from the trip, *Nairobi*, features footage of the ceremony in which Nairobi received its royal charter and became a city, filmed on the unit's final two days in East Africa (30 and 31 March 1950). The event was presented in the British press as a celebration of British imperial progress—the subheading in the *Times* was "From Swamp to City Within the Span of a Lifetime"—a view endorsed by the film's commentator, who opens *Nairobi* by stating that what was "less than fifty years ago . . . waste and swampy land" is now a "great African metropolis . . . a centre of ever-growing industry and nationwide commerce."[74] The film states categorically that "everywhere there is progress," from "motorcars parked where once the cattle roamed" to "huge hotels standing where once the skin huts of Masai herdsmen stood." As a final film from the unit, *Nairobi* reinforces this narrative of progress, of a country growing up (on British terms with the royal charter) and resorts to familiar stereotypes ("Nairobi's growth must seem near to magic"). Yet, this traditional, well-worn narrative is exposed both by the fractious end for the CFU in East Africa and by the escalating, though concealed, political tensions and unrest in the region.

Nairobi is framed by European businessmen driving into work and then returning to their "suburban homes" and completely ignores both the experiences of African communities and the strong local grievances expressed at the bestowal of the royal charter. The East African Trade Union Congress (EATUC) led a boycott against the celebrations, with its founder explaining that the workers "cannot be pleased by the Nairobi of the rich" and that "the so-called 'progress' is not the progress of the millions of toiling people but of a handful of capitalists."[75] Shortly afterwards, there was a nine-day general strike in the city, while the Kikuyu, who had already been forced to relocate to the city in large numbers, viewed the charter as damning evidence of further urban expansion and of the expropriation of their lands. For the frustrated CFU unit filming this event, while packing their bags, the colonial fantasies perpetuated on screen explain their own demise. The government, and indeed many of the filmmakers, were deeply skeptical of the CFU's development agenda here (in terms of developing local filmmakers and audiences), and ultimately it was the East African government's failure to support the costs of local production after 1950 that led to its closure.[76] The film's unashamedly British vision of the city, with Africans represented as superstitious, contented, loyal to the British crown, and grateful for British "progress," reveals a staggering lack of awareness both of the escalating criticisms and also of how film might best serve the government over the next few years. Presented here as a celebration and culmination of British work, *Nairobi* equally portends the government intransigence and repressed voices that would violently erupt and define the region over the next decade.

VISITING ENGLAND: THE COLONIAL FILM UNIT AT HOME

The postwar movement of film production into the colonies might appear to render the operations of the "home unit" increasingly anachronistic. When the CFU outlined the work of its home unit in 1946, it explained that it served two purposes. The first was to make films in Britain "illustrating the British way of life," and the second was "to cover events in this country involving Colonial peoples."[77] The first of these aims, so prevalent during war, now began to fade, with the more traditional productions held up or abandoned as personnel, attention, and funds moved overseas.[78] Instead the home unit focused on filming tours and events that showcased colonial people visiting, performing, and learning in Britain. In articulating new models of partnership and in showing British leadership training skilled African workers and performers, the films anticipated the CFU's training schools and the development of local units. Yet the films also often recalled prewar films of England, positioning and defining the Africans in relation to the imperial center. What we find then are often conflicted texts, rendered ambiguous by the uncertainty of the political shifts.

While the war may have made the empire's decline inevitable, the remainder of the decade revealed the rapidly accelerating pace of this process. Through two government conferences in 1948, both attended by the secretary of state for the colonies and CFU representatives, we can see the attempts to acknowledge and control the nature of this "end" and the part that film would play in this. First, in January 1948 the British Film Institute hosted the one-day conference in London on "The Film in Colonial Development" (see Figure 4.5). While speakers at the conference trotted out, as the journal *West Africa* termed it, "the old rusty arguments about primitive, illiterate peoples . . . ad nauseum," repeating familiar anecdotes about the "oversized" mosquito and expressing anxieties about the negative American influence on screen, they also recognized a shift in colonial film policy that was closely aligned to broader political developments.[79] "Throughout our Colonial Office policy we are working at one main thing," explained K.W. Blackburne, director of

> Board of Governors:
> F. W. Baker
> Sir W. Ross Barker, K.C.I.E., C.B.
> E. G. Barnard, M.A.
> A. C. Cameron, M.C., M.A.
>
> THE BRITISH FILM INSTITUTE
> 4 GREAT RUSSELL STREET, LONDON, W.C.1
> Telephone: MUSeum 0607/8
> President: THE DUKE OF SUTHERLAND, K.T.
>
> Prof. B. Ifor Evans, M.A., D.Litt.
> Sir Henry L. French, G.B.E., K.C.B
> W.R. Fuller
> J. H. Hay, M.P.
> The Hon. Eleanor Plumer, M.A.
>
> Director: Oliver Bell, M.A.   Chairman: Patrick Gordon Walker, M.A., B.Litt., M.P.   Secretary: R. W. Dickinson, M.A.

AGENDA

Conference on THE FILM IN COLONIAL DEVELOPMENT to be held at the Royal Empire Society Hall, Northumberland Avenue, W.C.2, on Friday, January 16th, 1948, 10 a.m. to 5 p.m.

MORNING SESSION: 10 a.m.—12.30 p.m.

CHAIRMAN:	Mr. Aidan M. Crawley, M.P., Parliamentary Private Secretary to the Secretary of State for the Colonies
OPENING ADDRESS:	The Rt. Hon. A. Creech Jones, M.P., H.M. Secretary of State for the Colonies
THE FILM AND PRIMITIVE PEOPLES:	Mr. John Grierson, Director of Mass Communications, U.N.E.S.C.O.
THE COMMERCIAL ENTERTAINMENT FILM AND ITS EFFECT ON COLONIAL PEOPLES:	Mr. Colin Beale, B.Sc. F.R.P.S., Secretary, Edinburgh House Bureau for Visual Aids.
THE MAKING OF FILMS FOR ILLITERATES IN AFRICA:	Mr. George Pearson, Hon. F.R.P.S., Colonial Film Unit.
SOME SPECIAL FEATURES OF COLONIAL FILM PRODUCTION:	Mr. Alan Izod, Films Division, Central Office of Information.
FINANCIAL PROBLEMS AND FUTURE POLICY IN BRITISH COLONIES:	Mr. K. W. Blackburne, C.M.G., O.B.E., Director of Information Services, Colonial Office.

AFTERNOON SESSION: 2.30 p.m.—4.30 p.m.

QUESTIONS AND DISCUSSION:	The Afternoon Session will be devoted to questions and discussion.

FIGURE 4.5. The agenda for "The Film in Colonial Development" conference held in London in January 1948. While the conference speakers called for more filmmakers and voices from the colonies, these speakers were, once more, exclusively white British men talking from the imperial center. In this way the conference is indicative of the tentative and ambiguous moves toward decentralized rule in this postwar period.

information services at the Colonial Office, "trying to teach the people of the Colonies to run the show themselves and doing precisely that thing in the film world as in every other field."[80] John Grierson further outlined the need to create "a genuine African Unit that can work with native units in other colonies," what he described as a "Colonial Film Unit with true regard for decentralization and the part which natives will play in it."[81]

The conference marks a public shift in colonial film policy at a moment when the British government was outlining concurrent changes in its political strategies toward Africa. In his opening address, Arthur Creech Jones, the secretary of state for the colonies, spoke twice of an efficient "discharge of responsibility" and reiterated not only the "enormous" economic advantages of colonial development but also the "constructive and positive" development of "nationhood," creating "colonial democracies" defined by the values of Western Europe and "supported by our social services and good economic conditions." Film was presented here as a weapon in a wider ideological battle against Communism, a battle brought into focus at this moment with the Communist "insurgency" in Malaya. Creech Jones argued that film could create "in the minds of the people in the Colonies a new sense of values," "obtaining their cooperation and goodwill," seeking to educate or to colonize the mind even as greater "freedoms" were offered. The sense of urgency was restated by the conference chairman, Labour MP Aidan Crawley (who would become the first editor-in-chief of ITN [Independent Television News] in 1955), when he concluded that "it seems to me, in the next few months, the survival or not of Western Civilisation, as we know it, will be decided."[82]

The cold war context runs throughout the speeches. Grierson warned against putting an "iron curtain" around the British Isles, seeing Britain as a population not of 50 million but of 113 million "white, black and others." While noting Britain's "shrinking horizons" (about as close as you will get to a mention of Indian independence), he stressed that Africa represents enormous "economic potential." As film historian Martin Stollery astutely shows, Grierson's position here straddled his current employment with UNESCO and his forthcoming appointment with the COI. In this latter respect, he appears diplomatic if somewhat underwhelmed by the "pioneer" work of the CFU. When discussing the need to produce films "from the inside, by and for the Colonial peoples themselves," he claims that "we start almost at scratch."[83]

While Grierson's calls for a decentralized CFU garnered some notice, he was hardly breaking new ground here. Alan Izod, occupying the post Grierson would soon assume at the COI, explained that the "official attitude" to film production in the colonies was "not merely making films for them, but helping them to help themselves."[84] As this event extolling decentralized leadership and increasing colonial involvement was held in London and contained exclusively white British men as its speakers, it may be safe to assume that there was still some way to go to match words with actions.[85] Indeed Grierson's calls for a "genuine African unit" still involved close European supervision, as he called for "a body of men who will make this their lifework," who "live and work with the African problem."[86]

Later in the year, Blackburne would speak about the CFU and the "grand job" it had done at the African Conference held at Lancaster House. The conference itself sought to reframe Britain's relationship with its African colonies. In the opening address, Deputy Prime Minister Herbert Morrison outlined: "We must wipe out the word 'exploitation'—put it amongst the antiques with 'piracy' and 'slavery'." In a speech that successfully riled Churchill, Morrison further acknowledged the need for rapid change. "Let us keep our eyes on the clock and calendar," he stated. "We in Britain are finding it difficult to adapt our ideas and ways and arrangements quickly enough to the greatly changed needs of the post-war world."[87] For his part, Blackburne highlighted the contribution of the CFU, finding "local lads who can be trained in film work, and to give local governments an opportunity, in the course of the next two or three years, of establishing their own units." While stressing the importance of locally made films, Blackburne also noted that the CFU was filming the official proceedings at the conference.[88] Here again we see the ambiguities of the moment as a conference calling for shifts in the centers and structures of colonial power coordinated an African leadership within the British establishment, while the calls for more "locally" made films were recorded in London.

The conference brought over delegates from Africa, many of whom, as *West Africa* noted on more than one occasion, "were not at all sure why they had been invited or what exactly they were going to discuss."[89] This was, to an extent, a publicity exercise after the loss of Britain's Asian colonies, showcasing the prominent position now afforded to the African colonies and, given the intensification of nationalist movements within Africa, encouraging loyalty among a British-approved leadership. One of the most prominently featured figures here was the Oni of Ife, described as the "spiritual head of all Yorubas," who featured across multiple films. His appearances foreground different and, at times, conflicting approaches from the CFU. In showcasing British primacy (for example, as he tours famous London sites in *African Visitors at the Tower of London*), his appearances recall interwar films of London, while at other times they acknowledge moves toward a newer model of African leadership (for example, when attending a reception with Nigerian students at the Royal Empire Society in *Colonial Cinemagazine* 20).[90] Indeed while the Oni of Ife represented a traditional figure—reports repeatedly emphasized that he wore "elaborate and pic-

FIGURE 4.6. The Oni of Ife watching films at the CFU offices in London, *Colonial Cinema*, March 1949, 14.

turesque" Yoruba ceremonial robes—he was crucially shown to embrace and work with the British government, an accepted and welcomed example of African leadership (his "broad smile and friendly manner gained him a lot of friends wherever he went"). He even attended a press show of CFU films with Sellers and Pearson to "provide a personal account of the use of the films from a native point of view" (see Figure 4.6). The official invitation to the screening showed how African leadership was used to legitimize the CFU's work, stating "who better to give a picture of the reactions of his people and their development, as a result of these films," than the Oni of Ife.[91]

The film of the African Conference, and those produced during the delegates' tour, positioned African leadership within a traditional image of Britain, but while these productions reiterate the historical primacy of Britain through this image of London, there were also important distinctions emerging. First, the central role of Africans on screen contrasted with their almost complete absence within interwar pictures of colonials within London. Africa was now positioned at the forefront of the empire. Secondly, this notion of the imperial center was supplemented by images of workers and performers traveling outside of the metropole. While the initial scenes in *An African Conference* highlight the formal nature of this imperial relationship, later sequences move away from the London landmarks, showing the leaders working with, and learning from, their British counterparts on farms and in factories.

The contrasts between these two sequences reveal the uneasy balance between a traditional relationship, controlled from the center, and this new model of imperial partnership. The sequences in London at official events (meeting the King and visiting London landmarks) conform to colonial hierarchies and highlight difference (for example through costume), but later sequences outside London reveal an apparent transgression across class and gender boundaries, as the Africans talk "firsthand" with British dignitaries, local farmhands, and women workers. This movement away from the center is not defined purely by agriculture but also takes in a trip to a car factory in Coventry, celebrating industrial Britain as "the modern way to progress."

Further home unit productions expose this tension between modern cooperation and traditional centralized leadership. For example, *Colonial Cinemagazine 14* shows colonial students meeting young farmers at Lampeter in Wales, but also a formal Colonial Office tea party in London. *Colonial Month* (1949) is bookended by staged shots of African and British men smoking and chatting informally in London. While supposedly promoting partnership and equality, the framing reveals a continued division. This is most acutely revealed in the final staged sequence, which shows the African and British men talking on either side of the frame, before walking off in opposite directions.

Staged in the summer of 1949, Colonial Month involved a series of events and publicity drives (including screenings of CFU films in the UK) and contained, as its centerpiece, an exhibition in Oxford Street in London. The exhibition offered a significantly scaled-down version of the 1924–25 British Empire Exhibition, as it sought to organize and display the colonies together within the city, allowing visitors to "make their way along a realistic jungle pathway" and to see life-sized models of Africans. In its form, it also mirrored much interwar documentary, defining the colonies by their economic value to Britain, usually in the form of an easily recognizable product. This economic value was prioritized on screen in *Colonial Month* through an exhibit that shows colonial raw materials used in Britain. The commentator notes here "that this section of the exhibition is most important. It shows very clearly that Britain and the colonies need each other today more than they have ever done before." The Colonial Office hoped that Colonial Month would not only stimulate interest in the colonies within Britain at a moment when public opinion was increasingly opposed to large-scale colonial expenditure, but would also then, partly through the CFU film, demonstrate this popular support back to the colonies.[92]

The Colonial Office directly emphasized the economic benefits of continued colonial investment and of housing colonial workers in Britain. This is foregrounded in Crown's *Spotlight on the Colonies* (1950), which while made for British cinemagoers, and sponsored by the Government's Economic Information Unit, uses CFU material. "To us in the factories at home, this plan for mutual exchange may seem remote," the commentator notes, "but we are—every one of us—a part of it; for if the colonies are to send us the food and raw materials we're short of, we must send them the tools to do the job." The press release for the film followed a similar rhetoric. "If the Colonies are given our continued help," the release concluded, "we shall in the coming years have staunch partners on our common road to progress."[93] In convincing colonial audiences of this "common road," the home unit productions presented imperial trade as a means of partnership. In *An African Conference*, the delegates visit the Bourneville factory and watch the export of "good African cocoa," seeing the "process through from beginning to end." The Colonial Office also, however, reframes this relationship within the context of its postwar development agenda. In one scene in *Colonial Month*, the commentator describes how "Eda, a little Malayan girl whose father is now studying at Oxford University, presented the Queen with a bouquet." The Queen, as the imperial figurehead, receives gifts from her colonies, yet the commentator also points out here Britain's role now in educating and training a colonial elite.

The Colonial Office also organized a series of tours, which sought to challenge British perceptions of the colonies and which, in turn, were filmed by the CFU. In May 1947, the Gold Coast Police Band embarked on a four-month trip to the UK, which was filmed within *Colonial*

Cinemagazine 9, while in August 1949 the Nigerian football team embarked on a five-week tour. Football writer Phil Vasili argued that the selectors "wanted the players to present a collective face to the British public that went some way to dispelling racial myths about Africans and which would also stand testament to the positive contribution made by the expatriates, confirming the legitimacy of their presence in the colony." Fourteen of the eighteen Nigerian footballers were civil servants, and another two were teachers. The team's player/secretary Kanno had been educated in England and had thus, it was deemed, "acquired the refinements necessary for the public engagements."[94] Historian Nate Plageman argued that the tour of the Gold Coast Police Band was similarly intended to highlight the "efficacy of Empire," demonstrating "colonialism's ability to transform 'backward peoples' into civilized subjects."[95]

In highlighting "successful" British leadership, these home unit films retain an overarching, colonial presence, both formally in deploying a British voiceover and also in their framing as they depict a collective African group gathered around, looking up at, and learning from, a single British figure. The Colonial Office was determined to stress that the Gold Coast Police Band's tour was a "colonial" rather than "African" group, "started from scratch," and Plageman notes the frustration in Whitehall when the white band leaders, foregrounded in COI photographs, were cropped from newspaper images. The bandleader Thomas Stenning argued, with evident frustration, that HMV intentionally took photos of the band in his absence and when promoting the band's recordings "hid the fact that a white man had anything to do with the band at all."[96] Plageman notes how colonial documentation privileges government intent, with boxes of material discussing the plans for these tours and often very little on what actually happened. This is, of course, equally true with the CFU—the preoccupation with film form over reception—and reminds us that these CFU home unit films endorse semi-fictionalized colonial narratives, which are, to an extent, written before the event.[97]

The tours served to showcase the export of British values. *Colonial Cinema* argued that the Nigerian footballers "did not take long to establish a fine reputation not only for fast, clever football but also for excellent manners and sporting behaviour on the field."[98] Writing to the English Football Association before the tour, the governor of Nigeria, John Macpherson, explained that when he watched matches in Nigeria, he was "invariably impressed by the good sportsmanship not only of the players but of the large and enthusiastic crowds of spectators" and looked forward to seeing the same "friendly sporting spirit" in England.

Macpherson saw the tour as a way for the people of Nigeria and the UK to "get to know each other" and concluded that the players would be "good ambassadors" for Nigeria and would "cement the friendly feelings between the peoples of the two countries."[99]

While these tours sought to define the Africans in relation to supposedly British ideals and customs, public responses to these tours often reasserted perceived African "characteristics," albeit in a regressive manner that played on established notions of primitivism. For example, newspaper reports of the Nigerian footballers' tour of England were preoccupied with the cultural differences between the Nigerian and English players, noting in particular that the Nigerians played barefoot. "If during the next month, you see a full back put a football on the spot for a goal kick and hoof it beyond midfield with his bare foot," a *Daily Mirror* report began, "there's no need to cringe. He likes doing it. In fact, he prefers it that way." A *Daily Mail* report, entitled "Five Goals, No Boots," simply noted the distances that the barefoot players had kicked the ball and quoted the opposition captain, who "soon found their feet were harder than our boots." While the commentary makes no mention of the lack of footwear, cameraman Sydney Samuelson, who filmed the tourists' first game against Marine Crosby in Liverpool, recalls specifically filming the feet of the Nigerians as they came on to the pitch.[100] Reports of the Gold Coast Police Band suggested that British audiences were particularly fascinated to know whether the musicians were playing the music from a score. One report even claimed that during a performance, the lighting crew switched off the lights "out of curiosity and doubtfulness." "To the surprise of the audience," the report added, "the band stopped playing abruptly."[101] Such assumptions and stereotypes were similarly evident in the press coverage of the tour. *African Affairs* commented on the "foolish British press descriptions of the Gold Coast Police Band as 'Jungle Musicians'."[102]

Sport features prominently across these home unit productions. An athletics meeting between Nigeria and the Gold Coast in *Colonial Cinemagazine 10* outlines national development through sport, suggesting "a day, not far distant, when West Africa will be able to compete in such great events as the Empire and Olympic Games." Both nations would compete for the first time at the 1952 Olympics in Helsinki, a further step toward full nationhood. The one-reel film of the Malayan badminton team's victory in the inaugural Thomas Cup (effectively the men's world championship) in Glasgow and Preston in 1949 played across multiple cinemas in Malaya and was shown to players and dignitaries at celebratory events. The item was followed by another a few months later of the victorious team welcomed at the Colonial Office, both highlighting Malaya's international achievement and then celebrating this within the halls of British power.[103]

Colonial Cinemagazine 4 shows the annual university football match between Oxford and Cambridge, played at Dulwich Hamlet in December 1945, which is noteworthy for the appearance of a Nigerian, Albert Osakwe, captaining the Oxford team. The film emphasizes Osakwe's acceptance and integration within the team and shows him leading his British teammates out. Osakwe appears as a role model for African leadership, trained and approved by Britain, and years later he would serve as permanent secretary of the Eastern Nigerian Public Service through independence (and would receive an OBE in 1963).[104] "He's an excellent captain," the British commentator notes. "After one match, one of the chief London newspapers said of him, 'he has led his team admirably and was the best forward on the field'."

The form used for a film of sporting performance—the action shots and those of the cheering crowds of white men ("thousands of people had gathered to cheer them on")—helps to showcase British support for, and to, the colonies, to promote imperial cooperation (teamwork) and, to extend the football analogy, present a "level playing field" across the empire. In this way, the films sought to dispel any notions of racial animosity, most notably in *Nigerian Footballers,* which shows seven thousand British and Africans cheering together in Liverpool, a site of race riots a year earlier. The films showcase African recognition and validation within Britain, concluding with shots of British crowds applauding the African performers and seeking to reassure African audiences of the care provided for those Africans now living within Britain. This is most notable in the uncomfortable analogy within *Colonial Cinemagazine 8,* which shows African animals well looked after in their new homes in London Zoo.

In 1950, the home unit produced its final film, *A Journey by a London Bus,* a fitting epitaph that encapsulates much of the unit's work over the previous decade. The film plays like a sequel to *An African in England,* taking two African students back to London from the countryside and offers a particularly fanciful advertisement for London Transport (the commentator repeatedly notes how the buses "run to carefully prepared timetables and are always punctual"). The film's function in 1950 is also ambiguous. It contains elements of the instructional film, explaining how to behave on a London bus (for example, in having the correct money to hand). In this way, the film might speak directly to (and of) postwar immigrants moving to Britain. In the following decade London Transport would directly recruit staff from the colonies, formalizing a recruitment scheme with the Barbados government in 1956 that would run until 1970. Yet significantly, given both fears within Britain over immigration and the moves toward self-government, these home unit films consistently define the Africans as "visitors" rather than immigrants. The films frequently depict Africans waving goodbye and note that the colonial men will take their accrued knowledge back "to their own country."

However, the film's status as an instructional film is usurped by its more general promotion of British values and by its repeated call for colonial cooperation. There is much that is familiar here, in the form (through Africans touring Britain), imagery (an emphasis on a quintessentially British technological symbol, the double-decker bus), and celebration of British primacy (London is introduced as "the largest city in the world"). The film again defines the British through a set of values—what better summation than the commentator's "people wait quietly in line"—showing how passengers enter in an "orderly manner" and show "thought to others," while the conductor controls everything in a "cheerful way." Audiences would do well to miss the message of cooperation—the commentator refers to the "friendly co-operation between bus driver and conductor," the "friendly co-operation" amongst passengers and, in the final line, praises the "orderly, willing and friendly co-operation by the travelling public." The film again shows educated African students and emphasizes their movement, albeit this time back to the imperial center. The home unit again implies here that the next journey for the students would be back to the colonies. For the CFU's home unit, this antiquated imperial fantasy would prove to be its last stop.

"HOW TO MAKE FILMS THE ENGLISHMAN'S WAY": PRODUCING FILMMAKERS AT THE CFU'S TRAINING SCHOOLS

The demise of the home unit coincided with the emergence of local film units, which were direct products of the CFU's training schools (see Figure 4.7). On Monday 13 September 1948, six African trainees began their first day at the CFU's inaugural training school in Accra. The trainees comprised three men from the Gold Coast (Sam Aryeetey, R. O. Fenuku, and Bob Okanta) and three from Nigeria (Alex Fajemisin,

FIGURE 4.7. Nigerian trainees learning the technical aspects of film production, courtesy of The National Archive (UK), INF 10/245/35.

J. A. Otigba, and Malam Yakuba Auna) who would then form the nucleus of their local government film units. The school trained these filmmakers in the CFU's "well tried methods of approach and technique," with the two main instructors: Ron Harris, who had been at Kodak for twenty years (where Sellers had trained while on leave in the 1930s), working on the technical training, and the CFU's Gareth Evans overseeing the "creative side of film production."[105] Trinidadian-born cinematographer Franklyn St. Juste, describing the second training school in Jamaica, argued that the trainees were taught "how to make films the Englishman's way."[106]

The aims and practices of the inaugural training school are represented in a short CFU film, *A Film School in West Africa* (1949), which in working through the various stages of the training course shows the gradual, moderated handing over of film apparatus. The students initially sit dutifully listening with pencils at the ready as the British instructor writes on the blackboard before later shooting scenes with the instructor on hand "not to teach now but ready to give help if asked." By the time the students are editing, the instructor "watches and is ready to give a kindly helping hand where aid is needed." Throughout this process, the instructor is rarely out of shot, often framed over the shoulder of the six trainees as the film idealizes a developing partnership between colonizer and colonized.

When first arriving in the classroom, the commentator states: "The students are welcomed cheerfully by the instructor and they, in turn, already feel that he is their friend." As with the home unit productions, the film's message of cooperation is inescapable. They are, we are repeatedly told, a "team," filmmaking is "above all a test of teamwork" and their success depends on "true co-operation with him [the British instructor] and with each other." Later the commentator reaffirms that the school is training character and values, as much as technique, explaining: "The development of the spirit of co-operation was one of the main purposes of the training for picture making is no one man job, it is teamwork throughout." This message was foregrounded in reports of subsequent training schools. "It cannot be too strongly stressed," the CFU wrote of the West Indies film school, "that this spirit of friendliness and co-operation went a very long way to make the school initially a great success."[107]

This message of cooperation is not simply between teacher and trainee, but also across the different regions represented within the school. The commentator makes a point of noting that the three young Nigerians, "a Hausa, a Yoruba and an Ibo, have been carefully chosen," and Harold Cooper, the public relations officer in Nigeria, admitted that the students were selected "with regionalization in mind." While *A Film School in West Africa* notes that the trainees "are all men of good education," and official reports heaped praise on them, Cooper spoke disparagingly of the "limited ability of the trainees." Highlighting the racial assumptions that stymied moves toward self-government, Cooper suggested at the course's outset that the trainees required at least a year's trial before taking on the roles of regional films officers.[108] In contrast, published accounts on the course argued that the films produced by the trainees "caused something of a mild sensation" in London, with the standard "much in advance" of expectation.[109]

While *A Film School in West Africa* shows African filmmakers behind the camera and at all stages of production, the footage of these African filmmakers was, once more, taken by a European, Lionel Snazelle, who would subsequently head the Nigerian Film Unit and train numerous students in ways articulated at the Accra school. The film's script was written by the CFU's H. M. K. Howson, who helped organize the school. The fantasies projected on screen do not yet stretch beyond the frame.

Furthermore, these shots conceal other repressed histories. The scriptwriting takes place away from Accra on the battlements of the old castle at Anomabu. While presented as a picturesque coastal setting, a relaxed environment for informal discussion around a table, the fort represented the center of British slave trading into the nineteenth century.

A Film School in West Africa talks directly to its African audience—the students are "writing what is called the film script"—and in this way also seeks to train and create film literate viewers, to make them aware of the processes and techniques of film. The training and development of filmmakers was closely aligned to this "development" of film audiences. When William Sellers first outlined proposals for a training school in the summer of 1946, he saw it also as a "means of training backward audiences to appreciate moving pictures."[110] Indeed the course curriculum addressed both the "psychology of the audience" and the "social content of films for Africans."[111] Writing in 1952, C. Y. Carstairs of the Colonial Office explained: "Trainees are turning out a type of straight-forward film, eschewing thrills, but strong in content and local touch, which very closely fits the stage of film education which their audience have reached."[112]

The commentator in *A Film School in West Africa* outlines the importance of the "local touch," arguing that by knowing "his fellow Africans," the African director can get his performers to "act and respond in a perfectly natural manner." When outlining the necessity of training Caribbean filmmakers, Gareth Evans argued the benefits for local audiences, who must not feel, "as is so often the case, that they are always on the outside looking in."[113] Sellers repeatedly argued that the "value of films" for colonial audiences would be considerably higher if made by colonials with an "intimate knowledge" of the local conditions, customs, and culture, but he also saw this "value" in economic terms, presenting the formation of local training schools as "the only practicable solution to the vital question of low production costs," particularly given the expense and difficulties of recruiting European technicians (see Figure 4.8).[114]

A Film School in West Africa is ultimately a fantasy of production, of citizens as much as celluloid, as it shows the production of filmmakers who would over the next decade be tasked with developing local film production in their own countries. The structure of *A Film School in West Africa* positions film alongside the other industries that the trainees were recording. *Copra,* made during the course "under guidance by the instructor," shows the industrial process of extracting oil and ker-

FIGURE 4.8. Nigerian trainees behind the camera. Courtesy of the National Archive (UK), INF 10/245/36.

nels from coconuts, while *Basket Making*, "made entirely without assistance" at the end of the course, focuses on students—much like those behind the camera—learning the process. While showing all stages of basket-making, the film concludes by emphasizing the economic value to the worker, showing the sale of the baskets at market. The films from the training school were, at once, formally and thematically consistent with the CFU's postwar output while also articulating the aims of the training school as part of the British government's gradual, controlled moves toward decolonization. *Welcome Home Soldiers* is a scripted film telling of brothers returning from war who hope to apply their training to civilian life, while *The Good Samaritan,* made by the Nigerian trainees in March 1949 at the end of their course, is an unsubtle allegory for the British in Africa, offering a parable of the titular Good Samaritan who helps an "unfortunate beggar," Kafi. The Good Samaritan provides a job and training for Kafi, who learns how to mix cement and thus becomes self-sufficient. After collecting his first paycheck, Kafi is "wise" and buys a blanket. The film concludes with a title outlining how the Good Samaritan tells Kafi "that he must work hard and help others as he has been helped." The trainee must now become a leader.[115]

The trainees from the Accra school would soon become members—if not yet leaders—of the emerging local units in West Africa. The CFU was quick to champion the school, not only for producing local filmmakers but for exemplifying wider colonial policy, a neat illustration of British government efforts to develop colonial training, foster local leaders, and support gradual moves toward self-government. Yet the plans for future training schools exposed the tensions and racial hierarchies that threatened this ideal, the disparity once more between the image projected on screen and the activities beyond the frame. The CFU abandoned plans to house its second film training school at Makerere College in Uganda in August 1949 after Sellers noted that government officials felt there would be "considerable difficulty" in finding suitable Africans equipped with the intelligence and capabilities to undertake the training. Sellers added that all officials "unanimously express such doubts without their opinion being asked."[116] Instead Sellers visited Jamaica in November 1949 with a view to setting up a training school and local production unit that would help "the people to a fuller life." Photographer Duncan Keith Corinaldi expressed some immediate resistance to this in the *Daily Gleaner*. "Let it not be said in the future," he wrote, "that the production of educational films in Jamaica was not a reality before the coming of the Colonial Film Unit." His words were certainly not heeded by those running the course, with Evans describing the Caribbean as "almost an untouched area" and "new ground." Viewing this intervention in political terms, Corinaldi asked why it was necessary to "woo, encourage and to beg for foreign capital on an important enterprise such as this for the betterment and enlightenment of our population."[117]

The colonial hierarchies that prevented East Africa from hosting the school were now applied in Jamaica. Corinaldi argued that "we in Jamaica are sufficiently advanced technically to produce pictures of this nature," and Evans ultimately reorientated the ideas for the Jamaica training school after determining that "films suitable for West African audiences were not suitable for West Indians." Evans now suggested that the approach adopted at Accra—described as "extreme simplicity" to cater to the "ignorance of cinema convention"—would be unsuitable for cosmopolitan West Indies, which was culturally exposed to "sophisticated" American and British influences.[118]

The West Indies film training school began on 6 March 1950, with trainees from Barbados (Isaac Carmichael), Trinidad (Wilfred Lee),

"Films *for*, *with*, and *by* Africans" | 189

British Guiana (R.H. Young), and Jamaica (Martin Rennalls, Trevor Welsh and Milton Weller), all of whom would go on to produce films in their own countries (and enjoy long careers in film).[119] (See Figure 4.9.) On his return to Barbados, Isaac Carmichael told the local press that the course should "mean much towards West Indian development, morally, socially and intellectually."[120] These motives are evident in the first film produced during the training school, which took as its subject the school's venue, the newly opened University of West Indies. Characteristically self-reflexive, the film highlights the training and development of local educated citizens, and initially focuses on the installation of Princess Alice, Countess of Athlone, as the university's first chancellor (a post she would hold until 1971). There are very clear parallels between the film training school and its subject here (the university), which is represented as a site of modern learning and cooperation (the film focuses on visiting male and female Trinidad students), all under overarching British supervision. In the next couple of years, the Jamaican trainees would produce another version of the film in color—now as part of the nascent Jamaica Film Unit—which focused more extensively on the students. In this later film, the commentator explicitly presents the university as a symbol of cooperation and nation-building—"men and women of many races and creeds come together to form a single community dedicated to the pursuit of knowledge"—and explains how the European lecturer works "to guide and to encourage the student to develop independence of thought." The film highlights the "modern methods" taught in science and agriculture and emphasizes that the students will apply this knowledge to help develop the region, whether studying Caribbean history or contributing through science to the "development of the British Caribbean." One of the stated aims of the university was to provide leaders and, in concluding with shots from the first graduation ceremony in 1953, the latter version outlines this gradual, moderated process: "Still with much to learn, he [the graduating student] goes out to serve the people."

The other films produced at the West Indies film training school again focus predominantly on industry and prioritize the economic productivity of the worker (and nation). They reveal both the circulation, and local adaptation, of colonial film conventions, so that while they repeatedly use the Mr. Wise and Mr. Foolish format, the films deviate from the specialized technique. The first film made by graduates in British Guiana was on the rice industry, celebrating new methods and machinery introduced through a cooperative scheme, while the trainees'

FIGURE 4.9. Reporting on the West Indies film training school, *Colonial Cinema*, September 1950, 66.

film on citrus foregrounded the economic effects on workers ("carelessness costs hard cash") through the Mr. Wise and Mr. Foolish format. Gareth Evans explained that the students were uncertain whether to show the more memorable "bad methods," and so represented these "by a quick montage of shots," which were indicative of the more ambitious techniques employed in the West Indies.[121]

There are strong similarities here with the first film produced in Trinidad, *Cocoa Rehabilitation*, which was directed by trainee Wilfred

FIGURE 4.10. The Trinidad Film Unit working on its first film, *Cocoa Rehabilitation* (1951). Courtesy of the National Archive (UK), INF 10/359/21.

Lee and made in collaboration with the Department of Agriculture (see Figure 4.10). The film, again following the Mr. Wise and Mr. Foolish format, is notably more ambitious in form than those from the Accra School—there are dissolves, panning, the use of a chart, shorter shot lengths, and even a match cut—and again defines work in economic terms. The commentator notes the "tidy sum" collected at payday and, as with the earliest interwar films for the colonies, celebrates the economic benefits of hard work ("high dividends for hard and honest labour"). Indeed, the film emphasizes the economic importance of industry to the individual ("Every bag produced means more dollars") but also to the nation, as the film concludes with shots of export (the well-worn image of the boat being loaded). "To win this battle and restore our export trade," the commentator explains, "every farmer must help." The economic effects on the individual are also prioritized in *Delay Means Death* (1951), a Mr. Wise and Mr. Foolish film about tuberculosis, which shows a laborer sacked after contracting the illness, then unable to pay his rent and evicted from home. The film is, in effect, a Jamaican-set version of *Fight Tuberculosis in the Home,* highlighting again the ways in which the training schools reworked themes, formats, and material across each island and for each territory.[122]

The next CFU training school began in Cyprus on 11 June 1951 and was again run by Harris and Evans. Realizing the CFU's aim to support filmmaking across the empire and to reach out to colonies previously beyond its line of view, the school consisted of five trainees from Cyprus (Wideson, Constantinides, Tsangarides, Pavlides, and Aziz), two Sudanese (Kemal and Gadalla), a Mauritian (Domaingue), and one from Hong Kong (Li). Many of these names, such as Antoine Domaingue, Gadalla Gubara, and Rene Wideson, would become leading visual chroniclers of their emerging nations.[123] Film historian Jonathan Stubbs suggested that Cyprus may have been chosen because of the growing anti-British sentiment in the area. He quotes Horace White, the public information officer in Cyprus, who argued that film could be "one of our most effective political weapons, especially in the villages," and would be all the more important in helping to "circumvent the largely hostile local press."[124] While the school followed a similar structure to the West Indies, it faced various challenges, from language barriers to the weather (first extreme heat and later incessant rain, which extended the course by two months). Sensitivity and anxiety over the political situation in Cyprus also provoked a particularly close, and evidently frustrating, scrutiny of each proposed topic.[125] The governor personally monitored the proposed subjects, which ranged from a filmstrip on road safety to a film on soil and water conservation ("Save the Soil"). A planned film on tuberculosis (yet another) was never completed, while the trainees' final production, *United We Stand*, promoted cooperative farming schemes. The film depicted a "foolish" carob farmer, who sells his crop to a merchant instead of the cooperative society, and outlined the historical developments under British rule (according to a draft, "the little island of Cyprus stands as a byword of steady progress and development").[126]

The Cyprus school would be the last of the CFU's overseas schools, although in 1954–55 George Pearson and Norman Spurr ran a six-month school at the CFU's offices in Soho Square for students from Somaliland (Farah), Sarawak (Morshedi), Haiti (Gueri), Tanganyika (Singh), and the Gold Coast (Allotey). Pearson described the course as traveling "full circle," a return to his roots as a schoolteacher.[127] By now, the CFU was on its last legs, no longer producing films of its own, operating out of London with a skeleton staff and set to disband in the next few months. This end was massaged here as a carefully staged handover, one that slightly preceded political independence, as its work had now been taken on by the local units that it had helped create. It was now the responsibility of these local units—from the Gold Coast and Nigeria to Jamaica and Malaya—to manage and contain the final, often tumultuous days of empire.

CHAPTER 5

Handover

Local Units through the End of Empire

When Harold Macmillan became prime minister early in 1957 on the back of the hugely damaging, epoch-defining Suez crisis, he immediately asked for an "audit of empire," a "profit and loss account" for each colonial territory. While Macmillan was keen to ascertain what Britain would likely "gain or lose" by each territory's "departure" (financially but also politically and strategically), it was largely unimaginable that over the next seven years of Conservative government, a dozen countries would secure independence from the British Empire. What's more, these celebrations would be replicated in a further dozen areas by the end of Harold Wilson's Labour government in June 1970.[1] This rapid disappearing act—which saw swathes of pink erased from the map—stretched across Africa from the Gambia to Nigeria, and down the East Coast from Uganda and Kenya (and previously Sudan in 1956) to Bechuanaland. Attempts to reframe the empire came and went, leaving behind what Francis Gooding terms "a rump, a far flung global archipelago where just a decade earlier there had been a near endless expanse of territory."[2]

While the speed of decolonization was largely unexpected—Wm. Roger Louis described the accelerated shifts during Iain Macleod's two-year term as secretary of state for the colonies (1959–61) as "no less than a revolution in colonial affairs"—this was a reimagining, rather than a removal, of empire.[3] Much of this was "rebranding"—Piers Brendon referred to a larger "campaign of linguistic cleansing"—transforming empire into commonwealth.[4] This was indicative of the desire and impulse from successive governments to conceal and to rewrite history, projecting a change that was often illusory. The CFU plays its part here. Into the 1950s, as the CFU trained and supported new local units, government film worked to perpetuate British social, economic, and political structures beyond colonialism. These films sought to envisage British models within the colonies, to instruct colonial citizens and promote continued economic partnership, often by obscuring or wiping political tensions from the screen. C. Y. Carstairs, a former director of information at the Colonial Office who was well versed in the work of the CFU, explained in 1961 when discussing the road to independence in Tanganyika that "collaboration with the U.K. . . . is what we are seeking to substitute for control."[5] The CFU was important in exercising this "soft power" as its goals mutated from imperialism to globalization. At the same time, the emerging local units, and the films they produced, exemplified the wider aims of the British government, mediating the shift from colonial to independent state and promoting continuity through this transition. In this way, this chapter will consider the "end" less as a point of rupture than of continuity.

NATION-BUILDING IN AFRICA: GRAHAM, GRIERSON, AND THE GOLD COAST FILM UNIT

A number of the local units that emerged across the empire in the 1950s shared a genealogy that stretched from the imperial roots of interwar nonfiction to the formation of film schools in the postwar colonies. This trajectory is outlined across the pages of this book, and these final moves, from the training schools to the local units, are seemingly the easiest to chart. The six trainees from the Accra school immediately formed the nucleus of the Gold Coast Film Unit and Nigerian Film Unit, while the trainees from the West Indian school worked on the first productions for their local units while at the school (including the Jamaica Film Unit's *Farmer Brown Learns Good Dairying*, 1951). They then returned to run the film operations in their own countries. There are, however, pronounced differences here in the scale, ideologies, and operating practices of the units, which often respond again to racial hierarchies across the empire. For example, while the West Indian trainees assumed leadership roles, in West Africa, British filmmakers were brought in to run these nascent units.[6]

Sean Graham, who was in his twenties when he traveled to West Africa to lead the Gold Coast Film Unit, was offered the post by his mentor John Grierson, the head of the Films Division at the COI. Graham suggested this career move was down to chance and timing—"the first bloke who walked into his office" after Grierson received a letter from the Gold Coast—but it would prove a hugely significant appointment.[7] Graham's approach and background in documentary was notably different from 32-year-old Lionel Snazelle, who would head the Nigerian Film Unit. Snazelle had already worked in Nigeria with the CFU on a number of its postwar tours. Both figures would remain in charge through to independence. Their units ostensibly reflect both the political differences—filmmaker Sydney Samuelson suggested that the Gold Coast Film Unit was "way ahead" of its Nigerian counterparts because Ghana was more advanced in its Africanization—and the different approaches to film, played out since the 1920s between Grierson and Sellers, the prestige documentarians and the instructional educators.[8]

In a recent interview Graham explained: "My competition, Lionel Snazelle and William Sellers, they were earnest people and they weren't storytellers, and I thought of myself as a storyteller; they came from a different milieu, they were educators really." Graham argued that Sellers was not a "filmmaker" but instead "used film in order to explain something on film," while Graham presented himself in contrast as "a filmmaker first" working with "educationalists whose work I respect but into whose sphere I would not presume to follow."[9] Graham's affinity with the Griersonian tradition is evident in his appointments in the Gold Coast, most notably as he brought in as his right-hand man the gregarious George Noble, a veteran of the British Documentary Movement.

Graham and Noble were a formidable team, working with their "three willing but inexperienced African assistants." Rejecting the specialized technique of Sellers and the CFU, Graham claimed that the GCFU operated without involvement from London. While this is not entirely accurate—all laboratory work was initially carried out in London and three local members of the unit traveled to England for six months in 1952 to work at a commercial studio—Graham worked largely without interference from overseas, and what interaction he did have with other colonial units served only to exacerbate their differences.[10] On visiting the Nigerian Film Unit, with whom he shared equipment, he concluded: "They are a rather unhappy lot, mainly because of personalities there. I don't think much can be expected from them."[11] Indeed Graham's writing reflects, and seeks to cement, his own position, distinct from other colonial units. When he visited the West Indies for UNESCO in 1955, he wrote disparagingly of the educational films produced by the local units, explaining that in Trinidad, "The audience seemed as bored as I was," while he was unable to sit through a Jamaican film on banana-growing: "It was not good, by any yard stick."[12]

While recent scholarship has acknowledged this distinction, highlighting the GCFU's more liberal politics and its break from colonial film orthodoxy, the vast majority of this scholarship has centered on its 1952 feature film *The Boy Kumasenu,* a film that has received substantial (and disproportionate) attention in the last few years.[13] The film's place in African film history, and in defining the work of this "African" unit, is partly a product of its claims to be a "first" within African cinema, its apparent deviation from existing colonial film orthodoxy and its international profile. On the last point, the film played at the Berlin Film Festival, gained a diploma at the Venice Film Festival, a nomination for the "Best Film from Any Source" at the 1953 BAFTA awards, and opened the International Film Festival in Durban in 1954. It was introduced at its British premiere at the Edinburgh Festival in August 1952 by its associate producer Basil Wright, one of the key figures of the British Documentary Movement. The film's debt and links to the British Documentary Movement further distinguished it from the dominant forms of colonial film, a point noted by C. Y. Carstairs, who suggested that the film was "hardly typical of the work of local units."[14]

Carstairs did, however, suggest that the film could be a "portent" for other African pictures as it "has commercial ambitions" and "has already had uproarious success in the Gold Coast."[15] This enormous success was noted by Sean Graham, who explained that the film had played to "a packed audience in the biggest cinema of Accra night after night," while *African Affairs* claimed in October 1952 that 40,000 people had seen the film at local cinemas in three weeks. The *New York Times* attributed this success to the "eagerness of the populace to see (and see again) themselves or their friends and their familiar surroundings and way of life on the screen." Local advertisements certainly played on this appeal—one that harks back to the earliest days of cinema and that was used by the CFU to justify the formation of local units—with an advert in the *Daily Graphic* advertising *The Boy Kumasenu* as a film "Acted by an All-African cast, drawn from the people you know. See yourself and your friends on the screen."[16]

Aside from its success and continued availability, *The Boy Kumasenu* dominates discussions of the GCFU because it offers a rather unsubtle allegory both for an emerging African cinema and the nation at large. As Carmela Garritano notes in her study of Ghanaian film culture, *The Boy*

Kumasenu's "creation and narrative stand between the final period of colonial rule and the beginning of Ghana's independence," while Peter Bloom and Kate Skinner examine Kumasenu's "march towards his place as citizen-subject along the horizon of decolonization."[17] The commentator certainly encourages such readings, describing Kumasenu as "a boy on a bridge, uncertainly and unhappily making his way from one world to another." After arriving in the city, where he is taken in by an educated doctor and his wife, the commentator repeatedly asks: "What of the boy's future?" explaining that he will need guidance as "he knows nothing of the world here." The doctor provides this guidance and represents a form of African leadership, a point also recognized by *West African Review*, which concluded that "only one of his own people who has already successfully crossed to the new world can guide the boy Kumasenu and others like him to a more hopeful future."[18] Bloom and Skinner situate this representation of "educated Africans mediating social adjustment" within the context of both developmentalist ideologies and the rising political influence of African nationalists.[19]

The film's premiere in the Gold Coast was attended by the prime minister, Kwame Nkrumah, who recognized the importance of the arts and film in promoting nationalism and took a close interest in the GCFU. Film historian Emma Sandon argues that the film, and its promotion of "highlife" and African personalities, were appropriated for Nkrumah's nationalist agenda, while the film's resolution in which "the child became a man" by standing up to his bullying oppressor could certainly be read within this context.[20] Reviews for the GCFU films in Britain invariably downplayed these messages (the films were often described as "quaint" and "simple") and when *The Boy Kumasenu* was released (and reviewed) in the UK years later in early 1957 at the time of Ghana's independence, *Kinematograph Weekly* suggested that this "dramatic documentary" served as a "warning against allowing uneducated African lads to run before they can walk." On seeing the film at Venice, the *Daily Mail* suggested it was "hardly the portentous Africa-at-the-crossroads study it claims to be," seeing it instead as "just a nice little Cinderella story of an African boy's difficulties in the big city."[21]

The Boy Kumasenu is one small part of the GCFU output and in prioritizing the exceptional aspects (its commercial and international popularity and its significance as a feature film), this focus privileges a particular African cinema history (commercial, fiction) and largely overlooks the many other ways in which the film represents the work of the GCFU. It is worth noting, for example, that *The Boy Kumasenu* was commissioned by the Department of Social Welfare and Community Development, a reminder that these films, regardless of their form, were produced to support specific government campaigns. The government had established the film unit at an initial cost of £129,581 (with a further £13,440 assigned for new cinema vans), primarily to produce "educational films." The GCFU would ask ministries "which problems or aspects of their activities they would like to have publicized in films," and Graham describes Saturday morning meetings, which he went to "against my will," at which various departments would make their requests. Graham specifically asked departments "the precise lesson" they wished to convey, the "order of priority," and the latest date by which the film was needed. From this, Graham selected the topics that interested him and, crucially, determined their treatment.[22] In this way, the GCFU constantly experimented with form and genre. "We have tried to make people come alive first, to dramatize their problems and stimulate their interest in whatever subject we were tackling," Graham explained. "We merely brought the question into focus and left it to other agencies to follow up with detailed instruction." Whether experimenting with color, animation, musical numbers, or using a crane he bought for £50 at an auction while on leave in London, Graham was always looking at new approaches, structures, and narrative devices to support these campaigns and to make audiences enthusiastic and receptive to the more detailed instruction.[23]

In a letter to the director of education in 1952 Graham asked for a meeting to discuss a "new type of film" which would be a "form of screen journalism on the lines of The March of Time or This Modern Age." Graham was characteristically pushing the boundaries here, looking to "present both sides to each problem" and with a "strong journalistic slant ... leave the audience to draw their own conclusions." It is very hard to imagine the CFU encouraging the audience to draw their own conclusions.[24] Another pet project of Graham's was "an African Grapes of Wrath," an unhappy story of "such unrelieved gloom," addressing migrant labor "which drifts in from the North." Graham recognized that this was unlikely to get made but it does reiterate both his affiliations with the Griersonian traditions and his desire to show, rather than conceal, local struggles and political problems. "As it is we are criticised—not loudly, but quietly, respectfully," he wrote in a letter to Basil Wright when discussing the possible film, "for showing an undue fascination for the seamy side of this place. This is really seamy."[25] One further example illustrates his approach to the sponsored model of government filmmaking. When heavily funded by "airways people" to make a film on air communications, Graham's plan was to produce a picture that "has nothing to do with planes, really," looking instead for "three or four little vignettes which can add up to something new on the subject." The plane would serve as a "continuity link"—connecting a Moslem pilgrim who has saved to make a trip to Mecca, a "blasé businessman" and "the woman who has family troubles, or husband trouble in another town."[26] It is also telling that when funding for the GCFU's films shifted in 1955, so that it now came from the sponsoring departments, Graham insisted on retaining creative control, supporting a model of sponsorship that was popularized by the British Documentarians in the 1930s.[27]

It is also important to stress that while GCFU films like *The Boy Kumasenu* did play on the festival circuit, their core audience would view these films through the mobile film units. In 1955 government reports claimed that the GCFU had visited 12,281 towns and villages and, with its twenty-one new vans, given 11,343 cinema shows and 3,535 talks to a total audience of over 3½ million. It had, by now, produced thirty-six films, which included short instructional films, "feature" films, and thirteen issues of its newsreel, *Gold Coast Review*.[28] A. R. G. Prosser, the chief social development officer for the Gold Coast, outlined the collaborative ways in which the GCFU's first production, *Amenu's Child,* which supported a campaign to reduce child mortality rates, was used by government to "train village leaders in Child Welfare." Prosser explained: "The Public Relations Officer made available a Mobile Cinema and crew; the Medical Department made available a trained Midwife and notes for the instructors on Child Welfare; the Chief Social Development Officer contributed two Assistant Mass Education Officers." This team recognized that the most effective way to use the film was to tell the story to the audience in advance and to use stills to stress pertinent points—for example, one poster on the board read "Wash your hands always"—before showing the film and then leading a discussion (see Figure 5.1).[29] The films themselves acknowledge the other media they work alongside. For example, in *I Will Speak English* (1954), viewers are urged to turn to specific pages of the accompanying textbook.

These screenings, and films, often participated in the processes of government. When *Ghana Today* noted in 1957 the "ubiquitous" work of the Department of Information Services, it explained that "the most important campaigns which it has undertaken have been in respect of

FIGURE 5.1. Discussion around a screening of *Amenu's Child* (1950). Photograph from Public Relations Office, Gold Coast.

the general election of 1954 when over 1½ million people saw the film on election procedure." As part of this "vigorous and prolonged campaign," *Progress in Kojokrom* (1953), a comedy about local government and tax collection, played widely, supported by government literature that included a pamphlet entitled "Your Council and Your Progress."[30] Teams of "six or seven" screened the film in the evening, before the next morning "all the people of the village" were invited to a meeting, usually attended by the local councilor, at which the team would explain "using visual aids" the ways in which they collect and spend the taxes.[31]

Progress in Kojokrom also includes a postscript delivered by the minister of local government, a device employed in other GCFU films such as *Mr. Mensah Builds a House* (1955). Dressed in a suit behind a desk, the minister talks directly to the camera and states, with a complete absence of screen charisma: "I would like to have a word with you before you go away and think about this film." This postscript seeks to contextualize the film—any development "depends on your cooperation and support"—and to direct the audience's responses to the film. It also highlights the ways in which these narratives were connected to contemporary campaigns. Often these local government figures would be on hand at the screening, but here the film again provides an opportunity to take these political figures on a wider tour, to rule remotely through film. This format would continue in postindependence films, such as the Ghana Film Production Corporation's *Your Police* (1962), which concluded with an equally stilted address to camera from E. R. T. Madjitey, the police commissioner. "One thing I ask for and that is your cooperation at all times," he says to the camera. "You will give it to us, won't you? I know, the answer is 'Yes'. Thank you." This device was also used by other units with mixed results. Martin Rennalls complained about the Jamaican government's insistence in the late colonial period of presenting ministers on screen delivering their message to camera. The messenger here proved a distraction, inviting a chorus of boos in areas with strong opposition support. "There was no concern for, or interest in the content of, the message," Rennalls explained. "Their concern was with who was delivering the message."[32]

The local council is represented in *Progress in Kojokrom* as an educated and benevolent group of Africans, converting the traditional skeptic to the modern ways of local government. From the opening moments when the suited returning officer announces the election results, the film projects models for the self-governing nation that are largely consistent with those adopted in Britain. A later film such as *I Will Speak English* (1954), made on behalf of the Department of Social Welfare, uses an almost entirely African cast, and depicts an African teacher instructing a group of African students. Yet, the subject of the film—presenting "a new technique to teach English to illiterate adult audiences"—positively encourages the retention of British influence (through language). These films mark a move away from British leadership and personnel while still endorsing the perpetuation of British structures and values. For example, in *Mr. Mensah Builds a House,* the titular protagonist appears dislocated from the African community as he enjoys British tea parties and chats informally with his British colleagues about his future plans ("oh I must look you up sometime"). At his retirement tea party, a British man presents Mr. Mensah with a clock "for his long and devoted service to the company." Throughout this, Mr. Mensah fails to monitor his wayward nephew who is supposed to be building his new house (see Figure 5.2). When he returns to his hometown and his unbuilt house, Mr. Mensah is dependent not on his former British colleagues, but on the plans, policies, and structures now put in place. Dressed in traditional clothing—as opposed to the shirt and tie he had previously worn—Mr. Mensah listens to the local officer

FIGURE 5.2. "Whatever Kofi wants, Kofi gets. . ." Kofi, Mr. Mensah's nephew, racking up debts in *Mr. Mensah Builds a House* (1955). Production still courtesy of Information Services Department, Ghana.

who outlines the new housing scheme by which the local community will work together to rebuild his house.

Sean Graham was alive to the unit's wider purpose to "interpret" the aims, policies, and activities of government, and saw this as a particularly important task "since the country today is in a state of transition from the age-old tribalism of the past into modern nationhood on the Western model."[33] Writing in 1955, Graham criticized the label "fundamental education" as a little "grandiose, a little vague." Instead he defined this work as "nation-building: an exciting and delicate process in which politicians, civil servants, writers, teachers, artists and propagandists alike are consciously involved." Graham recognized the role of film here in "[d]eliberately changing the direction of a society or accelerating the pace of evolution."[34]

It was not merely in its themes and narratives that these films were seeking to bridge this transition between old and new, to prepare for self-government, and to represent the development of skilled African leadership. The form of these films also reveals both a rising African voice and the ongoing ambiguities with these moves. First, the films pointedly reject the Sellers technique. The opening of *Progress in Kojokrom* includes crane shots and crowded frames, while a later film, such as *Mr. Mensah Builds a House,* opens at the end—the soundtrack explains "now his house is all but done, let me tell you how it all begun"—and parallel cuts between two stories, crediting the audience to relate and construct meaning from these images. Most notably Kofi's request to Mr. Mensah for more money to complete the building work

FIGURE 5.3. Filming on *Mr. Mensah Builds a House* (1955). Courtesy of Information Services Department, Ghana.

FIGURE 5.4. On set with the Gold Coast Film Unit in 1956. Courtesy of Information Services Department, Ghana.

on his house is immediately followed by a close-up of a trolley with alcohol and expensive beauty products.

Secondly, the new African voices become more vocal in these films as the decade progresses. In *The Boy Kumasenu* in 1951, the British commentator provides virtually the only voice. The opening of *Progress in Kojokrom* in 1953 now includes characters speaking in multiple languages, but it still retains a Voice of God narration ("All this didn't mean very much to us"). Basil Wright was critical of this "rather pompous commentary" and suggested that "if the visual incidents are sufficiently understood by the local audiences, would it be better to leave them to draw their own conclusions?"[35] In *Mr. Mensah Builds a House* in 1955, the narrative is told through the dialogue of the predominantly African characters. There is additional narrative guidance from the soundtrack—"Own your house and love your wife, you'll taste happiness all your life. Until a few weeks ago Mr. Mensah did not know"—but this is sung by African voices. Furthermore, the characters move between languages (with a lot of dialogue in Fante), without subtitles or attempts at translation.

The role of Africans behind the camera remains more ambiguous (see Figures 5.3 and 5.4). Official production stills from the set of *Progress in Kojokrom* reveal an almost exclusively African crew filming the African cast, yet the opening credits contain only European names.[36] Graham had cited a "lack of African creative talent" as "the major obstacle" for the unit's progress and speculated in 1952 that "perhaps it is

FIGURE 5.5. Staff at work for the Gold Coast Film Unit in 1956. Courtesy of Information Services Department, Ghana.

too early in a country still so largely concerned with the problems of survival and subsistence."[37] The unit employed "about 20 African junior technical staff" by the mid-1950s (see Figure 5.5) and the trainees from the Accra school receive credits on later films such as *Mr. Mensah Builds a House* (Sam Aryeetey as editor and R. O. Fenuku as camera operator), but the directors and writers remained almost exclusively European.[38]

There is a curious dichotomy within the GCFU, as it sought to lead and emblematize the moves toward self-government, while continuing to rely on British leadership and creative talent. Bloom and Skinner have challenged this reliance on European creativity, arguing, with reference to *The Boy Kumasenu,* that the unit's films invited creative local input and improvisation which permitted "alternative readings," while I have highlighted the need to look beyond the screen, at the integral "creative" role of the local commentator. Documentary historian Martin Stollery has usefully questioned the categorization of African staff and the binary of British and local personnel, noting that many of the African staff were themselves recruited from Achimota College, "an elite institution run along British public-school lines."[39]

Certainly Graham rejected comparisons with other "colonial" units, stating recently that "colonial was a dirty word in my vocabulary and we were a local unit."[40] The construction of the local here was as much about sensibility as personnel. George Noble explained in 1952: "Mostly, the films made by other units in the Colonies were small, single-reelers. Graham decided to make longer films, story films, films about the Africans themselves, played by themselves, in their own land, about their own people."[41] After his 1955 visit to the West Indies, in which he celebrated the "bubbling, robust, exuberance of Trinidad folk-lore," Graham was most perplexed by the failure of these other government film units to incorporate local culture into their films. He noted how young intellectuals in Trinidad, "with the problem of rapid change from Colonialism into nationhood, have understood the uniqueness and vigour of their calypsos, steel-bands and Carnival." Graham celebrated the fact that Trinidad youngsters were no longer imitating "Dickens, Pirandello and Shaw," but instead "have gone back to their own Trinidad to write in patois, drawing on the immensely rich folk-lore of that turbulent melting pot of so many races and cultures." Yet while hugely excited by the upsurge in music, drama, and art, Graham did not see this replicated in film. He complained about the complete lack of contact with local writers and artists and urged local units "not to stick to their dreary formulas."[42] By contrast Graham and Noble mixed socially, (romantically) and professionally with local Africans. Indeed Graham invariably complained that the European writers and filmmakers he brought out to assist the unit—including Ray Elton, Louis MacNeice, and Montgomery Tully—failed to understand the local culture. Writing in 1952 to Basil Wright, Graham complained about Tully's failure "to make any friends among the Africans." "The man is so sensitive that I cannot push him out into the village and tell him to make friends with the locals," Graham wrote. "Yet I cannot see what good it will do our scripts for Tully to swap confidences with the Europeans in the club."[43]

Yet Graham continued to rely on these creative figures from the UK. This is not to diminish the significance or progressive nature of the unit, but rather to recognize that the complexities of the nations were encapsulated not only in the films on screen (their themes, narrative, and forms) but also in the construction and development of the units themselves. This is equally true in Nigeria, where the film unit reflected, responded to, and recorded the broader constitutional changes across the last decade of colonial rule.

THE NIGERIAN FILM UNIT AND THE ONGOING INFLUENCE OF THE CFU

The Nigerian Film Unit was established in 1949 but was reorganized into regional units in line with the constitutional changes implemented in 1954. By 1957, when Western and Eastern Nigeria achieved self-government (Northern Nigeria would follow in 1959), the governments of the

Eastern, Western, and Northern regions all had production units, which were looking to manage the transition from colonial rule, predominantly on British terms. This was also the primary focus of the Federal Film Unit and nearly all of the thirteen films it released in 1957 covered official, formal ceremonies and state visits, with titles such as *Another Step Forward* (the Constitutional Conference), *Nigeria Hails Her Prime Minister* and *Tour of H. R. H., the Princess Royal*. The Western Nigeria government's first two major films, *Forward to a New Nigeria* (1958) and *Self-Government Celebrations for Western Nigeria* (1958), similarly celebrated the pageantry and performance of constitutional change as a way of simultaneously endorsing an enduring British influence.[44]

The nature and scale of these units varied. A report from William Sellers in 1958 estimated that while the Federal Film Unit produced seventy-five reels in both 35mm and 16mm a year, none of the regional units produced more than eight 35mm reels and the largest other 16mm producer, the Northern Nigeria Information Service, was making twenty-six 16mm reels annually. However, the Western Nigeria government reached by far the largest audience, operating forty-eight mobile units (Northern Nigeria had ten, the Federal and Eastern Nigerian units, two each).[45] *Film User* described the Western Nigeria government's growing fleet of mobile cinemas as "a veritable Aladdin's Lamp to millions of people living in the remote and almost inaccessible jungle and creek areas of undeveloped Africa." The Western Nigeria government launched six barges at Epe Boatyard in 1957, which joined their forty mobile cinema vans. These units reached 2,239 towns and villages and an estimated audience of more than five million in 1957 (another estimate placed the figure above ten million).[46] The extension and application of the CFU's work was then partly dependent on the priorities of the government. *Film User* credited the "progressive government" of Western Nigeria with ensuring that "millions of citizens living in the hinterland are now having regular glimpses of a wider world."[47]

The descriptions of these film shows reveal both the extension of government propaganda into new territories and the importance of those local figures working for the units. The barges traveled with a bargemaster, a projectionist/engineer, and a commentator. These crews were performing government work, using the films as part of "special publicity campaigns" and provided "weekly summaries of Government activities in English and the appropriate vernacular language." What is striking here is that they traveled largely unsupervised, with the Western Nigeria government employing ninety-six local staff in 1958 and only four "expatriates." The proportion shifted somewhat with the more production-led Federal Film Unit, where there were eleven expatriates alongside seventy-eight local staff.[48]

Despite the increasing local presence within these units, the Nigerian Film Unit and its regional offspring much more closely followed the conventions of the Colonial Film Unit than its Gold Coast counterparts. Its first production, *Smallpox* (1950), directed by Lionel Snazelle and photographed by Sydney Samuelson, became as emblematic of the Nigerian Film Unit as *The Boy Kumasenu* was for the Gold Coast. A dramatized Mr. Wise and Mr. Foolish film, *Smallpox* continues the work of William Sellers in Nigeria. It not only follows Sellers's specialized technique, but also, in functioning as part of a larger health campaign, mirrors his earliest work as a sanitary inspector. For example, *Smallpox* presents an African man carrying a sandwich board—with a finger on the poster image pointing at the viewer—reading "to escape smallpox you must be vaccinated." It shows the mobile vaccination van in operation (of course with smiling patients) and reiterates the personal dangers to each audience member.[49]

Smallpox was repeatedly cited by Sellers and the Colonial Office as *the* shining example of what these local units could achieve. The Colonial Office reported that *Smallpox* "has achieved a notable success. Critics in London described it as one of the best documentaries of its kind ever to be produced by a Colonial Unit," further adding that the film had "stimulated interest in vaccinations" throughout Nigeria.[50] C. Y. Carstairs later claimed that the film had been "shown all over Africa (as well as winning critical laurels elsewhere)," often under the auspices of UNESCO, while Sellers described it as "perhaps one of the best films that have been made by any unit connected with the Colonial Film Unit." Sellers also noted the film's widely quoted success in Tanganyika. Norman Spurr measured this success by the "marked increase in voluntary vaccination," which Carstairs said brought forward a crowd for vaccination after a screening in one part of Tanganyika "larger than the number of people who according to the census ought to be living there at all."[51]

It is hardly surprising that *Smallpox* became the defining film of the Nigerian Film Unit, as this was such a clear successor to the work of Sellers and the CFU, an example of what they wanted these units to produce. This model is followed in *Back to the Community* (1954), filmed over a few months in Oji. It tells the story of Okeke, a "very lucky man" with "the perfect life . . . a nice wife, a nice house, work and dancing," who contracts leprosy. The film shows, at great length, the process from when Okeke discovers (and fails to acknowledge) the disease, to his return to the cheering community three years later. The film is unfailingly earnest and devoid of the innovation, humor, or local vibrancy associated with its neighboring unit. It celebrates British medical interventions, presenting British researchers, nurses, and doctors "who have studied the disease for many years" working with suited Africans, and presents both British and African men and women within the operating theatre. The film rejects local tradition (the treatment from the medicine man Okeke initially visits is expensive, painful, and ineffective) in favor of modern British medicine, which the commentator repeatedly states elicits "no pain." However, there are a couple of striking points with this film. First, *Back to the Community* was directed by James Otigbah, with photography by Alex Fajemisin, both products of the Accra training school. The local filmmakers in Nigeria often assumed more senior roles than their Gold Coast counterparts and this further problematizes attempts to define the "local" or "African" nature of the unit by the nationality of its personnel. Secondly, while the film reveals government "intent," its effectiveness is less clear. Dr Arthur Garrett, an area superintendent in Oji River, complained that *Back to the Community* was seen more in London and Paris than in Africa, failing in its aims to "awaken the conscience of the African to the problems and the preventative measures of leprosy." The observation reminds us that while these films were primarily intended for local audiences, they often served instead to show educated European audiences the work in the colonies and to project a fantasy of colonial ideology in action.[52]

The clearest evidence of the NFU's debt to William Sellers's earlier work is in *Health and Baby Week, Lagos, 1956*, a virtual remake of Sellers's earliest prewar films, which celebrates the ongoing work of the British in colonial health. Health is again a metaphor for the nation— "healthy children mean a healthy future for Nigeria"—promoted both by government and the commercial companies that would continue to operate beyond independence (for example, a float promotes "Lux— the lovely white toilet soap"). The messages of cooperation and "progress" are played out on screen. One float shows an African dressed as St. George fighting "the dragon of ignorance, filth, disease and superstition," while the militarized parades of Africans (including girl guides, scouts, and nurses) display the nation ordered and contained under the watchful eye of the governor general. This order features commonly across other news items, such as *Nigeria's First Women Police* (1956), a projection of British authority that seeks to legitimize the police as a national authority in the face of escalating, unmentioned, challenges. These films appear to willfully misdirect, anaesthetizing the viewers through repetition (both visually and sonically). This is the art of looking the other way, of blocking out the rising sounds and images that are increasingly edging into the frame. Historian Charles Ambler argued that while the Department of Information in Kenya did expand its mobile cinema network during the Mau Mau uprising in the 1950s, there was no evidence of any significant change to its programming. Ambler's work suggests a government interest in the "spectacle of movie shows, rather than the movie content," and he argues that in Kenya many officials saw film shows as a way to "divert Africans from political activity."[53] Even if the films deliberately avoided showing tensions on screen, these tensions increasingly motivated the work of local units.

This is particularly evident in Malaya, where the Emergency (the anticolonial struggle that defined the last decade of colonial rule) shaped the work and operations of the Malayan Film Unit. Having produced nineteen films in its first three years, the MFU became an integral part of the government's Emergency propaganda campaign in 1950, producing fifty-two films in the year followed by 111 in 1951. Twenty-four of these were related to the Emergency. The Emergency Information Services added thirty public address vans and traveling cinemas to the twenty-three it already had in service in 1951 in a bid "to tell the story of the Emergency to people who live even in the remotest parts of the country." By 1954, there were ninety-two mobile units (giving a total of 17,092 shows during the year), extended to 123 by 1957 and 134 by 1959. The units played not only in Malay villages and kampongs but also in Chinese resettlement areas, as most of the MFU films were available in four languages—English, Malay, Tamil, and Mandarin Chinese. In short, the Emergency created, and accelerated, the infrastructure for the production, distribution, and exhibition of film across Malaya.[54]

While some of the MFU films responded directly to the Emergency, the MFU's response was equally tied up in instructional films highlighting the benefits of literacy (*The Letter,* 1953), the welfare of the blind (*Touch and Go,* 1953), the government's pension scheme (*Worry Free,* 1954), or rehabilitation through the prison services (*A Better Man,* 1953). In promoting self-sufficiency, modern welfare services, and a Western model of citizenship, the MFU assumed an active role in building the modern nation-state, combatting the communist threat by imagining a new, modern nation on British terms. "It has helped to train the people in the methods and standards of elections and census taking," MFU head Tom Hodge wrote at independence in 1957, "and to encourage a sense of responsible citizenship."⁵⁵

Crucially the MFU's work was also seen overseas—at festivals, in cinemas, and on TV broadcasts—keeping "Malaya's achievements in the eyes of the world." This served both to foster international support for Britain's continued (military) involvement in Malaya, and also to project this rhetoric of colonial development and welfare to other colonial audiences. In 1955, 121 MFU films played overseas (often reworked in newsreels) reaching fifty-four different countries in 1956.⁵⁶ Other units share this (often unspoken) interest in reaching international audiences. While the Nigerian Film Unit's Eastmancolor film of the Queen's 1956 tour to Nigeria, *Nigeria Greets the Queen*, was "made primarily for Nigerians," there was pressure to screen this in British cinemas. The *Daily Mail* asked, "Are other countries to see what will be an effective answer to Russian charges of Colonial oppression?" and was delighted to learn that America, Australia, Canada, and India had asked for copies.⁵⁷

The British crown feature prominently and repeatedly in these "local" productions, as a way of positioning and perpetuating a British lineage within the colonies. The Colonial Office reported that in Kenya the three color Royal Tour films, recorded in Swahili and English, were the most popular of 1957, while even in colonies with less organized production units, royal visits provided the catalyst for film work.⁵⁸ For example, the Visual Education branch of the Education Department in Mauritius produced a 16mm color film (processed in England), *And the Princess Came . . .* (1956), to commemorate the visit of Princess Margaret. The Colonial Office noted: "Never before had Mauritius received as much publicity as on this Royal Occasion," highlighting how these royal visits served to project a vision of the (loyal) colony overseas.⁵⁹ In Nigeria, the Princess Royal's tour was the subject of the Western region's ambitious 85-minute color documentary, *Self-Government for Western Nigeria* (1958). The film serves to endorse Britain's historical role and continuing influence within Nigeria. It promotes the region's "loyalty and affection to the Queen," shows cheering crowds waving the Union Jack and, as with films of independence days, shows the literal exchange (and continuation) of British traditions and customs. The region's premier, Chief Awolowo, acknowledges that the handing over of a ceremonial mace represents a "heritage of experience being passed to a young and forthright nation." Chief Awolowo is positioned within the British establishment throughout, dancing with the governor's wife and making speeches for the Princess Royal. Once more, any unrest is exorcised from the frame. Even when the commentator notes that the princess's visit to the University at Ibadan was cancelled, he does not explain the source or level of student unrest that forced the closure of the college for over a month.

The imported British traditions sit alongside images of the modern state, reflected here in the "new offices" of the Ministry of Home Affairs or the transportation advances (such as the repeated shots of planes). Brian Larkin shows how the films of Northern Nigeria served to "spectacularize" the infrastructural developments of the state, creating a "visual mantra, tying the construction of industry and infrastructure to the politics of national development."[60] This is evident in *Giant in the Sun*, a beautiful color documentary released to mark self-government in Northern Nigeria in 1959. The film was intended for British and international audiences with a longer version, *Our Land and People*, simultaneously produced and edited in London for Nigerian audiences. *Giant in the Sun* celebrates the social advances within Nigeria in industry, health, agriculture, and education, presenting a confluence of British and Nigerian influences, which is most clearly articulated in a staged sequence in which the British governor asks the premier to explain the new legislation. Recalling interwar colonial documentary, the editing serves to highlight "advances" in transport, housing, and agriculture—shots of the traditional replaced by the modern—while the film also seeks to present disparate cultures and religions together within the modern nation. Larkin refers to the "utopian ideal of a modern, yet still religious, Northern Nigeria," and the films show both Muslim and Christian celebrations, reaffirming that "complete religious toleration is enjoyed."[61]

Nation-building is imagined in myriad ways across these films, including health, religion, and policing. *Giant in the Sun* provides a particularly apposite example of the ways in which industry and national development are entwined. The commentary defines Nigeria through industry ("mechanised industry is more and more becoming a part of modern Nigeria") and explains that the Northern Region's government is "reconciling . . . modern production methods with the older skills." The film credits these modern methods and industries to the British (and "famous British firms") working closely with the regional government. Industry is a signifier of national growth. Over shots of modern industry, the commentator in *Giant in the Sun* concludes that Nigeria is moving toward "full nationhood within the British Commonwealth." This message is even more clearly outlined in the Northern

Nigerian Information Service's illustrated history of the region, also entitled *Giant in the Sun,* which features images from the film. The book contains a foreword by the governor, Sir Gawain Westray Bell, in which he notes "the trust and friendship which over half a century has held European and African in a common bond—a bond which is not to be severed at Self-Government." The book praises the historical role of the British and concludes that "self-government will not bring any lessening of friendship between the North and its old masters."[62]

In this way, industry is both the reason for self-government (the attainment of modern, economic *value*) and its most enduring tie, a colonial legacy that ensures that British interests and influence remain within the colony. Historian Francis Gooding considers the example of the mining industry within *Giant in the Sun.* While the film suggests that this industry will boost the newly independent Nigerian state, Gooding highlights how these British companies continued to operate with no discernible break, pocketing larger profits and, in his particular example, failing to mention, let alone worry about, independence within the company minutes.[63] Industry here is a means of working through the end of empire.

Film played an important part in this. For example, commercial companies increasingly saw the mobile cinema circuit as a productive way to advertise. In Nigeria, Mobile Films West Africa Ltd. put on free outdoor cinema shows, with its first tour in 1959 reaching an audience of 237,700 in towns and villages. The CFU had envisaged an audience receptive to government propaganda, and advertisers were now "quick to take advantage of this enthusiasm," still describing the cinema screen's "magic of novelty" and presenting the African viewer "as fresh and enthusiastic as our children." *Film User* reported that "snatches of advertising jingles are today being sung or whistled in the most out of way places," explaining that nine manufacturers of soap, petrol, cosmetics, and household appliances had paid for advertising during the two-hour show. The report noted increases in sales with mobile cinema staff redirecting those viewers eager to buy products on the spot to local stockists.[64] Charles Ambler noted a similar trend in Kenya in the late 1950s, with the Nairobi-based East African Film Services incorporating fifteen minutes of advertising in its ninety-minute entertainment show.[65] This is, of course, no great departure from earlier government uses of the vans, and while the specifics of what they were selling may change (a government scheme or soap), the broader purpose (economic) and sell (modern, Western ideology) remain the same, with film exercising its soft power to mediate between empire and commonwealth.

Film itself is often emblematic of this industrial continuity. *Giant in the Sun* was directed by Sydney Samuelson, a London-based former member of the CFU who worked for the Nigerian Film Unit a decade earlier on *Smallpox*. It was edited by Dennis Bowden, one of the postwar CFU trainees, and produced by Victor Gover, formerly the CFU's chief editor, who was commissioned to make the film by the Northern Nigerian Information Service. Gover now ran the Overseas Film and Television Centre (OFTVC), which emerged from the ashes of the Colonial Film Unit in 1954 and sought "to continue the work of the unit as a commercial enterprise." Gover had identified that the local overseas units would still need a technical agent working "in one of the world capitals." "It was explained to the overseas units that working alone they would, separately, be comparatively 'small voices'," Gover explained at a UNESCO conference in 1958, "but as members of a Central organisation, their existence and importance would be more easily recognised and, in consequence, their needs would be better served."[66] The models seen in other industries are here applied to film, arguing for, and realizing, the move from empire to commonwealth.

Alongside the federal and later regional units in Nigeria, the OFTVC also served government units in East Africa, in Uganda, Kenya, and Tanganyika as well as Sudan.[67] The production work in these colonies was generally on a much smaller scale. The unit in Kenya did produce some films (in six African languages) to support specific campaigns—like *Registration of Voters* and *How You Vote* in 1956—but its work often appeared to cater to expatriate or international audiences. This might be achieved through its own productions like *Samaki* (1959), which promoted fishing and "big game sport" in the region, or by helping visiting commercial units.[68] Other colonial units in the latter days of empire would also shift their focus to international audiences, most notably the Central African Film Unit. After the formation of the Central African Federation in 1953, its 16mm work for local African audiences, foregrounded in its first five years, was largely replaced by 35mm films produced almost exclusively for expatriate and overseas audiences.[69] These films promoted the formation and work of the federation overseas (*Two Generations*, 1955), celebrated and romanticized colonial rule (*See Saw Years*, 1963), or encouraged tourism and immigration (*Fairest Africa*, 1959). CAFU also produced a newsreel for European audiences, *Federal Spotlight,* until 1963, an anachronistic fantasy that pointedly failed to acknowledge the social and political changes within the federation but instead began the process of curating the memory of empire for British audiences.

The units in East Africa were often dependent on one or two men. In Uganda, this usually comprised one European producer/cameraman and an African assistant cameraman working for the Department of Information. The films it produced were largely consistent with the earlier work of the CFU, producing a cinemagazine (often with sporting scenes or visits from the governor or royalty), films for police recruitment (*Situma Joins the Police*), for industry (*The Preparation of Coffee* for the Bugisu Coffee Board), and a series of productions in advance of the 1958 elections (such as *How to Vote*). However, the unit's demise illustrates the rickety nature of these operations, dependent on both shifting political support and a few individuals. The Uganda Film Unit abruptly ceased production in the latter part of the 1950s when the producer returned to the UK and the Ugandan cameraman was killed in a car accident.[70]

It was a similar story in Tanganyika, where a series of government film initiatives in the first half of the 1950s dissipated as personnel left and government priorities shifted. Initially after the CFU's departure in 1950, it appeared to be business as usual. The commissioner for social development took on responsibility for film, and appointed Norman Spurr as his films research officer in July 1951. Spurr would continue the work he had performed for the CFU, again privileging visual storytelling and working closely with government departments. The success of these films was now determined by their impact in administering, and facilitating, government work. A typical example from Spurr was *Dipping* (1952), a 16mm color film produced at the request of the veterinary officer, which supported a scheme designed to combat the parasitic ticks causing cattle deaths. The film was deemed a success in most areas, prompting the veterinary officer to ask Spurr to produce a sequel of sorts, *We Benefit—We Pay*, which would show the economic benefits of dipping.[71] Other films produced during this period by the Department of Social Development recalled the earlier works of Sellers and the kinds of pageantry filmed by the NFU. For example, Governor Twining featured prominently in both *Northern Province Agricultural Show* (1952), inspecting the stalls and parades, and *The Sukumuland Trade and Agricultural Exhibition* (1954).

At the same time (from the second half of 1951), the Tanganyika government paid £13,000 a year to the Johannesburg-based African Film Productions to make "African entertainment films." One of the primary aims in Tanganyika was to see "how readily Africans could produce their own stories, scripts, casts and film technicians," providing the audience with "an essentially African story played almost entirely by his own African artistes."[72] This may sound like the development of a local unit, but given that the government had looked to apartheid South Africa and to African Film Productions (AFP), a company traditionally associated with the rise of Afrikaner nationalism, the reality was very different.[73] Donald Wynne, who oversaw the scheme for AFP, betrayed the unit's dominant racial prejudices when explaining that while there was no shortage of African labor in Tanganyika, "it is limited to fetching and carrying and any minor technical task of necessity has to be done by the European." As Norman Spurr earlier noted, "It does not follow that a film about Africans, and in which Africans take part, is an African film. It may be little more than Hollywood or Wardour Street with a change of cast."[74]

In its two and a half years in Tanganyika, AFP produced enough short comedies, newsreels, and feature films to fill four entertainment programs (between 90–120 minutes). In this work, they largely followed the Sellers technique, proving, according to one report, that "a straight forward story, simply presented, a slow tempo, is acceptable to unsophisticated audiences."[75] By the second half of the 1950s, these government units in East Africa prioritized their mobile exhibition, with their limited production work largely undertaken by government individuals working with specific departments. The units did retain a more literal connection with London through the OFTVC. Aside from processing, providing stock and replacement parts, the OFTVC undertook sound recording, titling, optical effects, and, to varying degrees, editing (see Figure 5.6). On other occasions, and especially on larger productions, it sent out additional European staff to support the units. Gover recalled his experiences on *Nigeria Greets the Queen*. The OFTVC filmed the Queen's departure from London before the NFU undertook all filming in Nigeria (with two cameramen loaned from the Gold Coast Film Unit). Gover outlined the scale of the OFTVC's job "to edit the film, write the commentary, record the narration using three different voices and the music and effects, cut the negative, make the optical effects and produce a top-grade Eastmancolour answer print," all within three weeks of the tour's completion.[76]

William Sellers praised the "highly satisfactory" work of the OFTVC, "happily" filling the gap left by the CFU. Over a period of almost forty years, through to the early 1990s, the OFTVC was responsible for about three thousand films. It also exercised a continuing influence across the former colonies through its extensive training programs, which fitted the development rhetoric used to defend and justify the British Empire.

FIGURE 5.6. The cover of *Colonial Cinema*, March 1953. Lionel Snazelle, head of the Nigerian Film Unit, flew to Soho Square to work with Vic Gover on a "census" film that was used as part of a propaganda campaign in Nigeria.

Speaking in 1958, Gover emphasized the long-term development of local filmmakers, stressing in language that was similarly used to temper the pace of moves toward independence, that time and experience were required, that "good training plus experience, and yet more experience, finally produces a filmmaker." Gover explained that this long process of "experience gathering" would not happen "overnight," but hoped that when the units were ready, the OFTVC would be on hand "backing up the technicians and ready to give them service and advice."[77]

The OFTVC offered, as a "start," a six-month training course to six Nigerian students in London in 1958. The principal teacher for this was 83-year-old George Pearson. Pearson wrote in very familiar terms of the aims, structure, and challenges of the course. "Their audiences will often consist of adults who cannot read or write," Pearson wrote, "are primitive in custom and environment, heirs of an age-long tradition of folk-lore, fetish and strange superstition." The students were expected to study the "accepted laws of mental progress," a reaffirmation of colonial ideology that emboldens a lineage from the earliest films of Sellers to the work of many units beyond independence. Indeed, the

OFTVC would continue to operate its training schools well beyond independence, establishing "a very big business" and produced students "that would come back to us eventually." The close links between the CFU and OFTVC continued into the 1960s, as this training work was performed during the decade by a new principal, Norman Spurr.[78]

GOVERNMENT IN ACTION: THE UNITS IN THE WEST INDIES

When Sean Graham visited the West Indies in 1955, he offered a damning verdict of the local units. Graham displayed some leniency toward the Trinidad Film Unit's "modest" two-person operation, but was less forgiving of the larger Jamaica Film Unit, determining that "it has not yet achieved professional standards, least of all in its scripts." Graham was particularly dismissive of *Let's Stop Them* (1953), in many ways the JFU's flagship production, which he tellingly misnamed "Stop It," complaining that "its craftsmanship is negligible, and the acting is pure caricature." Graham ultimately suggested that if there were no more funds, "or better talent," production should be abandoned as "premature."[79]

Graham's verdict was clearly shaped by his attitude toward documentary and his affiliation to a Griersonian model. Dismissing the ethos of the CFU, Graham wrote that film should "never be left as a plaything for amateurs," a view he said was borne out by his experiences in the West Indies. He was particularly critical of the pedagogical imperatives motivating this cinema. He noted that the Trinidad Film Unit was operated by the Ministry of Education and that the head of the Jamaica Film Unit, Martin Rennalls, "is primarily an Assistant Education Officer and does not pretend to be a film technician, let alone a writer or director." Graham's self-identification as a filmmaker shaped his value judgments, prompting him to dismiss the work of many other local units and to reject pointedly the principles of William Sellers.[80]

Graham was certainly right to foreground Martin Rennalls's background in education. Rennalls, who would head the JFU from its inception in 1951 until 1970, was every bit as important and influential in shaping Jamaican film culture as Graham and Snazelle were in West Africa. Rennalls was a former primary school headmaster who had initially looked to use film in the classroom, so successfully that the community raised money for a permanent projector and screening space to cater for additional evening shows. For this, Rennalls established a set of rules for school staff, consistent with the work of the CFU, explaining that "the film is an aid to be used in conjunction with other instructional materials" and that the film is "not intended to replace the warmth and personality of the teacher and his/her personal methods."[81]

Rennalls's desire to learn more about the use of films in schools took him to London for a year in 1948 on a scholarship to study "audio-visual education" at the Institute of Education. He then spent an additional three months at the end of 1949 training with George Pearson at Soho Square. His contemporary running the film operations in Barbados, Isaac Carmichael, had recently completed a course at the Visual Education Centre in Exeter through a British Council Scholarship before also spending time with the CFU in Soho Square.[82] Both would then attend the CFU's training school in Kingston, alongside the other founding members of the JFU, Milton Weller and Trevor Welsh. There are two immediate points to reiterate here. First that this government cinema in the West Indies was motivated by education, evidenced by Carmichael's title in Barbados, where he worked as "Supervisor of Visual Education." Secondly, these filmmakers were largely products of the CFU. In 1954 Rennalls spent a further six months in London training "at the feet" of George Pearson, whom he clearly viewed very fondly as a mentor. One of the striking features in Jamaica is that the CFU gained increasing influence after the war, in an almost complete reversal of the situation in the Gold Coast.[83]

On completing the CFU training school, Rennalls met with Alexander Bustamante, the chief minister of Jamaica, to launch a one-year trial of the Jamaica Film Unit from 1 October 1951. The formation of the JFU seemingly answered the escalating postwar calls for Jamaican productions. Mobile cinema operators repeatedly demanded local films to "further change the country for good," explaining that this was "of paramount importance to our work," while a conference at the Information Office late in 1945 on the "Production of Films" had outlined the need for a Central Film Organization (set up in 1946) "to promote the production and use of films and other visual aids."[84] Writing in 1953, Rennalls expounded the JFU's role in bridging a "great gap" in Jamaica's Visual Education Service. "Educational films from foreign sources are shrouded in an atmosphere of strangeness where our local population is concerned," he argued, suggesting that in contrast, when audiences see local productions "they cheer, they sympathise, they comment, they lament—seeing themselves for the first time, as others see them."[85] In responding to this need for "local" productions, the JFU, ironically, formalized closer affiliations with the CFU, particularly through its training. The JFU's mantra that it was producing "films in Jamaica, for Jamaicans and by Jamaicans," matched that proposed by Pearson, Grierson, and others at "The Film in Colonial Development" conference in 1948. In short, the vision of the local unit in Jamaica manifested the goals of the postwar CFU.

The influence of the CFU can certainly be seen across the JFU's work. There are practical reasons for this, as initially the JFU had to send all postproduction work to England. This meant, for example, that soundtracks were initially prepared and recorded in England, prompting some critics to label the music and voiceover as "inauthentic." A typical note from William Sellers in 1955, regarding the film of Princess Margaret's tour, provides a glimpse of the postproduction process. "Are you sending any recordings?" Sellers asked via telegram. "Do you particularly wish for a Jamaican commentator? Depending on early receipt from you of credit titles [we] hope [to] complete [the] film by end of next week."[86] The Jamaican government had supported the continuation of the CFU in 1953, contributing £200 a year to assist its "training and advisory activities," and determined that the Central Film Organization was "not yet able to stand on its own." When the CFU closed its doors a couple of years later, the OFTVC seamlessly stepped in, with the support of the director of education and Martin Rennalls. Rennalls later stated that this move "did not affect nor diminish the technical help and support we were previously receiving."[87]

The JFU did, however, develop and grow its local facilities. In November 1954, it received funding to expand its 35mm production in local cinemas and then, in 1957, to update its equipment, introducing synchronized sound, employing further staff (there were thirty-two members by 1959), doubling its production and extending its present accommodation (the unit was initially housed in premises above the racecourse before moving to Hanover Street). The number of mobile vans also increased, so that in 1959 there were 1,093 shows given to 128,611 people.[88] These developments would appear to indicate moves toward a more "local" cinema, the development of an increasingly autonomous, independent unit in step with the moves toward political independence. However, Rennalls's account of this period challenges such a view. Rennalls cites the early period—when most directly aligned to the CFU—as its apex, a time when the JFU operated with most freedom. In 1957, with Norman Manley and the People's National Party now in power, the Central Film Organization moved from the Ministry of Education to the recently formed public relations office, and Rennalls's role shifted from assistant education officer to films officer. Rennalls argued that the unit's work was "brought closer to propaganda than ever before," with ministers regularly appearing on screen and the unit "required to participate in propagandising the work of the government much more than it had ever done before." Rennalls also noted increased political intervention, with the JFU forced to shelve its "most ambitious and longest" production on family planning (*Too Late*, 1957) after completion, as the subject became a "political football" with the opposition party launching a campaign against family planning.[89] The shift may indicate differing approaches toward film propaganda. In the early years, Rennalls sat on (and was secretary of) the advisory committee that brought together representatives from various ministries and came up with a priority list of productions. This widely used model was scrapped by 1958 in favor of more direct government intervention. Of course, these JFU films were always intended to support and further government campaigns, but the CFU's approach was often to "sugar the pill," looking to foreground "education" and to embed rather than reveal its government workings.[90]

The films themselves reveal, and testify to, the complex moves toward independence. Film historian Terri Francis identifies four types of film produced by the JFU: story, news, instructional, and history.[91] These categories often overlap, and are united in their service to the nation-building process. *It Can Happen to You* (1956), a Mr. Wise and Mr. Foolish narrative showing two brothers with venereal disease, is a neat example of this. The personal, individual tale is always presented in relation to the nation as a whole. The film opens by showing active, internationally successful Jamaicans and states that these achievements can only continue if everyone gives of their best, which depends on the "mental and physical fitness of the individual." The commentator aligns the health of the individual with the health of the nation, next explaining: "It is in the field of health however that lies one of the greatest threats to the island's future prosperity." At the film's conclusion, a government minister provides the take-home message of the film, stating that "venereal disease is a national problem because it is retarding the development of the country."

In *Builders of the Nation* (1958), made with the Education Department, a prospective school teacher, Ted Williams, ponders his future. Evidently a project close to director Martin Rennalls's heart, the film presents teaching as an opportunity for "service, to help build and mold the lives of our people." The role of the teacher is to turn their pupils into "confident and useful citizens" and into "useful members of their community," seeing education as part of the citizenship process and again defining citizens by their usefulness to the nation. A later film shows how a classroom arithmetic exercise, in which the children play shops, serves in "developing habits of courtesy," revealing again the citizenship prerogatives motivating education. *Together We Build* (1953), which shows the more literal building of the nation through government self-help house-building schemes, concludes with a mantra sung over a montage of images: "The more we build together, the happier we shall be." These films are partly a response to the increased emigration of young men to England, a call for these men to stay and build their own nation. *Builders of the Nation* actually concludes with Ted departing for England on a scholarship (as Rennalls had done). While the commentator assures the viewers that Ted will return from his English university, England remains an aspirational land, in this case a place to train before returning as a "builder of the nation."[92]

Footage from *Builders of the Nation* also appears in *Education Programme Part One*, which is part of the later series "Our Government at Work." While the message may be familiar (the commentator emphasizes the need for "more qualified Jamaicans" to help develop "their Island home"), as a later JFU film the involvement of government is much more explicit. The film includes footage of a government meeting and a lengthy direct address to camera from a minister talking through a "Chart of Education System." The film's focus is now on promoting the part of government in the kinds of initiatives earlier shown in *Builders of the Nation*, stating, for example, that "government is spending about £300,000 to provide school places for 16,000 more pupils annually" and, over footage from *Builders of the Nation*, that "government is spending £70,000 to build 40 teachers cottages each year."

Other West Indian units similarly used film to promote government initiatives and, in particular, an economic model for nation-building that prioritized cooperative schemes. This reflected the welfare goals of the postwar Labour government and sought to stave off rising resistance and opposition to the colonial authorities by projecting a communal, egalitarian, participatory model for colonial workers.[93] This is evident in the films produced in British Guiana, which build on its initial production from the CFU training school, *Co-Operative Rice Farming*. *Building Homes Together* (ca. 1955), made with the "co-operation of the members of the Lancaster Aided Self-Help Housing Scheme," and *The Good Hope* (1955), made with the "co-operation of the members of the Good

Hope Livestock Rearers' Society," present government self-help schemes in housing and agriculture. These cooperative, modernization schemes also appear prominently across every issue of the Guiana Film Unit's newsreel. Titles include "Rupununi Shows Progress" (showing a self-help housing scheme), "Guided Self-Help Scheme in Essequibo Islands" (which focuses on the building of roads), "Self-Helpers at Wakenham Get Houses" (which shows the first self-help groups to complete their houses), and "A Community at Work," showing a community development project. These films often show government in action. They regularly feature district commissioners, show the formation of cooperative committees, and include speeches from ministers and the governor. They also promote and outline government work (as in *Houses Assemble*, 1961, which shows the functions of the various ministers) and encourage participation and engagement with these new models of government (for example, *How to Exercise Your Vote*, which was revised for future elections).[94] Election films were produced by most local units, with one of the first local productions in Trinidad, *To Vote Is a Great Duty*, used by electoral officers in the buildup to the 1950 elections.[95]

The JFU films also projected forms of government. *Let's Stop Them* (1953), the tale of Slippery Sam, a praedial thief, highlights the cooperative response from farmers to the theft of bananas. The film depicts numerous meetings and committees (a district committee is established and a chairman selected) and shows the democratic process as the farmers vote in support, before resolutions are taken up the chain to the minister of agriculture, who signs a new law. Terri Francis describes this as a "morality pageant of participation," showing and encouraging audience members to take action.[96] While addressing a particular problem (praedial larceny), the film is more broadly showing the community response and projecting a model of government for the emerging nation. In doing this, the film also promotes the JFU as a tool for government. In one sequence, the governor Sir Hugh Foot gives a JBC radio broadcast to camera, which is followed by a shot of Jamaicans listening to the radio. This shows both *how* media works and also, by further broadcasting the words of the governor, positions film as a valuable component of a wider media, performing government work. As was common in MFU films, *Let's Stop Them* shows a plethora of posters, pamphlets, and newspaper advertisements, which outline the various ways to stop thieves and encourage the community to report offenders.[97]

A number of these films served more directly as citizenship training. For example, a series of three road safety films in 1959 outlined the appropriate behavior in the car (*Drive with Care*), on bikes (*Ride with Care*), and as pedestrians (*Walk with Care*). The films, produced at the request of the Traffic Committee of St. James Church Parish for "school children, motorists and the general public," show the effects and dangers of rapid modernization.[98] However, they place the responsibility and blame for this not on the technology but on the citizens using it. The films' tone recalls American travelogues of the period, but in their format they largely follow the Mr. Wise and Mr. Foolish format. In *Ride with Care*, the good cyclist arrives safely at work while the bad cyclist is knocked down by a car, and in *Drive with Care*, the reckless speedy driver causes a death while the careful driver reaches his destination safely and on time. The "good driver" in *Drive with Care* lives an aspirational middle-class life with his wife and friends, and while this is an instructional film for motorists, it equally serves as modern citizenship training.

These films, like the unit producing them, also continued to negotiate Jamaica's relationship with Britain and her position within the empire. The first production from the Jamaican trainees, *Farmer Brown Learns Good Dairying* (1951), was presented in the local press as a film "made in Jamaica by Jamaicans." Yet this traditional Mr. Wise and Mr. Foolish film inevitably bears the marks of the CFU instruction and, through its British instructor, who demonstrates modern farming methods to Farmer Brown, promotes the need for continued British assistance.[99] The traditional imperial relationship is most clearly represented in the news films depicting tours, for example of Churchill's 1953 visit and Princess Margaret's trip two years later, which celebrate and revere British leadership. *Churchill Visits Jamaica* consists of numerous crowd scenes in which Churchill is framed centrally and watched by thousands of spectators. The film shows fainting spectators carried away, which through the commentary and editing, is credited to the popular excitement at seeing Churchill rather than the stifling heat. The film perpetuates an uncomplicated relationship between leader and public, reinforced by a commentary that promotes a homogenous crowd, unified in their support for Churchill and the empire ("spontaneous cheers," "cheers and shouts of welcome reached a deafening roar"). These postwar tours were imagined as a way of generating loyalty to Britain and, by extension, of decelerating change and deflecting nationalist support. This loyalty was replayed and extended long after the figures had departed through the numerous, circulating films.

Screenings of these films sought to reconnect both the public and the leadership in Jamaica with the absent British leaders and, in the process, to foster prestige for the JFU. When *Princess Margaret Visits Jamaica* received a "Grand Premiere" at the Carib Theatre in April 1955, a large advertisement in the *Gleaner* explained that the event would take place "in the distinguished presence of His Excellency The Governor, Sir Hugh Foot, K. C. V. O., K. C. M. G." As a "special attraction" Sir Horace and his Merry Knights would play calypsos that they had sung (and presented) to the princess including "Princess Margaret Welcome Song" and "Her Majesty's Visit," and Clyde Holt would also sing his composition "Salute to Princess Margaret" (see Figure 5.7).[100] The JFU advertised the presence of government ministers at these premieres. *It Can Happen to You* at the Odeon would take place "in the presence of the Hon. Dr. Ivan Lloyd, Minister of Education and Social Welfare [and] The Hon. C. L. A. Stuart, Minister of Health."[101] For Rennalls this was a very important and deliberate maneuver intended to change popular perceptions of the unit. Rennalls recognized the political value of the JFU films in "building a 'new Jamaica'" and in keeping the "forward movement of the country toward self-government," but he also realized that it was not only the films that performed this task but the ability to make films. Rennalls wanted his films to challenge the permeating impression that "Jamaicans were not capable of performing at a level equal to their foreign counterparts."[102] Reviews for a typical early JFU production, showing the Scout Jamboree in 1953, described "an inspiring documentary," inspiring not only in showing the scout movement and the "beauties of Jamaica," but in demonstrating "the high standards of efficiency and service" attained by the JFU.[103] The gala premieres and the entries in overseas festivals were an attempt to showcase the development of a Jamaican industry.

This process is replicated by other units. The first film produced by the Barbados Film Unit, *Give Your Child a Chance,* played at the Plaza cinema, Bridgetown (on 16mm) in 1952 before going on the mobile cinema circuit. The *Barbados Advocate* celebrated this "first locally produced film," which was "acted, produced and directed by Barbadians," and described this "simply told" tale of an expectant mother who visits a maternity hospital and, with help from the state, "produces a very healthy baby, and sets the stage for its usefulness in life." This "birth" narrative, creating "useful" citizens, is similarly articulated in the formation of the unit. The paper presents the film as "just a beginning," stating that the unit has "already proved its usefulness to the community and will become a permanent part of our educational set-up."[104]

```
═══════ CARIB ═══════
GRAND PREMIERE TOMORROW at 8.15.P.M
         IN THE DISTINGUISHED PRESENCE OF
         HIS EXCELLENCY THE GOVERNOR SIR HUGH FOOT,
                     K.C.V.O., K.C.M.G.

         THE MINISTER OF EDUCATION & SOCIAL WELFARE
                          PRESENTS
              THE JAMAICA FILM UNIT PRODUCTION

PRINCESS MARGARET VISITS JAMAICA

         THE MOST COMPREHENSIVE RECORD OF THE VISIT
                   OF HER ROYAL HIGHNESS

                    SCENES INCLUDE:
PORT ROYAL ..................... The Arrival
CORPORATE AREA .......... Ceremonial Drive
KNUTSFORD PARK ........ Royal Race Meeting
KING GEORGE V
  MEMORIAL PARK ............. Tree Planting
SPANISH TOWN ................. Civic Welcome
                          Visit To The Cathedral
UNIVERSITY COLLEGE ...... Scenes At The Ball
KING'S HOUSE ......... Tree Planting Ceremony
UP PARK CAMP .............. Military Display
DENBEIGH ............. Visit To Show Grounds
MANDEVILLE ................. Civic Welcome
                          Visit To Alumina Jamaica
                                 Barbecue Supper
MORANT BAY ....... ..Opening Of New Hospital
RIO GRANDE .......... Rafting Down The River
PORT ANTONIO ............... The Departure

DIRECTED BY M. A. RENNALLS. PHOTOGRAPHED BY
M. A. RENNALLS AND T. A. WELSH. EDITED BY THE
COLONIAL FILM UNIT, LONDON. COMMENTARY SPOKEN
BY NOEL VAZ. MUSIC BY THE JAMAICA MILITARY BAND
UNDER THE DIRECTION OF MAJOR R. G. JONES, M.B.E.

              EXTRA ADDED ATTRACTION
         ON THE CARIB STAGE • TOMORROW 8.15 P.M.
         ● SIR HORACE & His Merry Knights
         ● CLYDE HOYT singing his own compositions:
         "Princess Margaret Calypso", and for the first time in public
         "BIG FISH" theme song of the motion picture.
                     VERE JOHNS M.C.
```

FIGURE 5.7. An advertisement for the premiere of the Jamaica Film Unit's *Princess Margaret Visits Jamaica* (1955) from the *Daily Gleaner*, 27 April 1955, 4.

Taken together, the JFU films reveal the development of the unit and nation in the decade preceding independence. As one example, *The Jamaica Hope* (1960) addressed a very similar topic (milk production) to the JFU's first production, *Farmer Brown Learns Good Dairying*, but now revealed a technologically advanced model of industry. The CFU's "industrial process" film was barely mechanized, traditionally showing the process from the growth or manufacture of a product to its export, but by *The Jamaica Hope* (like *Giant in the Sun* in Nigeria) there is mechanized technology at the bottling factory and the latest scientific advances in the research laboratories. Similarly, *Eat Jamaican,* a film that the Ministry of Trade and Industry had been wanting to make for years, shows industrial mass production, with hypnotic shots of conveyor belts and a repeated emphasis on the latest, modern technology. The film itself is in many respects an update of *One Family* (though mercifully shorter), as the economic initiatives of the interwar Empire Marketing Board are adopted by the Jamaican government.

In recording and revealing the modernization of industry, these films also show their own industrial development: the development of film techniques, logic, and language. While the unit was a product of the CFU, it deviated from the Sellers technique and its films display formal flourishes. In the case of *It Can Happen to You,* an entirely typical colonial film in its story, Rennalls deploys dissolves, parallel editing between the two brothers, visual effects, point of view shots (for example, an out-of-focus image of the clock as Joe realizes he is going blind), and offers a darker narrative resolution (the "foolish" Joe shoots himself as his condition deteriorates). The effect of the earthquake in *Port Royal* is re-created through shaky camera work and disorientating close-ups of a screaming child, while *Eat Jamaican* includes animated, stop-motion footage. In *Builders of the Nation,* images from Ted's possible future are superimposed over a walking Ted as he contemplates another life. Later, this effect is achieved sonically as he hears dialogue and advice from his past while he contemplates a change of career. These moments may deviate from colonial doctrine but they ultimately attest to a filmmaker and unit developing new ways of communicating with its audience. As in the Gold Coast, the films deploy local songs and musical styles. Rennalls noted how the title song in *Let's Stop Them,* based on the Mento style, used lyrics in the Jamaican dialect and even "locally made" instruments.[105] Terri Francis cites the commentator's positioning among the audience (as an insider rather than outsider), the credited Jamaican cast and crews, and the articulation of Jamaica as "my country" as further evidence of an emerging local cinema.[106]

There is a marked attempt to define and celebrate this as a local Jamaican cinema. A review for one of the early JFU productions, *You Can Help Your Children* (1952), a self-help educational film, argued that the performers (including Lady Foot) had a "natural sincerity which gives them a real edge over all the elaborate technique of Hollywood sophistication." The distinct qualities of a Jamaican cinema are already defined and this process of presenting as local, and as authentic, is part of the British government's stage management at the end of empire. A significant part of the motivation for ceding authority here was to be *seen* as ceding authority, to project independence as a gift rather than a loss. Any "local" cinema continues to be shaped by the colonial powers, whether through personnel (British-educated educators and administrators trained through the CFU), equipment (particularly with the literal flow of film through the UK for processing), or ideology (both Sellers's "rules" and the dominant educational and instructional models of government filmmaking).

This colonial influence is equally prominent in the formation of the Trinidad Film Unit. Early in 1951, Harris and Evans, the CFU instructors from the Jamaica training school, visited Trinidad to organize "a local film production unit to carry on with the valuable work from which their unit was gradually withdrawing." They also took part in a discussion, with the local trainee Wilfred Lee, on filmmaking and film appreciation for local radio. Later in the year, William Sellers arrived for sixteen days, discussing technical details with Lee and meeting every possible minister and government official. His aim was both to "gauge" progress and also "to give advice to the various governments" on setting up film units. The process was far from smooth—in 1952, local film production was suspended—but with Lee as a driving force, working often with one or two assistants, the Trinidad Film Unit continued to produce films over the next few years.[107]

Lee's productions included films for overseas audiences, such as *Portrait of Trinidad* (1957), which was intended to coincide with, and celebrate, the launch of the West Indian Federation, and which helps to reveal the economic motivations behind these moves. While photographed and directed by Lee, the film was produced by Vic Gover, edited by Dennis Bowden, and credited to County Films Ltd. The film showcases Lee's undoubted ability as a filmmaker—this is an accomplished, beautifully shot picture of modern Trinidad—and projects a vision of Trinidad for British and overseas audiences that reworks the images and emphases of the local productions. The film serves up a fantasy of a contented people ("soon another day of work, music and laughter will begin"), of a "laughing, happy people" operating with the twin ambitions of "progress and learning." The film prioritizes industry, celebrating "modern machinery" and fetishizing the symbols of industrial progress and connectivity (the airport, pylons, factory machinery, road-building). While the shots of industry showcase and celebrate British developments, the focus is now on export and overseas markets, largely ignoring the "local benefit" invariably fostered in the "local" films. Industry is described as "a spider's web of wealth," as the film foregrounds the British government's economic aspirations and, in so doing, exposes the motivations behind the development narratives propagated in local productions. Ultimately *Portrait of Trinidad* is a well-crafted fantasy of impending "handover," presenting a land that is "moving with purpose and industry towards a well-planned and independent future."

At this stage, the Trinidad Film Unit was working on a "skeleton basis" and suffered whenever personnel left (for example in June 1957, the cameraman left the unit for Jamaica and the scriptwriter was seconded to the broadcasting unit, prompting production to halt for the rest of the year).[108] However, by the end of the decade, there was a new, expanded Trinidad and Tobago Government Film Unit that, as in Jamaica, was now operating as part of the Public Relations Department. The unit, seemingly without Wilfred Lee, was also more closely aligned to the work of government. It marked the moves toward independence by recording lengthy formal speeches, conferences, and the apparently amicable, planned "handover" of other institutes and industries. These included British West Indian Airways (largely bought by the government in 1961) and the Imperial College of Tropical Agriculture, which was transferred to the University College of the West Indies in 1960.

This transfer is the subject of *University in Trinidad* (1960), which through a succession of formal speeches shows the symbolic handing over of a casket to mark the "gift" of the university from the UK to the West Indies. The handover of power is contained within traditional British ceremonies and the well-established forms of nonfiction film that record them. *His Excellency the Governor* (1959) seemingly marks the moves toward independence by showing the swearing in of the first nonwhite governor of a British Crown Colony, Sir Soloman Hochoy, but the film is again framed by a lengthy opening that celebrates the "positive role" of the outgoing governor, Sir Edward Beetham, and concludes with another rendition of the British national anthem.

The speeches, ceremonies, and events leading to independence are compiled in the unit's *Road to Independence* (1962), which includes scenes in London filmed by (and credited to) the OFTVC. Further sequences marking independence show the continued support of the British government. A newsreel item depicts a delegate from the House of Commons visiting their Trinidadian counterparts with a gift. The parliamentary delegates present a collection of books that tell the story of British parliament and "enshrine the principles of parliamentary rule and the concept of government by consent," effectively handing over their model of government. Another newsreel item shows "useful gifts from Britain," including a silver and gold centerpiece and equipment to help technical training (and thus industrial and economic development) at the John S. Donaldson institute. In presenting independence as a "gift," these films help inform how Britain often continues to understand its past as a "benevolent" ruler.

The films preceding independence sought to obfuscate what empire had been, to simplify the narrative of "handover" by emphasizing cooperation, "British-led "development," and continued economic "partnership." This becomes even more apparent as the "end" grows nearer, with an increasing number of compilation films, organizing formal events, pageants and people as part of the narrative to independence. Hassan Muthalib shows how this process works in Malaya, while in Jamaica, films like *Towards Independence* (1962) that depicted the discussions in London, emphasized the British role in planning and administering these moves. As film historian Rachel Moseley-Wood astutely shows, in foregrounding and magnifying the importance of an individual London conference, *Towards Independence* starts the independence narrative in London, privileging the imperial center. In the JFU's *Government by the People* (1960), the governor reads a proclamation for the new constitution with a statue of Queen Victoria in the background, the first minister meets Princess Margaret, the ceremonial mace is carried into the new government buildings, while shots of ancient buildings, pictures, and historical statues further embalm British tradition and heritage within the modern nation.[109] These films served to create and curate screen memories, shaping both how the empire would be understood and the relationships that followed; a strategy that began in this late colonial period and continues today.

CHANGE AND CONTINUITY: INDEPENDENCE ON SCREEN

Speaking of his time with the Overseas Film and Television Centre, Tony Muscatt argued that independence "was very good for us." Not only did the OFTVC retain ties with many units but it also worked extensively on the ceremonies themselves, which were recorded and reused across multiple films.[110] The spectacle of colonial handover is a distinctly filmic moment and provides a visual shorthand for the move from colonial to independent state. In organizing and relaying these moments, film helps to imagine symbolically the new states and, in doing so, often divorces them from the politics that led to this point. These films, as Rachel Moseley-Wood argues in relation to the JFU's *A Nation Is Born* (1962), "conceive of independence as a moment rather than the result or part of a process," often omitting any mention of struggle and, in their totalizing language (repeatedly using phrases such as "every man, woman and child"), wiping any dissenting voices from the screen. The films do, however, follow a narrative built up by the local units in the previous decade, articulating a voluntary, British-controlled "handover," which enables Britain to qualify its loss by emphasizing its part in the development and emergence of the nation. Jonathan Trutor, in his analysis of COI films of Nigeria, sees this as an important distinction from France, arguing that "by citing the past, the British gained control over it."[111]

These independence films are then a culmination of the CFU's work over the previous two decades, of its management and myth-making on screen. The Trinidad and Tobago Film Unit's record of independence, *This Land of Ours* (1962), opens with a "quick glimpse at our everyday life," although this glimpse is evidently aimed predominantly at international audiences, highlighting tourist attractions (the Hilton Hotel and beaches for the "visitor's enjoyment") and shows the "expansion and modernisation of industry." Before addressing independence, the film considers the oil industry and shows the growth of Texaco in the region, a product of increased "foreign investment" that highlights economic continuity. The subsequent footage of independence is largely told through the experiences of the visiting Princess Royal, Princess Margaret, from her arrival at the airport to the military inspections and her "rousing welcome" at a youth rally. She witnesses the lowering of the British flag and delivers the throne speech at the opening of parliament, before handing over the constitutional instruments. The JFU's *A Nation Is Born* (1962) is very similar, showing cheering crowds as Princess Margaret arrives by plane before meeting the awaiting dignitaries. She becomes the attraction within the film, often appearing to direct proceedings (and the camera).

However, the *Gleaner's* review for *A Nation Is Born* recognized the underlying tensions behind the film, concealed within its formulaic treatment. The review criticized the commentary and editing for failing to "whip up some of the surge" and excitement of the event. "Certainly one might have been swept away more patriotically," the reviewer argued, "had much of 'Nation' not seemed to bend over backwards so abjectly to record activities of the two most important guests." While the review accepted the focus on the Princess Royal, "since she represented the institutional personage now cutting the young nation lose from her apron strings," it was less forgiving of the attention paid to the American vice president, Lyndon Johnson, who "perhaps represented the more practical business of purse strings!" The discussion illustrates the political and economic jostling within these moments, as economic superpowers used "independence" to imagine and secure their own interests within the nation's future.[112]

A Nation Is Born was, in some respects, a remake of a 1958 film of the same title, which was directed, scripted, and edited by Isaac Carmichael for the Barbados Film Unit. Carmichael's *A Nation Is Born* would by 1962 stand as a record of failure, commemorating the birth of the very short-lived West Indies Federation.[113] *A Nation Is Born* (1958) illustrates how Britain sought to mediate change and retain influence within the federation, particularly through the royal image. The film notes and displays the diverse population's "common loyalty to the British Crown." The central figure here is once again Princess Margaret, who from her arrival at the airport undertakes what would, within the next five years, become an extremely familiar tour. It is she who is credited with leading the people toward independent nationhood and with strengthening "attachment to the British Crown" within the Commonwealth. Her authority is enhanced by the specificity of the commentary (the princess arrived at "exactly two minutes to 11 o'clock"), while the places she visits in Trinidad (the Imperial College of Tropical Agriculture and a sugar factory on the Brechin Castle Estates) celebrate the perpetuation of British models of development. On her visit to the sugar factory, the commentator notes the "wealth stored in the land," describing sugar as the "mainstay of the economy." Significantly the factory and estate was owned by Caroni Limited, a subsidiary of the British company, Tate and Lyle. Tate and Lyle completely dominated the sugar industry in the region, buying up estates throughout the decade. In this way, the princess's visit formalizes and promotes an ongoing form of economic imperialism.[114]

This focus on the royal visitor is even more pronounced in *Nigeria Hails Independence* (1960), a color film from the Nigerian Ministry of Information, directed by Lionel Snazelle. The film follows Princess

Alexandra of Kent throughout and is, effectively, a film of her royal tour, concluding with her departure by plane. The film articulates this careful negotiation of tradition and modernization, continuity and change, through footage of the princess visiting the recently opened (in October 1959) studios of Western Nigeria TV. As an earlier government film on the launch of WNTV showed, the service was owned and operated through a partnership between the Western region government and the London-based Overseas Rediffusion Limited, which ran radio and TV stations across the empire from Malta to Barbados to Hong Kong. This media partnership, on the cusp of independence, exemplified the continued investment of British enterprise within the media. Indeed the footage of the WNTV launch showed Noel Sabine, formerly a senior figure at the Colonial Office, signing the agreement as a senior figure with Rediffusion. Sabine explained that this was a "complete 50–50 partnership," that it would involve paid advertising and largely foreign programming, and that Rediffusion would be "training African technicians partly in London and partly in Africa." The footage of the launch includes shots of the training in London and the instructor in question is George Pearson.[115]

The complex, contested, and often violent processes that led to independence are contained and eradicated within these films through the short visual displays, public celebrations, airport departures, and official ceremonies. The films often appear remarkably similar, but they also reveal the particular ideologies of the local units, the ways in which the work of the CFU was now reworked and repurposed across different territories. This is evident in two of the first films of independence from 1957, *Freedom for Ghana* and *Merdeka for Malaya*. *Freedom for Ghana*, the Ghana Film Unit's 35-minute color record of the events surrounding Ghanaian independence on 6 March 1957, opens with a shot of the new, fluttering Ghanaian flag, followed by a map, dignitaries arriving at the airport, a royal procession, and religious ceremonies within the stadium. Later there are formal state banquets, royal visits, the strike of the clock at midnight, and the unveiling of the national monument. In describing these independence ceremonies, Richard Rathbone noted the similar "quotients of military display, fireworks, pious sentimentality at midnight and the profoundly implausible pledges of eternal friendship between long-term antagonists."[116]

All of the above are also present in the Malayan Film Unit's *Merdeka for Malaya*, filmed five months later in August 1957. The film positively celebrates continued British influence, whether through shots of colonial architecture and sporting events or through the commentary, which notes the continued "close co-operation" between Britain and the Federation of Malaya. What is striking here is what lies beyond the frame, as any dissension or struggle is obfuscated in a narrative of racial harmony and nation-building. For example, the commentary offers one brief mention (and in the past tense) of the Emergency, thanking the troops that helped "rid the country of Communist terrorism." At the same time, the British are remembered with "gratitude" for their assistance "down our long path to nationhood." From this we can see that film not only records these major ceremonial events, but also carefully constructs a narrative that navigates "loss" by foregrounding the British involvement and by presenting the local populace as passive spectators. These films, and the events they depict, seek to perpetuate, to encourage continuity while visually marking this moment of change.[117]

While *Freedom for Ghana* is typical in what it shows, it is more ambitious in its form and outspoken in its commentary. For example, the commentary acknowledges and celebrates those who have lost their lives fighting for freedom and mythologizes Nkrumah's struggle to power ("The government put him in prison. They tried to forget him. They failed"). The differences between *Freedom for Ghana* and *Merdeka for Malaya* reveal the divergent practices and politics of the two units. The MFU increasingly produced short, instructional films, with its head, Tom Hodge, "openly critical" of the unit's founding Griersonian elements. By contrast, *Freedom for Ghana* is notably more poetic, both sonically and visually, which testifies to the unit's closer ties to the prestige work of the British Documentary Movement. Sean Graham was recently described by GCFU filmmaker Chris Hesse as a "rebel" within the Gold Coast Information Services, marked out by his integration within Ghanaian culture and his more liberal, humanist politics.[118] We see this in sequences in *Freedom for Ghana,* notably the formal dance at the Hotel Ambassador, which celebrates racial integration and the challenges to the existing order. The commentator gleefully champions the African influences now creeping into the European club, "that dear old department of the stiff upper lip."[119]

Freedom for Ghana appears to represent a bolder shift from colonial to independent state. After the raising of the Ghanaian flag at midnight, the film conveys the energy and excitement of the country through traveling shots, which follow Prime Minister Nkrumah's car, and the multiple cuts, which capture the urgency of the crowds. When the British flag is removed, the British commentator is replaced by a local voice stating "too long up there making us other people's property." The commentary was written by Basil Davidson, the radical journalist, noted African historian, and champion of liberation movements, and while uncharacteristically bold, it still looks to locate Britain's place within the newly independent state. As the procession moves through the streets, a British voiceover states: "I suppose we could have hung on of course, we could have gritted our teeth and called in the troops and somehow muddled through, shot our way through." The commentator concludes that such an approach is "out of date, greedy, stupid," divorcing Britain from these violent actions and projecting the still-enduring argument that Britain managed its end far better than other global powers (particularly France, with its continued, violent struggles in Algeria). An Indian voiceover recalls how the Indians felt about the British "before they decided to leave India." "We used to dislike the British, we don't now," he concludes. Instead the commentator outlines the "warmth of friendship that will continue to unite Ghana with Great Britain," looking to negotiate a peaceful handover. This is imagined partly through symbols such as the flag, although these symbols can also serve as a reminder of the anticolonial struggle that led to this point (in this case, the red represents the blood of those who fought for independence and the gold represents the mineral wealth of the country).[120]

The stakes are high in these films, not only in representing the new nation at home, but also in addressing those colonies still under British rule. The MFU claimed around this time that its films played in 68 different countries, while newspapers reported that *Merdeka for Malaya* would be seen by "millions of people throughout the world," as the MFU turned out 120 prints that would go initially to its agencies in America, Australia, England, India, and Jakarta.[121] *Freedom for Ghana* was presented as a positive call to arms for other nations. The Ghana Film Unit's catalogue recognized that the film "attempted more than the conventional record of a happy royal tour," setting a "pattern for the wider picture" and presenting Ghana "as a symbol for the whole of Africa."[122] The film's conclusion, which features Nkrumah's moonlit speech, represents a much more provocative and politicized moment than we see in most other films of independence. Nkrumah introduces the new national anthem over a shot of the Ghanaian flag, before proclaiming "freedom" with his right hand raised. The British commentator adds that Africa has "woken up" and that other countries will follow Ghana. "Courage, freedom, these are Ghana's words for you wherever you are, whoever you are ... humanity is indivisible. Indivisible."

Monthly Film Bulletin praised (and, in doing so, questioned) the COI for distributing *Freedom for Ghana,* a film which "in some parts of the world, might be considered positively inflammatory."[123]

The exhibition of these films also offered a way of performing nationhood, of organizing and bringing together this model of the new nation both on and off screen. The last governor of the Gold Coast, Sir Charles Arden-Clarke, attended both the Ghana and London premieres of *Freedom for Ghana,* which brought together "many important diplomats . . . who applauded the film enthusiastically." At the end of the event at the National Film Theatre in London, the audience of four hundred stood for the Ghana national anthem, "probably for the first time in any theatre in the UK."[124] The exhibition was thus a way to perform and validate the changes shown on screen and through its audience of British and Ghanaian dignitaries (there were also Ghanaians in "national costume" acting as ushers) acknowledge the continuities. The local units continued to play their part in mediating the shift played out in these films of independence. One of the first JFU productions after independence was a color trailer showing the Jamaican national anthem, which would now play in all cinemas at the start of the program. The trailer was bookended by footage of the Jamaican flag and included images of the band of the Jamaica Defence Force playing the anthem and shots of the police, Boy Scouts, and Girl Guides. The transition from colonial to nation-state was imagined and explained through symbols that often served to stabilize this fluid and contingent history.[125]

In the case of Uganda, the unit was resurrected for independence and indeed the first two films that the Uganda Film Unit produced were on the general election of 1961 and the independence celebrations of 1962. *Uganda Hails Independence* follows a familiar pattern, showing the prime minister laying the foundation stone of independence arch, the arrival and tour of the Duke and Duchess of Kent, the lowering and raising of flags, fireworks, and the opening of parliament. The unit was established here not only to record this historic event but also to navigate it. The celebrated British documentarian Alexander Shaw, who was the unit's producer, argued that when the government saw *Uganda Hails Independence,* it "began to realise that the Uganda Film Unit could be a useful part of their information set-up." The film was not only nation-building, but unit-building. Shaw outlined why he chose to leave the production of a color film showing the prime minister's wedding in 1963 entirely in the hands of the local trainees. "They would stand in front of three thousand people in the Cathedral," he explained, "and fifteen thousand at the reception so that everyone could see them doing the work themselves." Shaw saw this as a moment when the unit "was established." Like Martin Rennalls in Jamaica, Shaw derived the unit's value as much from its public appearance and performance off screen as from the images it produced on screen.[126]

A major part of Alexander Shaw's role in Uganda was to train filmmakers and to convince the government and public of the merits of these local units. Shaw saw the films as a way of unifying and defining the nation ("make the country people feel they are part of one country"), both through the films and through the efforts of government workers at the shows. The trainees produced fourteen "mass education" films in 1963, which with titles such as *Better Housing* and *The Two Friends,* made for the Ministry of Health and the Ministry of Community Development respectively, carried on the work of the CFU.[127] For decades, these films from Uganda were processed in London by the OFTVC. Tony Muscatt recalled "making films as we were asked to do" for the Ugandan government, including films for Idi Amin, which he described as "very hard propaganda stuff, almost like Nazi films."[128] The OFTVC would bear witness to the scars of empire and often participated in these struggles. It worked on films for both sides during the Biafran War (the Nigerian civil war in the late 1960s), processing films for the Eastern Nigerian Unit and the opposition, Federal Film Unit. OFTVC also processed numerous films for Gaddafi's Libyan government, with footage completely wiped in one instance after the film was put through X-ray machines at customs in London at a moment of heightened security and international tension.[129]

THE AFTERLIFE OF THE COLONIAL FILM UNIT

The films of independence mark this moment of transition from colonial to nation-state, a transition similarly played out behind the camera. The majority of those who assumed prominent positions in the postindependence units were products of their colonial predecessors. Sam Aryeetey and Reynold Ofoe (R.O.) Fenuku, both veterans of the inaugural CFU training school in Accra in 1948 and founding members of the Gold Coast Film Unit, would serve as managing directors of the Ghana Film Industry Corporation after independence (and into the 1980s) (see Figure 5.8). So too would Chris Hesse, who joined the GCFU shortly afterwards in 1952.[130] Aryeetey is often credited as the director of the first Ghanaian feature film, *No Tears for Ananse*

FIGURE 5.8. The changing of the guard. R. O. Fenuku, who first attended the Accra training school in 1948, bids farewell to a departing George Noble in 1958. Courtesy of Information Services Department, Ghana.

(1968). Manthia Diawara cited Aryeetey's film and Alhaji Adamu Halilu's *Shaihu Umar* (1976) as films that were "'specially' edited, with almost no ellipsis, in order not to confuse their African audiences," seeing "patterns of racist filmmaking" that perpetuated the work of earlier colonial filmmakers.[131] Halilu, who would head the Film Unit of the Northern Region in Nigeria, was trained in London at the Overseas Film and Television Centre and also at the Shell Film Unit.[132]

L. T. Fomson, writing in the early 1980s, noted that ten of the nineteen states in Nigeria had film units and "most of those working in these film units attended their courses at the Overseas Film and Television Centre." Dennis Bowden, formerly of the CFU and, until 1989, with the OFTVC, recalled his trips to Nigeria where he found that "most of the people with the units were trained by us."[133] Filmmaker and scholar Samantha Iwowo sees this influence in more contemporary cinema, positioning Nollywood and Neo-Nollywood as the "offspring" of the CFU, and cites an ongoing dependence on the West for training and filmmaking skills. In closely comparing the CFU's flagship title, *Mr. English at Home,* to more recent Nigerian cinema, Iwowo recognizes a genealogy from Sellers and the CFU to Neo-Nollywood through structure and form and through a reinforced "colonial mentality and discourse."[134]

In independent Ghana, Nkrumah placed enormous importance on the film unit, nationalizing production and distribution and building a cultural infrastructure, of which film was one part, with expensive modern facilities in Accra.[135] For Nkrumah, the unit was both an important tool for his government's nation-building and also a shiny, modern emblem of the new nation. He paraded the African film crews as a model for modern Ghana, suggesting that the film units were not only responsible for creating the new nation in the popular imagination but were also positively enacting this process, exemplars of the shift from colonial to postcolonial state. These narratives of change, however attractive to politicians of the time and historians today, oversimplify and conceal a more nuanced transition after independence, as the strong British influences often remained. Sean Graham claimed that Nkrumah had asked him to stay on after independence and, despite the government's stated desire to "make the film productions completely Ghanaian in character," the senior staff at the Ghana Film Industry Corporation in the early 1960s still consisted of five expatriate officers and six Ghanaians. The unit also continued to bring in European directors.[136] Barely a year after independence, Norman Spurr moved out to Ghana as a UNESCO expert working with, and training, the audiovisual unit of the Department of Social Welfare and Community Development.[137] One of the films Spurr collaborated on was *Enemy in the Night* (1960), a Ghana Film Unit production made "with the co-operation of UNESCO." *Enemy in the Night* was directed by Dennis Bowden, who filmed in the villages in Ghana before returning to the OFTVC in London for postproduction work. The film extended the pre-independence traditions in Ghana in its narrative, subject, and approach. Here was another malaria prevention story (with a literate Ghanaian hero), which outlined the merits of (and local resistance to) the World Health Organization's malaria eradication scheme. *Enemy in the Night* was again produced for government departments, in this case the Ministry of Health and the Department of Social Welfare and Community Development.[138]

The Ghana Film Production Corporation's *Your Police* (1962) further highlights this continuity, emphasizing that most police officers enjoy a "long record of service stretching back to the days prior to independence." The film is a fantasy of ruling by "kindness"—the police deploy "the helping hand, the happy smile" and "good humour and tact are his primary weapons"—while the criminal is caught by "efficient police work," a product of police training. The film was directed by Brian Salt (who soon after would become films officer of the Hong Kong Film Unit) and was produced for the Ghana Film Production Corporation by Victor M. Gover and Co. in London, with Tony Muscatt listed as the editor.[139] It is a similar story in Trinidad, where the films produced on either side of independence promote continuity through familiarity. *Two Royal Visits* offers a very traditional account of the Queen and

Prince Philip's 1966 tour, including a lengthy speech from the Queen at the state opening of Parliament, formal displays and traditional performances (one of these is the subject of its own twenty-minute film, *Command Performance All as One*). The commentator concludes that the royal visit symbolized "independence and commonwealth brotherhood," nuancing change and continuity together.[140] An earlier two-day tour from Prince Philip featured in the unit's newsreel from 1964, showing the prince "warmly welcomed and widely cheered by the thousands who saw him." The unit filmed conferences that marked the new (old) relationship, including the fifteenth Commonwealth Parliamentary Conference held in Trinidad in 1969, which featured much handshaking as 250 delegates and officials arrived in the spirit of "harmony and cooperation." There were also sporting events, filmed on either side of independence, including the Caribbean F.A.'s 1959 tour of England, which much like the CFU's *Nigerian Footballers in England* (1949) foregrounds the camaraderie and support for the touring sportsmen, and a postindependence film that shows the continued import of British instruction and culture, by detailing the rugby coaching offered in Trinidad by England international Martin Underwood.

Government film catalogues from the 1970s (in Ghana, Nigeria, and Jamaica) reveal both the continued circulation of colonial-era productions and the dominance of short, nonfiction forms, such as newsreels, documentaries, and instructional films, still playing predominantly to nontheatrical audiences. Cultural anthropologist Birgit Meyer noted the "clear continuity between colonial and postcolonial policies" in Ghana and these continuities are, in part, products of the funding channels and distribution networks that continued to be largely controlled by non-Africans.[141] Many of the colonial territories received mobile cinema vans and film equipment from overseas governments as independence gifts—for example, the US government donated mobile vans to Uganda and Kenya, the Canadian government provided Tanganyika with ten mobile cinema vans, while Sierra Leone received a van from the government of Sweden—as other countries (and especially America) sought, through film technology, to exercise economic and ideological influence in the midst of the Cold War and ultimately control cinema distribution channels within the former colonies.[142] One of the repercussions of this "control" is noted by Ikechukwu Obiaya, who defines the legacies of colonial filmmaking in Nigeria primarily by an "absence" (of funding, training, distribution, support, and infrastructure for feature-film production). Obiaya, in partial contrast to Iwowo, sees the more recent emergence of so-called Nollywood as a positive "rejection of a legacy."[143] In this way, the legacy of the NFU and of colonial cinema is not only in what it achieved and introduced, but also in how modern-day filmmakers have responded to its failings and restrictions.

In Malaya, the head of the MFU at (and beyond) independence, Ow Kheng Law, had traveled and trained with the Crown Unit in 1945–46 and was a founding member of the MFU, while Mohammed Zain Hussain, who would later become director general of the MFU, was a cameraman on the very earliest MFU productions like *The Kinta Story* (1949). In Jamaica, Martin Rennalls continued to lead what was now the Jamaica Information Services (JIS), and while the unit was rebranded and restructured, much of its work remained and covered familiar topics. As one example, the unit won the international Royal Society of Arts award in 1969 for the Rennalls' directed film *A Bright Tomorrow* (1967), which was made in conjunction with a family planning campaign (the subject of its earlier unreleased film, *Too Late*).[144] Some of the filmmakers recording independence would break from these traditions, such as Franklyn St. Juste, who having directed a number of JIS films in the 1960s, worked as cinematographer on the groundbreaking and enormously successful feature film *The Harder they Come* (1972). Elsewhere, there were many others responsible for filming their country's independence, like Gadalla Gubara, who would not only subsequently head the Sudan Film Unit but would also set up the country's first film studio (Studio Gad) and produce his nation's first feature films. Gadalla Gubara, who had traveled extensively with the CFU's mobile cinema vans, had trained at the CFU's Cyprus training school in 1951.[145]

At the same time, the fate of these colonial films highlights the continuing failure to confront and challenge this recent history. The vast majority of the films discussed within this book are located in British archives and, until recently, have been inaccessible to all but the most ardent (or well-funded) researchers. In 2015, filmmaker Didi Cheeka uncovered a batch of films "in the abandoned rooms of the old Colonial Film Unit in Lagos," now decomposed relics of an earlier period. Cheeka saw this locked archive as another closed door from history, a site of amnesia rather than memory, prompting him to ask, "What process of forgetting triggered this mass internment?"[146] Jennifer Blaylock documented her experiences in Ghana in 2010, working with a team of mostly volunteers sorting through the collections of the Information Services Department (ISD) Film Library. Of the 5,250 films found within the collection, only 626 (or 12%) were deemed salvageable.[147] The cliché of the decomposing film and neglected archive is a dusty one, often used as evidence of the failure of former colonies to care, or take responsibility, for their cultural heritage. And yet, it is not without merit as this cultural heritage, with all its complexities, is often neglected or removed from view. As a result, the fate and location of these films is very often unclear.

However, the afterlife of the Overseas Film and Television Centre challenges any tendency to privilege the British archive and further highlights the unstable nature of these films and memories. On the closure of the OFTVC, its library was sold to Film Images, a commercial archive in London, which primarily looked to sell the footage to media outlets for news reports and documentaries. Tony Muscatt explained that he would have been "only too pleased" to "repatriate" the films, but also concluded ten years later that if he had done so, they probably "would not exist today," given the storage conditions and constantly shifting priorities within the walls of former colonial governments.[148] Yet, holding the films in Britain was also fraught with problems, with the films themselves haunted by the after-effects of empire, often held in archives that were underfunded and that in a climate of austerity had to prioritize those few, celebrated materials, which were (believe it or not) more commercially lucrative than *Tropical Hookworm* or *Farmer Brown Learns Good Dairying*. After Film Images closed in 2007, Muscatt met with the British Film Institute but chose instead to donate the films to the British Empire and Commonwealth Museum, which itself closed a few years later, after a scandal that, in an apt metaphor for the empire it represented, allegedly involved the selling off of items loaned or donated to the museum. The OFTVC collections eventually found a new home at the Associated Press Archives in London, once more residing within a commercial archive. Now presented and sold by the foot, these images are rarely viewed as films or as a collection from the CFU and its successors, but as brief glimpses and records of historic moments. Once more the images are isolated and more often deemed valuable for what they show and record, rather than challenged for how they represent and conceal these histories. The commercial sale of footage continues to privilege a very small proportion of "exceptional" films.

The creation of the website Colonial Film: Moving Images of the British Empire in 2010 made some of these films freely available, without restriction, around the world and sought to connect and map the films and histories on screen. This was a significant step in bringing this footage out of the archive. However, the project's corpus was defined by those films contained within British archives, those films collected and stored in the imperial center, primarily by the British Film Institute and Imperial War Museum.[149] These are then historically curated histories, ultimately projections of government intent. The website itself only digitized a small proportion of the collections (approximately 5 percent) and so even this is a selected view. The history within this book is told not through the exceptional or celebrated films, but through the banal, revealed as much through repetition, through what is not shown and through the people beyond the frame (whether the colonizers producing and administering the films, or the colonized watching and responding to it). This is a largely neglected history of film, produced with government officials and played through mobile cinemas, in which the films are not viewed in isolation, but as part of a wider project of colonial governance, stretching across decades and continents, revealing the (often dramatic) evolution, dissolution, and continuities of empire.

It is essential that the government films discussed within this book—while recognized as partial histories—are not locked away or erased from public discourse but are revisited, studied, and challenged. While the statues of imperial figures stand prominently and visibly across the landscape of what was once the British Empire, the films are too often ignored or concealed from view. Yet the built, static space represented by towering imperial monuments, which is increasingly contested and confronted, is analogous to the moving space of film. These images may be government fantasies, concealing and removing dissenting voices, but they are also living monuments, which must be explicated and confronted if we are to understand our past and its presence within our ostensibly "postcolonial" present.

Notes

INTRODUCTION

1. George Pearson, *Flashback: The Autobiography of a British Filmmaker* (London: George Allen and Unwin, 1957), 215.
2. *Colonial Cinema*, December 1954, 74–75; George Pearson, "Hail and Farewell," *Colonial Cinema*, December 1954, 93–96. The secretary of state for the colonies argued in the House of Commons, when challenged by MP Tony Benn on its closure, that the CFU was a victim of its own success, as "its own pioneering work in stimulating the development of local film units overseas" now diminished the need for an advisory unit in London. "Colonial Film Unit Served Purpose Well," *Daily Gleaner*, 18 July 1955, 6. The *Times* published two letters complaining about the "deplorable" decision to close the unit, from John Bryan, the chairman of the British Film Academy (9 May 1955, 11), and W. Hamilton Whyte, who had worked in West Africa (12 May 1955, 11).
3. Paul Gilroy, "Great Games: Film, History and Working-Through Britain's Colonial Legacy," in *Film and the End of Empire*, edited by Lee Grieveson and Colin MacCabe (London: BFI, 2011), 14.
4. Lee Grieveson, *Cinema and the Wealth of Nations: Media, Capital and the Liberal World System* (Berkeley: University of California Press, 2018); Brian Larkin, *Signal and Noise: Media, Infrastructure and Urban Culture in Nigeria* (Durham, NC: Duke University Press, 2008).
5. Zoe Druick and Deane Williams, eds., *The Grierson Effect: Tracing Documentary's International Movement* (London: BFI, 2014), 4.
6. Priya Jaikumar, *Cinema at the End of Empire: A Politics of Transition in Britain and India* (Durham, NC: Duke University Press, 2006).
7. The main outputs were a website (www.colonialfilm.org.uk) and two edited collections: Grieveson and MacCabe, *Film and the End of Empire*, and Lee Grieveson and Colin MacCabe, eds., *Empire and Film* (London: Palgrave

MacMillan, 2011). For an excellent study of the French context, see Peter Bloom, *French Colonial Documentary: Mythologies of Humanitarianism* (Minneapolis: University of Minnesota Press, 2008).

8. Charles R. Acland and Haidee Wasson, eds., *Useful Cinema* (Durham, NC: Duke University Press, 2011), 4. For a further recent example in this area, see Haidee Wasson and Lee Grieveson, eds., *Cinema's Military Industrial Complex* (Berkeley: University of California Press, 2018). For work on industrial, sponsored, and educational film, see for example Vinzenz Hediger and Patrick Vonderau, eds., *Films That Work: Industrial Film and the Productivity of Media* (Amsterdam: Amsterdam University Press, 2009); Patrick Russell and James Piers Taylor, eds., *Shadows of Progress: Documentary Film in Post-War Britain* (London: British Film Institute, 2010); Jennifer Lynn Peterson, *Education in the School of Dreams: Travelogues and Early Nonfiction Film* (Durham, NC: Duke University Press, 2013).

9. Tom Rice, "Spotlight on the Colonies," www.colonialfilm.org.uk/node/757.

10. James Burns, *Flickering Shadows: Cinema and Identity in Colonial Zimbabwe* (Athens: Ohio University Press, 2002); Ian Aitken, *The British Official Film in South-East Asia: Malaya/Malaysia, Singapore and Hong Kong* (Basingstoke: Palgrave Macmillan, 2016). See also Ian Aitken and Camille Deprez, eds., *The Colonial Documentary Film in South and South East Asia* (Edinburgh: Edinburgh University Press, 2017).

11. David M. Anderson, "Mau Mau in the High Court and the 'Lost' British Empire Archives: Colonial Conspiracy or Bureaucratic Bungle?," *Journal of Imperial and Commonwealth History* 39.5 (2011): 699–716.

12. For example, see Amit Chaudhuri, "The Real Meaning of Rhodes Must Fall," *Guardian Online*, www.theguardian.com/uk-news/2016/mar/16/the-real-meaning-of-rhodes-must-fall (accessed 12 June 2017).

13. For media accounts relating Brexit to the British Empire, see Ishaan Tharoor, "Brexit and Britain's Delusions of Empire," *Washington Post*, 31 March 2017, www.washingtonpost.com/news/worldviews/wp/2017/03/31/brexit-and-britains-delusions-of-empire; David Olusoga, "Empire 2.0 Is Dangerous Nostalgia for Something That Never Existed," *Guardian Online*, 19 March 2017, www.theguardian.com/commentisfree/2017/mar/19/empire-20-is-dangerous-nostalgia-for-something-that-never-existed; Sally Tomlinson and Danny Dorling, "Brexit Has Its Roots in the British Empire—So How Do We Explain It to the Young?," *New Statesman*, 9 May 2016, www.newstatesman.com/politics/staggers/2016/05/brexit-has-its-roots-british-empire-so-how-do-we-explain-it-young.

14. Paul Gilroy, *After Empire: Melancholia or Convivial Culture?* (London: Routledge, 2004).

15. Native Administration Cinema Circuit, RG3/5/745, Ghana Public Records and Archives Administration Department, Accra.

16. I have explored the long histories of colonial cinema in entries on the Colonial Film website. Of particular relevance are those on *Panorama of Calcutta* (1899), www.colonialfilm.org.uk/node/275, and *Landing of Savage South Africa at Southampton* (1899), www.colonialfilm.org.uk/node/1186. The widely traveled films of Queen Victoria's Diamond Jubilee in 1897 offer an excellent example of the ways in which film provided a means of remote politi-

cal rule, taking the royals on a virtual tour of the empire. Film, and the royal image, also helped elicit an identification with the "mother country" that was crucial in securing allegiance and loyalty among colonized populations.

17. Hansard, H.C. Deb., vol. 362, cols. 51–64 (18 June 1940) [electronic version].

18. British Film Institute, *The Film in Colonial Development: A Report of a Conference* (London: BFI, 1948), 35.

CHAPTER 1: BEGINNINGS

1. *UK, Outward Passenger Lists, 1890–1960*, held at PRO and accessed through ancestry.com; W. Sellers, "Health Education," *Journal of the Royal Society for the Promotion of Health*, July 1955, 440–41.

2. Sellers, "Health Education." Sellers was awarded an MBE (Member of the Most Excellent Order of the British Empire) in 1938 and an OBE (Officer of the Most Excellent Order of the British Empire) in 1952.

3. John Grierson (credited as "The Moviegoer"), "Review of Moana," *New York Sun*, 8 February 1926.

4. For recent scholarship on the Empire Marketing Board, see Lee Grieveson, "The Cinema and the (Common)Wealth of Nations," in *Empire and Film*, edited by Lee Grieveson and Colin MacCabe (London: BFI, 2011), 73–114; Scott Anthony, *Public Relations and the Making of Modern Britain: Stephen Tallents and the Birth of a Progressive Media Profession* (Manchester: Manchester University Press, 2012).

5. See Mary Field, *Good Company: The Story of the Children's Entertainment Film Movement in Great Britain 1943–1950* (London: Longmans Green, 1952); Mary Field, "Commonwealth Unity of Thought through Films," *Journal of the Royal Commonwealth Society* 1.3 (September–October 1958): 231–36.

6. Stephen Tallents, credited as the founder of public relations in Britain and the man who brought Grierson to the Empire Marketing Board, argued that "no movement, I should be prepared to wager, has ever had a more clearly defined birthplace than that of the British documentary film; and the nursing home in which it first saw the light was Mr Amery's room at the Dominions Office." Stephen Tallents, "The Documentary Film," *Journal of the Royal Society of Arts*, 20 December 1946, 69.

7. Colonel Sir Arthur R. Holbrook, "British Films," *Royal Society of Arts Journal*, 3 June 1927, 684–709; Anthony, *Public Relations*, 37.

8. See Grieveson, "Cinema and the (Common)Wealth of Nations," 73–114.

9. John Grierson, "New Worlds for Cinema," 1931, G2:21; "Teach the World What We Have to Sell," 1931, G2:17:12, both John Grierson Archive, Special Collections, University of Stirling.

10. See Basil Wright, "Filming in Ceylon," *Cinema Quarterly* 2/4 (Summer 1934): 231–32.

11. Paul Rotha, *Documentary Film* (London: Faber and Faber, 1936), 18. See also Terry Bolas, *Screen Education: From Film Appreciation to Media Studies* (Bristol: Intellect Books, 2009), 11–36. Martin Stollery examines how Grierson's widely cited foundational text, "First Principles of Documentary," shaped

this categorization. Martin Stollery, "John Grierson's 'First Principles' as Origin and Beginning: The Emergence of the Documentary Tradition in the Field of Nonfiction Film," *Screen* 58.3 (2017): 309–31.

12. There are plenty of examples of individual enthusiasts and teachers, like Ronald Gow in Altrincham and W. H. George in Chesterfield making and renting films for schools. George would go on to publish *The Cinema in School* (London: Sir Isaac Pitman & Sons, 1935), with a foreword by Grierson.

13. See, for example, *Monthly Film Bulletin*, 1936, 162; 1937, 114; 1939, 64, 126. Some medical films produced by Spurr are available at the Wellcome Library, http://wellcomelibrary.org/item/b16759369#?.

14. James Fairgrieve, "The Use of Films in Teaching," *Geography* 17.2 (June 1932): 129–40; James Fairgrieve, *Geography in School* (London: University of London Press, 1926). Subsequent editions included a chapter entitled "Films in the Classroom." See also James Fairgrieve, "The Educational Film in England," *International Review of Educational Cinematography*, March 1932, 224–26.

15. Rosaleen Smyth, "Grierson, the British Documentary Movement, and Colonial Cinema in British Colonial Africa," *Film History* 25 (2013): 82–113.

16. Duncan Ross, who moved after the war from Paul Rotha's Films of Fact to work for the Documentary and Magazines Department of the BBC, suggested that television documentary could be considered Grierson's "own child." Quoted in Jo Fox, "From Documentary Film to Television Documentaries: John Grierson and This Wonderful World," *Journal of British Cinema and Television* 10.3 (2013): 518.

17. Memorandum Concerning the Use of the Cinema as an Aid to Increasing a Knowledge of the Empire, Imperial Education Conference 1927, ED121/134, TNA; "The Educational Uses of Cinematograph Films," Colonial Office Conference, May 1927, ED121/134, TNA.

18. Julian Huxley, *Africa View* (London: Chatto and Windus, 1931), 161.

19. Glenn Reynolds, *Colonial Cinema in Africa: Origins, Images, Audiences* (Jefferson, NC: McFarland, 2015), 175.

20. File 19/10 Medical: Report on the Work of the Mobile Cinema Unit of the Medical Health Service, Nigeria, IOR/R/20/B/251, British Library.

21. UK, *Outward Passenger Lists, 1890–1960*. See, for example, departure from Nigeria to Liverpool on 13 October 1931 and Liverpool to Lagos on 13 July 1940.

22. "Filming in Africa," *Colonial Cinema*, July 1943, 1–2.

23. James Burns, *Flickering Shadows: Cinema and Identity in Colonial Zimbabwe* (Athens: Ohio University Press, 2002), 27; Rachael Low, *The History of British Film, 1929–1939: Documentary and Educational Films of the 1930's* (New York and London: Bowker, 1979), 43; Rosaleen Smyth, "The Development of British Colonial Film Policy, 1927–1939, with Special Reference to East and Central Africa," *Journal of African History* 20.3 (1979): 437–50.

24. Marjorie Grant Cook, in collaboration with Frank Fox, *The British Empire Exhibition 1924: Official Guide* (London: Fleetway Press, 1924). See also John Mackenzie, *Propaganda and Empire: The Manipulation of British Public Opinion, 1880–1960* (Manchester: Manchester University Press, 1986), 96–120; Daniel Stephen, *The Empire of Progress: West Africans, Indians and Britons at*

the British Empire Exhibition, 1924–25 (New York: Palgrave Macmillan, 2013); Tom Rice, "Exhibiting Africa: British Instructional Films and the Empire Series (1925–1928)," in Grieveson and MacCabe, *Empire and Film*, 115–33.

25. "Two Films That Matter," *West Africa*, 26 April 1924, 393.

26. Edward Davson, "Empire Films," *The Times*, 10 October 1923, 11; "Memorandum by Graham Ball," CO 323/919/11, TNA.

27. "Encouragement in Production of British Films," 1927, CO 323/985/23, TNA.

28. *Kinematograph Weekly*, 19 November 1925; *Kinematograph Weekly*, 24 February 1927, 76.

29. See for example the BIF films, *Britain's Birthright* (1924), www.colonialfilm.org.uk/node/6219, and *Zanzibar and the Clove Industry* (1925), www.colonialfilm.org.uk/node/1050.

30. Fox, "From Documentary Film to Television Documentaries," 498–523.

31. *West Africa*, 19 February 1927, 175; Tom Rice, "Black Cotton (1927)," www.colonialfilm.org.uk/node/1322.

32. *Kinematograph Weekly*, 24 February 1927, 76.

33. "Films at Wembley," *The Times*, 15 October 1925, 15.

34. "Film and the Empire," *The Times*, 24 May 1926, xiv; "British Films in South Africa," *Bioscope*, 19 August 1926, 22. The Imperial Education Conference of 1927 acknowledged that *Britain's Birthright*, and by extension the Empire series, fell short in "conveying accurate knowledge of the Empire" since they depicted the regions in "gala dress" rather than under their "ordinary everyday aspect," effectively highlighting difference for British audiences and reaffirming traditional notions of "primitive" colonial subjects. "Memorandum on British Films," Imperial Education Conference, 1927, ED121/134, TNA.

35. "British Films," *The Times*, 15 November 1923, 10. When the Prince of Wales discussed the plight, and value, of British film across the empire in 1923 he stated that "we all know the catch-phrase 'Trade follows the film'." While acknowledging film's potential as an "aid to the development of imperial trade," he also noted its value as a pedagogical tool to "instruct children, and grown-ups too, by methods which no teacher or lecturer can achieve by the spoken word."

36. *Kinematograph Weekly*, 12 March 1925, 58.

37. Grierson, "Teach the World What We Have to Sell." Grierson argued that the meaning of the flag was also reconfigured by the EMB, replacing what he referred to as the "old flags of exploitation" with the "new flags of common labour." John Grierson, "The E. M. B. Film Unit," *Cinema Quarterly* 1.4 (Summer 1933): 203–8.

38. Letter from Crown Agents to the Under Secretary of State, Colonial Office, 11 July 1927, CO 323/985/23, TNA.

39. *Sight and Sound*, Summer 1972, 149; "Film Quotas (Amendment Order)," House of Commons, 30 March 1950, accessed from Hansard; Paul Swann, *The British Documentary Film Movement, 1926–1946* (Cambridge: Cambridge University Press, 1989), 35.

40. *Sight and Sound*, Summer 1972, 149; John Grierson, "Annual Report on the Activities of the Empire Marketing Board Film Unit, 1931," G2:8:4, John Grierson Archive, Special Collections, University of Stirling.

41. "One Family: A Film of the British Empire," *Manchester Guardian*, 8 July 1930, 6.

42. Creighton also produced the poetic one-reeler *A Southern April* from offcuts from the South African footage used in *One Family*, which was well received (described as "exquisite" by Mary Field) and continued in circulation for years.

43. Discussed in the *Educational Screen*, June 1926, 321–22; *The Age* (Melbourne), 27 February 1926, 6. Gervas Huxley, then of the EMB, sought to use extracts from the Empire series "for inclusion in new films" in 1931, which might serve as advertising in shop windows, while Colonel Levey pushed unsuccessfully for the films' rerelease in cinemas in the 1930s. Levey argued that showing the films in schools was "valueless propaganda," asserting that in cases where admission was not charged, a film was likely to be "regarded more in the nature of an advertisement and people took much less interest in it." Meeting at Crown Agents, 22 January 1931; Imperial Institute to Crown Agents, 28 May 1935, Colonial Films—Inclusion of, in, the Empire Series of Films, CSO 15/8/20, Ghana Public Records and Archives Administration Department, Accra (PRAAD).

44. Letter from Crown Agents to the Under Secretary of State, Colonial Office, 11 July 1927, CO 323/985/23, TNA.

45. CO 323/985/23, TNA.

46. British Instructional Films, *Catalogue of Films for Non-Theatrical Exhibition* (1928). A few years later in 1935, *Black Cotton* (and twenty-one other films from the Empire series) were handed over to the newly formed Empire Film Library (run by the Imperial Institute). This library, reaching out primarily to schoolchildren, was intended to "reveal the life, scenery and industries of the overseas Empire to the general public and particularly to the rising generation of the British Isles." Transfer of West African Government Films by Crown Agents for the Colonies, INF 17/47, TNA; CO 323/985/23, TNA; *Sight and Sound*, Summer 1935, 52; "The Cinema in Education: Popularizing the Imperial Institute," *The Times*, 31 October 1927, 8.

47. Huxley, *Africa View*, 59.

48. Priya Jaikumar, *Cinema at the End of Empire: A Politics of Transition in Britain and India* (Durham, NC: Duke University Press, 2006), 5.

49. *The Times*, 26 January 1928, 10; *The Times*, 23 January 1929, 14; *The Times*, 9 April 1930, 14.

50. *Times of India*, 15 August 1930, 12.

51. "This Place Called Hollywood," *Hollywood Filmograph*, 28 June 1930, 30.

52. Hesketh Bell, "Cinema in Africa," *The Times*, 4 October 1926, 15; Hesketh Bell, "Films in Tropical Africa," *The Times*, 10 July 1930, 15. Bell lamented the "deplorable antics of white women in a state of almost complete nudity" presented by "foreign" films, and suggested that this had "a shocking and dangerous effect on coloured youths and men in the earliest stages of culture who have hitherto been led to consider the white man's wife and daughters as patterns of purity and virtue."

53. *The Film in National Life: Being the report of an enquiry conducted by the Commission on Educational and Cultural Films into the service which the*

cinematograph may render to education and social progress (London: Allen and Unwin, 1932), 133.

54. *The Times,* 10 July 1930, 15.
55. *The Times,* 4 October 1926, 15.
56. "The Cinema in Africa," *The Times,* 5 October 1926, 10.
57. Julian S. Huxley, "Report on the Use of Films for Educational Purposes in East Africa," 1930, CO323/1252/15, TNA.
58. Huxley, *Africa View,* 57–60, 291–96; Huxley, "Report on the Use of Films for Educational Purposes in East Africa."
59. Ibid.
60. Huxley, "Report on the Use of Films for Educational Purposes in East Africa"; Huxley challenged William Sellers over this point in the 1940s.
61. *Film in National Life,* 135.
62. Huxley, *Africa View,* 158–63.
63. *Film in National Life,* 133; Colonial Films Committee: Report, Minutes, 1930, CO323/1091/10, TNA; "Colonial Films Committee," *The Times,* 10 April 1930, 14.
64. Passfield to Gold Coast Government, 18 August 1930, Course of Instruction to Officers on Leave in the Use of Cinematograph in Schools, CSO 15/8/41, PRAAD.
65. Reynolds, *Colonial Cinema in Africa,* 166.
66. A number of these proposals are discussed in the following works: Reynolds, *Colonial Cinema in Africa;* Smyth, "Development of British Colonial Film Policy, 1927–1939," 437–50; Rob Skinner, "'Natives are not critical of photographic quality': Censorship, Education and Films in African Colonies between the Wars," *University of Sussex Journal of Contemporary History* 2 (2001); Burns, *Flickering Shadows,* 37–59; James Burns, *Cinema and Society in the British Empire, 1895–1940* (London: Palgrave Macmillan, 2013), 93–132.
67. J. Russell Orr to the Under Secretary of State for the Colonies, 23 September 1931, CO323/1130/12, TNA.
68. CO 323/1130/12, TNA; "The Film in Empire Education," *United Empire* XXIII (1932): 691–92.
69. CO 323/1130/12, TNA. Mr. Allen suggested that Orr's background in Kenya, where he served as director of education, was not in his favor as "in spite of other excellent qualities he was not regarded as much of a 'doer'."
70. *Film in National Life,* 134.
71. J. Russell Orr, "The Use of the Kinema in the Guidance of Backward Races," *Journal of the Royal African Society* 30.120 (July 1931): 238–44; "Meetings of the Society," *Journal of the Royal African Society* 30.120 (July 1931): 301–11.
72. "Meetings of the Society," 302–3; "'Films' Proposed Experimental Scheme in Malaya," CO 323/1122/16, TNA. Vernon's scheme is discussed in Smyth, "Development of British Colonial Film Policy, 1927–1939," 441; Reynolds, *Colonial Cinema in Africa,* 166–67.
73. Films on Industrial, Social and Hygienic Education in West Africa, 1932–33, CO 554/92/15, TNA. Beresford Gale's letter to Hanns Vischer at the Colonial Office is dated 23 November 1932. Vischer responds on 23 January 1933.

74. Quoted in Zoe Druick, *Projecting Canada: Government Policy and Documentary Film at the National Film Board* (Montreal: McGill University Press, 2007), 37; *Sight and Sound*, Spring 1935, 37; letter from BFI to Colonial Secretary, Accra, 10 April 1935, Films made by Amateur Cinematographers—Request for Information Regarding, CSO 15/8/43, PRAAD.

75. British Film Institute: Dominions and Colonies Committee, 1934, CO 323/1252/15, TNA.

76. British Film Institute: Subcommittee on Local Cinematography Scheme in Africa, 1934, CO 323/1252/16, TNA; Reynolds, *Colonial Cinema in Africa*, 167–70; Smyth, "Development of British Colonial Film Policy, 1927–1939," 441.

77. BFI—Colonial Film Unit and the Machinery for the Circulation of Educational Films in the Empire, CO 323/1356/3, TNA.

78. Recent scholarship on the BEKE includes Aaron Windel, "The Bantu Educational Kinema Experiment and the Political Economy of Community Development," in Grieveson and MacCabe, *Empire and Film*, 207–26; Aboubakar Sanogo, "Colonialism, Visuality and the Cinema: Revisiting the Bantu Educational Kinema Experiment," in Grieveson and MacCabe, *Empire and Film*, 227–46; Reynolds, *Colonial Cinema in Africa*, 171–96; Luis Eslava, "The Moving Location of Empire: Indirect Rule, International Law and the Bantu Educational Kinema Experiment," *Leiden Journal of International Law* 31.3 (September 2018): 539–67; Tom Rice, BEKEFilm, "Colonial Film: Moving Images of the British Empire," www.colonialfilm.org.uk/production-company/bekefilm.

79. Skinner, "'Natives are not critical of photographic quality'," 5.

80. L. A. Notcutt and G. C. Latham, *The African and the Cinema: An Account of the Work of the Bantu Educational Cinema Experiment during the Period March 1935 to May 1937* (London: Edinburgh House Press, 1937); "Native Kinemas in East Africa," *Kinematograph Weekly*, 18 July 1935, 23.

81. Windel, "Bantu Educational Kinema Experiment," 211.

82. Latham was born in China in 1887, and was an accomplished sportsman who played first-class cricket at Oxford. He served with the North Rhodesian Police and in 1920 became the first inspector of schools in Northern Rhodesia, before becoming director of native education in 1925. He had attended the discussion on "The Film in Empire Education" in 1932 and was charged with overseeing the BEKE's exhibition circuit and gauging audience reactions to the films in his role as educational director.

83. Low, *History of British Film, 1929–1939*, 44.

84. All three films are available to view at "Colonial Film: Moving Images of the British Empire," www.colonialfilm.org.uk.

85. Notcutt and Latham, *The African and the Cinema*, 63, 132.

86. Notcutt and Latham, *The African and the Cinema*; Burns, *Flickering Shadows*, 27.

87. G. C. Latham, "Film for Africans," *Sight and Sound*, Winter 1936, 123–25; Reynolds, *Colonial Cinema in Africa*, 184.

88. Latham, "Film for Africans."

89. Notcutt and Latham, *The African and the Cinema*, 171; Reynolds, *Colonial Cinema in Africa*, 183.

90. Simon J. Potter, *Broadcasting Empire: The BBC and the British World, 1922–1970* (Oxford: Oxford University Press, 2012), 91–98, 59.

91. "Fifty Million African 'Fans': Big Scheme for Teaching Blacks by Film," *Commercial Film*, 1 April 1935, 2.

92. Smyth, "Development of British Colonial Film Policy, 1927–1939," 443. Latham noted that the audience's "joy at seeing actors of their own race in the familiar setting of tribal surroundings is tremendous." "African Films for Africa," *Today's Cinema*, 18 December 1935, 25.

93. Burns, *Cinema and Society in the British Empire, 1895–1940*, 128.

94. Reynolds, *Colonial Cinema in Africa*, 195.

95. The African and the Cinema—Observations on, 30 April 1938, Cinematograph—Use of in Schools, RG 3/5/998, PRAAD.

96. "African Films for Africans," *The Times*, 30 November 1937, 19.

97. Reynolds, *Colonial Cinema in Africa*, 195.

98. G. C. Latham, "The Cinema in African Education," *The Times*, 4 April 1939, 12.

99. Burns, *Cinema and Society in the British Empire, 1895–1940*, 120; M. A. Rennalls, "Development of the Documentary Film in Jamaica," unpublished thesis submitted for the Degree of Master of Science, School of Public Communication, Division of Broadcasting and Film, Boston University, 1967, 28–37.

100. M. A. Rennalls, "Development of the Documentary Film in Jamaica," 35.

101. "Jamaica Welfare Film Units Complete First Tour," *Daily Gleaner*, 23 May 1938, 16, 23.

102. "British Educational Films," *Sight and Sound*, Winter 1934, 131; "Filming the Caribbean for the Classroom," *Daily Gleaner*, 15 August 1936, 23.

103. *The Times*, 9 June 1938, 10.

104. There were also individual schemes proposed for schools within the colonies. H. M. Grace, the principal of Achimota school in the Gold Coast, wrote to the director of education in 1937 proposing to use films in teaching civics in secondary schools. His first proposed film, *Gold Coast Justice*, would stress that "co-operation between the two races is essential, and point out how native and foreign procedure and institutions have been combined into one system of judiciary." Grace hoped to work with the Education Department in developing "travelling cinema educational units" from large converted lorries. Cinematograph Films for Use in Teaching Civics—Making of, in the Gold Coast, CSO 15/8/45, PRAAD.

105. *Daily Gleaner*, 23 May 1938, 16, 23; "Ja. Welfare Ltd Now Functioning Actively," *Daily Gleaner*, 6 January 1938, 1.

106. Burns, *Cinema and Society in the British Empire, 1895–1940*, 120–121; Suggestion for a Test in the Use of Instructional Films, Carnegie Corporation: Progress Reports on Grants issued in 1936 and Applications for Further Grants for 1939, CO 137/838/3, TNA.

107. Letter from Eastwood, 5 June 1939, CO 137/838/3, TNA.

108. Oliver Bell, "Education by Film," *The Times*, 10 April 1939, 6.

109. Educational Use of Film in Africa, 1939–1940, CO 859/6/21, TNA.

110. Reynolds, *Colonial Cinema in Africa*, 197.

111. Note from G. Eastwood, 9 December 1939, Welfare Propaganda: West Africa, CO859/7/7, TNA; Minutes of Dominions, India and Colonies Panel, 19 July 1939, British Film Institute: Dominions and Colonies Panel, CO 859/6/11, TNA. Latham worked during the war for the MOI, but he was not directly involved with the CFU. He contacted the Colonial Office in a "personal capacity," offering his services, and urged them to plan for local film units in Africa "as soon as the war is over." He outlined a plan in January 1943 for the use of broadcasting and film in the colonies, which again warned that if Britain did not make use of film and broadcasting equipment, "America will, in a short time, completely dominate the market in these things." Latham to Blaxter, 20 January 1943; note from Blackburne, 13 January 1943; proposal from Latham, 6 January 1943, CO 859/46/9, TNA.

112. Eastwood was writing to Margaret Mace, who wanted to know of suitable people on leave for BBC broadcasts. He explained that Sellers was scheduled to be on leave until sometime in September. "Broadcast Talks by Members of the Colonial Service," CO 323/1651/19, TNA. Also quoted in Kate Morris, *British Techniques of Public Relations and Propaganda for Mobilizing East and Central Africa during World War II* (London: Edwin Mellen Press, 2000), 187.

113. William Sellers, "Making Films in and for the Colonies," *Royal Society of Arts Journal* 16 (October 1953): 829–37. Sellers was born on 7 November 1897. He had an older brother, Arthur, and married Bertha Bland in 1931, having three children over the next decade. See 1901 UK Census Collection and 1911 England and Wales Census Collection, and *England & Wales, Civil Registration Birth Index, 1837–1915*, accessed at ancestry.com.

114. William Sellers Service Record, no. 466415, *British Army WWI Service Records, 1914–1920*, accessed at ancestry.com. While serving, Sellers had seven teeth extracted before spending eighteen days in hospital during the Spanish flu outbreak of 1919.

115. The quote from 1935 comes from the acting director of the Medical Health Service, Dr. Thomson. Sellers adapted the lorry for Lagos health week in 1935 and the purpose-built van was produced in the UK during his next leave. File 19/10 Medical, IOR/R/20/B/251, British Library. For full details on the van, see Sancaster to Eastwood, 31 May 1939, British Film Institute: Further Development of Visual Education in the Colonies, CO 859/6/12, TNA.

116. Sellers had become a member of the Royal Sanitary Institute a few months earlier in December 1925.

117. Each trip was interspersed with approximately eighteen weeks of paid leave in the UK.

118. Sellers, "Health Education."

119. Memo from Governor Thompson, 26 September 1928, Sanitary Department: Special Plague Staff, CO 583/158/6, TNA.

120. Correspondence from the Crown Agents, 13 January 1930, Employment of Staff: Sanitary Department, 1930, CO 583/170/9, TNA. The Sanitary Inspectors' Association had taken up these questions with the Colonial Office at the end of 1929. Sellers's starting salary in 1926 was £400, which rose £12 a year to £436 by 1929.

121. Colonial Development Funding for Public Health Improvement Schemes, CO 583/204/4, TNA.

122. File 19/10 Medical, IOR/R/20/B/251.

123. Nadine Chan, "Making Ahmed 'Problem Conscious': Educational Film and the Rural Lecture Caravan in 1930s British Malaya," *Cinema Journal* 55.4 (2016): 84–107; Burns, *Cinema and Society in the British Empire, 1895–1940*, 93–132.

124. Ibid.; "Discussion on Conservancy in Rural Areas," *Journal of the Royal Society for the Promotion of Health*, June 1939, 267–68; W. H. Peacock, "Presidential Address on the Training and Place of Auxiliary Health Staff in Tropical Colonies," *Journal of the Royal Society for the Promotion of Health*, May 1936, 299–310.

125. File 19/10 Medical, IOR/R/20/B/251.

126. Ibid.; "Discussion on Conservancy in Rural Areas," 268.

127. Brian Larkin, *Signal and Noise: Media, Infrastructure and Urban Culture in Nigeria* (Durham, NC: Duke University Press, 2008), 85.

128. See Tom Rice, "Anti-Plague Operations, Lagos 1937," www.colonialfilm.org.uk/node/1526.

129. I accessed Sellers's films discussed in this section at the AP Archive in London (www.aparchive.com). It holds thirty-nine cans of early Sellers films, many of which are untitled. I identified many of these cans against lists that Sellers provided—for example, in his report of the Health Propaganda Unit (File 19/10 Medical, IOR/R/20/B/251)—while other bits of footage appear across productions. I am enormously grateful to James Kearney at the AP Archive for providing access to these films.

130. File 19/10 Medical, IOR/R/20/B/251.

131. Ibid.

132. Megan Vaughan, *Curing Their Ills: Colonial Power and African Illness* (Stanford, CA: Stanford University Press, 1991), 189.

133. Norman Spurr, "The Mobile Cinema Van Is a New Weapon in Mass Education," *Colonial Cinema*, March 1949, 9–16. When Sellers showed this film as part of the first CFU program in West Africa in 1940, he noted its popularity, with the "shouts and laughter from the audience almost deafening in a hall." Report of Visit of W. Sellers to West Africa, May 31st to August 14th 1940, Use of Mobile Cinema Units in West Africa, 1940, CO 323/1744/13, TNA, UK.

134. These criticisms were well established. The Ku Klux Klan had protested against Chaplin's appearance in *The Pilgrim* (1923) because it deemed that he "ridiculed" the Protestant ministry. Tom Rice, *White Robes, Silver Screens: Movies and the Making of the Ku Klux Klan* (Bloomington: Indiana University Press, 2015).

135. "Charlie Chaplin Films," *Colonial Cinema*, December 1942, 3.

136. See Tom Rice, "The Heart of an Empire," www.colonialfilm.org.uk/node/471.

137. "Discussion on Conservancy in Rural Areas," 268.

138. File 19/10 Medical, IOR/R/20/B/251.

139. Ibid.; note from G. Eastwood, CO 859/7/7, TNA.

140. File 19/10 Medical, IOR/R/20/B/251. At this stage, the training was restricted to operating the vans and the equipment with no mention of allowing Africans access to the cameras.

141. MOI planning for West Africa, 15 May 1939, Dissemination of Propaganda in War: West Africa, 1939, CO 323/1663/10, TNA.

142. Report from Malcolm MacDonald, 12 August 1939, Dissemination of Propaganda in War: West Africa, 1939, CO 323/1663/10, TNA.

143. Welfare Propaganda: West Africa, CO 859/7/7, TNA.

144. Bruce Woolfe, "I Remember," *Sight and Sound,* Spring 1941, 8–9.

145. *Atlantic* (1940) is available at http://film.britishcouncil.org/atlantic (accessed 5 September 2016).

146. Report from Malcolm MacDonald, CO 323/1663/10, TNA. MacDonald suggested that the projectors could also be transported on the eighty-one different bus routes in Nigeria or across the 1,900 miles of railroad. The buses and trains also provided "an opportunity for the display of posters," further performing the work of government as they travel.

147. Ibid.

148. Memorandum of the Cinema Branch of the Information Department Gold Coast and the Use of Mobile Cinema Units for Mass Information and Education, Colonial Film Unit, 1942–1943, CO 875/10/9, TNA.

149. Burns, *Cinema and Society in the British Empire, 1895–1940,* 121–22; letter from Oliver Bell, 29 March 1940, CO 1045/227, TNA. The BFI's Dominions, India and Colonies panel proposed a film library in Jamaica and Trinidad in the summer of 1939. J. Merle Davis, the visionary missionary behind the BEKE, argued that pictures of England would be of little value and what was instead needed were scenes of Jamaican life "in all its familiar sordidness, poverty and misery."

150. Note from C. G. Eastwood, 19 April 1940, CO 1045/227, TNA.

151. William Sellers, "Film Production," CO 1045/227, TNA; Sellers, "Health Education," 440.

152. Sellers, "Film Production."

153. Ibid.

154. George Pearson, *Flashback: The Autobiography of a British Filmmaker* (London: George Allen and Unwin, 1957), 199.

155. Ibid., 22.

156. "The Art of George Pearson," *Pictures and Picturegoer,* December 1924, 34.

157. Pearson, *Flashback,* 144.

158. Ibid., 204; George Pearson, "Ex Parte," *Documentary News Letter,* April 1941, 77–78.

159. Pearson, *Flashback,* 203.

CHAPTER 2: FILM RULES

1. See Tom Rice, "Mr. English at Home," www.colonialfilm.org.uk/node/1808.

2. *Colonial Cinema,* March 1948, 3; *Colonial Cinema,* December 1947, 87; John Maddison, "Le cinéma et l'information mentale des peuples primitives," *Revue Internationale de Filmologie* 1.3–4 (1948): 305–9.

3. William Sellers, "Making Films in and for the Colonies," *Royal Society of Arts Journal* 16 (October 1953): 829–37; William Sellers, "Film Use and Production in British Colonial Territories," in *Report on the Seminar on Visual Aids in Fundamental Education* (UNESCO, 1954).

4. George Pearson, "Memorandum re: Films for African Primitives," 29 October 1942, CO 875/10/9, TNA.

5. Provisional Film Programme, 1948/49, Colonial Film Unit: Expansion of Activities, CO 875/26/1, TNA; Progress Report, June 20–July 17, 1946, Monthly Meetings with Colonial Office, 1946–1949, INF 12/282, TNA.

6. *Colonial Cinema,* November 1944, 44. Also quoted in Rosaleen Smyth, "The British Colonial Film Unit and Sub-Saharan Africa, 1939–1945," *Historical Journal of Film, Radio and Television* 8 (1988): 285–98. A further report from Nigeria (*Colonial Cinema,* December 1945, 89) noted the popularity of the film, which had "specific lessons of domestic responsibilities to teach."

7. British Film Institute, *The Film in Colonial Development: A Report of a Conference* (London: BFI, 1948), 46.

8. *Colonial Cinema,* August 1944, 32; "Kumasi Kumbungu and John English," *Colonial Cinema,* June 1945, 46–48. The article described the film as "a picture of sturdy childhood, rightly encouraged to fend for itself in the happy atmosphere of parental care."

9. Stephen Tallents, *The Projection of England* (London, 1932), 11.

10. A report in *Colonial Cinema* in August 1944 (p. 32) noted the audience's fascination with the London bus. Highlighting British modernity and technological primacy, the report added that audiences "had never seen such a huge object on wheels. How the roads were wide enough for it was a mystery to them."

11. In noting the "comfortable living" Mr. English earned as a carpenter, an African viewer concluded that "this proves that Technical Education is valued and encouraged in the civilised world." *Colonial Cinema,* November 1944, 44.

12. *World Film News,* December 1937, 39; "No Pay—No Sleep," *World Film News,* January 1938, 36.

13. Sellers, "Making Films in and for the Colonies," 831. The report, written by Arthur Champion, was taken from an article he wrote in the *Crown Colonist,* February 1942. A two-paragraph extract of this article was sent to Sellers and appears in CO 875/10/9, TNA.

14. *Colonial Cinema,* June 1947, 28.

15. William Sellers to Mr. Mercier, 26 May 1941, Reorganisation of the Colonial Film Unit, INF 1/144, TNA.

16. Smyth, "British Colonial Film Unit and Sub-Saharan Africa, 1939–1945," 289. The CFU responded to three particular observations raised at the MOI screening. The first concerned the "anti-social" characters, depicted in isolation without showing other neighbors or shoppers. The CFU representatives responded that "the introduction of other people and other movements on the screen would lead to divided attention, and loss of the intended lesson of the

film." George Pearson, "Memorandum re: Films for African Primitives," 29 October 1942, CO 875/10/9, TNA.

17. Sellers was already defining the success of these films by his "rules." He argued that "the tempo is correct" for *Mr. English at Home,* in contrast to three of the other films viewed in West Africa in 1940. "Report of Visit of W. Sellers to West Africa, May 31st to August 14th, 1940," Use of Mobile Cinema Units in West Africa, 1940, CO 323/1744/13, TNA.

18. Colonial Film Unit: Distribution and Technical Questions: Replies to Questionnaire on Films Shown, CO875/10/11, TNA. John Wilson to Director of Education, Accra, 28 May 1942, Cinematograph—Use of in Schools, PRAAD. In 1943, E. A. L. Gaskin, who worked for the Information Service in Nigeria, listed the ten most popular films, placing Charlie Chaplin shorts in first place and *Mr. English at Home,* which he said could be shown repeatedly as it was "so popular," in second place. Gaskin to Bradshaw, 17 June 1943, CO 875/10/9, TNA.

19. *Colonial Cinema,* November 1942, 1.

20. *Documentary News Letter* was effectively an in-house organ for the British Documentary Movement and was launched a few months earlier by John Grierson.

21. "Films for Primitive Peoples: A New Technique," *Documentary News Letter* 1.3 (March 1940): 10–11. The article contained material from the recently completed report of the Health Propaganda Unit in Nigeria and also noted the pioneering efforts of Notcutt and Latham.

22. Sellers, "Films for Primitive Peoples," 1940, 11.

23. William Sellers, "Films for Primitive Peoples," *Documentary News Letter* 2.9 (September 1941): 173–74.

24. Ibid.; L. A. Notcutt and G. C. Latham. *The African and the Cinema: An Account of the Work of the Bantu Educational Cinema Experiment during the Period March 1935 to May 1937* (London: Edinburgh House Press, 1937), 146. James Burns charts the origins, and continued use, of these anecdotes. J. M. Burns, *Flickering Shadows: Cinema and Identity in Colonial Zimbabwe* (Athens: Ohio University Press, 2002), 44–50.

25. Sellers, "Films for Primitive Peoples," 1941, 174.

26. Ibid., 174–75. Sellers again uses unqualified "facts" to back this up. "It is well known that if an illiterate African is handed a photograph even of himself or some scene familiar to him he will invariably turn it the wrong way up in an effort to focus his eyes on the picture."

27. "Films for African Audiences," *Colonial Cinema,* June 1943, 1–2.

28. Sellers, "Films for Primitive Peoples," 1941, 175; William Sellers, "Audience Research," *Colonial Cinema,* September 1951, 55–56.

29. Sellers, "Making Films in and for the Colonies," 837. The question was asked by Tony Hodgkinson, a secondary modern schoolteacher interested in the educational uses of film.

30. *Colonial Cinema,* June 1943, 1.

31. See, for example, "The Production of Films for Primitive Peoples," *Oversea Education,* October 1941, 221–26, and an abridged version in the *Colonial Review,* March 1942. Sellers's appearance on the BBC Home Service,

during which he outlined how "we use a special technique in making films for these people ['primitive peoples']," was reported in the *Crown Colonist*, February 1942, 81, and in further detail in March 1942, 130.

32. *Colonial Cinema*, November 1942, 1.

33. Colonial Film Unit: Report for 1951, CO 875/52/3, TNA; *Colonial Cinema*, March 1945, 3.

34. William Sellers, "Making Films with the Africans," in *The Year's Work in the Film, 1950*, ed. Roger Manvell (London: Longmans, Green, 1951), 37–43; "Raw Stock Scheme," *Colonial Cinema*, September 1947, 68–70; personal interview by author with Dennis Bowden, 24 May 2016; interview by Mary Ingleby with Dennis Bowden, 9 August 2007, accessed at the Bristol Records Office.

35. "Filming in Africa," *Colonial Cinema*, July 1943, 1.

36. "Filming with an Object," *Colonial Cinema*, November 1943, 1. The article suggested: "The work of the informed amateur may be of more value than that of the experienced professional."

37. "Fundamentals of Filming," *Colonial Cinema*, August 1943, 1; "Fundamental Facts for Filmmakers," *Colonial Cinema*, January 1944, 1.

38. *Colonial Cinema*, November 1943, 1.

39. Memorandum of the Cinema Branch of the Information Department Gold Coast and the Use of Mobile Cinema Units for Mass Information and Education, CO 875/10/9, TNA. The document was credited to the information officer and dated 12 July 1943. Lironi also sent a detailed five-page response to the CFU's questionnaire in June 1943, which talked through each aspect of this technique and emphasized the division between "documentary" and CFU films. "The normal documentary film has far too fast a tempo, and is just not understood," he wrote. "Trick camera shots, reverse angles, dissolves and etc have not been used. These may add interest to normal documentaries but simply confuse an illiterate audience." Colonial Film Unit: Distribution and Technical Questions: Replies to Questionnaire on Films Shown, CO 875/10/11, TNA.

40. H. Lironi, "Learning to Film," *Colonial Cinema*, May 1943, 2; O. Waterfield, "Lessons to Learners," *Colonial Cinema*, December 1943, 1.

41. See Schedule for the West Indies Training School, Educational Films: showing of, 1953–55, 1B/44/1/104, Jamaica Archives, Spanish Town, Jamaica. The celebrated glaciologist Charles Swithinbank recalls attending a two-day training course with the CFU. "[I] do remember the fundamental lessons which is always use a tripod . . . if you're going to do a pan do it very slowly . . . you're allowed to follow movement by panning the camera . . . but otherwise you want to do a mixture of long shots and close ups." While Swithinbank's film was intended for British audiences, it shows the CFU training scientists and subject specialists to make films. Dr. Charles Swithinbank interviewed by Dr. Paul Merchant, *National Life Stories: An Oral History of British Science*, C1379/03, British Library, http://sounds.bl.uk/related-content/TRANSCRIPTS/021T-C1379X0003XX-0000A0.pdf (accessed 10 May 2017).

42. *Colonial Cinema*, May 1943, 1; BECTU History Project interview with Denny Densham by Margaret Thomson and John Legard, 4 June 1990, accessed at the BFI. Interviewed in 1990, Densham argued that "there is a grading system

in film. Lighting, cameraman, documentary, then below that came newsreels. But the bottom of the scale was a wartime organisation called The Colonial Film Unit."

43. *Colonial Cinema*, May 1943, 1. Sellers included an extract from a revised version of *Land and Water* when discussing the CFU technique on the BBC in 1948.

44. Note to Noel Sabine, 3 October 1942, CO 875/10/9, TNA; Minutes of Meeting on Films for the Colonies, MOI, 17 June 1943, CO 875/10/9. The first *Colonial Cinema* editorial from November 1942 (p. 1) acknowledged: "The new technique is a very debatable business altogether."

45. CO 875/10/11, TNA.

46. Colonial Film Unit: Replies to Questionnaire, CO 875/10/11, TNA; "On Laughter," *Colonial Cinema*, November 1943, 4. Arthur Champion in East Africa explained that he avoided showing sequences of wounded soldiers because he found the resultant laughter so upsetting. From this, he deduced: "The Kenyan natives have not yet reached a stage in which they are capable of feelings for others."

47. Colonial Film Unit: Replies to Questionnaire, CO 875/10/11, TNA.

48. "Mass Education in African Society," *Colonial Cinema*, February 1944, 1; Colonial Office, Advisory Committee on Education in the Colonies, *Mass Education in African Society* (London: HMSO, 1944).

49. Burns, *Flickering Shadows*, 52.

50. L. Van Bever, *Le Cinéma Pour Africains* (Brussels: G. Van Campenhout, 1952); Manthia Diawara, *African Cinema: Politics and Culture* (Bloomington: Indiana University Press, 1992), 13. See also the review for Van Bever's pamphlet in *Focus: A Film Review* (July 1951), 216. Van Bever noted the need for "simple" plots, long scenes, and clear continuity and argued that anything violent should be avoided as it rouses the "latent battle instinct." He also noted the importance of this cinema as a form of proactive censorship, countering negative representations of the "white man" on screen.

51. "C.F.U. Films at the University of Paris," *Colonial Cinema*, December 1947, 87; John Maddison, "Le cinéma et l'information mentale des peuples primitives," 305–9. Mark Koenigil's book *Movies in Society: Sex, Crime and Censorship* (New York: Robert Speller and Sons, 1962) includes a chapter on "African Movie Problems," which directly discusses Van Bever and Maddison's writings.

52. Ibid.; Peter Bloom, "Refiguring the Primitive: Institutional Legacies of the Filmology Movement," *Revues Cinémas: Journal of Film Studies* 19.2/3 (2009): 169–82. This argument is also presented by the German emigre Egon Larsen in 1946. Larsen quotes directly from Sellers and outlines the "special screen language, which like any other language has to be learned to be understood." He outlines that the work of the CFU is "to teach them [Africans who have "never seen a photograph or drawing, let alone a film"] the screen language." Egon Larsen, "Films for Africans," *See and Hear*, December 1946, 34, 38, 40.

53. Larkin, *Signal and Noise*, 111–18; Siegfried Kracauer, *Theory of Film: The Redemption of Physical Reality*, with an introduction by Miriam Bratu Hansen (Princeton, NJ: Princeton University Press, 1997, originally 1960), 53. Larkin quotes from Siegfried Kracauer, "Appeals to the Near and Middle East:

Implications of the Communications Studies along the Soviet Periphery. Report Prepared for the Bureau of Applied Social Research, Columbia University," May 1952. Larkin argues that Kracauer's use and articulation of Sellers's work positions these ideas within the field of mass communications in the United States, and the "rise of modernization theory more generally."

54. Andre Bazin, "A Contribution to an *Erotologie* of Television" (1954), in *Andre Bazin's New Media,* ed. and trans. Dudley Andrew (Berkeley: University of California Press, 2014), 107.

55. Mary Field, "Making Films for Children," *Educational Screen,* November 1946, 502–4; Mary Field, *Good Company: The Story of the Children's Entertainment Film Movement in Great Britain 1943–1950* (London: Longmans Green, 1952), 78–95; The infrared pictures formed the basis of Field's 1954 report on children's reactions to film. Mary Field, *Children and Films: A Study of Boys and Girls in the Cinema: A Report to the Carnegie United Kingdom Trustees on an Enquiry into Children's Response to Films* (Dunfermline, Fife: Carnegie United Kingdom Trust, 1954).

56. Field, "Making Films for Children," 502; Field, *Good Company,* 92.

57. Henri Storck, *The Entertainment Film for Juvenile Audiences* (Paris: UNESCO, 1950), 76; Roger Manvell, *Experiment in the Film* (London: Grey Walls Press, 1949), 258; James Fairgrieve, "Films for School," *Sight and Sound* (Summer 1946): 69–70.

58. Field, "Making Films for Children," 502.

59. Field, *Good Company,* 155.

60. "Leslie Meets Lesaoama," *The Times,* 28 November 1947, 6. See Tom Rice, "Basuto Boy," www.colonialfilm.org.uk/node/64. Through these CEF films, children came, somewhat unsubtly, to represent the wider empire, in need of education and paternal guidance as they "grow up" toward independence. They advanced a social and political modernization, which was fostered and supported on screen by British interests and which often featured in contrast to the traditional ways of their father or elders. Field later suggested that these films could play in the colonies and dominions, enabling non-British settlers to "acquire British ideals and sympathies." Mary Field, "Understanding the Commonwealth: Value of British Films for Children," letter in the *Times,* 2 May 1955, 18.

61. There is an important distinction in the intended application of the theories. Field was not attempting to train or reach nonprofessional filmmakers in her writing as Sellers was with the Raw Stock Scheme. "One does not make a film by just having a camera and taking moving pictures," she wrote, "any more than one writes a very powerful play by just having a piece of paper and a pencil." Mary Field, "Commonwealth Unity of Thought through Films," *Journal of the Royal Commonwealth Society* 1.3 (September–October 1958): 234.

62. Field, "Making Films for Children," 502; Field, *Good Company,* 90.

63. Field, "Commonwealth Unity of Thought through Films." By 1958, Field argued that this "Commonwealth point of view" had been diluted by the devolution of colonial administration as a generation of administrators—who largely shared an approach and background—were now replaced by disparate local voices. Field also used these well-established anxieties around the "harmful" influence of film as a way of justifying the necessary role of the CEF. Like

Sellers, she preempted and protected her work from criticism, arguing that this specialized form of filmmaking for children eschewed conventional judgments and "adult criticism." Field, "Making Films for Children," 503.

64. Field, "Making Films for Children," 503.

65. Field, *Good Company*, 86.

66. In the face of criticism from educational authorities, councils, and teachers, Rank explained his aims for the films: "We want to help the children in good citizenship and with an understanding of children in other parts of the Empire." "Teachers Disagree with Mr. Rank," *Daily Mail*, 1 April 1947, 3.

67. Minutes of the Colonial Film Committee, 1 June 1948, INF 12/282, TNA; letter from W. Sellers, 3 March 1942, CFU Staff and Expansion: 1941–42, INF 1/144, TNA.

68. George Pearson, *Flashback: The Autobiography of a British Filmmaker* (London: George Allen and Unwin, 1957), 204; Pearson, "The Making of Films for Illiterates in Africa," in *The Film in Colonial Development* (London: BFI, 1948), 24.

69. Author's interview with Bill Williams, 7 June 2016; author's interview with John Jochimsen, 17 May 2016.

70. Pearson, *Flashback*, 203; George Pearson, "Memorandum re: Films for African Primitives," 29 October 1942, and William Sellers to Noel Sabine, 2 November 1942, CO 875/10/9, TNA. Pearson explained that the aim of the unit was to raise "the primitive mind of the African native to a higher cultural standard." He argued that while the "Documentary technique" might be quite appropriate for its "cinema-minded audiences," it was "useless for ours" as it used a pictorial idiom "beyond the comprehension of the illiterate."

71. See Pearson, *Flashback;* Pearson, "Making of Films for Illiterates in Africa"; George Pearson, "Visual Education by Film in the Colonies," *United Empire*, 1950, 206–9; George Pearson, "Health Education by Film in Africa," *Health Education Journal*, March 1949, 39–42.

72. Norman Spurr, "Films for Africans—1910 or 1950?," a talk delivered at British Kinematograph Society on 15 March 1950. The full speech is contained in Colonial Film Unit—Audience Research, CO 875/51/7, TNA. An abridged version was published in *Journal of the British Kinematograph Society* 16.6 (June 1950): 185–88.

73. Ibid. This theory was partially put to the test in Jamaica in 1945, when Edwin S. Porter's *The Great Train Robbery* (1903) played to rural audiences on the mobile film circuit. The commentator's report recognized that audiences already had clear expectations, and "Invariably there was great disappointment." "Looking back to 1903 this film may be regarded as the forerunner of the modern western," it added. "It lacks, however, the thrill of the modern film." Exhibition Report on Non-Theatrical Films, Films and Reports from British Council Jamaica Agricultural Society Information Officer, 1943–1945, 3/24/145, Jamaica Archives, Spanish Town, Jamaica.

74. Norman F. Spurr, "Pamba," *Empire Cotton Growing Review*, June 1950, 172–76; N. F. Spurr, "Coating the Pill," *Colonial Cinema*, March 1951, 21–22.

75. Spurr, "Films for Africans—1910 or 1950?," CO 875/51/7, TNA.

76. See Minutes of the Colonial Film Unit Meeting—19 June 1946, 20 November 1946, 20 December 1946, 22 January 1947—Monthly Meetings with Colonial Office, 1946–1949, INF 12/282, TNA; *The Film in Colonial Development: A Report of a Conference* (1948), 46. Odunton was later appointed as press advisor to the Queen for her (postponed) trip to Ghana in 1959, reportedly the first African to become a member of the royal household. He subsequently served as director of Ghana Information Services.

77. G. B. Odunton, "One Step Ahead," *Colonial Cinema*, June 1950, 29–32; "Pupils Teaching Teachers," *West Africa*, 26 August 1950, 770.

78. Odunton, "One Step Ahead"; Sean Graham, *The Use of Film in the West Indies and Mexico: An Inquiry into Techniques of Film Production for Fundamental Education, 1955* (UNESCO, February–May 1955), 47.

79. Emma Sandon, Tom Rice, and Peter Bloom, "Changing the World: Sean Graham," *Journal of British Cinema and Television* 10.3 (2013): 524–36; Sean Graham, "The Work of the Gold Coast Film Unit," *Visual Aids in Fundamental Education: Some Personal Experience* (Paris: UNESCO, 1952), 77–87.

80. "A Gold Coast Experiment," *West Africa*, 20 May 1950, 435; "Power of the Film," *West Africa*, 28 October 1950, 986.

81. George Pearson, "Re . . . One Step Ahead," *Colonial Cinema*, June 1950, 32–33.

82. Odunton, "One Step Ahead," 31.

83. Sandon, Rice, and Bloom, "Changing the World: Sean Graham"; Graham, "Work of the Gold Coast Film Unit," 78.

84. "Colonial Film Unit Training School in the West Indies," *Colonial Cinema*, June 1951, 40–44; Martin Rennalls, *A Career Making a Difference* (1991), unpublished autobiography, National Library of Jamaica in Kingston, 107, 141.

85. Pearson, "Re . . . One Step Ahead," 32–33; Spurr, "Pamba," 173.

86. Norman F. Spurr, "Odunton's Article," *Colonial Cinema*, June 1950, 33–34; Norman Spurr, "The Mobile Cinema Van Is a New Weapon in Mass Education," *Colonial Cinema*, March 1949, 10; "Commentary and Commentators," *Colonial Cinema*, March 1948, 13–14.

87. Spurr, "Films for Africans—1910 or 1950?," *Journal of the British Kinematograph Society*, 188.

88. See for example: Norman Spurr, "A Report on the Use of Disney's Hookworm Film in Uganda," *Colonial Cinema*, June 1951, 28–33; N. Spurr, "Visual Aids: Colour or Monochrome," *Colonial Cinema*, June 1952, 41–44; Norman Spurr, "Talkies with the Magnetic Stripe Projector," *Colonial Cinema*, March 1954, 11–12; Myrtle Winter and Norman F. Spurr, *Film-Making on a Low Budget: The UNESCO-UNRWA Pilot Project* (Paris: UNESCO, 1960).

89. Spurr, "Mobile Cinema Van," 13–14.

90. Spurr, "Coating the Pill," 21; Spurr, "Odunton's Article," 33.

91. Arthur M. Champion, "Introducing Africans to the Cinema Screen," *Crown Colonist*, February 1942. In a 1948 article, Champion added that "the value of good commentary intelligible to them [local audience] cannot be over-rated and time spent on coaching commentators is not likely to be wasted." Arthur M. Champion, "With a Mobile Cinema Unit in Kenya," *Oversea Education*, October 1948, 792.

92. Charles Ambler, "Projecting the Modern Colonial State: Mobile Cinema in Kenya," in *Film and the End of Empire*, ed. Lee Grieveson and Colin MacCabe (London: Palgrave, 2011), 199–224; Brian Larkin, *Signal and Noise: Media, Infrastructure and Urban Culture in Nigeria* (Durham, NC: Duke University Press, 2008).

93. Sellers, "Films for Primitive Peoples," 174; W. Sellers, "Mobile Cinema Shows in Africa," *Colonial Cinema*, December 1951, 81.

94. "Programmes," *Colonial Cinema*, January 1944, 3.

95. "The Cinema and You," *Colonial Cinema*, March 1947, 20–21. A report of a screening in Afikpo in Nigeria, published in *Colonial Cinema* in January 1944 (p. 3), perpetuates the "first cinema" stereotypes on which both the film techniques and audience assumptions were founded. "Here the natives showed very great interest in this 'magic of the white man', as they call the cinema here," it stated, further quoting an elderly lady dragging herself to the screening: "I heard her say, 'If I can see this picture before I die, I shall thank my God'."

96. Sellers, "Films for Primitive Peoples," 74.

97. Sellers, "Mobile Cinema Shows in Africa," 79; Ambler, "Projecting the Modern Colonial State," 203. Arthur Champion presented footage of the King and Queen on their thrones as a finale, leading into the national anthem. He noted that the audience "stands bareheaded and if not as silent as one might wish, its murmurs are an expression of appreciation and not in any way disrespectful." A report in the *Mombasa Times* (17 March 1941) noted that "it is worthy of note that the natives are now beginning, instinctively, to stand to attention at the playing of the National Anthem." Arthur M. Champion, "Introducing Africans to the Cinema Screen," *Crown Colonist*, February 1942, 80; Kenya Mobile Cinema, CO 875/6/18, TNA; Report from A. McNair, Lecturer and Demonstrator, Cinema Unit, no. 3, 13 December 1940, Jamaica Welfare Limited—Cinema Unit and Film Education; Correspondence, Minutes, Reports, 4/60/10a/9, Jamaica Archives, Spanish Town, Jamaica.

98. H.N. Silver and L.A. Murray, "Plan for Collaboration between D.O. and Cinema Lecturer" (1948), Joint Film Committee, 1946–1958, 3/24/147, Jamaica Archives, Spanish Town, Jamaica.

99. *The Use of Mobile Cinema and Radio Vans in Fundamental Education* (Paris: UNESCO, 1949), 60. The UNESCO report quoted directly from A.M. Champion, "With a Mobile Cinema Unit in Kenya," *Oversea Education*, October 1948, 788–92. Captain Dickson, who ran the mobile propaganda unit for East Africa Command during the war, prioritized the lessons followed up by Askari after screenings. "Wireless, the printed word, and the cinema will all have an increasing role to play in informing and influencing African opinion. But the day is not yet past when the most important factor with the African is personal contact and example." Captain A.G. Dickson, "Askari Teach New Ways to East Africans," *Crown Colonist*, September 1945, 601–2.

100. Nadine Chan, "Making Ahmed 'Problem Conscious': Educational Film and the Rural Lecture Caravan in 1930s British Malaya," *Cinema Journal* 55.4 (2016): 100.

101. Reorganisation of the Colonial Film Unit, 1941–1945, INF 1/144, TNA.

102. Sellers, "Mobile Cinema Shows in Africa," 79; *Colonial Cinema,* March 1954, 19–22; "The Information Service in Kenya," *Colonial Cinema,* March 1954, 14–15.

103. *Use of Mobile Cinema and Radio Vans in Fundamental Education,* 86–87. The report explained: "One of the main difficulties appears to be the absence of any fixed standards for projectionists, the absence of a set course of training and the fact that the composition of the crews of the mobile cinema units is extremely varied."

104. Films for Mobile Film Units in West Africa, 1940, CO 323/1744, TNA. Sellers planned to train staff in "the technique of film demonstrations and audience control," hinting at the wider role of the cinema staff.

105. Spurr, "Report on the Use of Disney's Hookworm Film," 28–33.

106. Cinema Propaganda: Colonial Film Unit, CO875 10/9, TNA. See also here "Memorandum of the Cinema Branch of the Information Department Gold Coast and the Use of Mobile Cinema Units for Mass Information and Education."

107. Sandon, Rice, and Bloom, "Changing the World: Sean Graham"; interview with Sir Sydney Samuelson, conducted by Tom Rice and Emma Sandon, 15 June 2010; *Use of Mobile Cinema and Radio Vans in Fundamental Education,* 90.

108. "The Work of the African Section of the Kenya Information Office," 12 September 1941, CO 875/6/16; CO875 10/9, TNA.

109. Sellers, "Mobile Cinema Shows in Africa," 77; Arthur M. Champion, Report on Government Cinema Unit for W/E Sunday, March 16, 1941, Kenya: Films, 1940–1941, CO 875/6/18, TNA.

110. C. F. Strickland, "Instructional Films in India," *Journal of the Royal Society of Arts* 12 (January 1940): 204–15. Sellers also uses this example in "Films for Primitive Peoples" and in his report on the Health Propaganda Unit in Nigeria.

111. "Cinema in the Bush," *The Listener,* 23 September 1948, 441–42. Slater was out in Nigeria, working as a writer on *Daybreak in Udi.*

112. Rennalls, *A Career Making a Difference,* 108.

113. Proposal for Extension of the Film Projection Services of the Central Film Organization, 1954, 1B/31/1190, Jamaica Archives, Spanish Town, Jamaica.

114. Liam M. Buckley, "Cine-film, Film-strips and the Devolution of Colonial Photography in The Gambia," *History of Photography,* 34.2 (2010): 147–57.

115. Basic Training of Film Technicians, sent from the Secretary of State for the Colonies on 27 November 1953, Educational Films: showing of, 1953–55, 1B/44/1/104, Jamaica Archives, Spanish Town, Jamaica. The letter listed the advantages of the filmstrip in four words: "Intimacy. Clarity. Control. Flexibility."

116. George Pearson, "The Film Strip," *Colonial Cinema,* January 1952, 10–15.

117. Spurr, "Films for Africans—1910 or 1950?," 186–87.

118. Ibid.

119. "Commentary and Commentators," *Colonial Cinema,* March 1948, 13–14. John Wilson, the information officer in the Gold Coast, similarly concluded that "everything is dependent on his [the commentator's] skill." John Wilson, "Gold Coast Information," *African Affairs,* July 1944, 112.

120. Ambler, "Projecting the Modern Colonial State," 208. In "Films for Primitive Peoples" Sellers notes that all vans operating in the colonies "are identical in design" (174).

121. "Tanganyika," *Colonial Cinema*, September 1946, 62–64; George Pearson, "Visual Education by Film in the Colonies," *United Empire*, July/August 1950, 206–10; "Tanganyika: Wanderings of the Cinema Van," *Colonial Cinema*, March 1947, 9–10. The vans needed to be specially adapted, like the films they showed. When a new batch of MOI vans, used on England's "good roads," was dispatched to Africa at the end of the war, they were deemed "fundamentally unsuitable for use in a tropical climate." Precis of a letter from Mr. Sellers, 10–15 April 1946, INF 12/282, TNA.

122. Memorandum of the Cinema Branch, CO 875 10/9, TNA; *Colonial Cinema*, March 1954, 19–22.

123. A. G. Dickson, "Mass Education in Togoland," *African Affairs*, April 1950, 136–50.

124. Spurr, "Mobile Cinema Van Is a New Weapon," 9–16.

125. "The Mobile Cinema Van in the Villages," *Colonial Cinema*, March 1945, 11–14.

126. Larkin, *Signal and Noise*, 83.

127. Sellers, "Mobile Cinema Shows in Africa," 79.

128. An image from a film show in Palestine reveals women seated and viewing on the other side of the screen. See IWM K4164, Imperial War Museum, London.

129. Rennalls, *A Career Making a Difference*, 65, 80–83.

130. "The Units at Work," *Colonial Cinema*, November 1943, 2–3.

131. Sellers, "Mobile Cinema Shows in Africa," 81–82.

132. Tom Rice, "1955: The Year in Malaya," www.colonialfilm.org.uk/node/2545 (accessed 30 May 2013).

133. A Queen Is Crowned in Malta, FCO 141/10508, TNA. The governor's concerns centered on the fact that it depicted an Anglican ceremony. The coronation had already proved a politically contentious event in Malta. The prime minister revealed plans to boycott, and cut back local celebrations, after he was not initially offered a formal invitation. Further controversy over which Maltese flag to fly highlighted the political stakes at an event that brought together, displayed, and ordered shifting colonial hierarchies. See Philip Murphy, *Monarchy and the End of Empire: The House of Windsor, the British Government and the Postwar Government* (Oxford: Oxford University Press, 2013), 56–58.

134. Cinema Propaganda West Indies, CO 875/10/3, TNA.

135. Jamaica Welfare Limited—Cinema Unit and Film Education; Correspondence, Minutes, Reports, 4/60/10a/9.

136. Hugh Thomas to Colonial Secretary, 26 February 1947; response from Dixon, 8 March 1947, Films Passed by the Cinematograph Board of Control—Queries Regarding, C. S. O. 15/8/47, PRAAD. After the Chamber described the selection of the film as both "unwise and even improper," Dixon retaliated that the mobile van had provided years of entertainment for the mines "without complaint and apparently without gratitude." Dixon added that the van would stop touring the area.

137. Colonial Office, *Colonial Reports: Cyprus, 1955* (London: H.M.S.O., 1956), 76.

138. See correspondence in the file on Mobile Cinema, OPM 818/1962, National Archives of Malta.

139. Burns, *Flickering Shadows*, 133.

140. Personal correspondence with John Izod, March 2013.

141. Ambler, "Projecting the Modern Colonial State," 210. Ambler shows how the film equipment was now used for other purposes, most notably as nationalist leader Paul Ngei took the microphone at a film show in 1947 to advertise a forthcoming political meeting.

142. Terri Francis, "Sounding the Nation: Martin Rennalls and the Jamaica Film Unit, 1951–1961," *Film History: An International Journal* 23.2 (2011): 114; Jamaica Welfare Limited—Cinema Unit and Film Education; Correspondence, Minutes, Reports, 4/60/10a/9; Roger Marier, *Social Welfare Work in Jamaica: A Study of the Jamaica Social Welfare Commission* (Paris: UNESCO, 1953), 116. Quoted in M.A. Rennalls, "Development of the Documentary Film in Jamaica," unpublished thesis submitted for the Degree of Master of Science, School of Public Communication, Division of Broadcasting and Film, Boston University, 1967, 79.

143. Report of Cinema Lecturers Conference, 19 July 1946, Film Production, 1944–1948, 3/24/216, Jamaica Archives, Spanish Town, Jamaica. Commentators noted that the traveling films needed to be relatable to their audience and that this would vary by area. For example, the Kenya Information officer commented on a screening of *Life Cycle of the Newt* in February 1946 by simply stating "newts unknown in Africa." Comments on Films from BC Representatives Overseas, BW 4/29, TNA.

144. Cinema Propaganda: Colonial Film Unit, CO 875 10/9, TNA. See also *Colonial Cinema*, December 1943, 2; Sellers, "Mobile Cinema Shows in Africa," 80.

145. Ambler, "Projecting the Modern Colonial State," 206.

146. *Colonial Cinema*, September 1947, 59–62; Peter Morton-Williams, *Cinema in Rural Nigeria: A Field Study of the Impact of Fundamental-Education Films on Rural Audiences in Nigeria* (Lagos: Federal Information Services, 1952). The final report (p. 42) attributed unexpected audience laughter—for example, when a character dies in *Amenu's Child*—"in terms of the social norms and values on the audiences," so that laughter was not a critique, but rather "the appropriate reaction" in this context.

147. CO 875/51/7, TNA. The Colonial Office acknowledged: "We really have no control over the employment of local staff."

148. CO 875/51/7, TNA. See Davidson to Miss Loveless, dated 5 October 1951 and 18 October 1951; Governor's Deputy in Nigeria to Secretary of State in London, dated 8 May 1951.

149. CO 875/51/7, TNA. See letter from Acting Government of Nigeria to Secretary of State for the Colonies on 11 October 1951.

150. CO 875/51/7, TNA. See letter from Governor's Deputy, dated 8 May 1951.

151. CO 875/51/7, TNA. See K. W. Blackburne to Howson, dated 8 May 1950.

152. Morton-Williams, *Cinema in Rural Nigeria*, 29, 39; Tom Rice, "Amenu's Child," www.colonialfilm.org.uk/node/6730.

153. Mobile cinema operators in Jamaica in the 1940s regularly complained about technological problems. As an example from the first half of 1946, one unit had to abandon eighteen shows because of equipment faults, while another unit cancelled screenings because of power and projector problems. See Film Production, 1944–1948, 3/24/216, Jamaica Archives, Spanish Town, Jamaica.

154. Morton-Williams, *Cinema in Rural Nigeria*, 130–33.

155. Ibid., 73, 46.

156. Ibid., 45.

157. Ibid., 48, 100.

158. Ibid., 70.

159. Ibid., 32, 134.

160. Ibid., 48.

161. Ibid., 69, 50.

162. Ibid., 89.

163. Ibid., 45.

164. "Sound Track," *Colonial Cinema*, March 1950, 18.

165. Morton-Williams, *Cinema in Rural Nigeria*, 44, 45.

166. Sellers, "Film Use and Production in British Colonial Territories."

167. Graham, *Use of Film in the West Indies and Mexico*, 51, 45.

CHAPTER 3: MOBILIZING AN EMPIRE

1. Ashley Jackson, "The Colonial Film Archive and the British Empire at War, 1939–1945," paper presented at "Film and the End of Empire" Conference, University of Pittsburgh, September 2010, available at http://studylib.net/doc/8932424/the-colonial-film-archive-and-the-british-empire-at-war (accessed 22 March 2017).

2. Keith Jeffery, "The Second World War," in *The Oxford History of the British Empire*, vol. 4, *The Twentieth Century*, ed. Judith Brown and William Roger Louis (Oxford: Oxford University Press), 327. See also Lee Grieveson, "Introduction: Film at the End of Empire," in *Film and the End of Empire*, ed. Lee Grieveson and Colin MacCabe (London: Palgrave Macmillan, 2011); Ashley Jackson, *The British Empire and the Second World War* (London: Hambledon Continuum, 2006); Andrew Stewart, *Empire Lost: Britain, the Dominions and the Second World War* (London: Hambledon Continuum, 2008); David Killingray, *Fighting for Britain: African Soldiers in the Second World War* (Woodbridge: James Currey, 2010).

3. James Chapman, *The British at War: Cinema, State and Propaganda, 1939–1945* (London: I. B. Taurus, 1998), 13.

4. Colonial and Middle East Vote: Preparatory Expenditure on Ministry of Information Publicity Scheme in the Colonies: Cinema Vans, Film Publicity: Cinema Vans for the Colonies, INF 1/717, TNA.

5. Minutes from A.P. Waterfield, 10 November 1939, Staff Organisation: Film Division, INF 1/30, TNA; letter from D.G. Woodburn, 12 February 1940, CO 323/1744/13, TNA.

6. Letter from D.G. Woodburn, 12 February 1940; telegram from Secretary of State for the Colonies to Governor of Nigeria, 22 February 1940, Use of Mobile Cinema Units in West Africa, CO 323/1744/13, TNA.

7. Jo Fox, "John Grierson, His 'Documentary Boys' and the British Ministry of Information, 1939–1942," *Historical Journal of Film, Radio and Television* 25 (2005): 345–69.

8. Arthur Elton to Campbell, I July 1942, INF 1/144, TNA.

9. Sellers to Mercier, 26 May 1941, and responses and correspondence on this subject found in INF 1/144, TNA.

10. Sellers to Mercier, 26 May 1941.

11. Sellers to Mercier, 28 June 1941, INF 1/144.

12. Sellers to Mercier, 11 November 1941, INF 1/144.

13. Sellers to Beddington, 16 February 1942, INF 1/144.

14. Proposal from W. Sellers, 3 March 1942, and subsequent correspondence on the subject, contained in INF 1/144.

15. Mercier to Beddington, 6 February 1942, INF 1/144.

16. N.W.G. Tucker to G.G. Welch, 18 June 1942, INF 1/144.

17. E.R. Edmett, 26 February 1942, Proposals for Producing and Distributing Instructional Films, CO 859/46/9, TNA.

18. Edmett, 21 February 1942, CO 859/46/9; letter from W.S. Morgan, 7 December 1943, CO 859/46/9.

19. Edmett, 26 February 1942; Morgan, 7 December 1943.

20. Note to Blaxter, 4 February 1943; minutes of meeting, 29 January 1943 and further minutes from 1943, CO 875/10/9. *Documentary News Letter* (October 1942, 139) complained that the MOI is "at the mercy of half the petty officials in Whitehall" and so instead of shaping and directing propaganda, it was subservient to the "local, private and often conflicting notions of government departments."

21. Gervas Huxley to Noel Sabine, 31 May 1943; minutes of meeting held at MOI on 17 June 1943, CO 875/10/9. Huxley argued that if a mobile cinema tour took six months, there was absolutely no need for the CFU to produce four new films a month but instead "a small number of really good films which would not date over a period of six months or longer."

22. Huxley to Sabine, 31 May 1943, and Sabine to Huxley, 11 June 1943; minutes from 17 June 1943, CO 875/10/9; *Colonial Cinema,* May 1943, 3. Huxley ultimately argued that those within the MOI should "exercise a more continuous and direct control of the unit's work," urging closer supervision to ensure that time and money was not wasted on work that was "later bound to be rejected."

23. "The Colonies and the War," *Crown Colonist,* November 1939, 603.

24. Malcolm MacDonald, "Why the British Empire Is at War," *Crown Colonist,* November 1939, 607.

25. Report on Activities of Information Department, 6 September 1939, CO 323/1663/10, TNA.

26. Kate Morris, *British Techniques of Public Relations and Propaganda for Mobilizing East and Central Africa during World War II* (London: Edwin Mellen Press, 2000), 128–29.
27. Stephen Constantine, *The Making of British Colonial Development Policy, 1914–1940* (London: Frank Cass, 1984), 223.
28. The King stated in his Empire Day message in May 1940 that "there is a word that our enemies use against us—Imperialism." He argued instead that "our one object has always been peace—peace in which our institutions may be developed, the condition of our peoples improved." Cited in Wendy Webster, *Englishness and Empire 1939–1965* (Oxford: Oxford University Press, 2005), 26.
29. Cinema Photographic Unit in East Africa, CO 875/17/4, TNA.
30. Josephine Kamm, *Progress towards Self-Government in the British Colonies* (London, 1945). Cited in Rosaleen Smyth, "Britain's African Colonies and British Propaganda during the Second World War," *Journal of Imperial and Commonwealth History* 14 (1985): 70.
31. Smyth, "Britain's African Colonies and British Propaganda," 76; Morris, *British Techniques of Public Relations and Propaganda,* 238.
32. Campbell to May, 19 January 1943; paper no. 1679 and further correspondence on the hiring of African staff, INF 1/144.
33. Bradshaw to Fletcher, 29 September 1943 and 18 September 1945; letter to W. E. Phillips, 25 October 1945, INF 1/144.
34. *Colonial Cinema,* September 1945, 51; *Colonial Cinema,* December 1945, 75.
35. Arthur M. Champion, "Introducing Africans to the Cinema Screen," *Crown Colonist,* February 1942, 80; note to Primrose, 19 October 1939; Harlow to Primrose, 30 August 1939, H. M. The King, BW 4/9, TNA.
36. See, for example, Martin Rennalls, *A Career Making a Difference* (1991), 39–41; British News: Colonies, BW 4/12, TNA. *British News* comprised material edited from the ten weekly issues of the five British newsreel companies.
37. Letter from E. L. Mercier, 26 November 1941, Ministry of Information: Correspondence about Film Distribution, BW 4/64.
38. Films and Reports from British Council Jamaica Agricultural Society Information Officer, 1943–1945, 3/24/145, Jamaica Archives, Spanish Town, Jamaica.
39. Four British Council Films, BW 4/64; British Council Film Department, *Films of Britain, 1941;* Bracken to Robertson, 27 November 1941, BW 4/64. The British Council was not afraid to fight back. The director of its film department claimed the MOI had always been "antagonistic and jealous of the Council's activities" and "have tried by every means to bring about a complete cessation of our production and distribution activities." Others in the Council blamed the criticisms of on-screen representation on a perceived MOI "embargo" on war references in Council films. By early 1942 the MOI and British Council were urged to "get together and thrash things out. We are fighting a major war and the Council and the Ministry of Information simply must work together." Letter from Kearney, 10 December 1941, BW 4/64; Robertson to Bracken, 8 December 1941 and responses in BW 4/64; letter dated 16 February 1942, BW 4/64.

40. Gillan to Primrose, 23 February 1942, Film Committee: Meetings, BW 4/56. Malcolm Robertson further explained the council's role within the war effort: "We must show the World who we are and what we are fighting for, as well as how we are fighting." Robertson to Bracken, 8 December 1941, BW 4/64.

41. Minutes, 23 June 1943, Film Department Minutes, BW 4/54.

42. Sir Angus Gillan, 4 March 1943; minutes from W. S. Morgan, 2 April 1943, British Council Film Activities: Part I, CO 875/10/7, TNA; W. S. Morgan, 5 January 1944, British Council Film Activities: Part II, CO 875/10/8. W. S. Morgan at the Colonial Office also believed the need for the technique "exaggerated," stating: "I do not feel the British Council films could not be shown to other than educated or sophisticated audiences on the grounds of camera technique." While Morgan concluded that the CFU would be best placed to make "educational" films for the colonies, he concluded that it was best "to get as many films as possible, and not to discourage the Council in their desire to help."

43. Minutes, 17 February 1943; minutes, 17 June 1943, CO 875/10/9. The CFU filmed the agricultural school in the summer of 1944, released as *Education in England: A Secondary Modern School*. See "A School with Ideas," *Colonial Cinema*, March 1945, 6–10; *Colonial Cinema*, June 1945, 39.

44. Morgan, 31 January 1944, CO 875/10/8; Minutes of Meeting of Colonial Film Unit, 23 June 1943, CO 875/10/9. Sellers suggested replacing the British Council's planned works on "The Post Office" and "How a Book Is Made" with films entitled "How a Bicycle Is Made" (it is unclear if Sellers had shares in a bicycle company) and "British Boys and Girls' Games."

45. Minutes, 23 June 1943, CO 875/10/9.

46. This was one of two films initially designated "for the colonies." The program of fifty-six films in 1944–45 included four specifically "for the colonies." Minutes, 31 December 1943, Film Department: Minutes, BW 4/54. The film is available to view, alongside more than a hundred British Council films, at the excellent British Council website. See http://film.britishcouncil.org/local-government.

47. Girkins to Thomas, 14 August 1943, CO 875/10/8.

48. Thomas to Sabine, 23 August 1943, and further responses to the film in CO 875/10/8.

49. G. C. Miles, 6 August 1943; W. S. Morgan, 10 August 1943, CO 875/10/8.

50. Film Report on *Second Freedom*, 15 January 1946, Comments on Films from BC Representatives Overseas, BW 4/29, TNA.

51. The report further bemoaned the lack of films specifically prepared for overseas use (only twenty-seven out of 240 were specifically made for this purpose) and the absence of films that represent "not the government speaking *to* the people, but the people speaking through the government." *Documentary News Letter*, October 1942, 135.

52. Note dated 4 June 1942, CO 875/10/7.

53. Minutes of the 26th Meeting of the Film Committee, 7 April 1942, BW 4/54.

54. There are detailed historical essays on these films and, with the exception of *Community Development,* the films are available to view at www.colonial film.org.uk.

55. Hansard, H.C. Deb., vol. 401, cols. 821–25 (29 June 1944) [electronic version].

56. Hansard, H.C. Deb., vol. 414, col. 1991 (24 October 1945) [electronic version].

57. *Colonial Cinema,* March 1946, 9.

58. Fay Gadsden, "Wartime Propaganda in Kenya: The Kenya Information Office, 1939–1945," *International Journal of African Historical Studies* 19.3 (1986): 406.

59. Ibid., 407, 413. Gadsden also noted that the Information Office would avoid showing films that "revealed that American blacks were paid the same as whites."

60. "Propaganda: Kenya and the War," *East African Standard,* 10 October 1941; "The Work of the African Section of the Kenya Information Office," 12 September 1941, Kenya: The Information Office, CO 875/6/16. The Kenya Information Office was criticized for "costing the taxpayer about £16000 a year, much more than the expenditure on information and propaganda in adjoining territories" and was labeled in the weekly *East Africa and Rhodesias* as "so outstanding a case of failure."

61. The reports are found in Kenya: Films, CO 875/6/18; Champion, "Introducing Africans to the Cinema Screen." Champion used attendance figures as a "simple testimony to the popularity of the mobile cinema" and by 1942 stated that the unit had undertaken 250 displays to audiences of around 350,000.

62. *Mombasa Times,* 17 March 1941; Champion, Report on Cinema Unit, 3 March 1941, CO 875/6/18.

63. Champion, "Introducing Africans to the Cinema Screen"; A.M. Champion, "With a Mobile Cinema Unit in Kenya," *Oversea Education,* October 1948, 788–92.

64. Champion, "Mobile Cinema Unit in Kenya," 789.

65. Arthur M. Champion, Report of Government Mobile Cinema Unit for Fortnight Ending Sunday, June 22; Champion, Report from week ending January 19, 1941, CO 875/6/18; "The Work of the African Section of the Kenya Information Office," 12 September 1941, CO 875/6/16.

66. Champion, "Introducing Africans to the Cinema Screen."

67. "The Work of the African Section of the Kenya Information Office," CO 875/6/16; Dawe to Gurney, 12 January 1942, CO 875/6/16; Usill to Roper, 4 January 1943, CO 875/10/5.

68. "Making Films in Kenya," *Colonial Cinema,* December 1945, 87–88. This was originally published in the *East Africa Standard* in September 1945.

69. "Proceedings of the Conference of Information Officers, Nairobi, May 21st, 1941 and Following Days," Conference of Information Officers in Nairobi, CO 875/8/20.

70. Report of Conference of West African Information Officers, Achimota, 4–6 May 1943, CO 875/9/8.

71. Fraser to Usill, 26 May 1943; Fraser to Usill, 7 July 1943, Supply of Film Strips for the Colonies, INF 1/354.
72. Morgan, 7 December 1943, CO 859/46/9.
73. Usill to Grubb, 31 March 1943; Photographic Division, 7 October 1943, INF 1/354.
74. Evidence of Use Made of Filmstrips by Colonial Territories, Film Strip Service: Colonial Office, INF 12/428.
75. Ibid.; letter from Barbara MacFarlane, PR office, Bathhurst, 28 June 1945, INF 1/354.
76. INF 12/428.
77. The proposed subjects for the West Africa Photography Unit overlap with the CFU and include one demonstrating Western weaving techniques to an African village in Togoland, the subject of the 1946 CFU film *Weaving in Togoland*. The unit's early assignments, such as "A Day in the Life of a Native Administration Judge" and its less glamorous sequel "A Day in the Life of a Native Administration Treasurer," accompany Colonial Office articles and share the structures of CFU film and MOI filmstrips. See letter to Usill from West Africa, 11 December 1943, West Africa: Photographic Unit, CO 875/9/9.
78. See letter from PR Officer, Gambia to Evans, 1 July 1945, INF 1/354. The West Africa Photography Unit sought to source and access equipment in Africa, creating an infrastructure so that "photographs taken in West Africa can be processed on the spot and not, as at present, sent home." West Africa: Photographic Unit, CO 875/9/9.
79. Robinson, 13 May 1943, CO 875/9/9, Evans to Wathen, 25 October 1944; Evans to Wathen, 15 November 1944 and responses.
80. Fell to Usill, 22 December 1945, INF 1/354.
81. Bradshaw to Information Officer, Uganda, 1 December 1945, INF 1/354.
82. Colonial Distribution of Film Strips, INF 1/354. The scripts for the filmstrip of *Farmer Brown Learns Good Dairying* and other colonial titles are contained in a 1954 UNESCO report, *Filmstrip Commentary: Basic Education, Rural Education, Preventive Health Education in Various Developing Countries* (UNESCO, 1954).
83. William Sellers, "Advice on Filmstrip Production," *Colonial Cinema*, June 1951, 44–46. Sellers proposed an average of 40–50 pictures in each filmstrip with due emphasis on close-ups to provide detail.
84. Peter J. Bloom, "Elocution, Englishness and Empire: Film and Radio in Late Colonial Ghana," in *Modernization as Spectacle in Africa*, ed. Peter J. Bloom, Stephan F. Miescher, and Takyiwaa Manuh (Bloomington: Indiana University Press, 2014), 136–56.
85. Fred Pratt, "'Ghana Muntie!' Broadcasting, Nation-Building and Social Difference in the Gold Coast and Ghana, 1935–1985" (PhD diss., Indiana University, 2013), 48–49.
86. Extract from Colonial Press Summary Confidential, no. 23, West Africa, 10.1.41, Nigeria: Comparison with Gold Coast Services, CO 875/1/21, TNA.
87. Larkin, *Signal and Noise*, 48–49.
88. Pratt, "Ghana Muntie!," 51.

89. Wilson, "Gold Coast Information," 114; Wendell P. Holbrook, "British Propaganda and the Mobilization of the Gold Coast War Effort, 1939–1945," *Journal of African History* 26.4 (1985): 354.

90. Wilson, "Gold Coast Information," 111.

91. Simon Potter, *Broadcasting Empire: The BBC and the British World, 1922–1970* (Oxford: Oxford University Press, 2012), 110–43; Siân Nicholas "'Brushing Up Your Empire': Dominion and Colonial Propaganda on the BBC's Home Services, 1939–45," *Journal of Imperial and Commonwealth History* 31.2 (2003): 207–30; Thomas Hajkowski, *From the War to Westminster Abbey: The BBC and the Empire, 1939–53* (Manchester: Manchester University Press, 2010). The BBC shows included the roundtable discussion *Red on the Map*, the traditional fare of *Travellers' Tales, Dominion Commentary, The Empire's Answer, Meet the Empire: Bill and Bob at the BBC*, the light entertainment "quiz" *Brush Up Your Empire*, and the influential *Calling the West Indies* (later *Caribbean Voices*), which was hosted by Una Marson and filmed as part of a 1943 MOI film, *West Indies Calling*. For more on *West Indies Calling*, see Tom Rice, "West Indies Calling," www.colonialfilm.org.uk/node/5733, and Webster, *Englishness and Empire, 1939–1965*.

92. Potter, *Broadcasting Empire*, 132.

93. Morris, *British Techniques of Public Relations and Propaganda*, 115–17; Potter, *Broadcasting Empire*, 117.

94. Nicholas, "'Brushing Up Your Empire'," 214; Potter, *Broadcasting Empire*, 143.

95. Wilson, "Gold Coast Information," 111.

96. J. M. Burns, *Flickering Shadows: Cinema and Identity in Colonial Zimbabwe* (Athens: Ohio University Press, 2002), 34; H. Franklin, "The Central African Screen," *Colonial Cinema*, December 1950, 85–88. Franklin compared the average "native" adult to a ten-year-old European child, claiming that "anything subtle leaves them cold" and that a "native's mental perception is very limited."

97. Holbrook, "British Propaganda and the Mobilization of the Gold Coast War Effort, 1939–1945," 359–60.

98. Memorandum of the Cinema Branch, CO 875 10/9; Wilson to Davidson, 20 June 1941, CO 859/46/9. Wilson argued in 1941: "I am very doubtful if many films suitable for illiterate, semi-literate and even some literate Africans are to be found outside Sellers's production unit at the Ministry of Information."

99. See Morgan to Grossmith, 14 April 1943 and related correspondence, CO 875/10/9; Wilson to Evans, 17 March 1943, CO 875/10/8. The CFU views were evidently ingrained in Wilson. He rejected Gaumont British films as "they are very closely adapted to English ideas and the cinema idiom, e.g. fast cutting and method of shooting presupposes an audience well accustomed to the film." John Wilson to Minister of Education, 28 December 1942, Cinematograph—Use of in Schools, RG 3/5/998, PRAAD.

100. Morgan to Grossmith, CO 875/10/9; Report of Conference, CO 875/9/8.

101. A meeting at the MOI in December 1942 outlined the three functions of the CFU: first, "to produce films which would give an illustrative background

for colonial propaganda"; second, "to produce films of a war flavour, showing the efforts and achievements of the British Empire in particular and the United Nations in general"; and third, "to produce instructional films not necessarily connected with the war." Minutes of Meeting at MOI on 11 December 1942, CO 875/10/9.

102. Report of Conference, CO 875/9/8.

103. *Colonial Cinema,* November 1942, 2; *Colonial Cinema,* August 1943, 2.

104. Minutes of CFU Meeting at MOI, 16 July 1943, CO 875/10/9.

105. Morgan to Usill, May 1943, CO 875/10/9.

106. "Raw Stock Scheme," 23 July 1943, CO 875/10/9; "The Raw Stock Scheme: Retrospect and Prospect," *Colonial Cinema,* December 1945, 76–79. When new equipment was sent out in March 1945, Fiji and Northern Rhodesia were also included in the list. A report from Tanganyika in 1946 (*Colonial Cinema,* September 1946, 62–64) explained that "we are a country of amateurs" and in the "absence of a permanent professional," used a military officer to shoot films in Western Province and a member of the Labour office (Ballard) and wireless officer (Strickland) to shoot footage, largely of ceremonials in Dar-es Salaam (such as VE day, sports events, the opening of the legislative council). Robert Kingston Davies did travel around Tanganyika in 1945. He had previously produced films for British schools and would subsequently shoot material in East Africa for Crown after the war with Stewart McAllister.

107. See Tom Rice, "Plainsmen of Barotseland," www.colonialfilm.org.uk/node/1914; "Plainsmen of Barotseland," *Colonial Cinema,* June 1945, 42–43; Geoffrey Mangin, *Filming Emerging Africa: A Pioneer Cinematographer's Scrapbook—from the 1940s to the 1960s* (Cape Town: Author, 1998); Louis Nell, *Images of Yesteryear: Film-Making in Central Africa* (HarperCollins Zimbabwe, 1998).

108. Minutes of Meeting of the Colonial Film Unit Committee, 29 June 1943, CO 875/10/9. Usill argued that only when filmmaking became part of CFU's long-term policy and an area in which a "young man could make a career" would you get the "right kind of recruits." For an example of Schauder's work, see Tom Rice, "Father and Son," www.colonialfilm.org.uk/node/1755.

109. The Imperial War Museum holds a fascinating, extensive collection of these army rushes, along with the cameraman's "dope" sheets. For examples of Feilmann's work, see the Colonial Film website, www.colonialfilm.org.uk/node/5555 and www.colonialfilm.org.uk/node/2023.

110. "Raw Stock Scheme," 78.

111. Letter to H. V. Usill, 12 June 1943, CO 875/10/9.

112. "News Films," *Colonial Cinema,* April 1944, 15.

113. Rosaleen Smyth, "The British Colonial Film Unit and Sub-Saharan Africa, 1939–1945," *Historical Journal of Film, Radio and Television* 8.3 (1988): 290.

114. *Colonial Cinema,* June 1945, 27.

115. Memorandum of the Cinema Branch, CO 875 10/9.

116. Cited in Smyth, "Britain's African Colonies and British Propaganda," 350, and Smyth, "British Colonial Film Unit," 291. The final item in *Africa's Fighting Men*—"Pilot Officer Peter Thomas, R. A. F."—differs markedly and

was exceptional enough to warrant its own widely promoted CFU film. While the earlier items presented a collective African mass training overseas, this final item focuses on an individual African man excelling, the first to qualify for a commission in the R.A.F.

117. I have written extensively on Indian News Parade and on twenty individual issues of the newsreel on the colonial film website, www.colonialfilm.org.uk/production-company/indian-news-parade. IWM holds 138 issues of the newsreel and detailed commentary sheets. See also Philip Woods, "'Chapattis by Parachute': The Use of Newsreels in British Propaganda in India in the Second World War," *Journal of South Asian Studies* 23.2 (2000): 89–110; Jude Cowan, "'Women at Work for War . . . Women at Work for the Things of Peace': Representations of Women in the British Propaganda Newsreel in India in the Second World War, Indian News Parade" (unpublished master's thesis, Birkbeck College, University of London, 2001), accessed at the Imperial War Museum.

118. Sanjoy Bhattacharya, *Propaganda and Information in Eastern India, 1939–45: A Necessary Weapon of War* (London: Routledge, 2001); B.D. Garga, *From Raj to Swaraj: The Non-Fiction Film in India* (New Delhi: Penguin, 2007).

119. Minutes of Meeting at the Colonial Office, 18 March 1943, Colonial Film Unit: Film on Venereal Disease, CO 875/10/13. Both Dr. Paterson and Arthur Champion were mentioned as possible directors, although the Colonial Office thought that the MOI might demand professional filmmakers "to give the film a human story interest." See also Huxley to Morgan, 28 August 1943, CO 875/10/13.

120. Letter from Grossmith, 20 July 1943; Huxley to Morgan, 28 August 1943, CO 875/10/13.

121. Minutes, 18 March 1943; Sellers to Morgan, 22 April 1943; Huxley to Morgan, 28 August 1943, CO 875/10/13.

122. The CFU had previously stressed that any existing English or American films would be "inappropriate for showing to Africans." See minutes, 18 March 1943, CO 875/10/13.

123. Harry Franklin, 9 October 1943, CO 875/10/13. The director of education in the Gold Coast questioned the choice of names, stating that Mr. Wise was "far from wise in the first instance." While concluding that the film "might do good," he again suggested that much would rest on the commentator as "the vernacular commentaries will require the most detailed rehearsing." Director of Education, 17 August 1944, Cinematograph—Use of in Schools, RG 3/5/998 PRAAD.

124. *Colonial Cinema,* June 1947, 27; Exhibition Report on Non-Theatrical Films, Films and Reports from British Council Jamaica Agricultural Society Information Officer, 1943–1945, 3/24/145, Jamaica Archives, Spanish Town, Jamaica; Timbermen from Honduras, INF 6/43, TNA. There was also a film entitled *African Timber* (1945), which showed, to quote one audience member, "how African timber was helping to win the war." Norman Spurr, "A New Weapon in Mass Education," *Colonial Cinema,* March 1949, 9.

125. "Essex Village to 'Star' in Film for Colonies," *Essex Chronicle,* 24 August 1945, 5.

126. *Sight and Sound*, July 1944, 51–52; *Colonial Cinema*, July 1944, 1; *Colonial Cinema*, August 1944, 32; *Colonial Cinema*, September 1944, 36.

127. "Village School," *Colonial Cinema*, September 1946, 50–55; *Colonial Cinema*, March 1946, 13. The film was shown in senior schools in Africa and *Colonial Cinema* discussed the essays and reports from the students.

128. "African Girl as May Queen," *Colonial Cinema*, July 1944, 27; "Reports from Overseas," *Colonial Cinema*, June 1945, 40. *Colonial Cinema* reported on the enthusiastic response of African audiences to the film, noting that "the comment was heard that Aggrey's motto (black and white keys of the piano) was being put into practice in Britain."

129. "African Girl as May Queen," 27.

130. Marc Matera, *Black London: The Imperial Metropolis and Decolonization in the Twentieth Century* (Oakland: University of California Press, 2015), 305; "Essex Village to 'Star' in Film for Colonies," 5.

131. An African in England, INF 1/225; "Essex Village to 'Star' in Film for Colonies," 5. Filming took place elsewhere including Bishop Stortford, Clavering, and Arkston. John Jochimsen recalls filming the village hall sequence in his autobiography. Dennis Bowden featured in one sequence and Bob Paynter played the projectionist. John Jochimsen, *80 Years Gone in a Flash: The Memoirs of a Photojournalist* (London: MX, 2011), 45–47; interview by Mary Ingleby with Dennis Bowden, 9 August 2007, accessed at the Bristol Records Office; interview by Mary Ingleby with Bob Paynter, 18 September 2007, accessed at the Bristol Records Office.

132. An African in England, INF 1/225. The CFU also produced *Africans Study Social Work in Britain* in 1945, which shows how the skills learned in Britain can be applied back in Africa.

133. An African in England, INF 1/225.

134. "Colonial Film Unit," *Colonial Cinema*, June 1947, 27–31.

135. *Colonial Cinema*, September 1945, 54–55.

136. Work of 16mm Department, 20 June 1946 to 17 July 1946, INF 12/282, TNA.

137. Sabine to Sendall, 15 April 1946, Victory Parade, INF 6/226, TNA.

138. "Victory Celebrations: Special Supplement," *The Times*, 10 May 1946, 9.

139. *Colonial Cinema*, September 1945, 51.

140. Native Administration Cinema Circuit, RG 3/5/745, PRAAD.

141. Webster, *Englishness and Empire 1939–1965*, 59. The BBC reopened its television service with a two-hour broadcast of the ceremony.

142. This is reported in "Colonial Fighters to be Cut from Victory Parade Films," *Atlanta Daily World*, 14 September 1946, 1; Minutes of Colonial Film Unit Meeting, 17 July 1946, INF 12/282, TNA.

143. *Colonial Cinema*, September 1946, 47; *Colonial Cinema*, September 1947, 64.

144. *Colonial Cinema*, September 1946, 68.

145. Adrienne M. Israel, "Measuring the War Experience: Ghanaian Soldiers in World War II," *Journal of Modern African Studies* 25.1 (March 1987): 159–68.

146. Paul Gilroy, "Great Games: Film, History and Working-through Britain's Colonial Legacy," in Grieveson and MacCabe, *Film and the End of Empire*, 14.

CHAPTER 4: MOVING OVERSEAS

1. "Camera Unit in Africa," *Colonial Cinema*, June 1946, 24–27; George Pearson, "The Making of Films for Illiterates in Africa," in *The Film in Colonial Development: A Report of a Conference* (London: BFI, 1948), 26; Colonial Film Unit: Report for 1951, CO 875/52/3, TNA, UK.

2. *Colonial Cinema*, March 1946, 3; W. Sellers, "Address to the British Kinematograph Society," *Colonial Cinema*, March 1948, 9–13.

3. George Pearson, "Introduction," as part of "The Film in Colonial Development: Summary of Papers read to B.K.S. Sub-Standard Film Division on November 26 1947," *British Kinematography*, July 1948, 14.

4. *Colonial Cinema*, March 1946, 3; "Some Impressions," *Colonial Cinema*, September 1946, 48–50.

5. Interview by Mary Ingleby with Bob Paynter, 18 September 2007, accessed at the Bristol Records Office.

6. "Filming in Africa," *Colonial Cinema*, June 1947, 40–43; personal interview with Billy Williams, 7 June 2016.

7. Interview with Williams. Williams would use any space in packages to stuff food that would then be sent back to his mother in Surrey.

8. *Colonial Cinema*, March 1946, 3.

9. Interview by Mary Ingleby with Bob Paynter; *Colonial Cinema*, June 1946, 24–27; Bradshaw to Izod, 3 February 1947; Bradshaw to Sewell, 15 May 1947 and 3 June 1947, Shooting Units in Africa, 1946–1949, INF 12/281, TNA. Conditions were more favorable in some areas, such as Bathhurst, Gambia, where the humidity was "not unlike that in England" and so filming was not affected by "hard tropical shadows, the major problem when photographing in some tropical countries." "The Gambia," *Colonial Cinema*, March 1948, 5–8.

10. "The Gambia," 5–8; Donald Wynne, "Tanganyika's Film Experiment," *Colonial Cinema*, September 1952, 61–65; "Practical Hints to the Film Director," *Colonial Cinema*, March 1949, 3–5.

11. Bradshaw to Izod, 3 February 1947, INF 12/281; letter from COI to Grierson, 2 December 1949, G5:6:4, accessed at the John Grierson Archive, University of Stirling.

12. Colonial Film Unit Programme, 1947/48, Colonial Development and Welfare Act, Colonial Film Unit Scheme D819, T 220/1337, TNA.

13. Production Plan from H.L. Bradshaw, 1947–48, INF 12/293; Proposed Scheme for Training Colonials in 16mm Work, INF 12/282.

14. Estimates for 1948/49 from Bradshaw, INF 12/294; Work of 16mm Department, 20 June 1946–17 July 1946, INF 12/282; 16mm Report, 14 May 1947, INF 12/282.

15. Colonial Film Unit Programme, dated 1 July 1948, and related files, T 220/1337.

16. Estimates for 1948/49 from Bradshaw, INF 12/294; Mackay to Harding, 13 August 1948; Minutes of Meeting on 29 July 1948, T 220/1337.

17. Letter from Campbell, 10 November 1945, Colonial Film Unit—Visit of, to West Africa, CSO 15/8/33, Ghana Public Records and Archives Administration Department, Accra (PRAAD).

18. H. L. Gurney to Noel Sabine, 22 November 1945; letter from Campbell, 11 April 1946, Film of Achimota with Commentary by Julian Huxley—Representations Regarding, CSO 15/8/34, PRAAD.

19. "Colonial Fighters to be Cut from Victory Parade Films," *Atlanta Daily World*, 14 September 1946, 1.

20. J. L. Stewart to Colonial Secretary in Accra, 17 June 1946; Stewart to Campbell, 17 June 1946, Film and Script of "Fight for Life," CSO 15/8/36; letter from A. Campbell, 21 June 1944, Film of Native Administration and Department of Agricultural Activities in the Northern Territories, CSO 16/8/32, PRAAD.

21. Campbell to Colonial Secretary, Accra, 6 July 1946; Stewart to Colonial Secretary, Accra, 5 August 1946, CSO 15/8/36; letter from Campbell, 10 November 1945, CSO 15/8/33, PRAAD; *Fight for Life* (Life on Gold Coast, Accra), INF 6/88, TNA.

22. Hyde to Grierson, 23 March 1949, INF 12/282.

23. Minutes of the Meeting of the Colonial Film Committee, 24 March 1949, INF 12/282. *Here Is the Gold Coast* was also criticized in the Gold Coast Legislature in 1955 ("When it was shown, landladies gave students notices to quit"). The speaker asked, "How many films shown in this country depict the slum areas of, say, Manchester or Liverpool or 37 Upper Parliament Street?" Minutes of the Colonial Film Committee, 24 March 1949, INF 12/282, TNA; Gustav Jahoda, *White Man: A Study of the Attitudes of Africans to Europeans in Ghana before Independence* (Oxford: Oxford University Press, 1961), 67; see also Tom Rice, "Here Is the Gold Coast," www.colonialfilm.org.uk/node/1280.

24. Hyde to Grierson, 23 March 1949, INF 12/282.

25. Jack Ellis, *John Grierson: Life, Contributions, Influence* (Carbondale: Southern Illinois University Press, 2000), 229–39; Zoe Druick, *Projecting Canada: Government Policy and Documentary Film at the National Film Board* (Montreal: McGill-Queen's University Press, 2007), 93–100; Basil Wright, "Documentary Today," *Penguin Film Review* 2 (January 1947): 37–44.

26. John Grierson, "The Film and Primitive Peoples," in *Film in Colonial Development*, 9–15; Martin Stollery, "White Fathers Hear Dark Voices? John Grierson and British Colonial Africa at the End of Empire," in *The Grierson Effect: Tracing Documentary's International Movement*, ed. Zoe Druick and Deane Williams (London: BFI, 2014), 187–208.

27. Morgan to Grierson, 23 May 1949; Proposals for the Reorganisation of the Colonial Film Unit, Administration and Organisation, 1946–1949, INF 12/293. The listed failings of the CFU included rates of pay, overseas living conditions, insecurity, and variable budgets, which made it harder to recruit, retain, and train staff.

28. Ian Aitken, "The Griersonian Influence and Its Challenges: Malaya, Singapore, Hong Kong (1939–1973)," in Druick and Williams, *Grierson Effect*, 93–104.

29. "The Film Story of Malaya's Recovery," *Straits Times*, 4 August 1946, 4. For a discussion of this initial expedition in Malaya and its legacies, see Tom Rice, "Distant Voices of Malaya, Still Colonial Lives," *Journal of British Cinema and Television* 10.3 (2013): 430–51.

30. Letter from Ralph Elton to Basil Wright, 23 January 1946, accessed in Basil Wright file at BFI Special Collections; note from R. E. Tritton of the Films Division, COI, to Brock at India Office, 31 May 1946, File 462/14 Films for Publicity (IOR/L/I/1/686), India Office and Private Papers, accessed at the British Library.

31. "Malaya in Food Film," *Straits Times*, 21 June 1946, 5.

32. *Catalogue of Films Made by the Malayan Film Unit*, 1953 (Kuala Lumpur: Department of Information, 1953).

33. Colonial Development and Welfare Act: Revised Estimates for 1950/51, T 220/1337, TNA; Ian Aitken, *The British Official Film in South-East Asia: Malaya/Malaysia, Singapore and Hong Kong* (London: Palgrave Macmillan, 2016), 63–65.

34. Savings from Secretary of State for the Colonies to the Officer Administering the Government of the Gold Coast, 29 October 1945, 2 November 1945, CSO 15/8/33, PRAAD; "First Colonial Territory to Make Films," *Indian Daily Mail*, 8 August 1946, 4.

35. Sellers, "Address to the British Kinematograph Society," 11.

36. Precis of a letter from Mr. Sellers, 10–15 April 1946, INF 12/282, TNA. Sellers did fly out to Nigeria for five days in April to meet with the African staff of the cinema vans and to discuss the script for the tuberculosis film with local experts.

37. Rosaleen Smyth, "Images of Empires on Shifting Sands: The Colonial Film Unit in West Africa in the Post-War Period," in *Film and the End of Empire*, ed. Lee Grieveson and Colin MacCabe (London: Palgrave Macmillan, 2011), 155–75.

38. "Fight Tuberculosis in the Home," *Colonial Cinema*, December 1946, 62–64.

39. George Pearson, "Health Education by Film in Africa," *Health Education Journal* 7.1 (March 1949): 39–42.

40. Ibid.

41. Colonial Film Unit—Visit of, To West Africa, CSO 15/8/33.

42. "Swollen Shoot," *Colonial Cinema*, March 1947, 15–18. Sellers was initially concerned at a delay in receiving copies of the film from Kodak, fearing that "its usefulness, as a part of the Gold Coast campaign to prevent the spread of cocoa disease, would be lost for another twelve months." Minutes of the Colonial Film Unit Meeting, 19 June 1946, INF 12/282, TNA.

43. Francis K. Danquah, "Sustaining a West African Cocoa Economy: Agricultural Science and the Swollen Shoot Contagion in Ghana, 1936–1965," *African Economic History* 31 (2003): 43–74. This is also discussed in Smyth, "Images of Empires on Shifting Sands," 158.

44. *Colonial Cinema*, March 1948, 3.

45. The public relations officer in the Gold Coast hoped for an example other than Achimota, showing the part played by "other bodies in education." See letter from Campbell, 10 November 1945, CSO 15/8/33.

46. "Film to Educate Populations," *Colonial Cinema*, September 1947, 65–67.

47. Tom Rice, "Better Homes," www.colonialfilm.org.uk/node/1180.

48. Tour of W. Sellers, East Africa, 27 February to 6 April 1948, INF 12/294; West African Production Programme, 1947–48, INF 12/293.

49. Tour of W. Sellers, INF 12/294; "Demonstration Teams in Uganda," *Colonial Cinema*, March 1950, 5. The governor of Tanganyika wrote: "I am doubtful whether suitable African assistants can be found in Tanganyika." Saving Telegram from the Governor to Secretary of State for the Colonies, 10 September 1948, INF 12/294.

50. Tour of W. Sellers, INF 12/294; Colonial Film Unit: Estimates of Expenditure 1950–1951 and 1951–1952, CO 875/52/2, TNA. See also W.S. Morgan to Williams, 10 June 1948, INF 12/293.

51. N. Spurr, "Visual Aids: Colour or Monochrome?," *Colonial Cinema*, June 1952, 42; Rosaleen Smyth, "The Post-War Career of the Colonial Film Unit in Africa: 1946–1955," *Historical Journal of Film, Radio and Television* 12.2 (1992): 163–77; Tom Rice, "Why Not You?," www.colonialfilm.org.uk/node/1012.

52. Norman F. Spurr, "Pamba," *Empire Cotton Growing Review* (June 1950): 172–76.

53. "Health Education in Baganda," *Colonial Cinema*, September 1951, 56–59.

54. Spurr, "Pamba," 172; George Pearson, *Flashback: The Autobiography of a British Filmmaker* (London: George Allen and Unwin, 1957), 213; *Colonial Cinema*, March 1950, 4. Spurr saw Kapere as a way to use humor, which he felt was "sadly neglected to date in films for African peasants," but maintained that these films were "born of the class-room rather than of the entertainment world."

55. Minutes of the Colonial Film Unit Meetings, 15 May 1946, 19 June 1946, 17 July 1946, INF 12/282, TNA; Saving Telegram from Secretary of State for the Colonies, 2 November 1945, CSO 15/8/33, PRAAD.

56. Tom Rice, "Towards True Democracy," www.colonialfilm.org.uk/node/2529; Pearson, "Health Education by Film in Africa," 39.

57. Saving Telegram from Secretary of State for the Colonies, 20 January 1947; H.G. Johnson to Major Costello, 21 March 1947, Cinematograph Unit Department of Information: Cartoon Films, CSO 15/8/38, PRAAD; Minutes of Colonial Film Unit Meeting, 17 July 1946 and 20 December 1946, INF 12/282, TNA; Colonial Film Unit Programme, 1 July 1948, T 220/1337, TNA. Geoffrey Johnson noted that the Agricultural Department was "very interested in the project," but the director of medical services wished to "avoid all forms of propaganda" because he argued that the infrastructure was not yet in place to support the ideas or treatments shown within the films.

58. Note dated 3 February 1947; note from P.R.O., 18 November 1947; Johnson to Costello, 21 March 1947, CSO 15/8/38, PRAAD. The Johnsons worked closely with Sellers and also Lironi, who gave them "very sound advice about the production of films for the Gold Coast." They also discussed the requirements for African audiences with Norman Spurr in Nigeria.

59. Note from Acting Governor of Sierra Leone, 3 February 1948; note from P. R. O., 18 November 1947, CSO 15/8/38, PRAAD.

60. Investigation into the Production of Cartoon Films for African Colonies—Report of Mr Geoffrey Johnson on the Conclusion of a Three Months Tour in West Africa, CSO 15/8/38, PRAAD; Pearson, "Health Education by Film in Africa," 39.

61. Walt Disney, "Animated Cartoon," *Health Education Journal* 13.1 (March 1955): 70–77; Investigation into the Production of Cartoon Films for African Colonies, CSO 15/8/38, PRAAD. Alan Izod argued that the Disney films would be well suited to African audiences and claimed that the CFU only decided to make its own versions after failing to secure copies of the Disney films. Izod, "Some Special Features of Colonial Film Production," 32.

62. Disney, "Animated Cartoon," 71; Munro Leaf, *This Is Ann* (Washington, DC: War Department, U. S. Government Printing Office, 1943).

63. Norman Spurr, "A Report on the Use of Disney's Hookworm Film with an African Audience in the Western Province, Uganda," *Colonial Cinema*, June 1951, 28–33; Spurr also showed the film in Tanganyika. See his "Letter to the Editor," *Colonial Cinema*, December 1954, 86–87.

64. K. Pickering, "Another Walt Disney Experiment," *Colonial Cinema*, September 1954, 50–53.

65. Investigation into the Production of Cartoon Films for African Colonies, CSO 15/8/38, PRAAD.

66. Disney, "Animated Cartoon," 74.

67. Minutes of Colonial Film Unit Meetings, 18 September 1946, 26 February 1947, 26 March 1947, 14 May 1947, INF 12/282, TNA.

68. Colonial Development and Welfare Act: Revised Estimates for 1950/51, T 220/1337, TNA; Colonial Film Unit, October 1949—March 1950, INF 12/368, TNA. The CFU stopped all 35mm production at the end of March, but kept 16mm units in Kenya and Tanganyika until December.

69. Graham Stanford, "Talkies Rival Tom Toms," *Daily Mail*, 16 March 1949, 4. A report in the *Aberdeen Press and Journal* displayed familiar language, suggesting that these "members of the Colonial Film Unit are as much pioneers as the immortal Stanley." Derek Marks, "Scots Film Pioneers at Work in East African Territory," *Aberdeen Press and Journal*, 10 June 1949, 2. See also *Gloucestershire Echo*, 31 January 1949, 1.

70. Reorganisation of the Colonial Film Unit, INF 12/505, TNA; Report of Conference of Information Officers, INF 12/283, TNA.

71. Colonial Development and Welfare Act—Colonial Film Unit Estimates for 1950/51, CO875/52/2, TNA; letter from COI to Grierson, 2 December 1949, John Grierson Archive.

72. A Petition to the Controller, Films Division, Central Office of Information, in Protest against the Abandonment of Educational Film Production in East Africa, 6 January 1950, CO 875/52/4, TNA.

73. "They Made 35 Films: Colonial Office Unit Leaves Soon," *East African Standard*, 7 March 1950; Colonial Film Unit: Estimates of Expenditure 1950–1951 and 1951–1952, CO 875/52/2; *Manchester Guardian*, 11 March 1950. A follow-up report in the *Yorkshire Post and Leeds Mercury* (13 May 1950, 4)

complained that "another socialist experiment undertaken at the expense of the taxpayer has had an unhappy ending." Having met two of the returning men ("poorer yet wiser"), the writer noted how unfortunate it was that all their "energy and enthusiasm" should be thrown away.

74. "Royal Charter for Nairobi: From Swamp to City within the Span of a Lifetime," *The Times*, 30 March 1950, 7; Tom Rice, "Nairobi," www.colonialfilm.org.uk/node/1698.

75. Makhan Singh, *History of Kenya's Trade Union Movement to 1952* (Nairobi: East African Publishing House, 1969), 254.

76. In contrast, the Gold Coast and Nigerian governments agreed to meet the cost of their production units.

77. Letter from Margaret Bucknall to Alan Izod, 9 May 1946, INF 12/283.

78. Minutes of Colonial Film Unit Committee, 18 June 1947, INF 12/282; Minutes of Colonial Film Unit Meeting, 19 June 1946, INF 12/282. There are still a few films of British life, such as the George Pearson–directed *Young Farmers' Clubs*. See "Young Farmers Filmed," *Bedfordshire Times and Standard*, 5 September 1947, 7; "Young Farmers' 'Mock Auction'," *Biggleswade Chronicle and Bedfordshire Gazette*, 10 October 1947, 1.

79. "Film Talk . . . African Outlets . . . Non-White Britons," *West Africa*, 24 January 1948, 59; *Film in Colonial Development*.

80. K. W. Blackburne, "Financial Problems and Future Policy in British Colonies," in *Film in Colonial Development*, 35.

81. John Grierson, "Film and Primitive Peoples," 13.

82. The Rt. Hon. A. Creech Jones, "Opening Address," *Film in Colonial Development*, 4–8; *Film in Colonial Development*, 52. Creech-Jones explained: "Empire (if we continue to use that particular term) is not an opportunity for exploitation to our material advantage, but the occasion of service, the discharge of responsibility in building up the economic and social conditions of the peoples in our control."

83. Grierson, "Film and Primitive Peoples," 9–15; Stollery, "White Fathers Hear Dark Voices?," 189. Blackburne ("Financial Problems and Future Policy in British Colonies," 33), representing the Colonial Office, restated the claim that "we are starting very much from scratch," although he also offered a caveat, claiming that 20 million people see CFU films each year.

84. Izod, "Some Special Features of Colonial Film Production," 32.

85. Grierson would appear to be conscious of this and concludes with a quote ("Film and Primitive Peoples," 15) from the actor Richard Wright, stating: "I conclude in the dark voice of Richard Wright, and not in my own white one."

86. Grierson, "Film and Primitive Peoples," 13.

87. "Colourful Scene as the Delegates Arrive," *West Africa*, 2 October 1948, 996.

88. African Conference, Lancaster House, Minutes of Sessions 1–12, CO 879/153, TNA.

89. *West Africa*, 2 October 1948, 996.

90. The Oni of Ife also features in *Colonial Cinemagazine* 21 visiting London Zoo.

91. *Colonial Cinema*, September 1948, 69–70; *Colonial Cinema*, December 1948, 75; *Colonial Cinema*, March 1949, 15; Films: Copies of Colonial Cinema and Miscellaneous Papers, CO 1045/227, TNA.

92. Colonial Month—1949, and letter from Colonial Office, February 1949, Home Publicity: Colonial Exhibition, INF 12/350, TNA.

93. Spotlight on the Colonies, INF 6/1337, TNA.

94. Phil Vasili, "Colonialism and Football: The First Nigerian Tour to Britain," *Race and Class* 36.4 (1995): 60–61. See also Tom Rice, "Nigerian Footballers in England," www.colonialfilm.org.uk/node/1444; Tom Rice, "Colonial Cinemagazine No. 9," www.colonialfilm.org.uk/node/211.

95. Nate Plageman, "A Failed Showcase of Empire?: The Gold Coast Police Band, Colonial Record Keeping, and a 1947 Tour of Great Britain," *African Music* 10.2 (2016): 57.

96. Plageman, "Failed Showcase of Empire?," 70.

97. Ibid., 58–59.

98. An editorial in the magazine added that "of even greater importance than their technical ability was the fine atmosphere of sportsmanship they left along their trail." "Nigerian Footballers in England," *Colonial Cinema*, December 1949, 68; *Colonial Cinema*, December 1949, 55.

99. Macpherson to the Football Association, 2 May 1949, https://medium.com/@olaojo15/the-nigerian-governor-s-1949-letter-to-the-english-fa-4a5codf6a820 (accessed 23 July 2017). Olaoja Aiyegbayo offers an excellent account of the tour on Horeb International, www.horebinternational.com/the-story-of-the-1949-nigerian-football-teams-uk-tour/. He notes that some of the players would return to the UK and "become the first generation of Nigerian footballers to play for English clubs."

100. "Bare Feet Give Them a Kick," *Daily Mirror*, 30 August 1949, 6; "Five Goals, No Boots," *Daily Mail*, 1 September 1949, 1; personal interview with Sir Sydney Samuelson, conducted by Tom Rice and Emma Sandon, 15 June 2010.

101. "Police Band," Ghana Police website, http://64.226.23.153/others/band.htm (accessed 21 January 2009).

102. Henry Swanzy, "Quarterly Notes," *African Affairs*, October 1947, 188.

103. "Cup Men at the Theatre," *Straits Times*, 31 May 1949, 11. Advertisements in the *Straits Times* on 20 March 1949 (p. 11) showed the film playing concurrently in three cinemas.

104. "New Year Honours," *The Times*, 1 January 1963, 4.

105. "The School of Instruction, Accra, Gold Coast," *Colonial Cinema*, December 1948, 78–80; "The School of Instruction, Accra, Gold Coast," *Colonial Cinema*, September 1949, 43–45; Colonial Film Unit: Courses of Instruction, INF 12/284, TNA; School of Instruction, Accra, INF 12/285, TNA. Cameraman Fred Lagden, who would work with the Nigerian Film Unit during the 1950s, gave the initial instruction on photography.

106. Franklyn "Chappie" St. Juste, "Through the Camera's Eye: The Making of *The Harder They Come*," *Caribbean Quarterly: A Journal of Caribbean Culture* 61.2–3 (2015): 137.

107. "Colonial Film Unit Training School in the West Indies," *Colonial Cinema*, June 1951, 43.

108. H. M. K. Howson to W. S. Sellers, Future Film Section Organisation in Nigeria in Relation to the Accra Training School, INF 12/285, TNA.
109. *Colonial Cinema,* September 1949, 44.
110. Proposed Scheme for Training Colonials in 16mm Work, INF 12/282, TNA.
111. Film Training School, Accra, INF 12/285.
112. C. Y. Carstairs, "Edinburgh Film Festival," *Colonial Cinema,* December 1952, 78.
113. Gareth Evans, "The Colonial Film Unit's West Indian Training Course in Jamaica," in *Visual Aids in Fundamental Education: Some Personal Experiences* (Paris: UNESCO, 1952), 131.
114. Proposed Scheme for Training Colonials in 16mm Work, INF 12/282.
115. One of the trainees, James Otigbah, discussed the filming of *The Good Samaritan* in the village of Annum, Accra, while training in London under a UNESCO fellowship in 1951. "Filming the Good Samaritan," *The Listener,* 13 September 1951, 409.
116. Tour of W. Sellers, INF 12/294.
117. "Colonial Film Unit Man from London on Survey," *Daily Gleaner,* 4 November 1949, 12; Duncan Keith Corinaldi, "Local Films—A Reality 11 Years Ago," *Daily Gleaner,* 5 December 1949, 8; Evans, "Colonial Film Unit's West Indian Training Course in Jamaica," 131.
118. Corinaldi, "Local Films—A Reality 11 Years Ago"; Evans, "Colonial Film Unit's West Indian Training Course in Jamaica," 133.
119. "The West Indies Film Training School," *Colonial Cinema,* September 1950, 66–69; "Colonial Film Unit Training School in the West Indies," *Colonial Cinema,* June 1951, 40–44; "West Indies," *Colonial Cinema,* March 1950, 19–21.
120. "Visual Aid Courses Will Mean Much to W. I. Development—Carmichael," *Barbados Advocate,* 19 December 1950, 6.
121. Evans, "Colonial Film Unit's West Indian Training Course in Jamaica," 130–39.
122. *Delay Means Death* was also used as a part of a TB campaign by the medical department in Trinidad.
123. Rene Wideson would briefly serve as Head of Films for the Cyprus Broadcasting Television Service in the 1950s. He relocated to the UK where he eventually became head of film operations for the BBC.
124. Jonathan Stubbs, "'Did You Ever Notice This Dot in the Mediterranean?' Colonial Cyprus in the Post-war British Documentary," *Historical Journal of Film, Radio and Television* 35.2 (2015): 240–56. *Commonwealth Survey* explained that the Public Information Service had operated a mobile cinema over the past decade in Cyprus that had given more than five thousand performances and had proved "very popular in the more remote villages and in the schools." The article stated that the new training school would "encourage larger audiences by producing and making available films of special local interest." "Film Making in the Dependencies," *Commonwealth Survey,* 20 July 1951, 27–28.
125. "The Cyprus Film Training School, 1951," *Colonial Cinema,* December 1951, 87–90. See also "Film-Making in the Dependencies," *Commonwealth Survey,* 20 July 1951, 27–28.

126. Stubbs, "'Did You Ever Notice This Dot in the Mediterranean?'," 247–48; UNESCO, "Seminar on Visual Aids in Fundamental Education at Messina, September 1953: List of Films" (Paris: UNESCO, 1954).

127. Pearson, *Flashback*, 215.

CHAPTER 5: HANDOVER

1. T. Hopkins, "Macmillan's Audit of Empire, 1957," in *Understanding Decline: Perceptions and Realities of British Economic Performance*, ed. P. Clarke and C. Trebilcock (Cambridge: Cambridge University Press, 1997), 234–60. Macmillan was succeeded by Alec Douglas-Home in November 1963. The dozen countries to achieve independence under this Conservative administration stretch from Ghana on 6 March 1957 to Malta on 21 September 1964. Zambia celebrated independence barely a week after Wilson came to power in October 1964 and the Kingdom of Tonga was the last under his administration in June 1970.

2. Francis Gooding, "Missing the End: Falsehood and Fantasy in Late Colonial Cinema," in *Film and the End of Empire*, ed. Lee Grieveson and Colin MacCabe (London: Palgrave Macmillan, 2011), 287–92.

3. Wm. Roger Louis, "The Dissolution of the British Empire," in *The Oxford History of the British Empire*, vol. 4, *The Twentieth Century*, ed. Judith M. Brown and Wm. Roger Louis (Oxford: Oxford University Press, 1999), 351; Ronald Hyam, *Britain's Declining Empire: The Road to Decolonisation, 1918–1968* (Cambridge: Cambridge University Press, 2006).

4. Piers Brendon, *The Decline and Fall of the British Empire, 1781–1997* (London: Jonathan Cape, 2007), 539. This typically infuriated Churchill, who complained in 1948 of "Socialist and Left-Wing forces" who "gird at the word Empire and espouse the word Commonwealth," and noted the Labour government's "calculated omission" of three words: "Empire," "Dominion," and "British." Hansard, H. C. Deb., vol. 457, cols. 242–50 (28 October 1948) [electronic version].

5. Louis, "Dissolution of the British Empire," 352.

6. "The School of Instruction, Accra, Gold Coast," *Colonial Cinema*, December 1948, 78–80; "Colonial Film Unit Training School in the West Indies," *Colonial Cinema*, June 1951, 40–44.

7. Emma Sandon, Tom Rice, and Peter Bloom, "Changing the World: Sean Graham," *Journal of British Cinema and Television* 10.3 (2013): 525.

8. Personal interview with Sir Sydney Samuelson, conducted by Tom Rice and Emma Sandon, 15 June 2010.

9. Sandon, Rice and Bloom, "Changing the World: Sean Graham," 526; Sean Graham, *The Use of Film in the West Indies and Mexico: An Inquiry into Techniques of Film Production for Fundamental Education, 1955* (UNESCO, 1955), 2. Graham further argued that "film-making is story telling. No more—and no less." Sean Graham, "The Work of the Gold Coast Film Unit," *Visual Aids in Fundamental Education: Some Personal Experience* (Paris: UNESCO, 1952), 77.

10. George Noble, "Cameraman on the Gold Coast," *Colonial Cinema*, June 1952, 36–39; "Gold Coast Film Men Train in Britain," *West Africa*, 22 March 1952, 261.

11. Sean Graham to Basil Wright, 8 August 1952, BFI Special Collections, BCW 1/16/1.

12. Graham, *Use of Film in the West Indies and Mexico,* 8, 29.

13. See Carmela Garritano, *African Video Movies and Global Desires: A Ghanaian History* (Athens: Ohio University Press, 2013); Emma Sandon, "Cinema and Highlife in the Gold Coast: The Boy Kumasenu (1952)," *Social Dynamics: A Journal of African Studies* 39.3 (2013): 496–519; Peter Bloom and Kate Skinner, "Modernity and Danger: *The Boy Kumasenu* and the Work of the Gold Coast Film Unit," *Ghana Studies* 12/13 (2009): 121–54; Martin Stollery, "White Fathers Hear Dark Voices? John Grierson and British Colonial Africa at the End of Empire," in *The Grierson Effect: Tracing Documentary's International Movement,* ed. Zoe Druick and Deane Williams (London: BFI, 2014), 187–208.

14. "All Black Cast," *Rand Daily Mail,* 4 August 1954, 10; C. Y. Carstairs, "Edinburgh Film Festival," *Colonial Cinema,* December 1952, 76–80.

15. Carstairs, "Edinburgh Film Festival," 78.

16. Graham to Basil Wright, 10 July 1952, BFI Special Collections, BCW 1/16/1; Henry Swanzy, "Quarterly Notes," *African Affairs,* October 1952, 279; Stephen Watts, "On the African Movie Menus," *New York Times,* 26 April 1953, II, 4; *Daily Graphic,* 19 July 1952, 4.

17. Garritano, *African Video Movies and Global Desires,* 25; Bloom and Skinner, "Modernity and Danger," 122.

18. "Film Production in the Gold Coast," *West African Review,* September 1952, 888–89.

19. Bloom and Skinner, "Modernity and Danger," 148.

20. *West African Review,* September 1952, 888; Sandon, "Cinema and Highlife in the Gold Coast."

21. "The Boy Kumasenu," *Kinematograph Weekly,* 31 January 1957, 20; Fred Majdalany, "Canada Has an 8-Minute Winner," *Daily Mail,* 22 August 1952, 2.

22. "The Impact of Information Services on the People of Ghana," *Ghana Today* 1.22 (25 December 1957): 4–5; Establishment of Priorities for Films to be Made by the Gold Coast Film Unit, 1954–1955, 22 December 1953, Cinematograph and Visual Aids—Use of in Schools, Policy, RG 3/5/182, PRAAD; Sandon, Rice, and Bloom, "Changing the World: Sean Graham," 527.

23. Graham, "Work of the Gold Coast Film Unit," 79; Sandon, Rice, and Bloom, "Changing the World: Sean Graham," 527.

24. Sean Graham to Director of Education, 4 September 1952, Use of Films and Film Strips in Post-Primary Institutions, RG 3/5/181, PRAAD.

25. Sean Graham to Basil Wright, 28 July 1952, BFI Special Collections, BCW 1/16/1.

26. Ibid.

27. The Future Procedure for the Production of Films by the Gold Coast Film Unit, 15 July 1955, RG 3/5/182, PRAAD.

28. "Impact of Information Services on the People of Ghana," 4–5; Gold Coast Film Unit, "Gold Coast Film Catalogue, 1949–1954" (1954).

29. A. R. G. Prosser, "An Experiment in Community Development," *Community Development Bulletin* 2.3 (June 1951): 52–53. Graham recognized the

influence of *Amenu's Child* in helping "to shape the basic principles which govern our approach to film-making: the campaign-film telling a story in the idiom of the country." Graham, "Work of the Gold Coast Film Unit," 84.

30. See Tom Rice, "Progress in Kojokrom," www.colonialfilm.org.uk/node/2566; "Impact of Information Services on the People of Ghana," 4–5; Colonial Office, "Report on the Gold Coast for the Year 1954" (London: HMSO, 1954), 120; Henry Swanzy, "Quarterly Notes," *African Affairs* 53.212 (July 1954): 195. Sean Graham was unhappy with the script for *Progress in Kojokrom*, complaining that the "more we mess about with it, the worse it gets." Graham to Wright, 28 July 1952, BFI Special Collections, BCW 1/16/1.

31. Colonial Office, "Report by Her Majesty's Government in the United Kingdom of Great Britain and Northern Ireland to the General Assembly of the United Nations on the Administration of Togoland, 1954" (London: HMSO, 1954), 35.

32. Martin Rennalls, *A Career Making a Difference* (1991), unpublished autobiography, National Library of Jamaica in Kingston, 173.

33. Graham, "Work of the Gold Coast Film Unit," 81.

34. Graham, *Use of Film in the West Indies and Mexico*, 2.

35. Basil Wright to Sean Graham, 9 September 1952, BFI Special Collections, BCW 1/16/1.

36. See "Impact of Information Services on the People of Ghana."

37. Graham, "Work of the Gold Coast Film Unit," 87.

38. "Gold Coast Film Catalogue, 1949–1954."

39. Bloom and Skinner, "Modernity and Danger," 123; Stollery, "White Fathers Hear Dark Voices?," 193.

40. Sandon, Rice, and Bloom, "Changing the World: Sean Graham," 530.

41. Noble, "Cameraman on the Gold Coast," 36.

42. Graham, *Use of Film in the West Indies and Mexico*, 10, 17–18, 51.

43. Sean Graham to Basil Wright, 28 July 1952.

44. Colonial Office, *Federal Nigeria: Annual Report, 1957* (Lagos: HMSO, 1957), 143–44; "The Jungle Showboat: Western Nigeria Educates with 46 Mobile Schools," *Film User*, January 1959, 19–20.

45. William Sellers, "The Production and Use of Films for Public Informational and Educational Purposes in British African Territories," Colloquy of the Official Information Services in Black Africa, Brussels, 1958, International and Universal Exhibition, Brussels, July 1958.

46. "Jungle Showboat," 19–20; Government of Western Nigeria, *Report of the Western Region Government, 1957* (Ibaden, Western Nigeria: Government Printer, 1957), 24. The figure of ten million is quoted by William Sellers in "The Production and Use of Films for Public Informational and Educational Purposes in British African Territories." The Public Relations Department's mobile cinema vans showed films to audiences of "well over one million" in 1950, rising to three and a half million in 1954, while the NFU also now supplied its films for free in the forty-four commercial cinemas within Nigeria. Colonial Office, *Annual Report on the Colonies: Nigeria, 1950* (London: HMSO, 1950), 109; Colonial Office, *Annual Report on the Colonies: Nigeria, 1954* (London: HMSO, 1954), 188.

47. "Jungle Showboat," 19–20.
48. Ibid.; Sellers, "Production and Use of Films."
49. Tom Rice, "Smallpox," www.colonialfilm.org.uk/node/770.
50. Colonial Office, *Annual Report, 1950*, 109.
51. C. Y. Carstairs, "Information Services as an Aid to Administration," *Journal of African Administration*, 1953, 4; Sellers, "Making Films in and for the Colonies," 835; Norman Spurr, "Multiplication: The Use of 8mm. Film in Community Development," *Community Development Journal*, January 1966, 29–32. Carstairs noted that the film had also been shown without a vaccinator handy in Northern Nigeria. "Here is a moral," he concluded. "Do not show a film—or indeed engage in any other form of persuasion—unless practical action can follow."
52. "Dr Garret [sic] of Oji River," *West Africa*, 14 December 1957, 1181.
53. Charles Ambler, "Projecting the Modern Colonial State: Mobile Cinema in Kenya," in Grieveson and MacCabe, *Film and the End of Empire*, 199, 212.
54. Kumar Ramakrishna, *Emergency Propaganda: The Winning of Malayan Hearts and Minds 1948–1958* (Richmond, Surrey: Curzon Press, 2002), 110–11; "Vintage Year for Malayan Film Unit," *Kinematograph Weekly*, 10 March 1955; Tom Hodge, "Eleven Years of the Malayan Film Unit: A Record of Solid Achievement," *Educational Screen and Audio-Visual Guide*, November 1957, 538; Malayan Film Unit, *Catalogue of Documentary Films in the Federal Film Library* (Kuala Lumpur: Department of Information, Federation of Malaya, 1959), 3; "Propaganda War on Reds Will Be Intensified," *Straits Times*, 16 January 1951, 4.
55. Hodge, "Eleven Years of the Malayan Film Unit," 539.
56. Ibid.; "Malayan Film Unit," *Commonwealth Survey*, 5 February 1957, 127–28.
57. "Tour Film," *Daily Mail*, 6 February 1956; "Riddle of Royal Film Decision," *Daily Mail*, 20 March 1956, 7. Copies of the NFU's news films, such as *Nigeria's New Constitution*, were also sent to universities in America "where there are Nigerian students," revealing a desire to address educated expatriate students. *Report on Nigeria for the Year 1952*, 121.
58. Colonial Office, *Kenya, 1957: Report for the Year* (London: HMSO, 1957), 118.
59. Colonial Office, *Report on Mauritius, 1956* (London: HMSO, 1957), 110.
60. Brian Larkin, *Signal and Noise: Media, Infrastructure and Urban Culture in Nigeria* (Durham, NC: Duke University Press, 2008), 102.
61. Ibid., 101. In *Self-Government for Western Nigeria*, a service at the central mosque in Kabana underlines "the essential unity of the people of Western Nigeria regardless of their own beliefs and creeds," while the commentator remarks upon the governor's arrival that "all creeds were combining together at this important stage" of the country's development.
62. Ronald Baxter, *Giant in the Sun: The Story of Northern Nigeria which Becomes a Self-Governing Region on March 15, 1959* (London; Tonbridge: Brown Knight and Truscott, 1959).
63. Gooding, "Missing the End," 290–91.

64. Doris Waddilove, "Cinema on Safari," *Film User*, June 1959, 293–94. *Film User* saw this advertising as a further point of identification between the African and British viewer, suggesting that the British television viewer would be "sharing for a moment the same experience as thousands of Nigerians in their tropic heat with the dark sky above them and the rustling, chattering African night all around."

65. Ambler, "Projecting the Modern Colonial State," 216.

66. Victor Gover, "A Brief Review of the Services provided by the Overseas Film and Television Centre for Film Units working in Africa," Colloquy of the Official Information Services in Black Africa, Brussels, 1958, International and Universal Exhibition, Brussels, July 1958.

67. Ibid.

68. Colonial Office, *Kenya, 1957*, 118; Colonial Office, *Kenya, 1958* (London: HMSO, 1958), 100.

69. J.M. Burns, *Flickering Shadows: Cinema and Identity in Colonial Zimbabwe* (Ohio: Ohio University Press, 2002), 97. Filmmaker Geoffrey Mangin suggested that "only about five new films a year" catered for African audiences. Geoffrey Mangin, *Filming Emerging Africa: A Pioneer Cinematographer's Scrapbook—from the 1940s to the 1960s* (Cape Town: Author, 1998), 29.

70. Alexander Shaw, "The Uganda Film Unit: Final Report on the Project—Period September 1961 to December 1964" (Paris: UNESCO, 1965); Colonial Office, *Uganda: Report for the Year, 1956* (London: HMSO, 1956), 128; Colonial Office, *Uganda: Report for the Year, 1960* (London: HMSO, 1960), 117; Colonial Office, *Uganda: Report for the Year, 1959* (London: HMSO, 1959), 122.

71. Norman F. Spurr, "Experience with Two Films in Tanganyika," *Health Education Journal* 13.1 (March 1955): 81–85. Norman Spurr, "Talkies with the Magnetic Stripe Projector," *Colonial Cinema*, March 1954, 11–12. For this latter film, Spurr used a magnetic stripe as part of a UNESCO experiment on film sound, which allowed him to record a commentary from the chairman of the Hehe council "in the tribal language." Spurr also collaborated with, and followed the lead of, the East African Literature Bureau that was producing a series entitled "Custom and Tradition in East Africa." Andrew Michael Ivaska, "Negotiating Culture in a Cosmopolitan Capital: Urban Style and the Tanzanian State in Colonial and Postcolonial Dar es Salaam" (PhD diss., University of Michigan, 2003).

72. "Tanganyika Film-Making Experiment: Entertainment Films for Africans," *Commonwealth Survey*, 2 April 1954, 49–50; Donald Wynne, "Tanganyika's Film Experiment," *Colonial Cinema*, September 1952, 62–65.

73. See Jacqueline Maingard, *South African National Cinema* (London: Routledge, 2007), 90–105. Maingard shows how AFP was increasingly looking to "exploit developing black cinema audiences" in South Africa. It had been the main commercial distributor in East Africa since the 1920s and also made films for the Kenyan Government, such as the 1954 Donald Swanson film, *Mau Mau*. See Tom Rice, "Mau Mau," www.colonialfilm.org.uk/node/3233.

74. Wynne, "Tanganyika's Film Experiment," 64–65; Norman Spurr to Member for Social Service, 29 August 1950, Tanzania National Archives

41128,9. Quoted in Ivaska, "Negotiating Culture in a Cosmopolitan Capital," 84. Spurr believed an "African" film was one rooted in "African psychology."

75. "Tanganyika Film-Making Experiment," 50; Colonial Office, *Annual Report, 1954* (London: HMSO, 1954), 18. Quote in Mike Ssali, "The Development and Role of an African Film Industry in East Africa, with Special Reference to Tanzania, 1922–1984" (PhD diss., University of California, Los Angeles, 1988), 91. The AFP experiment ended in 1954, the same year that Julius Nyerere's Tanganyika African National Union (TANU) formed.

76. Gover, "Brief Review of the Services Provided by the Overseas Film and Television Centre."

77. Sellers, "Production and Use of Films"; Gover, "Brief Review of the Services Provided by the Overseas Film and Television Centre."

78. George Pearson, "Overseas Film and Television Centre Training School," Colloquy of the Official Information Services in Black Africa, Brussels, 1958, International and Universal Exhibition, Brussels, July 1958; interview by Mary Ingleby with Tony Muscatt, 9 August 2007.

79. Graham, *Use of Film in the West Indies and Mexico*, 6–7, 28, 49.

80. Ibid., 48, 28.

81. Rennalls, *A Career Making a Difference*, 87. Rennalls never lost his interest in education. He eventually left Jamaica to undertake a master's at Boston University's School of Public Communication (as did Sydney Hill, a prominent director for the Trinidad and Tobago Unit in the 1960s), completing his thesis on the "Development of the Documentary Film in Jamaica," and ended his career as a professor at the Rochester Institute of Technology, teaching film production.

82. Ibid.; *Colonial Cinema*, September 1947, 52.

83. Rennalls, *A Career Making a Difference*. Rennalls explained that Pearson "had helped me so much in assisting me with my career" (141).

84. Exhibitor report written by Rupert E. Meikle, Cinema Lecturer Unit 2, Film Production, 1944–1948, 3/24/216; Report of Cinema Lecturers' Conference, 19 July 1946, Film Production, 1944–1948, 3/24/216; Central Film Organisation: Establishment of: 1947–48, 1B/44/1/110, Jamaica Archives, Spanish Town, Jamaica.

85. M. A. Rennalls, "Visual Education in Jamaica," *Colonial Cinema*, March 1953, 16.

86. Telegram from Sellers, 4 March 1955, Educational Films: showing of, 1953–55, 1B/44/1/104, Jamaica Archives, Spanish Town, Jamaica.

87. Contribution by Government of Jamaica to the Colonial Film Unit, 1B/31/395, Jamaica Archives, Spanish Town, Jamaica; Rennalls, *A Career Making a Difference*.

88. Executive Council Submission: Jamaica Film Unit, 1956, Document re the Future Scope and Activities of the Jamaica Film Unit, 1B/31/48, Jamaica Archives, Spanish Town, Jamaica; Rennalls, *A Career Making a Difference*.

89. Rennalls, *A Career Making a Difference*, 167–73.

90. See Advisory Committee of Film Unit, 1955; 1956, 3/24/899, Jamaica Archives, Spanish Town, Jamaica.

91. Terri Francis, "Sounding the Nation: Martin Rennalls and the Jamaica Film Unit, 1951–1961," *Film History: An International Journal* 23.2 (2011): 116.

92. When Rennalls left to study in America in the late 1960s, he explained that he intended to become an "expert from within" and wished to "return home and lead Jamaica on in her historical making of film history." However, he would remain in America. Michael L. Hayes, "A Pioneer in Jamaican Film-Making," *Daily Gleaner*, 20 February 1967, 6.

93. For an African context, see Rohland Schuknecht, *British Colonial Development Policy after the Second World War: The Case of Sukumaland, Tanganyika* (Berlin: Lit Verlag, 2010). The Barbados Film Unit production *Let's Build Their Future* (1959) combines the literal construction of the land with the development of people, as it shows both the construction of the modern school and the work of students inside it.

94. Colonial Office, *Report on British Guiana, 1955* (London: HMSO, 1955). In 1961, a revised version of *How to Exercise Your Vote* was shown as part of the How to Vote campaign. See Colonial Office, *Report on British Guiana, 1961* (London: HMSO, 1961).

95. Colonial Office, *Annual Report on Trinidad and Tobago, 1951* (London: HMSO, 1951), 146.

96. Francis, "Sounding the Nation," 120.

97. The JFU were involved in the production of this other media; for example, it collaborated with the "All Island Banana Growers Association" on a pamphlet entitled "Leaf Spot Control," which accompanied a JFU film. "Pamphlet on Leaf Spot Control," *Daily Gleaner*, 25 June 1954, 16.

98. "Film on Road Safety Suggested," *Daily Gleaner*, 19 March 1958, 3.

99. "Home-made Documentary for the Screen," *Daily Gleaner*, 15 February 1952, 5.

100. *Daily Gleaner*, 27 April 1955, 4.

101. *Daily Gleaner*, 6 February 1956, 4. The *Gleaner* often listed the invited guests and headlined their reports on these films by noting the attendance of the governor.

102. Rennalls, "Visual Education in Jamaica," 17; Rennalls, *A Career Making a Difference*, 119.

103. *Daily Gleaner*, 15 May 1953, 14.

104. Paul Foster, "Give Your Child a Chance: First Locally Produced Film," *Barbados Advocate*, 30 January 1952, 2; *Colonial Cinema*, June 1952, 26; *Sunday Advocate*, 3 February 1952, 3. The film was made with the Department of Medical Services. The Barbados Film Unit posited familiar colonial topics in a local context, such as *Better Living* (1952), a Mr. Wise and Mr. Foolish film.

105. Rennalls, *A Career Making a Difference*, 124.

106. Francis, "Sounding the Nation," 120, 122, 125.

107. Information Office, *Annual Report of the Information Officer, Trinidad and Tobago, 1951* (1951), 13–18; Information Office, *Annual Report of the Information Officer, Trinidad and Tobago, 1952* (1952), 15–19; Information Office, *Annual Report of the Information Officer, Trinidad and Tobago, 1950* (1950), 10–13.

108. Colonial Office, *Annual Report of Trinidad and Tobago for the Year 1957* (London: HMSO, 1957), 132–33.

109. Hassan Muthalib, "The End of Empire: The Films of the Malayan Film Unit in 1950s British Malaya," in Grieveson and MacCabe, *Film and the End of Empire,* 177–96; Rachel Moseley-Wood, "Ambivalence in the Image: The Jamaica Film Unit and the Narrative of the Emerging Nation," *Jamaican Historical Review* 26 (2013): 47–66.

110. Interview by Mary Ingleby with Tony Muscatt, 9 August 2007.

111. Moseley-Wood, "Ambivalence in the Image"; Jonathan William Trutor, "Please Stand By: Reconstruction, Decolonization and Security in British and French Public Information Films in the Postwar Era, 1945–1965" (unpublished diss., University of Minnesota, 2011), 184–98.

112. Norman Rae, "Historic Moments," *Sunday Gleaner,* 3 March 1963, 17.

113. Two further films on the advent of the federation were produced by the National Board of Canada in 1958: *New Nation in the West Indies* and *The Bright Land.* See Renee A. Nelson, "Promotion of the West Indian Federation: The Federal Information Service, 1957–1961," in *Ideology, Regionalism, and Society in Caribbean History,* ed. Shane J. Pantin and Jerome Teelucksingh (London: Palgrave Macmillan, 2017), 41–68.

114. See Philippe Chalmin, *The Making of a Sugar Giant: Tate and Lyle 1859–1989,* trans. Erica E. Long-Michalke (London: Routledge, 1990), 347–64.

115. The Western Nigerian government took sole control of WNTV at the end of 1961, buying out Overseas Rediffusion. Rediffusion often performed the work of colonial government. In Malaya it broadcast fifteen minutes of official government announcements each day and during the Emergency its radio services targeted Chinese communities. Matthew H. Brown, "The Enchanted History of Nigerian State Television," in *State and Culture in Postcolonial Africa: Enchantings,* ed. T. Olaniyan (Bloomington: Indiana University Press, 2017), 100; Drew O. McDaniel, *Broadcasting in the Malay World: Radio, Television, and Video in Brunei, Indonesia, Malaysia, and Singapore* (Norwood, NJ: Ablex, 1994), 137–39.

116. Richard Rathbone, "Casting 'the Kingdome into Another Mold': Ghana's Troubled Transition to Independence," in *The Iconography of Independence: Freedoms at Midnight,* ed. Robert Holland, Susan Williams, and Terry Barringer (Abingdon: Routledge, 2009), 57.

117. I examine these films in greater detail in "Merdeka for Malaya: Imagining Independence across the British Empire," in *The Colonial Documentary Film in South and South-East Asia,* ed. Ian Aitken and Camille Deprez (Edinburgh: Edinburgh University Press, 2016), 73–98.

118. Ian Aitken, "British Governmental Institutions, the Regional Information Office in Singapore and the Use of the Official Film in Malaya and Singapore, 1948–1961," *Historical Journal of Film, Radio and Television* 35.1 (2015): 34; Stollery, "White Fathers Hear Dark Voices?," 193.

119. While the film again showcased British royalty and parliamentary traditions, local responses focused on the images of Nkrumah. A *Daily Graphic* review wrote in capitals: "BUT PROBABLY THE MOST STIRRING PICTURES OF THE FILM ARE THOSE HISTORIC SHOTS SHOWING THE PRIME MINISTER LIKE A CAPTAIN WITH HIS CHIEF OFFICERS FLOODLIT

UPON THE BRIDGE OF THE SHIP OF STATE THEY HAVE FINALLY LAUNCHED INTO THE RESPONSIBLE FREEDOM OF THE INTERNATIONAL WATERS OF THE WORLD." "Ghana Film Unit Did Excellent Work," *Daily Graphic,* 11 May 1957, 7.

120. The British government was eager to claim credit for independence and to highlight international approval for its efforts. *Commonwealth Survey* listed tributes paid "to the part played by the United Kingdom in bringing the new state into being." It quoted US vice president Richard Nixon, who labeled Britain's action in "granting" independence as "perhaps as good an example of colonial policy at its best that the world has seen." Nehru was also quoted: "We may criticize them for other things, as we sometimes do, but undoubtedly this has been something which deserves congratulations." "The New State of Ghana," *Commonwealth Survey,* 19 March 1957, 242–45.

121. *Catalogue of Documentary Films,* 1959, 3; "'Merdeka' Film for Foreign Lands," *Straits Times,* 19 September 1957, 7; "Free Merdeka Films for Free World," *Straits Times,* 20 July 1957, 7.

122. *Films We Have Produced* (Accra: Ghana Film Industry, 1974), 1.

123. "Freedom for Ghana," *Monthly Film Bulletin,* July 1957, 92.

124. "800 See Birth of Nation," *Daily Graphic,* 10 May 1957, 2; "'Freedom for Ghana' Show in London," *Daily Graphic,* 31 May 1957, 6.

125. "Seaga Sees National Anthem Film," *Daily Gleaner,* 20 October 1962, 2.

126. Alexander Shaw, "Uganda Film Unit." The presence of Alexander Shaw in Uganda further highlights the postwar movement across the empire of British documentarians, including Denny Densham who was making films in Tanganyika at independence. Shaw was invested in nation-building throughout his career, from his films at GPO and Strand to his unit-building roles overseas, most notably setting up production work for the Government of India's Film Advisory Board in 1940–41. His period as head of Crown after the war was followed by a long career with UNESCO, which included time in Egypt and Sudan in the 1950s setting up film and filmstrip production as part of fundamental education projects. See Alexander Shaw, "Letter to India," *Documentary News Letter,* February 1942, 24–25; "White Man of the West," *Filmindia,* July 1942, 3–8; Alexander Shaw, "Visual Aids for the Egyptian Village," *Visual Aids in Fundamental Education: Some Personal Experiences* (Paris: UNESCO 1952), 15–24; see also Ravi Vasudevan, "A British Documentary Film-Maker's Encounter with Empire: The Case of Alexander Shaw, 1938–1942," *Historical Journal of Film, Radio and Television* 38.4 (2018): 743–761.

127. Shaw, "Uganda Film Unit." After Shaw's departure in 1964, the unit struggled to recruit a new producer, and when Basil Wright visited for UNESCO at the start of 1967, he described the unit as "one of stagnation and demoralisation." Wright described newsmagazines lying in vaults awaiting completion and four new Canadian mobile cinema vans "standing idle." Basil Wright, *The Uganda Film and Its Development, 18 November–22 December 1966* (Paris: UNESCO, 1967).

128. Shaw, "Uganda Film Unit"; interview by Mary Ingleby with Tony Muscatt, 9 August 2007.

129. Interview by Mary Ingleby with Tony Muscatt, 9 August 2007.

130. Bloom and Skinner, "Modernity and Danger," 137.
131. Manthia Diawara, *African Cinema: Politics and Culture* (Bloomington: Indiana University Press, 1992), 5–11.
132. Francoise Balogun, *Cinema in Nigeria* (Enugu: Delta, 1987), 68.
133. L. T. Fomson, "Documentary Films in Nigeria," *Our Pride*, 1984, 7–10; interview by Mary Ingleby with Dennis Bowden, 9 August 2007, and personal correspondence with Dennis Bowden.
134. Samantha Nkechi Iwowo, "Colonial Continuities in Neo-Nollywood: A Postcolonial Study" (PhD diss., University of Bristol, 2018).
135. Garritano, *African Video Movies and Global Desires*, 46–56.
136. *Ghana: An Official Handbook*, 1961, 114.
137. "Annual Report of the Department of Social Welfare and Community Development, 1963" (Accra: Ministry of Information and Broadcasting, 1964), 34.
138. Personal interview with Dennis Bowden, 24 May 2016.
139. On Brian Salt's work in Hong Kong, see Ian Aitken, *The British Official Film in South-East Asia: Malaya/Malaysia, Singapore and Hong Kong* (Basingstoke: Palgrave Macmillan, 2016), 76, 175–83.
140. The other royal visitor was Haile Selassie, Emperor of Ethiopia, and spiritual head of Jamaica's growing Rastafarian movement, who through the film is situated alongside the British royalty.
141. Birgit Meyer, *Sensational Movies: Video, Vision, and Christianity in Ghana* (Berkeley: University of California Press, 2015), 44–46.
142. *African World*, January 1963, 15; *Sierra Leone Trade Journal*, May 1961, 9.
143. Ikechukwu Obiaya, "A Break with the Past: The Nigerian Video-Film Industry in the Context of Colonial Filmmaking," *Film History: An International Journal* 23.2 (2011): 129–46.
144. Rennalls, *A Career Making a Difference*; "JIS Wins Film Award," *Daily Gleaner*, 25 November 1969, 26. The local units often responded differently to wider technological developments. While the Jamaican Information Services reverted to 16mm work for local television, in British Guiana 16mm production was totally replaced by 35mm by the 1960s. Manthia Diawara argued that the dominance of 35mm, which was not as accessible and affordable, stalled the development of a local, independent cinema in Ghana. Diawara, *African Cinema: Politics and Culture*, 10.
145. Omar Zaki, "Gadalla Gubara—a Forgotten Filmmaking Legend," *Africa News Service*, 16 September 2012. In Frédérique Cifuentes's film *Cinema in Sudan: Conversations with Gadalla Gubara*, Gadalla Gubara explains that he "believed that the cinema was the best media to take the message to the ignorant people who cannot read or cannot write."
146. Didi Cheeka, "Re-encountering Biafra in Film Archives," Africa Is a Country, http://africasacountry.com/2017/07/memory-stored-in-a-can-re-encountering-biafra-in-film-archives/ (accessed 20 November 2017).
147. Jennifer Blaylock, "ISD Sort Finished," Mobile Cinema: African Politics in Transit, https://cinemaintransit.wordpress.com/2011/05/22/isd-sort-finished/ (accessed 20 November 2017).

148. Interview by Mary Ingleby with Tony Muscatt, 9 August 2007.

149. "Colonial Film: Moving Images of the British Empire," www.colonialfilm.org.uk. I have written about this project and some of these curatorial decisions in "Opening the Colonial Film Archive," *Frames* 1.1 (2012), http://framescinemajournal.com/article/opening-the-colonial-film-archive/.

Selected Bibliography

ARCHIVES AND COLLECTIONS

(for individual references see endnotes)

Associated Press (AP) Archive, London (www.aparchive.com). This includes *films of the Colonial Film Unit and Overseas Film and Television Centre.*
Bristol Records Office. This includes *British Empire and Commonwealth Collection* (including Oral History interviews).
British Council Film Collection (http://film.britishcouncil.org). This includes *films and publications.*
British Film Institute, London. This includes *films, Special Collections (including Basil Wright papers and George Pearson papers), and BECTU interviews.*
British Library, London. This includes *India Office Records, Annual Reports for the Colonies, private papers, and audio archives.*
Colonial Film, Moving Images of the British Empire (www.colonialfilm.org.uk).
Ghana Public Records and Archives Administration Department, Accra. This includes *correspondence, papers, and records.*
Imperial War Museum, London. This includes *films, photographs, and Special Collections.*
Information Services Department, Ghana. This includes *reports and photographs.*
Jamaica Archives, Spanish Town, Jamaica. This includes *government papers and records.*
John Grierson Archive, Special Collections, University of Stirling. This includes *papers and unpublished manuscripts.*
Media History Digital Archive (http://mediahistoryproject.org).
National Archives, London. This includes *Records created or inherited by the Central Office of Information (INF). Records of the Colonial Office, Commonwealth and Foreign and Commonwealth Offices, Empire Marketing*

Board, and related bodies (CO). Records of the Foreign and Commonwealth Office and Predecessors (FCO). Records of the British Council (BW). Records created or inherited by HM Treasury (T). Records created or inherited by the Department of Education and Science (ED). Additional materials accessed through ancestry.com including UK, Outward Passenger Lists, 1890–1960; UK Census Collections, England and Wales; Civil Registration Birth Index, 1837–1915; British Army WWI Service Records, 1914–1920.

National Archives of Malta.

National Archives of Trinidad and Tobago. This includes *Annual Reports from the Information Officer.*

National Library of Jamaica. This includes *films, publications, and unpublished manuscripts.*

UNESCO, Paris, France (www.unesco.org/archives/new2010/index.html). This includes *publications and conference materials.*

Wellcome Library, London (http://wellcomelibrary.org). This includes *films.*

NEWSPAPERS AND PERIODICALS

Aberdeen Press and Journal
Africa News Service
African Affairs
African World
Age (Melbourne)
Atlanta Daily World
Barbados Advocate
Bedfordshire Times and Standard
Biggleswade Chronicle and Bedfordshire Gazette
Bioscope
British Kinematography
Colonial Cinema (1942–1954)
Colonial Review
Commercial Film
Commonwealth Survey
Crown Colonist
Daily Gleaner (Jamaica)
Daily Graphic
Daily Mail
Daily Mirror
Documentary News Letter
East Africa and Rhodesias
East African Standard
Educational Screen (subsequently *Educational Screen and Audio-Visual Guide*)
Essex Chronicle
Filmindia
Film User
Focus: A Film Review
Ghana Today (previously *Gold Coast Today*)

The Guardian
Hollywood Filmograph
Indian Daily Mail
Journal of African Administration
Journal of the Royal African Society
Journal of the Royal Society for the Promotion of Health
Kinematograph Weekly
The Listener
Manchester Guardian
Mombasa Times
Monthly Film Bulletin
New Statesman
New York Times
Oversea Education
Pictures and Picturegoer
Rand Daily Mail
Royal Society of Arts Journal
Sight and Sound
Singapore Free Press
Straits Times
The Times
Times of India
Today's Cinema
United Empire
Washington Post
West Africa
West African Review
World Film News
Yorkshire Post and Leeds Mercury

SELECTED BOOKS, ARTICLES, AND OTHER SOURCES

Acland, Charles R., and Haidee Wasson, eds. *Useful Cinema*. Durham, NC: Duke University Press, 2011.

Aitken, Ian. "The Griersonian Influence and Its Challenges: Malaya, Singapore, Hong Kong (1939–1973)." In *The Grierson Effect: Tracing Documentary's International Movement,* edited by Zoe Druick and Deane Williams, 93–104. London: BFI, 2014.

———. "British Governmental Institutions, the Regional Information Office in Singapore and the Use of the Official Film in Malaya and Singapore, 1948–1961." *Historical Journal of Film, Radio and Television* 35.1 (2015): 27–52.

———. *The British Official Film in South-East Asia: Malaya/Malaysia, Singapore and Hong Kong*. Basingstoke: Palgrave Macmillan, 2016.

Ambler, Charles. "Projecting the Modern Colonial State: Mobile Cinema in Kenya." In *Film and the End of Empire,* edited by Lee Grieveson and Colin MacCabe, 199–224. London: Palgrave, 2011.

Anderson, David M. "Mau Mau in the High Court and the 'Lost' British Empire Archives: Colonial Conspiracy or Bureaucratic Bungle?" *Journal of Imperial and Commonwealth History* 39.5 (2011): 699–716.
Anthony, Scott. *Public Relations and the Making of Modern Britain: Stephen Tallents and the Birth of a Progressive Media Profession.* Manchester: Manchester University Press, 2012.
Balogun, Francoise. *Cinema in Nigeria.* Enugu: Delta, 1987.
Baxter, Ronald. *Giant in the Sun: The Story of Northern Nigeria Which Becomes a Self-Governing Region on March 15, 1959.* London: Brown Knight and Truscott, 1959.
Bazin, Andre. "A Contribution to an *Erotologie* of Television" (1954). In *Andre Bazin's New Media,* edited and translated by Dudley Andrew. Berkeley: University of California Press, 2014.
Bhattacharya, Sanjoy. *Propaganda and Information in Eastern India, 1939–45: A Necessary Weapon of War.* London: Routledge, 2001.
Bloom, Peter. *French Colonial Documentary: Mythologies of Humanitarianism.* Minneapolis: University of Minnesota Press, 2008.
———. "Refiguring the Primitive: Institutional Legacies of the Filmology Movement." *Revues Cinémas: Journal of Film Studies* 19.2–3 (2009): 169–82.
———. "Elocution, Englishness and Empire: Film and Radio in Late Colonial Ghana." In *Modernization as Spectacle in Africa,* edited by Peter J. Bloom, Stephan F. Miescher, and Takyiwaa Manuh, 136–56. Bloomington: Indiana University Press, 2014.
——— and Kate Skinner. "Modernity and Danger: *The Boy Kumasenu* and the Work of the Gold Coast Film Unit." *Ghana Studies* 12/13 (2009): 121–54.
Bolas, Terry. *Screen Education: From Film Appreciation to Media Studies.* Bristol: Intellect Books, 2009.
Brendon, Piers. *The Decline and Fall of the British Empire, 1781–1997.* London: Jonathan Cape, 2007.
British Council Film Department. *Films of Britain.* London: British Council Film Department. Individual years from 1939–1949.
British Film Institute. *The Film in Colonial Development: A Report of a Conference.* London: BFI, 1948. [Individual papers listed in endnotes.]
British Instructional Films. *Catalogue of Films for Non-Theatrical Exhibition* (1928).
Brown, Matthew H. "The Enchanted History of Nigerian State Television." In *State and Culture in Postcolonial Africa: Enchantings,* edited by Tejumola Olaniyan, 94–110. Bloomington: Indiana University Press, 2017.
Buckley, Liam M. "Cine-film, Film-strips and the Devolution of Colonial Photography in The Gambia." *History of Photography* 34.2 (2010): 147–57.
Burns, J. M. *Flickering Shadows: Cinema and Identity in Colonial Zimbabwe.* Athens: Ohio University Press, 2002.
———. *Cinema and Society in the British Empire, 1895–1940.* London: Palgrave MacMillan, 2013.
Chalmin, Philippe. *The Making of a Sugar Giant: Tate and Lyle 1859–1989.* Translated by Erica E. Long-Michalke. London: Routledge, 1990.

Champion, Arthur M. "Introducing Africans to the Cinema Screen." *Crown Colonist* (February 1942).
———. "With a Mobile Cinema Unit in Kenya." *Oversea Education* (October 1948): 788–92.
Chan, Nadine. "Making Ahmed 'Problem Conscious': Educational Film and the Rural Lecture Caravan in 1930s British Malaya." *Cinema Journal* 55.4 (2016): 84–107.
Chapman, James. *The British at War: Cinema, State and Propaganda, 1939–1945*. London; New York: I. B. Taurus, 1998.
Colloquy of the Official Information Services in Black Africa, Brussels, 1958. International and Universal Exhibition, Brussels, July 1958. [Individual papers listed in endnotes.]
Colonial Office reports from 1925–1970. [Individual colonies, departments, and years listed in endnotes.]
Commission on Education and Cultural Films. *The Film in National Life: Being the Report of an Enquiry Conducted by the Commission on Educational and Cultural Films into the Service which the Cinematograph May Render to Education and Social Progress*. London: Allen and Unwin, 1932.
Constantine, Stephen. *The Making of British Colonial Development Policy, 1914–1940*. London: Frank Cass, 1984.
Cook, Marjorie Grant, in collaboration with Frank Fox. *The British Empire Exhibition 1924: Official Guide*. London: Fleetway Press, 1924.
Cowan, Jude. "'Women at Work for War . . . Women at Work for the Things of Peace': Representations of Women in the British Propaganda Newsreel in India in the Second World War, Indian News Parade." Master's thesis, Birkbeck College, University of London, 2001.
Danquah, Francis K. "Sustaining a West African Cocoa Economy: Agricultural Science and the Swollen Shoot Contagion in Ghana, 1936–1965." *African Economic History* 31 (2003): 43–74.
Department of Information, Federation of Malaya. *Catalogue of Films Made by the Malayan Film Unit, 1953*. Kuala Lumpur: Department of Information, 1953.
———. *Catalogue of Documentary Films in the Federal Film Library*. Kuala Lumpur: Department of Information, 1959.
Diawara, Manthia. *African Cinema: Politics and Culture*. Bloomington: Indiana University Press, 1992.
Disney, Walt. "Animated Cartoon." *Health Education Journal* 13.1 (March 1955): 70–77.
Druick, Zoe. *Projecting Canada: Government Policy and Documentary Film at the National Film Board*. Montreal: McGill University Press, 2007.
Ellis, Jack. *John Grierson: Life, Contributions, Influence*. Carbondale: Southern Illinois University Press, 2000.
Eslava, Luis. "The Moving Location of Empire: Indirect Rule, International Law and the Bantu Educational Kinema Experiment." *Leiden Journal of International Law* 31.3 (September 2018): 539–67.

Evans, Gareth. "The Colonial Film Unit's West Indian Training Course in Jamaica." *Visual Aids in Fundamental Education: Some Personal Experiences*, 130–39. Paris: UNESCO, 1952.
Fairgrieve, James. *Geography in School*. London: University of London Press, 1926.
———. "The Educational Film in England." *International Review of Educational Cinematography* (March 1932): 224–26.
———. "The Use of Films in Teaching." *Geography* 17.2 (June 1932): 129–40.
———. "Films for School." *Sight and Sound* (Summer 1946): 69–70.
Field, Mary. "Making Films for Children." *Educational Screen* (November 1946): 502–4.
———. *Good Company: The Story of the Children's Entertainment Film Movement in Great Britain 1943–1950*. London: Longmans Green, 1952.
———. *Children and Films: A Study of Boys and Girls in the Cinema: A Report to the Carnegie United Kingdom Trustees on an Enquiry into Children's Response to Films*. Dunfermline, Fife: Carnegie United Kingdom Trust, 1954.
———. "Commonwealth Unity of Thought through Films." *Journal of the Royal Commonwealth Society* 1.3 (September–October 1958): 231–36.
Fomson, L. T. "Documentary Films in Nigeria." *Our Pride* (1984): 7–10.
Fox, Jo. "John Grierson, His 'Documentary Boys' and the British Ministry of Information, 1939–1942." *Historical Journal of Film, Radio and Television* 25 (2005): 345–69.
———. "From Documentary Film to Television Documentaries: John Grierson and This Wonderful World." *Journal of British Cinema and Television* 10.3 (2013): 498–523.
Francis, Terri. "Sounding the Nation: Martin Rennalls and the Jamaica Film Unit, 1951–1961." *Film History: An International Journal* 23.2 (2011): 110–28.
Franklin, H. "The Central African Screen." *Colonial Cinema* (December 1950): 85–88.
Gadsden, Fay. "Wartime Propaganda in Kenya: The Kenya Information Office, 1939–1945." *International Journal of African Historical Studies* 19.3 (1986): 401–20.
Garga, B. D. *From Raj to Swaraj: The Non-Fiction Film in India*. New Delhi: Penguin, 2007.
Garritano, Carmela. *African Video Movies and Global Desires: A Ghanaian History*. Athens: Ohio University Press, 2013.
George, W. H. *The Cinema in School*. London: Sir Isaac Pitman & Sons, 1935.
Ghana Film Industry Corporation. *Films We Have Produced*. Accra: Ghana Film Industry, 1974.
Gilroy, Paul. *After Empire: Melancholia or Convivial Culture?* London: Routledge, 2004.
———. "Great Games: Film, History and Working-Through Britain's Colonial Legacy." In *Film and the End of Empire*, edited by Lee Grieveson and Colin MacCabe, 13–34. London: BFI, 2011.
Gold Coast Film Unit. *Gold Coast Film Unit, 1949–1953*. Gold Coast, 1953.
———. *Films from the Gold Coast, 1954–1955*. Gold Coast, 1955.

Gooding, Francis. "Missing the End: Falsehood and Fantasy in Late Colonial Cinema." In *Film and the End of Empire,* edited by Lee Grieveson and Colin MacCabe, 287–92. London: BFI, 2011.

Graham, Sean. "The Work of the Gold Coast Film Unit." In *Visual Aids in Fundamental Education: Some Personal Experiences,* 77–87. Paris: UNESCO, 1952.

———. *The Use of Film in the West Indies and Mexico: An Inquiry into Techniques of Film Production for Fundamental Education, 1955.* UNESCO, February–May 1955.

Grierson, John. "The E.M.B. Film Unit." *Cinema Quarterly* 1.4 (Summer 1933): 203–8.

Grieveson, Lee. "Introduction: Film at the End of Empire." In *Film and the End of Empire,* edited by Lee Grieveson and Colin MacCabe, 1–12. London: Palgrave Macmillan, 2011.

———. "The Cinema and the (Common)Wealth of Nations." In *Empire and Film,* edited by Lee Grieveson and Colin MacCabe, 73–114. London: BFI, 2011.

———. *Cinema and the Wealth of Nations: Media, Capital and the Liberal World System.* Berkeley: University of California Press, 2018.

Hajkowski, Thomas. *From the War to Westminster Abbey: The BBC and the Empire, 1939–53.* Manchester: Manchester University Press, 2010.

Holbrook, Wendell P. "British Propaganda and the Mobilization of the Gold Coast War Effort, 1939–1945." *Journal of African History* 26.4 (1985): 347–61.

Hopkins, T. "MacMillan's Audit of Empire, 1957." In *Understanding Decline: Perceptions and Realities of British Economic Performance,* edited by P. Clarke and C. Trebilcock, 234–60. Cambridge: Cambridge University Press, 1997.

Huxley, Julian. *Africa View.* London: Chatto and Windus, 1931.

Hyam, Ronald. *Britain's Declining Empire: The Road to Decolonisation, 1918–1968.* Cambridge: Cambridge University Press, 2006.

Israel, Adrienne M. "Measuring the War Experience: Ghanaian Soldiers in World War II." *Journal of Modern African Studies* 25.1 (March 1987): 159–68.

Ivaska, Andrew Michael. "Negotiating Culture in a Cosmopolitan Capital: Urban Style and the Tanzanian State in Colonial and Postcolonial Dar es Salaam." PhD dissertation, University of Michigan, 2003.

Iwowo, Samantha Nkechi. "Colonial Continuities in Neo-Nollywood: A Postcolonial Study." PhD dissertation, University of Bristol, 2018.

Jackson, Ashley. *The British Empire and the Second World War.* London: Hambledon Continuum, 2006.

Jahoda, Gustav. *White Man: A Study of the Attitudes of Africans to Europeans in Ghana before Independence.* Oxford: Oxford University Press, 1961.

Jaikumar, Priya. *Cinema at the End of Empire: A Politics of Transition in Britain and India.* Durham, NC: Duke University Press, 2006.

———. "An 'Accurate Imagination': Place, Map and Archive as Spatial Objects of Film History." In *Film and the End of Empire,* edited by Lee Grieveson and Colin McCabe, 167–88. London: Palgrave Macmillan, 2011.

———. *Where Histories Reside: India as Filmed Space.* Durham, NC: Duke University Press, 2019.
Jeffery, Keith. "The Second World War." In *The Oxford History of the British Empire,* vol. 4, *The Twentieth Century,* edited by Judith Brown and Wm. Roger Louis, 306–28. Oxford: Oxford University Press, 1999.
Jochimsen, John. *80 Years Gone in a Flash: The Memoirs of a Photojournalist.* London: MX, 2011.
Killingray, David. *Fighting for Britain: African Soldiers in the Second World War.* Woodbridge: James Currey, 2010.
Kracauer, Siegfried. *Theory of Film: The Redemption of Physical Reality,* with introduction by Miriam Bratu Hansen. Princeton, NJ: Princeton University Press, 1997 (originally 1960).
Larkin, Brian. *Signal and Noise: Media, Infrastructure and Urban Culture in Nigeria.* Durham, NC: Duke University Press, 2008.
Larsen, Egon. "Films for Africans." *See and Hear* (December 1946).
Louis, Wm. Roger. "The Dissolution of the British Empire." In *The Oxford History of the British Empire,* vol. 4, *The Twentieth Century,* edited by Judith M. Brown and Wm. Roger Louis, 329–56. Oxford: Oxford University Press, 1999.
Low, Rachael. *The History of British Film, 1929–1939: Documentary and Educational Films of the 1930's.* New York: Bowker, 1979.
Mackenzie, John. *Propaganda and Empire: The Manipulation of British Public Opinion, 1880–1960.* Manchester: Manchester University Press, 1986.
Maddison, John. "Le cinéma et l'information mentale des peuples primitives." *Revue Internationale de Filmologie* 1.3–4 (1948): 305–9.
Maingard, Jacqueline. *South African National Cinema.* London: Routledge, 2007.
Mangin, Geoffrey. *Filming Emerging Africa: A Pioneer Cinematographer's Scrapbook—From the 1940s to the 1960s.* Cape Town: Author, 1998.
Manvell, Roger. *Experiment in the Film.* London: Grey Walls Press, 1949.
Marier, Roger. *Social Welfare Work in Jamaica: A Study of the Jamaica Social Welfare Commission.* Paris: UNESCO, 1953.
Matera, Marc. *Black London: The Imperial Metropolis and Decolonization in the Twentieth Century.* Berkeley: University of California Press, 2015.
McDaniel, Drew O. *Broadcasting in the Malay World: Radio, Television, and Video in Brunei, Indonesia, Malaysia, and Singapore.* Norwood, NJ: Ablex, 1994.
Meyer, Birgit. *Sensational Movies: Video, Vision, and Christianity in Ghana.* Berkeley: University of California Press, 2015.
Morris, Kate. *British Techniques of Public Relations and Propaganda for Mobilizing East and Central Africa during World War II.* London: Edwin Mellen Press, 2000.
Morton-Williams, P. *Cinema in Rural Nigeria: A Field Study of the Impact of Fundamental-Education Films on Rural Audiences in Nigeria.* Lagos: Federal Information Services, 1952.
Moseley-Wood, Rachel. "Ambivalence in the Image: The Jamaica Film Unit and the Narrative of the Emerging Nation." *Jamaican Historical Review* 26 (2013): 47–66.

Murphy, Philip. *Monarchy and the End of Empire: The House of Windsor, the British Government and the Postwar Government.* Oxford: Oxford University Press, 2013.

Muthalib, Hassan. "The End of Empire: The Films of the Malayan Film Unit in 1950s British Malaya." In *Film and the End of Empire,* edited by Lee Grieveson and Colin MacCabe, 177–96. London: Palgrave Macmillan, 2011.

Nell, Louis. *Images of Yesteryear: Film-Making in Central Africa.* Harper Collins Zimbabwe, 1998.

Nelson, Renee A. "Promotion of the West Indian Federation: The Federal Information Service, 1957–1961." In *Ideology, Regionalism, and Society in Caribbean History,* edited by Shane J. Pantin and Jerome Teelucksingh, 41–68. London: Palgrave Macmillan, 2017.

Nicholas, Siân. "'Brushing Up Your Empire': Dominion and Colonial Propaganda on the BBC's Home Services, 1939–45." *Journal of Imperial and Commonwealth History* 31.2 (2003): 207–30.

Noble, George. "Cameraman on the Gold Coast." *Colonial Cinema* (June 1952): 36–39.

Notcutt, L. A., and G. C. Latham. *The African and the Cinema: An Account of the Work of the Bantu Educational Cinema Experiment during the Period March 1935 to May 1937.* London: Edinburgh House Press, 1937.

Nowell-Smith, Geoffrey, and Christophe Dupin, eds. *The British Film Institute, the Government and Film Culture, 1933–2000.* Manchester: Manchester University Press, 2012.

Obiaya, Ikechukwu. "A Break with the Past: The Nigerian Video-Film Industry in the Context of Colonial Filmmaking." *Film History: An International Journal* 23.2 (2011): 129–46.

Odunton, G. B. "One Step Ahead." *Colonial Cinema* 8.2 (June 1950): 29–32.

Pearson, George. "Health Education by Film in Africa." *Health Education Journal* 7.1 (March 1949): 39–42.

———. "Visual Education by Film in the Colonies." *United Empire* (July–August 1950): 206–9.

———. *Flashback: The Autobiography of a British Filmmaker.* London: George Allen and Unwin, 1957.

Pickering, K. "Another Walt Disney Experiment." *Colonial Cinema* (September 1954): 50–53.

Plageman, Nate. "A Failed Showcase of Empire?: The Gold Coast Police Band, Colonial Record Keeping, and a 1947 Tour of Great Britain." *African Music* 10.2 (2016): 57–76.

Potter, Simon J. *Broadcasting Empire: The BBC and the British World, 1922–1970.* Oxford: Oxford University Press, 2012.

Pratt, Fred. "'Ghana Muntie!' Broadcasting, Nation-Building and Social Difference in the Gold Coast and Ghana, 1935–1985." PhD dissertation, Indiana University, 2013.

Prosser, A. R. G. "An Experiment in Community Development." *Community Development Bulletin* 2:3 (June 1951): 52–53.

Ramakrishna, Kumar. *Emergency Propaganda: The Winning of Malayan Hearts and Minds 1948–1958.* Richmond, Surrey: Curzon Press, 2002.

Rathbone, Richard. "Casting 'the Kingdome into Another Mold': Ghana's Troubled Transition to Independence." In *The Iconography of Independence: Freedoms at Midnight,* edited by Robert Holland, Susan Williams, and Terry Barringer, 57–70. Abingdon: Routledge, 2009.

Rennalls, M. A. "Development of the Documentary Film in Jamaica." Unpublished master's thesis, Boston University, 1967.

Rennalls, Martin. *A Career Making a Difference.* Unpublished, 1991. Accessed at the National Library of Jamaica in Kingston.

Reynolds, Glenn. *Colonial Cinema in Africa: Origins, Images, Audiences.* Jefferson, NC: McFarland, 2015.

Rice, Tom. "Exhibiting Africa: British Instructional Films and the Empire Series (1925–1928)." In *Empire and Film,* edited by Lee Grieveson and Colin MacCabe, 115–33. London: BFI, 2011.

———. "Opening the Colonial Film Archive." *Frames* 1.1 (2012).

———. "Distant Voices of Malaya, Still Colonial Lives." *Journal of British Cinema and Television* 10.3 (2013): 430–51.

———. "Merdeka for Malaya: Imagining Independence across the British Empire." In *The Colonial Documentary Film in South and South-East Asia,* edited by Ian Aitken and Camille Deprez, 73–98. Edinburgh: Edinburgh University Press, 2016.

Rotha, Paul. *Documentary Film.* London: Faber and Faber, 1936.

Russell Orr, J. "The Use of the Kinema in the Guidance of Backward Races." *Journal of the Royal African Society* 30.120 (July 1931): 238–44.

Sandon, Emma. "Cinema and Highlife in the Gold Coast: *The Boy Kumasenu* (1952)." *Social Dynamics: A Journal of African Studies* 39.3 (2013): 496–519.

———, Tom Rice, and Peter Bloom. "Changing the World: Sean Graham." *Journal of British Cinema and Television* 10.3 (2013): 524–36.

Sanogo, Aboubakar. "Colonialism, Visuality and the Cinema: Revisiting the Bantu Educational Kinema Experiment." In *Empire and Film,* edited by Lee Grieveson and Colin MacCabe, 227–46. London: BFI, 2011.

Schuknecht, Rohland. *British Colonial Development Policy after the Second World War: The Case of Sukumaland, Tanganyika.* Berlin: Lit Verlag, 2010.

Sellers, William. "Films for Primitive Peoples." *Documentary News Letter* 2.9 (September 1941): 173–74.

———. "Address to the British Kinematograph Society." *Colonial Cinema* (March 1948): 9–13.

———. "Making Films with the Africans." In *The Year's Work in the Film, 1950,* edited by Roger Manvell, 37–43. London: Longmans, Green, 1951.

———. "Advice on Filmstrip Production." *Colonial Cinema* 9.2 (June 1951): 44–46.

———. "Mobile Cinema Shows in Africa." *Colonial Cinema* 9.4 (December 1951): 77–82.

———. "Making Films in and for the Colonies." *Royal Society of Arts Journal* (16 October 1953): 829–37.

———. "Film Use and Production in British Colonial Territories." In *Report on the Seminar on Visual Aids in Fundamental Education,* 42–46. Paris: UNESCO, 1954.

———. "Health Education." *Journal of the Royal Society for the Promotion of Health* (July 1955): 440–41.
Shaw, Alexander. "The Uganda Film Unit: Final Report on the Project—Period September 1961 to December 1964." Paris: UNESCO, 1965.
Singh, Makhan. *History of Kenya's Trade Union Movement to 1952*. Nairobi: East African Publishing House, 1969.
Skinner, Rob. "'Natives are not critical of photographic quality': Censorship, Education and Films in African Colonies between the Wars." *University of Sussex Journal of Contemporary History* 2 (2001): 1–9.
Smyth, Rosaleen. "The Development of British Colonial Film Policy, 1927–1939, with Special Reference to East and Central Africa." *Journal of African History* 20.3 (1979): 437–50.
———. "Britain's African Colonies and British Propaganda during the Second World War." *Journal of Imperial and Commonwealth History* 14 (1985): 65–82.
———. "The British Colonial Film Unit and Sub-Saharan Africa, 1939–1945." *Historical Journal of Film, Radio and Television* 8 (1988): 285–98.
———. "The Post-War Career of the Colonial Film Unit in Africa: 1946–1955." *Historical Journal of Film, Radio and Television* 12.2 (1992): 163–77.
———. "Images of Empires on Shifting Sands: The Colonial Film Unit in West Africa in the Post-War Period." In *Film and the End of Empire*, edited by Lee Grieveson and Colin MacCabe, 155–75. London: Palgrave Macmillan, 2011.
———. "Grierson, the British Documentary Movement, and Colonial Cinema in British Colonial Africa." *Film History* 25 (2013): 82–113.
Spurr, Norman. "The Mobile Cinema Van Is a New Weapon in Mass Education." *Colonial Cinema* 7.1 (March 1949): 9–16.
———. "Films for Africans—1910 or 1950?" *Journal of the British Kinematograph Society* 16.6 (June 1950): 185–88.
———. "Pamba." *Empire Cotton Growing Review* (June 1950): 172–76.
———. "Coating the Pill." *Colonial Cinema* (March 1951): 21–22.
———. "A Report on the Use of Disney's Hookworm Film in Uganda." *Colonial Cinema* (June 1951): 28–33.
———. "Visual Aids: Colour or Monochrome." *Colonial Cinema* (June 1952): 41–44.
———. "Experience with Two Films in Tanganyika." *Health Education Journal* 13.1 (March 1955): 81–85.
———. "Multiplication: The Use of 8mm. Film in Community Development." *Community Development Journal* (January 1966): 29–32.
Ssali, Mike. "The Development and Role of an African Film Industry in East Africa, with Special Reference to Tanzania, 1922–1984." PhD dissertation, University of California–Los Angeles, 1988.
Stephen, Daniel. *The Empire of Progress: West Africans, Indians and Britons at the British Empire Exhibition, 1924–25*. New York: Palgrave Macmillan, 2013.
Stewart, Andrew. *Empire Lost: Britain, the Dominions and the Second World War*. London: Hambledon Continuum, 2008.

St Juste, Franklyn "Chappie." "Through the Camera's Eye: The Making of *The Harder They Come.*" *Caribbean Quarterly: A Journal of Caribbean Culture* 61.2–3 (2015): 134–42.

Stollery, Martin. "John Grierson's 'First Principles' as Origin and Beginning: The Emergence of the Documentary Tradition in the Field of Nonfiction Film." *Screen* 58.3 (2017): 309–31.

———. "White Fathers Hear Dark Voices? John Grierson and British Colonial Africa at the End of Empire." In *The Grierson Effect: Tracing Documentary's International Movement*, edited by Zoe Druick and Deane Williams, 187–208. London: BFI, 2014.

Storck, Henri. *The Entertainment Film for Juvenile Audiences*. Paris: UNESCO, 1950.

Strickland, C. F. "Instructional Films in India." *Journal of the Royal Society of Arts* (12 January 1940): 204–15.

Stubbs, Jonathan. "'Did You Ever Notice This Dot in the Mediterranean?' Colonial Cyprus in the Post-war British Documentary." *Historical Journal of Film, Radio and Television* 35.2 (2015): 240–56.

Swann, Paul. *The British Documentary Film Movement, 1926–1946*. Cambridge: Cambridge University Press, 1989.

Tallents, Stephen. *The Projection of England*. London, 1932.

———. "The Documentary Film." *Journal of the Royal Society of Arts* (20 December 1946): 68–85.

Trutor, Jonathan William. "Please Stand By: Reconstruction, Decolonization and Security in British and French Public Information Films in the Postwar Era, 1945–1965." PhD dissertation, University of Minnesota, 2011.

UNESCO. *The Use of Mobile Cinema and Radio Vans in Fundamental Education*. Paris: UNESCO, 1949.

———. *Filmstrip Commentary: Basic Education, Rural Education, Preventive Health Education in Various Developing Countries*. Paris: UNESCO, 1954.

———. "Seminar on Visual Aids in Fundamental Education at Messina, September 1953." Paris: UNESCO, 1954.

Van Bever, L. *Le Cinéma Pour Africains*. Brussels: G. Van Campenhout, 1952.

Vasili, Phil. "Colonialism and Football: The First Nigerian Tour to Britain." *Race and Class* 36.4 (1995): 60–61.

Vaughan, Megan. *Curing Their Ills: Colonial Power and African Illness*. Stanford, CA: Stanford University Press, 1991.

Webster, Wendy. *Englishness and Empire 1939–1965*. Oxford: Oxford University Press, 2005.

Windel, Aaron. "The Bantu Educational Kinema Experiment and the Political Economy of Community Development." In *Empire and Film,* edited by Lee Grieveson and Colin MacCabe, 207–26. London: Palgrave Macmillan, 2011.

Winter, Myrtle, and Norman F. Spurr. *Film-Making on a Low Budget: The UNESCO-UNRWA Pilot Project*. Paris: UNESCO, 1960.

Woods, Philip. "'Chapattis by Parachute': The Use of Newsreels in British Propaganda in India in the Second World War." *Journal of South Asian Studies* 23.2 (2000): 89–110.

Wright, Basil. "Filming in Ceylon." *Cinema Quarterly* 2/4 (Summer 1934): 231–32.
———. "Documentary Today." *Penguin Film Review* 2 (January 1947): 37–44.
———. *The Uganda Film and Its Development, 18 November–22 December 1966*. Paris: UNESCO, 1967.
Wynne, Donald. "Tanganyika's Film Experiment." *Colonial Cinema* (September 1952): 61–65.

INTERVIEWS

Bowden, Dennis. 24 May 2016. Personal interview.
Bowden, Dennis. 9 August 2007. Interview by Mary Ingleby, accessed at the Bristol Records Office.
Densham, Denny. 4 June 1990. Interview by Margaret Thomson and John Legard. BECTU History Project, accessed at BFI.
Graham, Sean. 5 February 2010. Personal interview by Peter Bloom, Tom Rice, and Emma Sandon.
Izod, John. March 2013. Personal correspondence.
Jochimsen, John. 17 May 2016. Personal interview.
Muscatt, Tony. 9 August 2007. Interview by Mary Ingleby, accessed at the Bristol Records Office.
Paynter, Bob. 18 September 2007. Interview by Mary Ingleby, accessed at the Bristol Records Office.
Samuelson, Sir Sydney. 15 June 2010. Personal interview by Tom Rice and Emma Sandon.
Williams, Bill. 7 June 2016. Personal interview.

SELECTED FILMOGRAPHY

Square brackets list the archive from which the film was accessed and, where applicable, its online availability. Abbreviations: British Film Institute (BFI); Imperial War Museum (IWM); Associated Press Archives (AP); National Library of Jamaica (NLJ).

The online sites are:
Colonial Film: Moving Images of the British Empire (colonialfilm), accessed at http://colonialfilm.org.uk
British Council (BC), accessed at http://film.britishcouncil.org/british-council-film-collection
BFI Player, accessed at https://player.bfi.org.uk
The National Archives (TNA), accessed at www.nationalarchives.gov.uk/films
/Internet Archive, accessed at archive.org

GENERAL (BY DATE)

Panorama of Calcutta (Warwick Trading Co. GB, 1899) [BFI, colonialfilm]
Landing of Savage South Africa at Southampton (British Mutoscope and Biograph Company, 1899) [BFI, colonialfilm]

Secrets of Nature (British Instructional Films, 1922–1933) [BFI]
Fathoms Deep beneath the Sea (H. M. Lomas, British Instructional Films, 1922) [BFI]
Britain's Birthright (British Instructional Films, 1924) [IWM, BFI]
Black Cotton (British Instructional Films, 1927) [BFI, colonialfilm]
The Oil Palm Industry (Dr. Thomas, n.d.)
Drifters (John Grierson, Empire Marketing Board, 1929) [BFI]
One Family (Walter Creighton, British Instructional Films, 1930) [BFI, colonialfilm]
Song of Ceylon (Basil Wright, GPO Film Unit, 1934) [BFI, colonialfilm]
The Heart of an Empire (Alexander Shaw, Strand, 1935) [BFI, colonialfilm]
African Peasant Farms—the Kingolwira Experiment (Leslie Notcutt, BEKEFILM, 1936) [BFI, colonialfilm]
Tropical Hookworm (Leslie Notcutt, BEKEFILM, 1936) [BFI, colonialfilm]
The Veterinary Training of African Natives (Leslie Notcutt, BEKEFILM, 1936) [BFI, colonialfilm]
Anti-Plague Operations, Lagos (William Sellers, 1937) [BFI, colonialfilm]
William Sellers's films including *Anti-Malaria Field Work* (ca. 1933), *Infant Welfare Work in Nigeria* (ca. 1933), *Young Nigeria* (ca. 1937), *Dirt Brings Sickness—Cleanliness Brings Health* (ca. 1935), *Slum Clearance and Town Planning* (ca. 1933), *A Day with an English Baby Boy* (ca. 1937). [All accessed at AP].
Jamaican Harvest (Frank Bundy, Gaumont British Instructional, 1938) [BFI, colonialfilm]
Atlantic (Mary Field, Gaumont British Instructional, 1940) [BFI, BC]
British News (1940–1967) [BFI, sample online at BC]
Indian News Parade (1943–1946) (126 issues) [IWM, and several at colonialfilm]
The Winged Scourge (Disney, 1943) [archive.org]
Local Government (Bernerd Mainwaring, Signet Pictures, 1943) [BC]
Hello West Indies (John Page, Paul Rotha Productions, 1943) [BFI, BFI Player]
Jonathan Builds a Dam (Kenya Information Office, 1944). Reedited as *Kenya Village Builds a Dam* by the Colonial Film Unit.
Kenya Daisies (Kenya Information Office, 1944). Reedited by Colonial Film Unit.
Achimota (John Page, Crown Film Unit, 1945) [BFI]
District Officer (Kenneth Villers, Information Films of India, 1945) [BFI, colonialfilm]
Fight for Life (John Page, Crown Film Unit, 1946) [BFI]
Basuto Boy (Aubrey Singer, Gaumont-British Instructional, 1947) [BFI, colonialfilm]
Here Is the Gold Coast (John Page, COI, 1947) [BFI, colonialfilm]
Voices of Malaya (Ralph Elton, Crown Film Unit, 1948) [BFI, IWM, colonialfilm]
Nigerian Cocoa Farmer (1948) [BFI, colonialfilm]
Daybreak in Udi (Terry Bishop, Crown, 1949) [BFI, colonialfilm]

Spotlight on the Colonies (Diana Pine, Crown Film Unit, 1950) [BFI, colonialfilm]
A Queen Is Crowned (Michael Waldman, Castleton Knight, 1953) [BFI]

COLONIAL FILM UNIT FILMS

(All CFU except those listed as part of training schools. The numbers were assigned by CFU and relate to their order of release.)

1. *Mr. English at Home* (Gordon Hales, 1940) [BFI, colonialfilm]
7. *Progress in the Colonies: An African Hospital* (Sellers, 1941) [earlier version ca. 1933 at AP]
8. *An African in London* (1941)
11. *This Is a Barrage Balloon* (1941)
17. *These Are London Firemen* (1942) [IWM]
19. *Early Training of African Troops* (Arthur Champion, 1942)
20. *African Troops on Active Service* (1942)
23. *Uganda Police* (Roberts, 1942)
32. *Charlie the Rascal* (1943)
32a. *The Man Hunt* (1943)
35. *Machi Gaba* (William Sellers, 1943) [AP—reedited from earlier Sellers material]
36. *Timbermen from Honduras* (1943)
42. *Barless Incinerator* (William Sellers, 1943) [AP—reedited from earlier Sellers material]
46. *Africa's Fighting Men* (1943) [BFI, colonialfilm]
Home Guards (William Sellers, 1943) [AP]
50. *Sam the Cyclist* (1943)
53. *Mr Wise and Mr Foolish Go to Town* (1943) [AP]. Reedited version of *The Two Brothers* (1940).
The British Empire at War (Issues 1–39, 1943–45)
55. *Springtime in an English Village* (1944) [BFI, colonialfilm]
56. *Plainsmen of Barotseland* (Nell, 1944) [BFI, colonialfilm]
57. *West Indians with the R.A.F. in Britain* (1944)
65. *Basuto Troops on Active Service* (1945), [BFI]
67. *Home Guard Stand Down* (1945) [BFI]
69. *Boy Scouts in Uganda* (1945) [AP]
71. *Boy Scouts* (1945)
74. *Freed War Prisoners Return to Africa* (1945)
77. *Education in England: A Village School* (1945) [AP]
Colonial Cinemagazine (1–28, 1945–1949) [some at BFI, AP, colonialfilm]
85. *Welcome Home* (1946)
88. *Deck Chair* (1946)
90. *Victory Parade* (1946) [BFI, BFI Player]
91. *Swollen Shoot* (1946) [AP]
92. *An African in England: An English Village* (1945) [AP]

93. *Weaving in Togoland* (1946) [BFI, AP]
94. *Fight Tuberculosis in the Home* (1946) [BFI]
103. *Towards True Democracy* (1947) [BFI]
104. *Good Business* (1947) [BFI]
109. *Better Homes* (1948) [BFI]
111. *West African University* (1948)
113. *Mixed Farming* (1948) [BFI]
115. *African Conference in London, 1948* (1948) [BFI, colonialfilm]
124. *University College of the Gold Coast* (1948)
125. *Foundation Day at Ibadan University College* (Nigeria, 1948) [BFI]
126. *African Visitors at the Tower of London* (1949) [BFI, BFI Player]
128. *Better Pottery* (1949) [AP]
130. *Nigerian Footballers in England* (1949) [BFI, colonialfilm]
131. *Colonial Month* (1949) [BFI, colonialfilm]
135. *A Film School in West Africa* (Lionel Snazelle, Gold Coast, 1949) [AP]
136. *Basket Making* (Gold Coast, 1949) [AP]
137. *Copra* (Gold Coast, 1949) [AP]
Welcome Home Soldiers (Gold Coast, 1949) [AP]
The Good Samaritan (Nigeria, 1949) [AP]
Childbirth Today (Rollo Gamble, Tanganyika, 1949) [AP]
146. *Pamba* (Spurr, Uganda, 1950) [AP]
147. *A Journey by a London Bus* (1950) [TNA, archive.org]
155. *Why Not You?* (Norman Spurr, Uganda, 1950) [BFI]
161. *Community Development in Awgu Division* (Alex Fajemisin, Nigeria Film Unit, 1950). Also listed as *Awgu Marches Forward* [BFI]
168. *Smallpox* (Lionel Snazelle, Nigerian Film Unit, 1950) [BFI, colonialfilm]
173. *A Challenge to Ignorance* (Norman Spurr, Uganda, 1950) [AP]
188. *Nairobi* (Kenya, 1950) [BFI, colonialfilm]
191. *University College of the West Indies* (West Indies Training School, 1951) [AP]
193. *Delay Means Death* (Jamaica Film Unit, 1951) [AP]
194. *Cocoa Rehabilitation* (Wilfred Lee, Trinidad and Tobago Film Unit, 1951) [AP]
195. *Give Your Child a Chance* (Isaac Carmichael, Barbados Film Unit, 1951) [AP]
196. *Co-Operative Rice Farming* (R.H. Young, British Guiana Film Unit, 1951) [AP]
197. *Farmer Brown Learns Good Dairying* (Martin Rennalls, Jamaica Film Unit, 1951) [BFI, colonialfilm]

CENTRAL AFRICAN FILM UNIT

Two Farmers (Stephen Peet, 1948) [BFI, colonialfilm]
Wives of Nendi (Stephen Peet, 1949) [BFI, colonialfilm]
Two Generations (1955) [BFI]
Fairest Africa (Geoffrey Mangin, 1959) [BFI]
Rhodesian/Federal Spotlight newsreel (1957–1963) [Many at BFI]
See Saw Years (Dick Raynor, 1964) [BFI]

GOLD COAST FILM UNIT

Amenu's Child (Sean Graham, 1950) [BFI]
The Boy Kumasenu (Sean Graham, 1952) [BFI, colonialfilm]
Progress in Kojokrom (Sean Graham, 1953) [IWM, colonialfilm]
I Will Speak English (1954) [BFI, colonialfilm]
Mr. Mensah Builds a House (Seam Graham, 1955) [BFI, colonialfilm]
Freedom for Ghana (Sean Graham, 1957) [AP]
Enemy in the Night (Dennis Bowden, Ghana Film Unit, 1960) [AP]
Your Police (Brian Salt, Ghana Film Production Corporation, 1962) [AP]
No Tears for Ananse (Sam Aryeetey, Ghana Film Industry Corporation, 1968).

NIGERIAN FILM UNIT

Back to the Community (James Otigbah, Federal Information Service Production Unit, 1954) [AP]
Health and Baby Week, Lagos, 1956 (Federal Information Service Production Unit, 1956) [AP]
Nigeria's First Women Police (Federal Information Service Production Unit, 1956) [BFI, colonialfilm]
Nigeria Greets the Queen (Lionel Snazelle, 1956) [BFI]
Another Step Forward (The Constitutional Conference) (Federal Information Service Production Unit, 1957)
Nigeria Hails Her Prime Minister (Federal Information Service Production Unit, 1957)
Tour of H.R.H., the Princess Royal (Federal Information Service Production Unit, 1957)
Forward to a New Nigeria (Information Services of Western Nigeria, 1958)
Self-Government for Western Nigeria (Cedric Williams, Information Services of Western Nigeria, 1958) [BFI]
Giant in the Sun (Sydney Samuelson, Northern Nigerian Information Service, 1959) [BFI, colonialfilm]
Our Land and People (Sydney Samuelson, Northern Nigerian Information Service, 1959)
Nigeria Hails Independence (Lionel Snazelle, Nigeria Ministry of Information, 1960) [AP]
Shaihu Umar (Adamu Halilu, Nigeria Film Corporation, 1976)

KENYA INFORMATION OFFICE, FILM SECTION

Registration of Voters (1956)
How You Vote (1956)

UGANDA FILM UNIT

Situma Joins the Police (1957)
The Preparation of Coffee (1957)
How to Vote (1957)

Uganda Hails Independence (1962)
Better Housing (1963)
The Two Friends (1963)

TANGANYIKA FILM UNIT

Dipping (Norman Spurr, 1952)
Northern Province Agricultural Show (1952) [AP]
We Benefit—We Pay (Norman Spurr, 1953)
The Sukumuland Trade and Agricultural Exhibition (1954) [AP]

EDUCATION DEPARTMENT, MAURITIUS

And the Princess Came . . . (1956)

JAMAICA FILM UNIT

You Can Help Your Children (Martin Rennalls, 1952) [AP]
Together We Build (1953) [AP]
Churchill Visits Jamaica (1953) [BFI, colonialfilm]
Let's Stop Them (Martin Rennalls, 1953) [NLJ]
Princess Margaret Visits Jamaica (1955) [AP]
It Can Happen to You (Martin Rennalls, 1956) [NLJ]
Too Late (1957) [AP]
Builders of the Nation (Martin Rennalls, 1958) [AP]
Our Government at Work: Education Programme Part One (1959) [AP]
Drive with Care (1959) [NLJ]
Ride with Care (1959) [AP]
Walk with Care (1959) [AP]
The Jamaica Hope (1960) [NLJ]
Government by the People (1960) [AP]
Eat Jamaican (Martin Rennalls, Jamaica Information Service Production, n.d.) [NLJ]
Port Royal (Martin Rennalls, Albert Miller, n.d.) [NLJ]
Towards Independence (1962) [NLJ]
A Nation Is Born (1962) [NLJ]
A Bright Tomorrow (Martin Rennalls, Jamaican Information Services, 1967) [AP]

BARBADOS GOVERNMENT FILM UNIT

A Nation Is Born (Isaac Carmichael, 1958) [AP]

TRINIDAD AND TOBAGO GOVERNMENT FILM UNIT

To Vote Is a Great Duty (Trinidad Film Unit, 1950)
Portrait of Trinidad (Wilfred Lee, County Films Ltd., 1957) [BFI]

His Excellency the Governor (1959) [BFI]
University in Trinidad (1960) [BFI]
Road to Independence (1962) [BFI]
This Land of Ours (1962) [BFI]
Two Royal Visits (1966) [BFI]
Command Performance All as One (1966) [BFI]

BRITISH GUIANA FILM UNIT

Building Homes Together (ca. 1955) [AP]
How to Exercise Your Vote (1955) [AP]
The Good Hope (1955) [AP]
British Guiana Cinemagazine (1955) (issues at AP]
Houses Assemble (1961)

MALAYAN FILM UNIT

The Kinta Story (Harry Govan, 1949)
A Better Man (1953) [IWM]
The Letter (1953)
Touch and Go (1953) [IWM]
Worry Free (1954) [IWM]
1955: The Year in Malaya (1955) [IWM, colonialfilm]
Merdeka for Malaya (1957) [IWM]

Index

Films for the Colonies Tom Rice *fig.* refers to figures

Accra, 126–27, 151–52, 197, 238, 285n115
Accra (1948), 138
Accra training school (1948), xvi, 12, 183–88, 195, 205, 209, 237, 238*fig.*
Achimota, 123–24, 130
Achimota (1945), 157, 310
Achimota College, 164, 205, 280n45
Acland, Charles R., 5
Adams, Robert, 141–42
Aden, 123, 155
Adventurer, The (1917), 52
advertisements, 15–16, 75, 76*fig.*, 197, 213, 290n64
Africa: absences, 133, 141–42; *An African in England: An English Village* (1945), 140–44; BEKE, 35–41, 43; BIF, 28–29; *Black Cotton* (1927), 19–20, 27–31; *The Boy Kumasenu* (1952), 197–98; British Empire, 133–34, 140, 144, 178; British film, 19, 28–29; Central African Federation, 97, 214; CFU, 10, 130, 133, 151–56, 162, 167, 277n132; *Colonial Cinema* (1942–54), 130, 134; Colonial Office, 150–51; colonies, 116; Davidson, Basil, 235; *Early Training of African Troops* (1942), 130–31; economics, 175; education, 36–37; *Education in England: A Village School* (1945), 139, 277n127; *Fairest Africa* (1959), 214, 312; film units, 69, 108, 149–57, 254n111; *Freed War Prisoners Return to Africa* (1945), 144; *The Good Samaritan* (1949), 187–88; Huxley, Elspeth, 115; imperialism, 133–34, 135; independence, 167–68, 194; instructional films, 34; mobile exhibition, 108, 122–23, 207; modernization, 162, 164, 167; MOI, 43; *Mr. English at Home* (1940), 61, 113; nationhood, 195–206; Orr, James Russell, 43; political control, 95; postwar, 135, 152; practices/principles/policies, 149; Prince of Wales, 22; proposals, 34; radio, 126; Raw Stock Scheme, 130–37, 154; sanitation, 46; Schauder, Leon, 132; self-reliance/co-operation, 161–73; Sellers, William, 43, 108; *Smallpox* (1950), 208; *Springtime in an English Village* (1944), 140–41; Spurr, Norman F., 17; *Victory Parade* (1946), 147; Woolfe, Harry Bruce, 34; World War II, 126, 130–37, 276n124. *See also* African cinema; East Africa; West Africa; *individual countries; individual film units*
African Affairs (publication), 181, 197
African and the Cinema, The (1937) (report), 37, 38*fig.*, 40

317

African audiences: AFP, 290n73; *An African in England: An English Village* (1945), 141; agriculture films, 150; animation, 168–70; *Back to the Community* (1954), 209; BEKE, 36–41; bicycle films, 113; *Black Cotton* (1927), 27–31; British film, 18–19, 28–29, 124; British primacy, 52–53, 66, 67; Central African Federation, 214; CFU, 1–2, 28, 36, 52, 64, 67, 79, 104, 134, 213; Champion, Arthur, 87; Chaplin, Charlie, 52; children, 72–80; *Le Cinéma Pour Africains* (pamphlet), 73; citizenship, 35, 150; COI, 170; *Colonial Cinema* (1942–54), 68–72, 264n95; *Colonial Cinemagazine* (newsreels), 151; Colonial Office, 150–51; documentaries, 71; East African Film Unit, 171; education, 67–68; Empire Transcription Scheme, 128; Feilmann, Captain, 132; *A Film School in West Africa* (1949), 186; "Films for Africans—1910 or 1950?" (speech), 79; "Films for Primitive Peoples" (articles), 65–68, 84–85, 258n21; film/specialized techniques, 31, 36, 61, 73, 75, 103; *The Heart of an Empire* (1935), 52; house construction, 150; Huxley, Julian, xv, 19, 28, 30–31, 36–37; information office/rs, 123; instructional films, 75; Johnson, Geoffrey and Mina, 281n58; labor, 150; *Land and Water* (1944), 71; Latham, Geoffrey, 37–38; local voices, 87, 127; London, 52–53; media, 65; mobilization, 132–33; MOI, 134; Morton-Williams, Peter, xvi; *Mr. English at Home* (1940), 61–65, 257n11; Nell, Louis, 131–32; *Nigerian Footballers in England* (1949), 182; Notcutt, Leslie, 38; Odunton, J. B., 80–81; Pearson, George, 78; practices/principles/policies, 72–80; race, 10; Sellers, William, 10–11, 31, 52–53, 56, 61, 64, 78, 110; *Shaihu Umar* (1976), 238; *Springtime in an English Village* (1944), 140; Tanganyika, 71; *Theory of Film* (Kracauer), 73; VD films, 136; *Victory Parade* (1946), 146; World War II, 127, 133–34. *See also* primitivity, theories on

African cinema, 39, 103, 149, 173–83, 197, 198, 204–5, 215–16. *See also* film units; individual film units

African Conference in London, (1948) (film/event), 151, 176–78, 179, 312

African Film Productions (AFP), 215–16, 290n73, 291n75

African in England: An English Village, An (1945), 140–44, 182, 311

African in London, An (1941), 52–53, 141–42, 311

African Troops on Active Service (1942), 130, 311

"African Village School, An" (film concept), 162

African Visitors at the Tower of London (1949), 176, 312

Africa's Fighting Men (1943), 133–34, 275n116, 311

agriculture: *Achimota* (1945), 157; BEKE, 36, 37, 42; British Guiana Film Unit, 222–23; CFU, 5, 35, 142, 161–62; *Cocoa Rehabilitation* (1951), 190–91; *Colonial Cinema* (1942–54), 69–70; *Colonial Cinemagazine* (newsreels), 152; *Co-Operative Rice Farming* (1951), 222–23; *Giant in the Sun* (1959), 212; Imperial College of Tropical Agriculture, 229, 232; information office/rs, 123; instructional films, 43; JFU, 189; *Let's Stop Them* (1953), 223; Nigeria, 212; *The Oil Palm Industry* (n.d.), 51–52; Raw Stock Scheme, 19; Sellers, William, 54; Tanganyika, 215; *United We Stand* (1953), 192; useful cinema, 149–50

agriculture films, 28–29, 37, 122. *See also* individual films

Aitken, Ian, 7, 160, 161

Alakija, O. B., 142

Alexandra of Kent, Princess, 232–33

Ambler, Charles, 84, 91, 97, 98, 210, 213, 267n141

Amenu's Child (1950), 81–82, 99–100, 200, 201fig., 267n146, 287n29, 313

America. *See* Hollywood's cultural imperialism; United States

Amery, Leo, 31–32

Anderson, Gerry, 116

And the Princess Came . . . (1956), 211, 314

animation, 168–70, 199, 227, 282n61

Another Step Forward (The Constitutional Conference) (1957), 207, 313

Anstey, Edgar, 161

anti-colonialism, 129, 210–11, 235

Anti-Malaria Field Work (ca. 1933), 47–48, 310

Anti-Plague Operations, Lagos (1929, 1932, 1933, 1937), 47, 48–49, 53, 162–63, 310

Index | 319

archival materials, 6, 7–8, 241–43, 255n129
Arden-Clarke, Charles, 236
Aryeetey, Sam, 183–84, 205, 237–38
Associated Press Archives, 242, 255n129
Atlantic (1940), 55, 310
audience research, 19, 71–72, 83, 98–103. *See also* Morton-Williams, Peter
audiences, international, 211, 212, 214, 228, 231, 235, 236
Auna, Malam Yakuba, 183–84
Australia, 25, 28, 146–47, 160, 235
Awolowo, Chief, 211–12
Azikiwe, Nnamdi, 147, 168

Back to the Community (1954), 208–9, 313
Baldwin, Stanley, 15–16
Ball, Graham, 20–21
Bantu Educational Kinema Experiment (BEKE), xv, 35–43, 252n82, 256n149. *See also* Davis, John Merle
Barbados, 5, 101*fig.*, 183, 188–89, 219, 233, 292n93, 314
Barbados Advocate (newspaper), 225
Barbados Film Unit (BFU), 225, 232, 292n93, 292n104, 314
barges, 207
Barkas, Geoffrey, 32
Barless Incinerator (1943), 53, 130, 311
Basket Making (1949), 186–87, 312
Basuto Boy (1947), 75, 76*fig.*, 310
Basuto Troops on Active Service (1945), 135, 311
Bazin, Andre, 73–74
BBC (British Broadcasting Corporation): British Empire, 128; CFU, 4, 126, 128; Colonial Office, 126; colonies, 39, 103, 126–28; education, 126; Empire Service, 39, 126; Empire Transcription Scheme, 128; filmstrips, 125; imperialism, 39, 128; Ormsby-Gore, William, 40; primitivity, theories on, 61, 68, 126; propaganda, 39, 128; race, 128; radio, 39, 126, 127, 128; Sellers, William, 44, 61, 111, 258n31; shows, 274n91; Wideson, Rene, 285n123
Beddington, Jack, 71, 111, 113, 151
Belgian Congo, 73, 123
Bell, Gawain Westray, 213
Bell, Hesketh, 29–30, 31–32, 250n52
Bell, Oliver, 43
Bengal famine, 135–36
Better Homes (1948), 150, 165, 312
Better Housing (1963), 237, 314

Better Man, A (1953), 210
Better Pottery (1949), 164, 312
Bever, L. Van, 73
Bhattacharya, Sanjoy, 136
bicycle films, 113–14, 223–24, 271n44
bin Shamsuddin, Osman, 161
biopolitics, 3, 7, 18, 41, 74. *See also* political control
Blackburne, K. W., 99, 173–74, 176, 283n83
Black Cotton (1927), 15, 19–31, 55, 250n46, 310. *See also* Empire series (1925–1928)
Blaylock, Jennifer, 241
Bloom, Peter, 73, 126, 197–98, 205
Bowden, Dennis, 69, 116, 155*fig.*, 214, 228, 238, 239, 277n131
Boy Kumasenu, The (1952), xvi, 197–200, 204–5, 313
Boy Scouts, 138, 209, 225, 236, 311
Boy Scouts/in Uganda (1945), 138, 311
Bracken, Brendan, 117–18, 120
Bradshaw, Hugh L., 155*fig.*, 165
Brendon, Piers, 194
Bright Tomorrow, A (1967), 241, 314
Britain's Birthright (1924), 24, 249n34, 310
British Commonwealth. *See* Commonwealth
British Council: CFU, 4, 11, 116–21, 138–39; colonies, 118–20, 271n46; economics, 108; educational films, 118; England, projection of, 140; Field, Mary, 97; film collection, 309; film techniques, 271n42; Gillan, Angus, 71, 118, 120; Huxley, Gervas, 114; Jamaica, 117; mobile exhibition, 117; MOI, 117–19, 140, 270n39; primitivity, theories on, 118, 271n42; Sellers, William, 112, 116–17, 118, 120, 271n44; TIDA, 108, 116; trade, 55; World War II, 116–21, 270n39, 271n40. *See also individual films*
British Documentary Movement: Anstey, Edgar, 161; British film, 16; CFU, 57–58; Colonial Office, 159; Graham, Sean, 200; Grierson, John, 4–5, 14–15, 18, 35, 159; Grierson, Marion, 35; Highet, A. G., 108; instructional films, 18, 157; MFU, 161; MOI, 64; Noble, George, 196; postwar, 294n126; Tallents, Stephen, 62, 247n6; Taylor, Donald, 35; Wright, Basil, 197. *See also Documentary News Letter* (publication); *individual films*

British Empire: Africa, 133–34, 140, 144, 178; archival materials, 242; *Atlantic* (1940), 55; BBC, 128; BIF, 22–23; *Black Cotton* (1927), 20–27; Boy Scouts, 138; British film, 6, 7, 9–10, 14–15, 17, 19–20, 28, 32, 54–55, 106, 107; CAFU, 214; CFU, 1–4, 9, 11, 12, 55, 65, 84–85, 104–8, 115–16, 120, 130, 136, 148, 150–51, 274n101; Cinematograph Act (1927), 28–29; *Colonial Cinema* (1942–54), 85; *Colonial Cinemagazine* (newsreels), 151; Colonial Film: Moving Images of the British Empire (website), 242–43; colonies, 9–10, 106, 107, 144–45, 147, 151; Commonwealth, 3, 8, 11, 75, 194–95, 213, 214, 286n4; Communism, 115, 150; Creech-Jones, Arthur, 283n82; documentaries, 14–15; Dominions, India and Colonies (panel), 34; economics, 15, 20, 52, 142–43, 213, 230, 283n82; educational films, 14–15; *Education in England: A Village School* (1945), 139; Field, Mary, 14; film history, 243; film units, 193; *Freed War Prisoners Return to Africa* (1945), 144; Gilroy, Paul, 3; Gold Coast, 114, 132; *Government By the People* (1960), 230; *The Heart of an Empire* (1935), 52, 310; Hollywood's cultural imperialism, 15, 128; Huxley, Gervas, 114; Imperial Education Conference (1927), 18, 249n34; Imperial Institute, 27; independence, 150, 194, 231, 294n120; local voices, 84–91; London, 151; media, 11, 233; mobile exhibition, 84–85, 94; MOI, 114–15; *Mr. English at Home* (1940), 104; newsreels, 136; OFTVC, 216, 237; *One Family* (1930), 25–26; Overseas Rediffusion Limited, 233; postwar, 107, 111, 114, 115, 144, 149; Scenes in the British Empire (series), 20–21; schoolchildren, 42, 250n46; Sellers, William, 13–14, 54, 72–73, 74; sports, 182; *Springtime in an English Village* (1944), 140; tours, 180; useful cinema, 5; *Victory Parade* (1946), 144–45; war and CFU, 11, 55, 106–8, 136; World War II, 55, 84–85, 106–8, 114–15, 136, 173. *See also* British primacy; decolonization; Empire series (1925-1928); imperialism; postcolonialism; *individual countries*

British Empire and Commonwealth Museum, 242

British Empire at War, The (newsreel), 132, 133, 311

British Empire Exhibition (Wembley, 1924–25), xv, 20–21, 22, 23–24, 25, 178–79

British film: Africa, 19, 28–29; African audiences, 18–19, 28–29, 124; biopolitics, 18, 74; British Documentary Movement, 16; British Empire, 6, 7, 9–10, 14–15, 17, 19–20, 28, 32, 54–55, 106, 107; British primacy, 2, 9–10, 91; Caribbean, 29; CFU, 4–5, 7, 33, 61, 130, 173; Cinematograph Act (1927), 28–29; citizenship, 17, 35, 47, 253n104; Colonial Office, 18; commercial markets, 24–25; documentaries, 10; economics, 15, 18, 74, 138, 195; education, 30–31, 33, 34, 36, 74, 249n35, 258n29; educational films, 10; film history, 243; filmstrips, 124, 126; global film, 5; *The Heart of an Empire* (1935), 52; Hollywood's cultural imperialism, 58, 254n111; imperialism, 6, 10, 14, 23, 28, 243; information office/rs, 121; labor, 14, 18, 36; London, 52–53; modernization, 48–51, 55, 91; MOI, 117; *One Family* (1930), 26–27; Pearson, George, 58; political control, 32, 94–98, 192, 195, 246n16; postcolonialism, 12; postwar, 138; practices/principles/policies, 28, 65–72; primitivity, theories on, 31–32, 124–25, 127; propaganda, 31, 123, 264n99; school/children, 27, 75–78, 249n35, 250n43; *Times*, 24; trade, 10, 14, 15–16, 21, 24, 32, 249n35; war and CFU, 55, 129; West Africa, 94, 127; World War II, 106–8, 117, 138. *See also* colonies and British film; *individuals*; *individual film types*

British Film Institute (BFI): archival materials, 6, 242–43; BEKE, 36, 37; Bell, Oliver, 43; Colonial Film project, 5; establishment, 34; Fairgrieve, James, 17; "The Film in Colonial Development" (conference), xvi, 12, 160, 173–74; geography films, 17; war and CFU, 56. *See also* Dominions, India and Colonies (panel)

British Guiana, 189–90, 222–23, 295n144

British Guiana Film Unit, 222–23, 315

British Instructional Films (BIF), 14, 21–23, 25, 27–29, 32. *See also* Empire series (1925-1928); *individual films*

British Kinematograph Society, 79
British Movietone News, 146–47
British News (newsreel), 117, 310
British primacy: African audiences, 52–53, 66, 67; An African Conference in London (1948) (film/event), 176, 178; *An African in London* (1941), 52–53; BIF, 22; *Black Cotton* (1927), 23; British film, 2, 9–10, 91; CFU, 2, 65, 162; colonies, 67; "Films for Primitive Peoples" (articles), 66; *A Journey by a London Bus* (1950), 183; Oni of Ife, 176; *Victory Parade* (1946), 145. See also British Empire; imperialism
Buckley, Liam M., 90
Builders of the Nation (1958), 221–22, 227, 314
Building Homes Together (ca. 1955), 222–23, 315
Bundy, Frank, 42
Bureau of Applied Social Research (BASR), 73
Burns, James, 7, 39, 42, 46, 72–73, 96–97, 129
Bustamante, Alexander, 219

Campbell, Alan, 156, 157, 158
Canada, 14, 160, 240, 293n113, 294n127
Caribbean, 2, 29, 186, 188, 189, 190fig., 240. See also West Indies; *individual countries*
Carnegie Corporation, 36
Carstairs, C. Y., 186, 195, 197, 208, 289n51
Castleton-Knight Productions, 146
Central African Federation, 97, 214
Central African Film Unit (CAFU), xvi, 7, 100, 129, 131, 214, 312–13
Central Film Organis/zation, 112, 219, 220–21. See also Colonial Film Unit (CFU)
Central Film Service (Jamaica), 94
Central Office of Information (COI), xvi, 61, 73, 158, 160, 168, 170–71, 175, 180, 195–96, 231, 236
Ceylon, 16, 134, 310
Challenge to Ignorance, A (1950), 167, 312
Champion, Arthur: African audiences, 87; CFU, 122, 131; citizenship, 264n97; Kenya, 87, 88, 89, 122, 131, 260n46; local voices, 87, 88, 89, 263n91; mobile exhibition, 87, 122, 272n61; *Mr. English at Home* (1940), 83–84; primitivity, theories on/propaganda, 122; Raw Stock Scheme, 130–31; *Royal Review* (1939), 116–17; Sellers, William, 131; VD films, 276n119
Chan, Nadine, 46, 87
Chaplin, Charlie, 52, 255n134, 258n18
Chapman, James, 108
Charlie the Rascal (1942), 52, 311
Cheeka, Didi, 241
Chelsea Colour Films, 146
children: African audiences, 72–80; *Amenu's Child* (1950), 200; *Basuto Boy* (1947), 75; British film, 75–78; CFU, 75; citizenship, 75, 225, 262n66; colonies and British film, 75, 77–78; Commonwealth, 75; education, 139; *Give Your Child a Chance* (1951), 225–27, 292n104, 312; *Health and Baby Week, Lagos, 1956* (1956), 209, 313; Hollywood's cultural imperialism, 76; "Making Films for Children" (article), 74; modernization, 261n60; *Mr. English at Home* (1940), 75; Nigeria, 209; Pearson, George, 77–78; practices/principles/policies, 72–80; Rank, J. Arthur, 262n66; Sellers, William, 77–78; specialized techniques, 74–75; *Springtime in an English Village* (1944), 140; *You Can Help Your Children* (1952), 228, 314. See also Field, Mary; schoolchildren
Children's Entertainment Films (CEF) (1944-1950), 14, 74, 75, 77, 261n60, 261n63. See also *Basuto Boy* (1947)
Christian Science Monitor (publication), 27
Churchill, Winston, 11, 176, 224, 286n4, 314
Churchill Visits Jamaica (1953), 224, 314
cinema clubs, 77
Cinéma Pour Africains, Le (pamphlet), 73
Cinematograph Act (1927), 28–29
cinema vans. See mobile exhibition
citizenship: African audiences, 35, 150; *The Boy Kumasenu* (1952), 197–98; British film, 17, 35, 47, 253n104; *Builders of the Nation* (1958), 221–22; CEF, 14; CFU, 84, 104, 140, 150; Champion, Arthur, 264n97; colonies, 46, 47, 75; East Africa, 86; economics, 46; *Education in England: A Village School* (1945), 139; *Give Your Child a Chance* (1951), 225; Grierson, John, 17; JFU, 223–24; Malaya, 46; media, 3, 4; MFU, 210–11; mobile exhibition, 86, 104; Orr, James Russell, 43; school/children,

citizenship: African audiences *(continued)* 14, 75, 225, 253n104, 262n66; Sellers, William, 11, 47, 104; *Springtime in an English Village* (1944), 140; tours, 180; *Towards True Democracy* (1947), 167

Cocoa Rehabilitation (1951), 190–91, 312

Cold War, 77, 175, 240. See also Communism

Colonial Cinema (1942–54): Africa, 130, 134; African audiences, 68–72, 264n95; African cinema, 149; agriculture, 69–70; audience research, 98; *Basuto Troops on Active Service* (1945), 135; BBC, 103; Beddington, Jack, 113; bicycle films, 113; British Empire, 85; census film, 217fig.; CFU, xvi, 2, 68, 144, 145, 152; Chaplin, Charlie, 52; Colonial Office, 111; colonies, 68–69, 94–95, 152; *Education in England: A Village School* (1945), 139, 277n127; filmstrips, 126; final issue cover, 3fig.; Franklin, Harry, 129; *Freed War Prisoners Return to Africa* (1945), 144; house construction, 69–70; hygiene, 69–70; Lironi, H. E., 70; local voices, 87; Maddison, John, 73; modernization, 257n10; *Mr. English at Home* (1940), 64–65; Odunton, J. B., 80–81; Oni of Ife, 177fig.; primitivity, theories on, 98; Raw Stock Scheme, 19, 69, 133; Sellers, William, 70, 71, 85fig., 94–95, 126; specialized techniques, 69–70; *Springtime in an English Village* (1944), 140–41; tours, 180, 284n98; trainees, 116; *Victory Parade* (1946), 147; *Weaving in Togoland* (1946), 164

Colonial Cinemagazine (newsreels), 151–52, 176, 178, 179–80, 181, 182, 311

Colonial Development and Welfare Acts (1940, 1945), 115, 149, 154, 155, 168

Colonial Development Fund, 54–55

Colonial Film Committee, 158, 160

Colonial Film: Moving Images of the British Empire (website), 242–43

Colonial Films Committee, 28–29, 31–32, 33. See also individuals

Colonial Film Unit (CFU), 54–59, 60–105, 173–83; *Aberdeen Press and Journal*, 282n69; absences, 6, 130–37; Africa, 10, 130, 133, 151–56, 162, 167, 277n132; African audiences, 1–2, 28, 36, 52, 64, 67, 79, 104, 134, 213; An African Conference in London (1948) (film/event), 176–78; "An African Village School" (film concept), 162; afterlife, 237–43; agriculture, 5, 35, 142, 161–62; archival materials, 241–42; audience research, 19, 71–72, 98–103; BBC, 4, 126, 128; BEKE, 37; biopolitics/political control, 7, 41, 98, 168; Blackburne, K. W., 99, 176, 283n83; Bracken, Brendan, 120; British Council, 4, 11, 116–21, 138–39; British Documentary Movement, 57–58; British Empire, 1–4, 9, 11, 12, 55, 65, 84–85, 104–8, 115–16, 120, 130, 136, 148, 150–51, 274n101; British film, 4–5, 7, 33, 61, 130, 173; British primacy, 2, 65, 162; Caribbean, 2; Carmichael, Isaac, 219; Carstairs, C. Y., 195; Champion, Arthur, 122, 131; Chaplin, Charlie, 52; children, 75; *Le Cinéma Pour Africains* (pamphlet), 73; citizenship, 84, 104, 140, 150; closure, xvi, 1, 2, 14, 103–5, 170, 172, 192–93, 245n2; COI, xvi, 170–71; Colonial Development and Welfare Acts (1940, 1945), 115, 149, 154, 155; Colonial Films Committee, 33; Colonial Month, 178–79; Colonial Office, 70, 107, 110–14, 120, 144–45, 171, 179; comedy films, 170; Commonwealth, 3, 115; Crown Film Unit, 11, 70–71, 109–10, 158, 160–61; Cyprus training school (1951), 192; decolonization, 170–71; Densham, Denny, 259n42; disciplinary expertise, 259n41; Disney, 282n61; documentaries, 4–5, 71, 259n39; Dominions, India and Colonies (panel), 34; East Africa, 41, 132, 153, 165–66, 170–71, 172, 282n73; economics, 2, 3, 4, 9, 120–21; education, 5, 17, 79, 112, 125, 221; educational films, 118, 120–21, 271n42; establishment, xv, 1, 15, 54–59, 108, 115, 148; exhibition, 84, 87–88, 98–99, 104, 107; fascism, 107; *The Film in National Life* (1932) (report), 33; film school, 90; "Films for Primitive Peoples" (articles), 66; films of, 311–12; filmstrips, 90, 107–8, 126; film techniques, 28, 57, 63–64, 75, 154; film units, xvi, 12, 73, 90, 104–5, 149–57, 162, 173, 192–93, 195; GCFU, 70; global film, 2–3, 4, 5; globalization, 150, 195; Gold Coast, 1–2, 161, 162, 219; GPO, 63; Grierson, John, 4–5, 160, 175; Hammond, S. A., 35; health, 5, 35, 125, 142; home unit, xvi, 52–53,

173–83; house construction, 62–63; Huxley, Gervas, 113–14, 131, 269n21; Huxley, Julian, 30, 55; hygiene, 4; imperialism, 1–5, 7, 106–7, 143, 150, 183, 195; independence, 2–3, 5, 12, 150, 168, 188, 195, 233, 237; industrial films, 227; industries, 164; information office/rs, 121–24, 129–30, 171; instructional films, 1–2, 43, 136, 143–44, 157, 274n101; instruction courses, 70, 111; interwar Britain, 59, 106; JFU, 219–20, 221; labor, 7; Lagos, 241; Latham, Geoffrey, 41, 43; Legislative Council, 167; libraries, 57, 111; Lironi, H. E., 70, 163, 259n39; local voices, 11, 87, 91, 98–99, 101–2, 104; London, 56–59, 151; media, 2, 4, 9; Mediterranean, 155; MFU, 161; mobile exhibition, 2, 4, 5, 9, 84, 104, 269n21; modernization, 7; MOI, 11, 106–21, 129–30, 131, 257n16, 274n101; Morgan, W. S., 271n42; Morton-Williams, Peter, xvi; nationhood, 104, 150, 151–61, 237; Nell, Louis, 131–32; NFU, 206–18; Notcutt, Leslie, 43; Odunton, J. B., 80–83; OFTVC, xvi, 214, 218, 220; Oni of Ife, 176–77; Pearson, George, 1, 2, 4, 58–59, 150, 155*fig.*, 168; political events, 146; postwar, 2, 12, 107, 115, 120–23, 125, 136, 142–48, 150–52, 164, 167, 187, 219; primitivity, theories on, 28, 53, 67, 68, 72, 111, 153, 260n52; propaganda, 14, 106–8, 112, 113–14, 132, 213, 274n101; proposals, 32, 33, 35, 106; race, 116, 153; radio, 107–8, 128; Raw Stock Scheme, xv, 32, 34, 57, 69, 130–32; Rennalls, Martin, 219; Reynolds, Glenn, 32; Snazelle, Lionel, 155*fig.*, 196; soil erosion, 170; Sowande, Fela, 87; specialized techniques, 63–64, 71–72, 103–5, 118, 169, 184, 196; Spurr, Norman F., 17, 79–80, 99, 166, 215, 218, 220; staff, 56, 59, 116, 154, 155*fig.*, 279n27; Swithinbank, Charles, 259n41; Taylor, John, 160; *Times*, 245n2; tours, 179–81; trade, 4, 179; trainees, 116, 275n108; UFU, 237; UNESCO, 4; universities, 150; useful cinema, 149–50; Usill, H. V., 275n108; VD films, 136–37; welfare, 2; West Africa, xvi, 2, 45, 56, 129–30, 132, 153*fig.*, 164; West Africa Photography Unit, 273n77; West Indies, 155; West Indies training school, 185. *See also Colonial Cinema* (1942–54); colonies and CFU; practices/principles/ policies; Sellers, William: CFU; training schools; war and CFU; *individual countries; individual films*

Colonial Month (1949), 151, 178–79, 312

Colonial Office: *Achimota* (1945), 157; Africa/n audiences, 150–51; animation, 168; BBC/Empire Service, 126; BEKE, 35–36, 39; Blackburne, K. W., 173–74; British Documentary Movement, 159; British film, 18; Carstairs, C. Y., 186, 195; Central Film Organis/zation, 112; CFU, 70, 107, 110–14, 120, 144–45, 171, 179; Champion, Arthur, 131; *Colonial Cinema* (1942–54), 111; *Colonial Month* (1949), 179; colonies, 18, 159, 179; Eastwood, Christopher, 54; economics, 18, 179; film units, 173–74; Gale, Beresford, 33–34; Girkins, G. A., 72; Grierson, John, 161; health, 18; health films, 136; *Hello West Indies* (1943), 95–96; information office/rs, 122–23; Kenya, 122–23, 158, 211; Latham, Geoffrey, 254n111; *Local Government* (1943), 119; local voices, 98–99; Malaya, 155–56, 161; media, 130; MFU, 161; mobile exhibition, 33–34; MOI, 11, 111–13; Morgan, W. S., 124, 131, 271n42; *Mr. English at Home* (1940), 64; Odunton, J. B., 80; Orr, James Russell, 32, 43; postwar, 179; race, 159; Sabine, Noel, 118, 128, 233; Sellers, William, 54, 108, 109–10, 112, 120; *Smallpox* (1950), 208; sports, 182; tours, 179–81; training schools, 186; Usill, H. V., 130; VD films, 276n119; Vernon, Roland, 33, 35–36; *Victory Parade* (1946), 145; West Indies, 56, 137

colonies: absences, 146–47, 178; Africa, 116; An African Conference in London (1948) (film/event), 176–78; *An African in England: An English Village* (1945), 142–43; Aitken, Ian, 160; anti-colonialism, 129, 210–11, 235; archival materials, 241–42; *Back to the Community* (1954), 209; BBC, 39, 103, 126–28; BIF, 22–23, 28–29; *Black Cotton* (1927), 20; *The Boy Kumasenu* (1952), 197–98; *Britain's Birthright* (1924), 24; British Council, 118–20, 271n46; British Empire, 106, 107,

colonies: absences *(continued)*
144–45, 147, 151; British Movietone News, 146–47; British primacy, 67; Campbell, Alan, 157; CEF, 261n60; citizenship, 46, 47, 75; *Colonial Cinema* (1942–54), 68–69, 94–95, 152; Colonial Development and Welfare Acts (1940, 1945), 115, 149, 154, 155, 168; *Colonial Month* (1949), 178–79, 312; Colonial Office, 18, 159, 179; Creech-Jones, Arthur, 72, 175; *Daily Comet* (newspaper), 147–48; economics, 3, 25, 27, 138, 159, 161–62, 164, 175, 179, 194, 195, 213, 222; education, 18, 74, 179; educational films, 17, 30–31, 271n42; *Education in England: A Village School* (1945), 139; Empire Service (BBC), 39; Empire Transcription Scheme, 128; fascism, 107; film history, 243; "The Film in Colonial Development" (conference), xvi, 80, 160, 173–75; filmstrips, 125–26; film units, 174, 205; *Freedom for Ghana* (1957), 234; Gillan, Angus, 120; Graham, Sean, 205–6; Grierson, John, 24, 159, 175; health/films, 5, 10, 48–49, 51; *The Heart of an Empire* (1935), 52; Hollywood's cultural imperialism, 43, 254n111; home unit, 183; imperialism, 173; independence, 150, 231, 234–35, 237, 294n120; information office/rs, 121, 123–24, 129; instructional films, 18, 48; interwar Britain, 179; Iwowo, Samantha, 238; *A Journey by a London Bus* (1950), 183; labor, 3–4, 7, 41–42, 161–62; *Local Government* (1943), 119, 120; local voices, 87; London, 158; London Transport, 183; Macleod, Iain, 194; Macmillan, Harold, 194; "Mass Education in the Colonies" (memorandum), 72; Mau Mau uprising, 7–8; media, 7, 121, 126; MFU, 233–34; mobile exhibition, 49–50, 84–88, 91–98, 240; modernization, 48–51, 55–56; MOI, 108, 117, 131, 271n51, 274n101; *Nigeria Greets the Queen* (1956), 211; OFTVC, 216; *One Family* (1930), 25; Overseas Rediffusion Limited, 293n115; Pearson, George, 59; political control, 17, 94–98, 195, 246n16; postwar, 72, 115, 138, 144–48, 159; practices/principles/policies, 28, 65–72, 151, 173–75, 188; primitivity, theories on, 158; *Progress in the Colonies: An African Hospital* (ca. 1933), 51, 53, 130, 311; propaganda, 31, 111, 115, 119, 125, 128, 274n101; radio, 127–28; royal family, 211; *Royal Review* (1939), 116–17; schoolchildren, 253n104; *See Saw Years* (1963), 214; Sellers, William, 48, 53, 54, 56–57, 72, 77, 91, 112; specialized films, 14–15; sports, 182; *Spotlight on the Colonies* (1950), 6, 179, 311; *Springtime in an English Village* (1944), 140; *This Wonderful World* (1958–65), 23; *Timbermen from Honduras* (1943), 138; *Times*, 24; tours, 179–81; trade, 21, 25, 27; training schools, 185, 192; VD films, 136–37; *Victory Parade* (1946), 144–48; war and CFU, 54, 106–7, 120, 129, 133, 137–44; World War II, 106–8, 114, 117, 119, 128. *See also* colonies and CFU; decolonization; Dominions, India and Colonies (panel); nationhood; postcolonialism; *individual countries*; *individual film units*

colonies and British film: African audiences, 28; BBC, 103; BEKE, 39; BIF, 22–23, 28–29; *Britain's Birthright* (1924), 24; British Empire, 9–10, 106, 107; CFU, 1–2, 3–5, 61, 173; children, 75, 77–78; citizenship, 47; *Colonial Cinema* (1942–54), 68–69; Colonial Development Fund, 54–55; Colonial Office, 18; Crown Film Unit, 110; disciplinary expertise, 19; education, 18, 74; Gold Coast, 31–32; Hollywood's cultural imperialism, 254n111; independence, 231; Latham, Geoffrey, 43; "Mass Education in the Colonies" (memorandum), 72; mobile exhibition, 49–50, 93–96; modernization, 48–51; MOI, 117; *Mr. English at Home* (1940), 61, 62, 64–65; Orr, James Russell, 43; Pearson, George, 59, 79; political control, 94–98, 195, 246n16; practices/principles/policies, 28, 65–72; propaganda, 31; Sellers, William, 54, 73–74, 91–92, 94–95, 110–11; trade, 21; West Africa, 94; World War II, 106–8, 117. *See also Colonial Cinema* (1942–54)

colonies and CFU: archival materials, 6; British Empire, 1–4, 104–5; economics/labor, 7, 161–62; educational films, 271n42; England, projection of,

Index | 325

138–39; establishment, 1–2, 15, 115; *The Film in National Life* (1932) (report), 33; home unit, 173; imperialism, 1–5, 7; independence, 150; information office/rs, 129–30; mobile exhibition, 2, 84; Pearson, George, 79; postwar, 120–21, 151–52; propaganda, 274n101; proposals, 35; Sellers, William, 54, 77; staff, 116; tours, 180; training schools, 192; VD films, 136; World War II, 107–8, 142–48
comedy films, 37, 52, 170, 201, 216
Comet (newspaper), 157
Command Performance All as One (1966), 239–40, 315
commentators. *See* local voices
Commission on Educational and Cultural Films, 32
Commonwealth, 3, 7–8, 11, 14, 75, 76–77, 114–15, 194–95, 213, 214, 286n4
Commonwealth Parliamentary Conference (1969), 240
Communism, 95, 115, 150, 175, 210–11, 234
community development, 41, 143–44, 149, 198–99, 223, 231, 237, 239, 289n51. *See also* Colonial Development and Welfare Acts (1940, 1945)
Community Development in Awgu Division, Nigeria (1949), 100, 120, 150, 312
Constantine, Stephen, 115
Cooper, Harold, 185
Co-Operative Rice Farming (1951), 222–23, 312
Copper, Duff, 114–15
Copra (1949), 186–87, 312
Corinaldi, Duncan Keith, 188
Cotton Growing in Nigeria. See Black Cotton (1927)
County Films Ltd., 228
Crawley, Aidan, 174fig., 175
Creech-Jones, Arthur, 72, 174fig., 175, 283n82
Creighton, Walter, 25, 31–32, 250n42
Crown Colonist (publication), 114
Crown Film Unit: *Achimota* (1945), 157; CFU, 11, 70–71, 109–10, 158, 160–61; colonies and British film, 110; *Daybreak in Udi* (1949), 63, 159, 160, 310; Densham, Denny, 71; documentaries, 106–7, 158; *Fight for Life* (1946), 157–58; film units, 157–59; Kheng Law,

O. W., 241; Kingston Davies, Robert, 275n106; Malaya, 160–61; MFU, 160–61; MOI, 109; *Mr. English at Home* (1940), 63; Pearson, George, 110; Sellers, William, 64, 108–10; Shaw, Alexander, 294n126; *Spotlight on the Colonies* (1950), 6, 179, 311; World War II, 63, 106–7
cultural imperialism. *See* Hollywood's cultural imperialism
Cyprus, 96, 119–20, 144, 192, 241, 285n123, 285n124
Cyprus training school (1951), 192–93, 241, 285n124

Daily Comet (newspaper), 147–48
Daily Gleaner (newspaper), 188, 225–26, 231–32, 292n101
Daily Graphic (newspaper), 197, 293n119
Daily Mail (newspaper), 171, 181, 198, 211
Daily Mirror (newspaper), 181
Daily Service (newspaper), 127
Danquah, Francis K., 163
Davidson, Basil, 235
Davis, John Merle, 36, 39, 256n149
Davson, Edward, 20
Daybreak in Udi (1949), 63, 159, 160, 310
Day with an English Baby Boy, A (ca. 1937), 53, 310
Deck Chair (1946), 170, 311
decolonization, 1, 3, 7–8, 149, 151, 170–71, 187, 194, 197–98. *See also* independence; postcolonialism
Delay Means Death (1951), 90, 191–92, 285n122, 312
Densham, Denny, 71, 160, 259n42, 294n126
Department of Social Welfare and Community Development (Ghana), 198–99, 239
Diary for Timothy, A (1946), 63
Diawara, Manthia, 238, 295n144
Dickson, A. G., 93, 134, 264n99
Dipping (1952), 215, 314
Dirt Brings Sickness—Cleanliness Brings Health (ca. 1935), 51, 310
disciplinary expertise, 17, 19, 36, 57, 165, 259n41
Disney, 83, 169–70, 282n61
District Officer (1945), 120, 310
documentaries: *Achimota* (1945), 157; African audiences, 71; Aitken, Ian, 160; *Black Cotton* (1927), 27; British Empire, 14–15; British film, 10; CFU,

documentaries *(continued)*
    4–5, 71, 259n39; COI, 158; commercial markets, 24; Crown Film Unit, 106–7, 158; economics, 15; education, 16–17; educational films, 19, 58; education/fiction hybrids, 26–27; EMB, 20; film techniques, 63, 259n39; Gamage, Faulder (Fred), 63; Ghana, 240; Graham, Sean, 81, 196, 218; *The Heart of an Empire* (1935), 52; imperialism, 15, 16, 23; instructional films, 32, 58, 109, 110–11; interwar Britain, 27, 179; Jamaica, 240, 291n81; Malaya, 160–61; mobile exhibition, 16; *Mr. English at Home* (1940), 62; Nigeria, 240; Pearson, George, 58–59; Sellers, William, 53, 71, 82; Shaw, Alexander, 236–37; specialized techniques, 16; Tallents, Stephen, 247n6; television documentaries, 18, 248n16; trade, 15; World War II, 63. *See also* British Documentary Movement; Grierson, John; Stollery, Martin
Documentary Film (Rotha), 16–17
Documentary News Letter (publication), xv, 65–66, 120, 258n20, 271n51
Domaingue, Antoine, 192
Dominions, India and Colonies (panel), 34, 35–36, 43, 256n149
Drifters (1929), 16, 26–27, 310
Drive with Care (1959), 223–24, 314
Druick, Zoe, 5

Early Training of African Troops (1942), 130–31, 311
East Africa: AFP, 290n73; African cinema, 149; Barkas, Geoffrey, 32; BEKE, xv, 43; *Better Homes* (1948), 165; CFU, 41, 132, 153, 165–66, 170–71, 172, 282n73; citizenship, 86; film units, 115, 154, 165–66, 170–72, 215, 216; health, 18; Huxley, Julian, xv, 19, 28; information office/rs, 123; instructional films, 165; Kingston Davies, Robert, 131, 275n106; labor, 18; mobile exhibition, 216, 264n99; *Mr. English at Home* (1940), 63; *Nairobi* (1950), 150, 172–73; Notcutt, Leslie, 36; OFTVC, 214; Paterson, A. R., 18, 36; primitivity, theories on, 165–66; race, 165; Sellers, William, 165; Spurr, Norman F., 166–67, 290n71; *Towards True Democracy* (1947), 150; trade, 34–35; training schools, 165, 166; *Victory Parade* (1946), 147; West Africa, 165–66. *See also* Africa
East Africa Command Mobile Propaganda Unit, 134
East African Film Services, 213
East African Trade Union Congress (EATUC), 172
East Africa Standard (newspaper), 171
Eastern Nigerian Guardian (newspaper), 127
Eastern Nigerian Public Service, 182
Eastern Nigerian Unit, 237
Eastwood, Christopher, 42, 43, 44, 54, 56
Eat Jamaican (n. d.), 227, 314
economics: advertisements, 213; Africa, 175; *Basket Making* (1949), 187; British Council, 108; British Empire, 15, 20, 52, 142–43, 213, 230, 283n82; British Empire Exhibition (Wembley, 1924–25), 20; British film, 15, 18, 74, 138, 195; CFU, 2, 3, 4, 9, 120–21; citizenship, 46; *Cocoa Rehabilitation* (1951), 191; *Colonial Month* (1949), 179; Colonial Office, 18, 179; colonies, 3, 25, 27, 138, 159, 161–62, 164, 175, 179, 194, 195, 213, 222; Commonwealth, 213; Creech-Jones, Arthur, 283n82; documentaries, 15; EMB, 14, 20; filmstrips, 125; health, 10, 164; imperialism, 7, 8, 232; independence, 213, 230–32; industries, 191; information office/rs, 121; interwar Britain, 179; Jamaica, 227; labor, 161–62, 191; mobile exhibition, 34; MOI, 108; nationhood, 222; *One Family* (1930), 25; *Portrait of Trinidad* (1957), 228–29; postcolonialism, 7; postwar, 12, 222; proposals, 32, 33, 34, 35; *This Land of Ours* (1962), 231–32; training schools, 186; Trinidad, 232; United States, 240; West Indies training school, 189–90; World War II, 106, 138. *See also* trade
Edmett, E. R., 111–12
education: Africa, 36–37; African audiences, 67–68; animation, 170; BBC, 126; BEKE, 36, 40–41; BFU, 225; British film, 30–31, 33, 34, 36, 74, 249n35, 258n29; *Builders of the Nation* (1958), 221–22; CFU, 5, 17, 79, 112, 125, 221; children, 139; *Colonial Cinemagazine* (newsreels), 152; Colonial Development and Welfare Acts (1940, 1945), 149; colonies, 18, 74, 179; Dickson, A. G., 93; documentaries, 16–17; Dominions, India and Colonies

(panel), 34; education/fiction hybrids, 24–25, 26–27; filmstrips, 125; *Giant in the Sun* (1959), 212; Gold Coast, 40–41; Graham, Sean, 81; imperialism, 8; information office/rs, 129; instructional films, 16–17, 24–25; Jamaica, 222; labor, 41; Latham, Geoffrey, 36; "Mass Education in the Colonies" (memorandum), 72; mobile exhibition, 83, 93, 253n104; *Mr. English at Home* (1940), 61; Nigeria, 212; Pearson, George, 58, 59; political control, 33–34; radio, 126–27; Rennalls, Martin, 218–19, 291n81; Sellers, William, 46, 74; Shaw, Alexander, 294n126; *Towards True Democracy* (1947), 167; Vernon, Roland, 33; West Indies, 219. *See also* Imperial Institute
educational films: BEKE, 42; Blackburne, K. W., 99; *Black Cotton* (1927), 27; British Council, 118; British Empire, 14–15; British film, 4, 10; CFU, 118, 120–21, 271n42; colonies, 17, 30–31, 271n42; commercial markets, 24–25; Commission on Educational and Cultural Films, 32; documentaries, 19, 58; Dominions, India and Colonies (panel), 34; Field, Mary, 14–15; film units, 165–66; Gold Coast, 199; Graham, Sean, 196–97; Grierson, John, 18; imperialism, 23, 27; interwar Britain, 27; Jamaica, 42, 188; JFU, 196–97; labor, 42; political control, 17, 42; race, 17, 28, 32, 34; Rennalls, Martin, 219; specialized techniques, 118; Spurr, Norman F., 17; UFU, 237; UNESCO, 150; Vernon, Roland, 33; Waterfield, O., 70; *You Can Help Your Children* (1952), 228. *See also* British Instructional Films (BIF); instructional films; "useful" cinema
education/fiction hybrids, 24–25, 26–27
Education in England: A Village School (1945), 139, 162, 277n127, 311
Education Programme Part One (1959), 222, 314
Edward VIII, Prince of Wales, 22, 236, 249n35. *See also* royal family
Egypt, 123, 294n126
election films, 214, 215, 223, 315
Elizabeth II (queen), 95, 179, 211, 216, 239–40, 263n76, 311, 313. *See also* royal family
Elton, Arthur, 25–26, 109
Elton, Ralph, 160

Elton, Ray, 109, 206
emigration, 21–22, 214
Empire Marketing Board (EMB): BIF, 29; documentaries, 20; *Eat Jamaican* (n. d.), 227; economics, 14, 20; Grierson, John, xv, 14, 26–27, 247n6, 249n37; Hankin, G. T., 34; Huxley, Gervas, 250n43; Huxley, Julian, 19; Imperial Institute, 27; imperialism, 23; mobile exhibition, 16, 55; *One Family* (1930), 25; trade, 14, 16
Empire series (1925–1928), 20–21, 22, 24, 32, 55, 132, 167, 249n34, 250n43, 250n46. *See also* British Instructional Films (BIF)
Empire Service (BBC), 39, 126
Empire Transcription Scheme, 128
Enemy in the Night (1960), 239, 313
England, projection of, 137–44. *See also individual films*
Essex Chronicle (newspaper), 142
Eunoto (n. d.), 171
Evans, Gareth, 184, 186, 188, 190, 192, 228
exhibition, 2, 84, 88–89, 94, 98–102, 104, 107, 136. *See also* mobile exhibition
Experiment in the Film (1949) (study), 75

Fairest Africa (1959), 214, 312
Fairgrieve, James, 17, 36, 75, 77
Fajemisin, Alex, 183–84, 209
family planning campaigns, 221, 241
Farmer Brown Learns Good Dairying (1951/film) (filmstrip), 126, 195, 224, 242, 273n82, 312
Fathoms Deep beneath the Sea (1922), 28, 310
Federal Film Unit (Nigeria), 207–8, 237. *See also* Nigerian Film Unit (NFU)
Federal Spotlight (newsreel), 214
Feilmann, Captain, 132
Fell, Barbara, 126
Fenuku, R. O., 183–84, 205, 237, 238fig.
Field, Mary, 14–15, 55, 74–77, 97, 250n42, 261n60, 261n61, 261n63
Fight for Life (1946), 157–58, 310
Fight Tuberculosis at Home (1946), 162–63, 191–92, 312
Fiji, 144, 275n106
Film and Photo Bureau, 73
film festivals, 197, 200, 211, 225
"Film in Colonial Development, The" (conference, 1948), xvi, 12, 80, 160, 173–75, 220

Film in Empire Education, The (meeting), 32, 252n82
Film in National Life, The (1932) (report), 29, 31, 32, 33
Film School in West Africa, A (1949), 184–87, 312
"Films for Africans—1910 or 1950?" (speech), 79, 83
"Films for Primitive Peoples" (articles), xv, 65–68, 84–85, 258n21. *See also* African audiences; primitivity, theories on; specialized techniques
filmstrips, 11, 13, 83, 90, 107–8, 121, 124–26, 294n126
film techniques: African audiences, 31, 36, 61, 73, 75, 103; *Amenu's Child* (1950), 82; audience research, 100, 103; British Council, 271n42; CFU, 28, 57, 63–64, 75, 154; *Colonial Cinema* (1942–54), 69–70; documentaries, 63, 259n39; Gambia, 154; GBI, 274n99; Kracauer, Siegfried, 73; *Local Government* (1943), 119; modernization, 227; *Mr. English at Home* (1940), 63–65; OFTVC, 216; primitivity, theories on, 1–2, 36, 65–68, 75, 259n39, 262n70, 274n99; Rennalls, Martin, 227; Sellers, William, 65–68, 69, 72; *Shaihu Umar* (1976), 238; Spurr, Norman F., 83; Swithinbank, Charles, 259n41; West Indies training school, 190–91. *See also* "Films for Primitive Peoples" (articles); specialized techniques
Film Unit of the Northern Region (Nigeria), 238. *See also* Nigerian Film Unit (NFU)
film units, 194–243; Africa, 69, 108, 149–57, 254n111; audiences, international, 211, 214; Blackburne, K. W., 176; British Empire, 193; CFU, xvi, 12, 73, 90, 104–5, 149–57, 162, 173, 192–93, 195; Colonial Office, 173–74; colonies, 174, 205; Crown Film Unit, 157–59; East Africa, 115, 154, 165–66, 170–72, 215, 216; educational films, 165–66; film size, 295n144; films of, 312–15; filmstrips, 90, 126; Gambia, 154–55, 156fig., 278n9; Ghana, 199, 238–39; Gold Coast, 154, 156–58, 193, 199; Gover, Victor, 214; Graham, Sean, 196–97, 205–6; Grierson, John, 154, 159–60, 174, 175–76; health, 169; home unit, 183; independence, 192–93, 195, 233, 236; interwar Britain, 195; Jamaica Welfare Ltd, 41, 42; Kenya, 122–23, 154, 165; Latham, Geoffrey, 254n111; Malaya, 193; Nigeria, 153–54, 193, 206–8, 209, 238; Nkrumah, Kwame, 238–39; OFTVC, 216, 238; political events, 210; postwar, 195; race, 195; Sellers, William, 82, 162, 228; *Smallpox* (1950), 208; Tanganyika, 165, 215–16; training schools, 149, 183–84, 195; Uganda, 154, 165, 215, 236–37; West Africa, 188, 195; West Indies, 218–30; West Indies training school, 195; Wright, Basil, 159–60; Zanzibar, 165. *See also* African cinema; mobile exhibition; *individual film units*
Film User (publication), 207, 213, 290n64
Fomson, L. T., 238
Foot, Hugh, 223
Forward to a New Nigeria (1958), 207, 313
Foundation Day at Ibadan University (1948), 150, 312
Fox, Jo, 23, 109
France, 73, 114, 231, 235
Francis, Terri, 97, 221, 223, 227
Franklin, Harry, 129, 131, 137, 274n96
Freedom for Ghana (1957), 233–36, 293n119, 313
Freed War Prisoners Return to Africa (1945), 144, 311

Gaddafi, Muammar, 237
Gadsden, Fay, 121
Gale, Beresford, 33–34
Gale, W. D., 129
Gamage, Faulder (Fred), 63
Gambia, 90, 125, 131, 144, 154–55, 156fig., 194, 278n9
Garrett, Arthur, 209
Garritano, Carmela, 197–98
Garvey, Marcus, 39
Gaskin, E. A. L., 258n18
Gaumont-British Instructional (GBI), 35, 36, 42, 132, 274n99
Gaumont British News, 132
gender, 48, 52, 61–62, 77, 139, 142, 178
General Post Office (GPO) Film Unit, 14, 57–58, 63, 294n126
geography films, 17, 20, 25, 27
Geography in School (Fairgrieve), 17
Ghana: Africa, 235; anti-colonialism, 235; archival materials, 6; Blaylock, Jennifer, 241; Bowden, Dennis, 239; *The Boy Kumasenu* (1952), 197–200; documentaries, 240; Elizabeth II (queen),

263n76; *Enemy in the Night* (1960), 239; film size, 295n144; film units, 199, 238–39; *Freedom for Ghana* (1957), 233–36, 293n119, 313; Graham, Sean, 234; independence, xvi, 198, 233–36, 238–39, 286n1; instructional films, 240; newsreels, 240; *No Tears for Ananse* (1968), 237–38; Odunton, J. B., 263n76; postcolonialism, 240; Samuelson, Sydney, 196; Spurr, Norman F., 239; *Your Police* (1962), 239. *See also* Gold Coast; Nkrumah, Kwame

Ghana Film Industry/Production Corporation, 202, 237, 239

Ghana Film Unit (GFU), 235, 239. *See also* Gold Coast Film Unit (GCFU)

Ghana Today (publication), 200–201

Giant in the Sun (1959), 212–14, 313

Gillan, Angus, 71, 118, 120

Gilroy, Paul, 3, 8–9, 148

Girkins, G. A., 72

Give Your Child a Chance (1951), 225–27, 292n104, 312

Gold Coast: *An African in England: An English Village* (1945), 142; *Amenu's Child* (1950), 100; animation, 170; anti-colonialism, 129; archival materials, 6; Arden-Clarke, Charles, 236; BEKE, 40–41; BIF, 28; *Black Cotton* (1927), 20; *The Boy Kumasenu* (1952), 197, 198; British Empire, 114, 132; British Empire Exhibition (Wembley, 1924–25), 20, 21fig.; CFU, 1–2, 161, 162, 219; colonies and British film, 31–32; Dickson, A. G., 93; education, 40–41; educational films, 199; film units, 154, 156–58, 193, 199; Grace, H. M., 253n104; Graham, Sean, 81, 88; Gurney, H. L., 157; *Here Is the Gold Coast* (1947), 158, 279n23, 310; information office/rs, 123; Johnson, Geoffrey and Mina, 281n58; Legislative Council, 167; Lironi, H. E., 70; local voices, 84–85, 88; mobile exhibition, 9, 54, 56, 70, 92–93, 94, 95fig., 96, 98, 101fig.; modernization, 55–56; MOI, 54; *Mr. English at Home* (1940), 64; Nigeria, 181; Nkrumah, Kwame, 198; Odunton, J. B., 80; Page, John, 158; *Progress in Kojokrom* (1953), 120; Prosser, A. R. G., 200; radio, 126–27; Raw Stock Scheme, 131; Sellers, William, 149, 167; Stewart, J.L., 157; *Swollen Shoot* (1946), 163, 280n42; training schools, xvi, 162, 183–84, 192; tuberculosis, 162; UGCC, 163; *University of the Gold Coast* (1948), 150, 312; VD films, 276n123; *Victory Parade* (1946), 146, 147; *Welcome Home* (1946), 144; World War II, 9, 84–85, 126–27, 132–33, 134. *See also* Ghana

Gold Coast Chamber of Mines, 96, 266n136

Gold Coast Film Unit (GCFU), 195–206; Accra, 195; African cinema, 204–5; *Amenu's Child* (1950), 81–82, 99–100; Aryeetey, Sam, 237; *The Boy Kumasenu* (1952), xvi, 197–200; CFU, 70; Dickson, A. G., 93; establishment, xvi; Fenuku, R. O., 237; Graham, Sean, 93, 195–96, 199–200, 204–5; Grierson, John, 12; Hesse, Chris, 234, 237; independence, 168; instructional films/mobile exhibition, 200; *Mr. Mensah Builds a House* (1955), 201, 204fig.; *Nigeria Greets the Queen* (1956), 216; Odunton, J. B., 80, 81; practices/principles/policies, 197; *Progress in Kojokrom* (1953), 120; Samuelson, Sydney, 196; staff, 204–5

Gold Coast Information Services, 114, 234

Gold Coast Justice (n. d.), 253n104

Gold Coast Police Band, 179–80, 181

Gold Coast Review (newsreels), 200

"Gold Coast: Soap from Cocoa" (newsreel), 132

Good Hope, The (1955), 222–23, 315

Gooding, Francis, 194, 213

Good Samaritan, The (1949), 187–88, 285n115, 312

Gordonu, J. S. D., 137

Gover, Victor, 214, 216–17, 228, 239

Government By the People (1960), 230, 314

Grace, H. M., 253n104

Graham, Sean, 81, 82, 88, 93, 104, 195–206, 218, 234, 239, 286n9, 287n29, 288n30

Grierson, John, 159–61; British Documentary Movement, 4–5, 14–15, 18, 35, 159; CFU, 4–5, 160, 175; citizenship, 17; COI, 160, 175, 195–96; Colonial Office, 161; colonies, 24, 159, 175; Communism, 175; documentaries, 16, 18, 248n16; *Documentary News Letter* (publication), 258n20; EMB, xv, 14, 26–27, 247n6, 249n37; film units, 154, 159–60, 174, 175–76; GCFU, 12; GPO, 14; Graham, Sean, 81, 195–96, 199, 218; Hodge, Tom, 234; Huxley, Julian,

Grierson, John *(continued)*
  159; Hyde, John, 158–59; JFU, 220; mobile exhibition, 16, 55; MOI, 109; nationhood, 159, 195–206; postwar, 159; primitivity, theories on, 174fig.; Sellers, William, 159, 160; *This Wonderful World* (1958–65), 23; trade, 14; UNESCO, 17, 159–60, 174fig., 175; World War II, 14. *See also individual films*
Grierson, Marion, 35
Grierson, Ruby, 52
Grierson Effect, The (Druick and Williams), 5
Grieveson, Lee, 4
Grossmith, C. A., 112–13
Gubara, Gadalla, 192, 241, 295n145
Guedalla, Phillip, 117
Guiana Film Unit. *See* British Guiana Film Unit
Gurney, H. L., 157

Hales, Gordon, 63
Halilu, Alhaji Adumu, 238
Hammond, S. A., 35
Hankin, G. T., 34, 36
Harder they Come, The (1972), 241
Harris, Ron, 184, 192, 228
health: BEKE, 36, 37, 42; CFU, 5, 35, 125, 142; *Colonial Cinemagazine* (newsreels), 152; Colonial Office, 18; colonies, 10, 48, 51; East Africa, 18; economics, 10, 164; filmstrips, 125; film units, 169; Grierson, John, 18; information office/rs, 129; Kenya, 18; labor, 18, 162; modernization, 51; nationhood, 209, 212; Nigeria, 10, 45, 212; *Pamba* (1950), 166; Pearson, George, 169; rural health units, 46–47, 48, 50; Sellers, William, 10, 13–14, 18–19, 27–28, 45–51, 54, 158, 169; useful cinema, 149–50. *See also individual films*
Health and Baby Week, Lagos, 1956 (1956), 209, 313
Health and Baby Weeks, 45–46, 48, 50
Health Congress (Bournemouth, 1955), 13–14
health films, xv, 5, 28–29, 45, 47–51, 136, 169–70. *See also* medical films; VD films; *individual films*
Health Propaganda Unit (Nigeria), xv, 13, 45–46, 54, 255n129, 258n21. *See also* Sellers, William

Heart of an Empire, The (1935), 52, 310
Hello West Indies (1943), 95–96, 310
Here Is the Gold Coast (1947), 158, 279n23, 310
Hesse, Chris, 234, 237
Highet, A. G., 108
His Excellency the Governor (1959), 229, 315
Hodge, Tom, 210–11, 234
Holbrook, Wendell P., 127, 129
Hollywood's cultural imperialism: BEKE, 36; British Empire, 15, 128; British Empire Exhibition (Wembley, 1924–25), 23–24; British film, 58, 254n111; children, 76; colonies, 43, 254n111; "The Film in Colonial Development" (conference), 173; India, 29; Parr, James, 29; Pearson, George, 58; Sellers, William, 169; Stewart, J.L., 157–58; Tallents, Stephen, 62; *Times*, 23, 43; Vernon, Roland, 33
Home Guards, 138, 311
home unit (CFU), xvi, 52–53, 173–83
Hong Kong, 7, 160, 192, 233, 239
hookworm, 31, 35, 37, 169–70, 242
house construction, 31, 62–63, 69–70, 150, 165, 166, 202–4, 222–23, 312, 313
Howson, H. M. K., 171, 185
How to Exercise Your Vote (1955), 223, 292n94, 315
How to Vote (1957), 215, 313
How You Vote (1956), 214, 313
Hussain, Mohammed Zain, 241
Huxley, Elspeth, 115, 136
Huxley, Gervas, 71, 113–14, 115, 131, 250n43, 269n21, 269n22
Huxley, Julian, xv, 18, 19, 28, 30–31, 36–37, 55, 71, 157–58, 159
Hyde, John, 158–59
hygiene, 4, 19, 32, 34, 43, 61, 69–70, 200. *See also* health; sanitation

"illiterate" audiences, theories on, 67, 118. *See also* African audiences; primitivity, theories on
Impahim, T. K., 147–48
Imperial College of Tropical Agriculture, 229, 232
Imperial Conference (1926), 16, 28
Imperial Education Conference (1927), 18, 249n34
Imperial Institute, 21–22, 27, 250n46
imperialism: Africa, 133–34, 135; An African Conference in London (1948)

Index | 331

(film/event), 178; BBC, 39, 128; BIF, 22; *Black Cotton* (1927), 23; British Empire Exhibition (Wembley, 1924-25), 20; British film, 6, 10, 14, 23, 28, 243; CFU, 1-5, 7, 106-7, 143, 150, 183, 195; Cinematograph Act (1927), 28; colonies, 173; *Daily Comet* (newspaper), 147; documentaries, 15, 16, 23; economics, 7, 8, 232; education, 8; educational films, 23, 27; EMB, 23; Field, Mary, 75; *Fight for Life* (1946), 157; *Freed War Prisoners Return to Africa* (1945), 144; India, 135; Jamaica, 42, 224; *Local Government* (1943), 119; local voices, 87; media, 128; mobile exhibition, 16; *Mr. English at Home* (1940), 62; *Nairobi* (1950), 172; neocolonialism, 8; *One Family* (1930), 25; radio, 127; royal family, 179; sports, 182; trade, 14, 179; training schools, 5; *Victory Parade* (1946), 145, 147; war and CFU, 106-8, 133, 144; World War II, 106, 115, 138, 270n28. *See also* British Empire; British primacy
Imperial War Museum, 5, 6, 242-43
independence, 230-37; Africa, 167-68, 194; British Empire, 150, 194, 231, 294n120; CFU, 2-3, 5, 12, 150, 168, 188, 195, 233, 237; colonies, 150, 231, 237, 294n120; economics, 213, 230-32; film units, 192-93, 195, 233, 236; GCFU, 168; Graham, Sean, 196, 239; *His Excellency the Governor* (1959), 229; Impahim, T. K., 147-48; JFU, 236; media, 233; MFU, 168, 233-35; mobile exhibition, 96, 97, 240; NFU, 168; OFTVC, 217-18; political control, 202, 231; *Portrait of Trinidad* (1957), 229; postcolonialism, 239; *Road to Independence* (1962), 229-30, 315; Sellers, William, 13-14; Snazelle, Lionel, 196; TFU, 228-30; *Towards Independence* (1962), 230, 314; *Towards True Democracy* (1947), 167-68; training schools, 188; Trinidad and Tobago Government Film Unit, 229, 231. *See also* nationhood; *individual countries*
India: British Movietone News, 146-47; CFU, 7; *District Officer* (1945), 120; Hollywood's cultural imperialism, 29; imperialism, 135; independence, 6, 150, 175, 235, 294n120; Information Films of India, 168; instructional films, 28, 89; Kipling, Rudyard, 128; Shaw, Alexander, 294n126. *See also* Dominions, India and Colonies (panel)
Indian News Parade (newsreel), 135-36, 310
industrial films, 5, 51-52, 132, 152, 227, 310. *See also individual films*
industries: *Black Cotton* (1927), 20, 27; CFU, 164; *Colonial Cinemagazine* (newsreels), 152; economics, 191; *Giant in the Sun* (1959), 212; Jamaica, 225, 227; modernization, 162, 164, 178, 227; nationhood, 212-13; Nigeria, 212-14; *Portrait of Trinidad* (1957), 229; *Swollen Shoot* (1946), 163; *This Land of Ours* (1962), 231; training schools, 186-87; UFU, 215; useful cinema, 149-50; West Indies training school, 189-90. *See also* mines; *Weaving in Togoland* (1946)
Infant Welfare Work in Nigeria (ca. 1933), 48-49, 50, 310
Information Films of India, 168
information office/rs, 56, 70, 121-30, 131, 171, 272n60. *See also individuals*
Information Services Department (ISD) Film Library, 241
Innes, Geoffrey, 171
Institute of Amateur Cinematographers, 17
instructional films: Africa, 34; African audiences, 75; agriculture, 43; BEKE, 37; *Better Homes* (1948), 165; BIF, 28-29; British Documentary Movement, 18, 157; British film, 4, 10, 16-17, 27; Ceylon Tea Propaganda Board, 16; CFU, 1-2, 43, 136, 143-44, 157, 274n101; colonies, 18, 48; documentaries, 32, 58, 109, 110-11; East Africa, 165; education, 16-17, 24-25; educational films, 58; GCFU, 200; Ghana, 240; Graham, Sean, 81, 199; India, 89; Jamaica, 240; JFU, 221; *A Journey by a London Bus* (1950), 182-83; Malaya, 28; MFU, 161, 210-11, 234; mobile exhibition, 97; *Mr. English at Home* (1940), 62-63; Nigeria, 240; *One Family* (1930), 25; Rotha, Paul, 16-17; Sellers, William, 48, 107, 157, 196; Spurr, Norman F., 17; UNESCO, 97, 150; useful cinema, 4, 5; war and CFU, 55, 107. *See also* Paterson, A. R.
intertitles, 22-23

interwar Britain, 13–59; absences, 178; BEKE, 35; *Black Cotton* (1927), 27; CFU, 59, 106; colonies/economics, 179; documentaries/educational films, 27, 179; film units, 195; *The Heart of an Empire* (1935), 52; labor, 30; World War II, 134
It Can Happen to You (1956), 137, 221, 225, 227, 314
I Will Speak English (1954), 200, 202, 313
Iwowo, Samantha, 238, 240–41
Izod, Alan, 174fig., 175, 282n61
Izod, John, 97

Jackson, Ashley, 106
Jaikumar, Priya, 5, 28
Jakarta, 235
Jamaica: archival materials, 6; BEKE, 41–42; British Council, 117; British Empire, 224, 228; Central Film Service, 94; CFU, 188, 219, 220; *Churchill Visits Jamaica* (1953), 224, 314; *Delay Means Death* (1951), 191–92; documentaries, 240, 291n81; Dominions, India and Colonies (panel), 256n149; economics, 227; education, 222; educational films, 42, 188; Graham, Sean, 104; imperialism, 42, 224; independence, xvi, 220–21, 225, 227, 228, 236; industries, 225, 227; instructional films, 240; *It Can Happen to You* (1956), 221; labor, 41–42, 97; local voices, 86, 90, 227–28; Margaret, Princess, 3–4, 220, 224–26, 230, 231, 314; mobile exhibition, 41, 86, 94, 96, 97, 219, 220, 268n153; modernization, 224, 225; nationhood, 227, 236; newsreels, 240; political control, 202; Rennalls, Martin, 237, 241, 291n81, 292n92; Selassie, Haile, 295n140; Sellers, William, 188; specialized techniques, 228; training schools, xvi, 184, 188–89; *West Indians with the R. A. F. in Britain* (1944), 137
Jamaica Film Unit (JFU), 218–28; agriculture, 189; CFU, 219–20, 221; citizenship, 223–24; *Delay Means Death* (1951), 90; educational films, 196–97; establishment, xvi, 219; films of, 314; *Government By the People* (1960), 230; independence, 236; *It Can Happen to You* (1956), 137; media, 223, 292n97; modernization, 189, 224; nationhood, 221–22; *A Nation is Born* (1962), 231–32; Pearson, George, 220; postwar, 219; propaganda, 221; Rennalls, Martin, 41, 82, 90, 218; Sellers, William, 188, 220; university films, 189. See also *Farmer Brown Learns Good Dairying* (1951/film) (filmstrip)
Jamaica Hope, The (1960), 227, 314
Jamaica Information Services (JIS), 241, 295n144
Jamaican Harvest (1938), 42, 310
Jamaica training school (1950), 188, 228
Jamaica Welfare Ltd, 41, 42
J. Arthur Rank Organisation Limited, 76fig. See also Rank, J. Arthur
Jeffrey, Keith, 106
Jennings, Humphrey, 63
Jochimsen, John, 78, 116, 277n131
Johnson, Geoffrey and Mina, 168–70, 281n57, 281n58
Johnson, Lyndon, 232
Jonathan Builds a Dam (1944), 123, 310
Journey by a London Bus, A (1950), 182–83, 312

Keepers of the Peace (n. d.), 131–32
Kenya: advertisements, 213; AFP, 290n73; BEKE, 35, 37, 39–40, 42; *Black Cotton* (1927), 30; Boy Scouts, 138; CFU, 5; Champion, Arthur, 87, 88, 89, 122, 131, 260n46; Colonial Office, 122–23, 211; film units, 122–23, 154, 165; Gadsden, Fay, 121; health, 18; independence, 194; Innes, Geoffrey, 171; local voices, 88; Mau Mau uprising, 7–8, 210; mobile exhibition, 5, 43, 87, 89, 97, 98, 116–17, 122, 210, 240, 267n143; *Mr. English at Home* (1940), 64; Northern Frontier film, 158; OFTVC, 214; Orr, James Russell, 32, 251n69; Paterson, A. R., 18; political control, 98, 210; proposals, 33; Raw Stock Scheme, 131; Scott, H. V., 136; World War II, 121, 122, 123
Kenya Daisies (1944), 123, 310
Kenya Information Office, 88, 121–23, 272n60, 313
Kheng Law, O. W., 161, 241
Kinematograph Weekly (publication), 22fig., 23, 24, 198
Kingston Davies, Robert, 131, 275n106
Kinta Story, The (1949), 241, 315
Kipling, Rudyard, 25, 39, 128
Kodak, 19, 53, 184
Kracauer, Siegfried, 73, 260n53

labor: African audiences, 150; BEKE, 36, 41–42; *Better Pottery* (1949), 164;

biopolitics, 18; *Black Cotton* (1927), 20, 23, 30; British film, 14, 18, 36; CFU, 7; colonies, 3–4, 7, 41–42, 161–62; East Africa, 18; economics, 161–62, 191; education, 41; educational films, 42; *Education in England: A Village School* (1945), 139; Graham, Sean, 199; health, 18, 162; Huxley, Julian/Notcutt, Leslie, 18; interwar Britain, 30; Jamaica, 41–42, 97; *Mr. English at Home* (1940), 62, 65; nationhood, 41–42; *The Oil Palm Industry* (n.d.), 52; Paterson, A. R., 34–35; useful cinema, 150; war and CFU, 107

Lagos, 45, 47–49, 51, 127, 209, 241, 254n115

Land and Water (1944), 71

Larkin, Brian, 4, 47, 73, 84, 127, 212, 260n53

Larson, Egon, 260n52

Latham, Geoffrey, 36–38, 39, 41, 43, 55, 66, 252n82, 254n111

Lee, Wilfred, 188–91, 228, 229

leprosy, 208–9

Let's Build Their Future (1959), 292n93

Let's Stop Them (1953), 218, 223, 227, 314

Letter, The (1953), 210, 315

Life History of a Mosquito, The (n.d.), 53

Life History of the Onion (1943), 97

Life of a Plant, The (1926), 28

Lironi, H. E., 70, 80, 131, 163, 168–69, 259n39, 281n58

Listen to Britain (1942), 63

Local Government (1943), 118–20, 136, 141, 310

local voices, 84–91; African audiences, 87, 127; audience research, 99, 100–103; Blackburne, K. W., 99; *The Boy Kumasenu* (1952), 204; CFU, 11, 87, 91, 98–99, 101–2, 104; Champion, Arthur, 87, 88, 89, 263n91; *Colonial Cinema* (1942–54), 87; Colonial Office, 98–99; colonies/imperialism, 87; *Freedom for Ghana* (1957), 234–35; Gold Coast/Kenya, 88; Jamaica, 86, 90, 227–28; *Let's Stop Them* (1953), 227; Malaya, 87; mobile exhibition, 56, 84–91, 93–94, 263n91; *Mr. Mensah Builds a House* (1955), 204; *Progress in Kojokrom* (1953), 204; radio, 127; Sellers, William, 87, 88–89, 104, 186; Spurr, Norman F., 88, 90–91, 93; training schools, 186; Wilson, John, 265n119

London, xvi, 52–53, 56–69, 117, 125–26, 133, 151, 158, 230, 236. *See also* African Conference in London, (1948) (film/event); *African in London, An* (1941); *African Visitors at the Tower of London* (1949); *Journey by a London Bus, A* (1950); *These Are London Firemen* (1942)

London 1942 (1943), 117

Louis, Wm. Roger, 194

Lucas, Charles, 27

MacDonald, Malcolm, 54, 55–56, 256n146

Machi Gaba (1943), 53, 89, 130, 311

Macleod, Iain, 194

Macmillan, Harold, 194, 286n1

MacNeice, Louis, 206

Macpherson, John, 180–81

Maddison, John, 61, 73–74

Madjitey, E. R. T., 202

Maingard, Jacqueline, 290n73

"Making Films for Children" (article), 74

malaria, 43, 47–48, 152–53, 154, 169–70, 239, 310

Malaya: anti-colonialism, 210–11; Burns, James/Chan, Nadine, 46; Colonial Office, 155–56, 161; colonies, 211; Communism, 175; Crown Film Unit/documentaries, 160–61; film units, 193; independence, xvi, 210–11, 230, 233–35, 241; instructional films, 28; local voices, 87; *Merdeka for Malaya* (1957), 233–35, 315; mobile exhibition, 210; *1955: The Year in Malaya*, 95, 315; Overseas Rediffusion Limited, 293n115; race, 234; Sellers, William, 161; sports, 181–82; Vernon, Roland, 33

Malayan Emergency, 95, 155–56, 210–11, 234, 293n115

Malayan Film Unit (MFU), xvi, 160–61, 168, 210–11, 233–35, 241, 315

Malta, 95, 96, 126, 233, 266n133, 286n1

Manchester Guardian (newspaper), 26, 171

Man Hunt, The (1943), 52, 255n133, 311

Manley, Norman, 220–21

Manvell, Roger, 61, 75

Margaret, Princess, 3–4, 211–12, 220, 224–26, 230, 231–32, 314. *See also* royal family

Marier, Roger, 97

Marson, Lionel, 103

mass communications, 17, 73, 159, 260n53, 261

"Mass Education in the Colonies" (memorandum), 72
Mau Mau uprising, 7–8, 210
Mauritius, 121, 126, 154–55, 192, 211, 314
media, 121–30; African audiences, 65; BASR, 73; biopolitics, 3; British Empire, 11, 233; CFU, 2, 4, 9; citizenship, 3, 4; Colonial Office, 130; colonies, 7, 121, 126; Film Images, 242; Gubara, Gadalla, 295n145; independence, 233; information office/rs, 123; *I Will Speak English* (1954), 200; JFU, 223, 292n97; propaganda, 125; race, 124, 125; Sellers, William, 74; war and CFU, 107–8, 121–30; *Why Not You?* (1950), 166; World War II, 127, 128–29. *See also individual media; individual media companies/organizations*
medical films, 17, 18, 32, 43, 50–51. *See also health films; individual films*
Medical Health Service, 45, 254n115
Mediterranean, 155
Mercier, E. L., 110, 111
Merdeka for Malaya (1957), 233–35, 315
Meyer, Birgit, 240
Middle East, 147
mines, 36, 96, 213, 266n136
Ministry of Health, 48, 237
Ministry of Information (MOI), 106–21; *Achimota* (1945), 156–57; Africa, 43; African audiences, 134; British Council, 117–19, 140, 270n39; British Documentary Movement, 64; British Empire, 114–15; CFU, 11, 106–21, 129–30, 131, 257n16, 274n101; *Colonial Cinemagazine* (newsreels), 151; Colonial Office, 11, 111–13; colonies, 108, 117, 131, 271n51, 274n101; Crown Film Unit, 109; *Documentary News Letter* (publication), 120; economics, 108; filmstrips, 124–26; Gold Coast, 54; Grierson, John, 109; Huxley, Gervas, 71, 131, 269n22; information office/rs, 124; Latham, Geoffrey, 43, 254n111; *Local Government* (1943), 119; mobile exhibition, 108, 122, 266n121; *Mr. English at Home* (1940), 61, 64, 257n16; Nigeria, 54; primitivity, theories on, 109, 274n98; propaganda, 269n20; radio, 128; Raw Stock Scheme, 131; Sellers, William, 43, 56, 88, 108, 111, 112, 113, 120, 274n98; specialized techniques, 71; *Springtime in an English Village* (1944), 140; VD films, 276n119; war and CFU/World War II, 54, 106–21, 270n39, 274n101
Mixed Farming (1948), 102, 312
mobile exhibition, 91–98; advertisements, 213; Africa, 108, 122–23, 207; barges, 207; BEKE, 35, 38; *Black Cotton* (1927), 55; *The Boy Kumasenu* (1952), 200; British Council, 117; British Empire, 84–85, 94; Canada, 294n127; CFU, 2, 4, 5, 9, 84, 104, 269n21; Champion, Arthur, 87, 122, 272n61; citizenship, 86, 104; Colonial Office, 33–34; colonies, 49–50, 84–88, 91–98, 240; Cyprus, 285n124; documentaries, 16; East Africa, 216, 264n99; economics, 34; education, 83, 93, 253n104; Egypt, 123; EMB, 16, 55; film history, 243; filmstrips, 124, 125, 126; Gale, Beresford, 33–34; GCFU, 200; Gold Coast, 9, 54, 56, 70, 92–93, 94, 95fig., 96, 98, 101fig.; Grace, H. M., 253n104; Grierson, John, 16, 55; Gubara, Gadalla, 241; "Handbook of Instructions for Mobile Cinema and Travelling Projector Vans," 88; Huxley, Gervas, 269n21; imperialism, 16; independence, 96, 97, 240; information office/rs, 122–23; instructional films, 97; Jamaica, 41, 86, 94, 96, 97, 219, 220, 268n153; Kenya, 5, 43, 87, 89, 97, 98, 116–17, 122, 210, 240, 267n143; Lironi, H. E., 70; local voices, 56, 84–91, 93–94, 263n91; MacDonald, Malcolm, 55–56, 256n146; Malaya, 210; Mauritius, 121; mines, 96, 266n136; modernization, 55; MOI, 108, 122, 266n121; nationhood, 104; Nell, Louis, 131; Nigeria, 5, 44, 47, 54, 109fig., 207, 213, 256n146, 264n95; Northern Rhodesia, 96; Nyasaland, 96–97; Odunton, J. B., 80; Pearson, George, 92; political control, 94–98; political events, 85–86, 93; propaganda, 93; Rennalls, Martin, 90; resistance, 91–98; *Royal Review* (1939), 116–17; rural health units, 46–47; sanitation, 46; Sierra Leone, 240; Slater, Montagu, 89–90; Spurr, Norman F., 83; staff, 56; *Swollen Shoot* (1946), 163; Tanganyika, 38fig., 92, 240; Tanzania, 97; trade, 16; Uganda, 123, 240; UNESCO, 87–88, 265n103; United States, 240; war and

Index | 335

CFU, 55; West Africa, 33–34, 94; Zanzibar, 123. *See also* Sellers, William: mobile exhibition
Mobile Films West Africa Ltd., 213
modernization: Africa, 162, 164, 167; An African Conference in London (1948) (film/event), 178; *The Boy Kumasenu* (1952), 198; British film, 48–51, 55, 91; British Guiana, 223; CEF, 261n60; CFU, 7; children, 261n60; colonies, 48–51, 55–56; film techniques, 227; Gold Coast, 55–56; health, 51; industries, 162, 164, 178, 227; Jamaica, 224, 225; JFU, 189, 224; Kracauer, Siegfried, 260n53; mobile exhibition, 55; *Mr. English at Home* (1940), 62–63, 257n10; *Nairobi* (1950), 172–73; Nigeria, 55–56, 212, 233; *Portrait of Trinidad* (1957), 229; radio, 127; *This Land of Ours* (1962), 231; *Weaving in Togoland* (1946), 164
Mombasa Times (newspaper), 122
Monthly Film Bulletin (publication), 236
Morgan, W. S., 112, 119, 124, 131, 271n42
Morris, Kate, 115
Morrison, Herbert, 176
Morton-Williams, Peter, xvi, 98–103
Moseley-Wood, Rachel, 230, 231
Mr. English at Home (1940), 60–65; Africa, 61, 113; African audiences, 61–65, 257n11; British Empire, 104; CFU, xv, 59, 60–61, 64, 113, 238, 257n16, 311; Champion, Arthur, 83–84; Colonial Office, 64; colonies and British film, 61, 62, 64–65; *A Day with an English Baby Boy* (ca. 1937), 53; education, 61; film techniques, 63–65; Gaskin, E. A. L., 258n18; gender, 61–62; hygiene, 61; Iwowo, Samantha, 238; labor, 62, 65; Maddison, John, 73; modernization, 62–63, 257n10; MOI, 61, 64, 257n16; Pearson, George, 61; primitivity, theories on, 63–64; school/children, 64, 75; Sellers, William, 61–64, 83–84, 258n17; West Africa, 64, 258n17
Mr. Mensah Builds a House (1955), 201–5, 313
Mufulira Copper Mines, 36
Muscatt, Tony, 230–31, 237, 239, 242
Muthalib, Hassan, 230

Nairobi, 123, 165, 171, 172, 213
Nairobi (1950), 150, 172–73, 312
National Baby Week Council, 48

National Film Board of Canada, 14
nationalism, 6, 8, 41, 163, 198, 216, 224
nationhood, 151–61, 195–206; Africa, 195–206; *The Boy Kumasenu* (1952), 197; *Builders of the Nation* (1958), 221–22, 227, 314; CFU, 104, 150, 151–61, 237; Creech-Jones, Arthur, 175; economics, 222; *Freedom for Ghana* (1957), 236; Ghana, 238–39; *Government By the People* (1960), 230; Graham, Sean, 203, 206; Grierson, John, 159, 195–206; health, 209, 212; industries, 212–13; Jamaica, 227, 236; JFU, 221–22; labor, 41–42; Larkin, Brian, 212; *Let's Stop Them* (1953), 223; Malaya, 234; Margaret, Princess, 232; *Merdeka for Malaya* (1957), 236; MFU, 210–11; mobile exhibition, 104; *A Nation is Born* (1958/1962), 231–32, 314; Nigeria, 212; Nkrumah, Kwame, 238–39; postwar, 161; religion, 212; Shaw, Alexander, 294n126; sports, 181; *Together We Build* (1953), 222; Trinidad, 206, 232; *Uganda Hails Independence* (1962), 236–37; University of West Indies, 189; West Indies, 222. *See also* independence
Nation Is Born, A (1958), 232, 314
Nation Is Born, A (1962), 231–32
Native Welfare (n. d.), 131
Nell, Louis, 131–32
newsreels, 136, 138, 211, 214, 216, 223, 230, 240. *See also* individual newsreels
New York Times (newspaper), 197
New Zealand, 25, 28–29, 48, 146–47, 160
Nigeria: absences, 240; African cinema, 149; *An African in London* (1941), 141; agriculture, 212; audience research, 99; Azikiwe, Nnamdi, 147, 168; barges, 207; Barkas, Geoffrey, 32; Bell, Hesketh, 29; Biafran War, 237; BIF, 28; *Black Cotton* (1927), 20, 27, 30; Bowden, Dennis, 238; Boy Scouts, 138; British Empire Exhibition (Wembley, 1924–25), 20, 21fig.; Carstairs, C. Y., 289n51; CFU, 4, 5, 6, 153–54, 161, 162, 238; children, 209; *Comet* (newspaper), 157; *Community Development in Awgu Division, Nigeria* (1949), 100, 120, 150, 312; Cooper, Harold, 185; *Daily Comet* (newspaper), 147–48; *Daybreak in Udi* (1949), 63, 159, 160, 310; documentaries, 240; Eastern Nigerian Unit, 237; education, 212; Federal Film Unit,

Nigeria: absences *(continued)*
207–8, 237; Film Unit of the Northern Region, 238; film units, 153–54, 193, 206–8, 209, 238; *Forward to a New Nigeria* (1958), 207, 313; *Giant in the Sun* (1959), 212–14; Gold Coast, 181; Gordonu, J. S. D., 137; health, 10, 45, 212; *Health and Baby Week, Lagos, 1956* (1956), 209; health films, 50; independence, 168, 194, 206–7, 209, 211– 13, 231, 232–33, 313; industries, 212–14; *Infant Welfare Work in Nigeria* (ca. 1933), 48–49, 50, 310; information office/rs, 124; instructional films, 240; Larkin, Brian, 212; Legislative Council, 167; Macpherson, John, 180–81; mines, 213; mobile exhibition, 5, 44, 47, 54, 109*fig.*, 207, 213, 256n146, 264n95; modernization, 55–56, 212, 233; MOI, 54; Morton-Williams, Peter, xvi, 98; *Mr. English at Home* (1940), 64; nationhood, 212; newsreels, 240; Nollywood, 238, 240–41; Northern Nigeria Information Service, 207, 212–13, 214; Obiaya, Ikechukwu, 240–41; Osakwe, Albert, 182; *Our Land and People* (1959), 212; propaganda, 207, 217*fig.*; radio, 127; Raw Stock Scheme, 131; religion, 212, 289n61; Samuelson, Sydney, 88; sanitation, 45–46; *Self-Government for Western Nigeria* (1958), 207, 211–12, 313; Sellers, William, xv, 5, 10, 13–14, 19, 27–28, 31, 37–38, 43–55, 65–66, 70, 89, 108, 130, 154, 162, 208, 238, 280n36; Slater, Montagu, 89–90; *Smallpox* (1950), 208; Snazelle, Lionel, 196; Spurr, Norman F., 79, 83; tours, 179–81; training schools, 183–84, 185, 187*fig.*; Waterfield, O., 70; WNTV, 233, 293n115; *Young Nigeria* (ca. 1937), 50–51, 310. *See also* Central Office of Information (COI); Health Propaganda Unit (Nigeria)
Nigeria Greets the Queen (1956), 211, 216, 313
Nigeria Hails Her Prime Minister (1957), 207, 313
Nigeria Hails Independence (1960), 232–33, 313
Nigerian Cocoa Farmer (1948), 150, 310
Nigerian Film Unit (NFU), xvi, 12, 82, 99, 168, 185, 195–96, 206–18, 241, 288n46, 289n57, 313. *See also* Federal Film Unit (Nigeria); *individual films*

Nigerian Footballers in England (1949), 151, 182, 240, 312
Nigerian football team, 179–81, 182, 284n98, 284n99
Nigeria's First Women Police (1956), 209–10, 313
1955: The Year in Malaya, 95, 315
Nkrumah, Kwame, 198, 234, 235, 238–39, 293n119
Noble, George, 196, 205, 206, 238*fig.*
Nollywood, 238, 240–41
nonfiction films. *See* British film; *individual film types*
Northern Nigeria Information Service, 207, 212–13, 214
Northern Province Agricultural Show (1952), 215, 314
Northern Rhodesia, 35, 36, 39–40, 96, 123, 129, 131, 137, 252n82, 275n106, 286n1
Notcutt, Leslie, 18, 36–43, 66
No Tears for Ananse (1968), 237–38, 313
Nyasaland, 35, 39–40, 96–97, 123, 134

Obiaya, Ikechukwu, 240–41
Odunton, J. B., 80–83, 263n76
Oil Palm Industry, The (n.d.), 51–52, 310
Okanta, Bob, 183–84
Oldham, Joseph, 19
One Family (1930), 25–27, 128, 250n42, 310
"One Step Ahead" (article), 80–81
Oni of Ife, 176–77
Ormsby-Gore, William, 40
Orr, James Russell, 32–33, 43, 55, 251n69
Osakwe, Albert, 182
Otigba, J. A., 183–84, 209, 285n115
Our Government at Work (series), 222, 314
Our Land and People (1959), 212, 313
Overseas Film and Television Centre (OFTVC), xvi, 214, 216–18, 220, 229–31, 237, 238, 239, 242
Overseas Rediffusion Limited, 233, 293n115

Page, John, 156–58, 159
Pamba (1950), 166–67, 281n54, 312
Parr, James, 29
Paterson, A. R., 18, 31, 34–35, 36, 276n119
Paynter, Bob, 116, 152–53, 277n131
Pearson, George, 77–80; African cinema, 149; *An African in England: An English Village* (1945), 143*fig.*; British film, 58;

CFU, 1, 2, 4, 58–59, 77–80, 150, 155*fig.*, 168; colonies, 59; Crown Film Unit, 110; *Fight Tuberculosis at Home* (1946), 162–63; "The Film in Colonial Development" (conference), 160, 220; filmstrips, 90; health, 169; JFU, 220; mobile exhibition, 92; *Mr. English at Home* (1940), 61; Odunton, J. B., 82–83; OFTVC, 217; Oni of Ife, 177; *Pamba* (1950), 166–67; primitivity, theories on, 59, 78–79, 174*fig.*, 217, 262n70; Rennalls, Martin, 219; training schools, 192; WNTV, 233
Peng, Chin, 95
Plageman, Nate, 180
plague, 13, 44, 47. *See also* Anti-Plague Operations, Lagos (1929, 1932, 1933, 1937)
Plainsmen of Barotseland (1944), 131, 132, 311
political control: Africa, 95; British film, 32, 94–98, 192, 195, 246n16; CFU, 41, 98, 168; colonies, 17, 94–98, 195, 246n16; education, 33–34; educational films, 17, 42; independence, 202, 231; *I Will Speak English* (1954), 202; Kenya, 98, 210; Latham, Geoffrey, 41; mobile exhibition, 94–98; *Mr. Mensah Builds a House* (1955), 201–2; schoolchildren, 42; Sellers, William, 47. *See also* biopolitics
Portrait of Trinidad (1957), 228–29, 314
Port Royal (n. d.), 227, 314
postcolonialism, 7, 8–9, 12, 149, 239, 240, 243. *See also* independence; nationhood
postwar: Africa, 135, 152; British Documentary Movement, 294n126; British Empire, 107, 111, 114, 115, 144, 149; British film, 138; CFU, 2, 12, 13, 107, 115, 120–23, 125, 142–48, 150–52, 164, 167, 187, 219; Champion, Arthur, 122; Colonial Office, 179; colonies, 72, 115, 138, 144–48, 159; economics, 12, 222; "The Film in Colonial Development" (conference), 174*fig.*; film units, 195; Grierson, John, 159; information office/rs, 123; JFU, 219; Malaya, 160; Morrison, Herbert, 176; nationhood, 161; tours, 224
Potter, Simon, 39, 128–29
practices/principles/policies, 60–105; African audiences, 72–80; audience research, 98–103; British film, 28, 65–72; CFU, 4, 10–11, 99, 102, 103–5,
116, 129–30, 151, 152, 188; children, 72–80; colonies, 28, 65–72, 151, 173–75, 188; GCFU, 197; *Mr. English at Home* (1940), 63–65; orthodoxy challenges, 80–84; resistance, 91–98; Sellers, William, 61, 64, 74; voices, 84–91. *See also* specialized techniques
Pratt, Fred, 126–27
primitivity, theories on, 31–35; AFP, 216; African audiences, 29–31, 52–53, 65–68; animation, 168–70; BBC, 61, 68, 126; BEKE, 37–38, 41; Bell, Hesketh, 29–30; BIF, 28; *Britain's Birthright* (1924), 249n34; British Council, 118, 271n42; British film, 31–32, 124–25, 127; CFU, 28, 53, 67, 68, 72, 111, 153, 260n52; Champion, Arthur, 83–84, 122; *Colonial Cinema* (1942–54), 98; colonies, 158; Davis, John Merle, 36; East Africa, 165–66; "The Film in Colonial Development" (conference), 173; "Films for Primitive Peoples" (articles), 65–68, 84–85, 258n21; filmstrips, 124–25; film techniques, 1–2, 36, 65–68, 75, 259n39, 262n70, 274n99; Franklin, Harry, 274n96; Graham, Sean, 81; Grierson, John, 174*fig.*; Gubara, Gadalla, 295n145; health films, 48; Larson, Egon, 260n52; Latham, Geoffrey, 37–38, 41; Lironi, H. E., 70; "Mass Education in the Colonies" (memorandum), 72; MOI, 109, 274n98; *Mr. English at Home* (1940), 63–64; Notcutt, Leslie, 41; Odunton, J. B., 80–81; Orr, James Russell, 32; Passfield (Lord), 31–32; Pearson, George, 59, 78–79, 174*fig.*, 217, 262n70; proposals, 31–35; radio, 126–27; Sellers, William, xv, 29, 37–38, 48, 53, 61, 65–68, 72, 78, 87, 118, 124, 186, 258n26, 258n31, 274n98; Spurr, Norman F., 79–80; tours, 180–81; VD films, 136; Vernon, Roland, 33; *Victory Parade* (1946), 146; Wilson, John, 274n98; *The Winged Scourge* (1943), 169. *See also* specialized techniques
Prince of Wales. *See* Edward VIII, Prince of Wales
Princess Margaret Visits Jamaica (1955), 225–26, 314. *See also* Margaret, Princess
Production of Films (conference, 1945), 219

Index

Progress in Kojokrom (1953), 120, 201–4, 288n30, 313
Progress in the Colonies: An African Hospital (ca. 1933), 51, 53, 130, 311
Projection of England, The (Tallents) (pamphlet), 62
propaganda: *Amenu's Child* (1950), 100; animation, 170; BBC, 39, 128; British film, 31, 123, 264n99; Ceylon Tea Propaganda Board, 16; CFU, 14, 106–8, 112, 113–14, 132, 213, 274n101; Champion, Arthur, 122; colonies, 31, 111, 115, 119, 125, 128, 274n101; Dickson, A. G., 264n99; East Africa Command Mobile Propaganda Unit, 134; *Fight for Life* (1946), 157; filmstrips, 124, 125; health films, 45–46; information office/rs, 121, 123–24; JFU, 221; media, 125; Mercier, E. L., 111; MFU, 210; mobile exhibition, 93; MOI, 269n20; nationalism, 41; Nigeria, 207, 217fig.; *Pamba* (1950), 166; radio, 127–28; schoolchildren, 250n43; Sellers, William, 112, 169; Smyth, Rosaleen, 115; Spurr, Norman F., 83, 93; Tanzania, 97; training schools, 70; Uganda, 237; war and CFU, 107–8; *We Want Rubber* (1943), 131; World War II, 54–55, 111, 119, 127, 128, 264n99; Wright, Basil, 159. *See also* Health Propaganda Unit (Nigeria); Ministry of Information (MOI)
Prosser, A. R. G., 200

Queen Is Crowned, A (1953), 95, 311. *See also* Elizabeth II (queen); royal family

race: AFP, 216; African audiences, 10; *An African in England: An English Village* (1945), 140–42; *Africa's Fighting Men* (1943), 133–34; animation, 168–69; audience research, 71, 98; BBC, 128; BEKE, 39; Bell, Hesketh, 250n52; CFU, 116, 153; Chaplin, Charlie, 52; Colonial Office, 159; Cooper, Harold, 185; East Africa, 165; educational films, 17, 28, 32, 34; filmstrips, 125; film units, 195; *Freedom for Ghana* (1957), 234; Gale, W. D., 129; *Gold Coast Justice* (n. d.), 253n104; *Hello West Indies* (1943), 95–96; Impahim, T. K., 147; Malaya, 234; media, 124, 125; *Mr. English at Home* (1940), 62; nationalism, 8; *Nigerian Footballers in England* (1949), 182; *Shaihu Umar* (1976), 238;
specialized techniques, 71; *Springtime in an English Village* (1944), 140; staff, 116; tours, 180, 181; training schools, 188; Van Bever, L., 260n50; West Africa, 195; World War II, 106. *See also* African audiences; primitivity, theories on
radio, 11, 39, 107–8, 121, 124, 126–29, 223, 233
Rank, J. Arthur, 74, 76fig., 77, 262n66
Rathbone, Richard, 233
Raw Stock Scheme, 130–37; Africa, 130–37, 154; Caribbean, 190fig.; CFU, xv, 32, 34, 57, 69, 130–32; Champion, Arthur, 130–31; *Colonial Cinema* (1942–54), 69, 133; Dominions, India and Colonies (panel), 34; Gambia, 131, 144, 154; information office/rs, 131; London, 133; MOI, 131; Northern Rhodesia, 275n106; Passfield (Lord), 32; Sellers, William, 19, 69; Sierra Leone, 131, 154; specialized techniques, 69; Tanganyika, 275n106; victory celebrations, 144; war and CFU, 130–37. *See also individual films*
Registration of Voters (1956), 214, 313
religion, 212, 255n134, 289n61
Rennalls, Martin, 41, 82, 90, 188–90, 202, 218–21, 225–27, 237, 241, 291n81, 292n92
resistance, 91–98. *See also* independence; political control
Revue Internationale de Filmologie, La (publication), 61, 73
Reynolds, Glenn, 18, 32, 41
Ride with Care (1959), 223–24, 314
Road to Independence (1962), 229–30, 315
Roan Antelope Mines, 36
Roberts, Captain, 130, 131
Robertson, Malcolm, 271n40
Rotha, Paul, 16–17, 19, 21, 248n16
Royal Commonwealth Society, 76
Royal Empire Society, 42, 176
royal family, 125, 128, 211, 236, 295n140. *See also individuals; individual films*
Royal Review (1939), 116–17
Royal Sanitary Institute, 13
Royal Society of Arts (RSA), 33, 61
rules. *See* practices/principles/policies; Sellers, William: rules; specialized techniques
rural health units, 46–47, 48, 50

Sabine, Noel, 113, 118, 128, 157, 158, 233
St. Juste, Franklyn, 184, 241

Salt, Brian, 239
Samaki (1959), 214
Samuelson, Sydney, 88, 116, 181, 196, 208, 214
Sandon, Emma, 198
sanitation, 13, 32, 33, 44–48, 51, 162–63, 208, 209, 310. *See also* health
Sargent, Peter, 152, 155fig.
Scenes in the British Empire (series). *See* Empire series (1925–1928)
Schauder, Leon, 132
schoolchildren: British Empire, 42, 250n46; British film, 27, 249n35, 250n43; citizenship, 14, 253n104; colonies, 253n104; *Education in England: A Village School* (1945), 139, 277n127; GBI, 42; George, W. H., 248n12; Huxley, Julian, 30; *Let's Build Their Future* (1959), 292n93; *Mr. English at Home* (1940), 64; political control, 42; propaganda, 250n43; sanitation, 46. *See also* children
Scott, H. V., 136
Second Freedom (1943), 119–20
Secrets of Life/Nature (series), 14, 21, 28, 34, 310
See Saw Years (1963), 214, 312
Selassie, Haile, 295n140
self-government. *See* independence; nationhood
Self-Government for Western Nigeria (1958), 207, 211–12, 313
Sellers, William, 44–59; Africa, 43, 108; African audiences, 10–11, 31, 52–53, 56, 61, 64, 78, 110; agriculture, 54; audience research, 100; BBC, 44, 61, 111, 258n31; British Council, 112, 116–17, 118, 120, 271n44; British Empire, 13–14, 54, 72–73, 74; Burns, James, 72–73; Campbell, Alan, 158; CFU, 5, 13–15, 19, 29, 46, 47, 51, 53, 54–59, 61, 103–4, 108–10, 113, 120, 123, 149–50, 155fig., 160; Champion, Arthur, 122, 131; children, 77–78; *Le Cinéma Pour Africains* (pamphlet), 73; citizenship, 11, 47, 104; *Colonial Cinema* (1942–54), 70, 71, 85fig., 94–95, 126; *Colonial Cinemagazine* (newsreels), 151; Colonial Office, 54, 108, 109–10, 112, 120; colonies, 48, 53, 54, 56–57, 72, 77, 91, 112; colonies and British film, 54, 73–74, 91–92, 94–95, 110–11; Crown Film Unit, 64, 108–10; documentaries, 53, 71, 82; East Africa, 165; Eastwood, Christopher, 44, 54, 56; Edmett, E. R., 112; education, 46, 74; exhibition, 84, 88–89; Federal Film Unit (Nigeria), 207; Field, Mary, 74–75; *Fight Tuberculosis at Home* (1946), 162; "Films for Primitive Peoples" (articles), xv, 65–66, 84–85; films of, 310; film/specialized techniques, 10–11, 38, 53, 65–68, 69, 72, 77–78, 98, 103–4, 108, 118, 162, 196, 258n31; filmstrips, 126; film units, 82, 162, 228; Gold Coast, 149, 167; GPO, 58; Graham, Sean, 81, 82, 196, 218; Grierson, John, 159, 160; health, 10, 13–14, 18–19, 27–28, 45–51, 54, 158, 169; Health Congress (Bournemouth, 1955), 13–14; health films, 45, 47–51; Health Propaganda Unit (Nigeria), xv, 45–46, 54, 255n129; Hollywood's cultural imperialism, 169; Home Guards, 138; Huxley, Julian, 71; independence, 13–14; instructional films, 48, 107, 157, 196; Iwowo, Samantha, 238; Jamaica, 188; JFU, 188, 220; Johnson, Geoffrey and Mina, 281n58; Kracauer, Siegfried, 260n53; Larkin, Brian, 47; Lee, Wilfred, 228; Lironi, H. E., 70; local voices, 87, 88–89, 104, 186; Maddison, John, 73; malaria, 169; Malaya, 161; "Mass Education in the Colonies" (memorandum), 72; media, 74; MFU, 161; mobile exhibition, 44, 46–47, 49fig., 54, 56, 92–93, 94–95, 98, 104, 254n115; 288n46; MOI, 43, 56, 88, 108, 111, 112, 113, 120, 274n98; NFU, 12; Odunton, J. B., 80; OFTVC, 216; Oni of Ife, 177; Pearson, George, 59, 77–78; plague, 44, 47; political control, 47; practices/principles/policies, 61, 64, 74; propaganda, 112, 169; Raw Stock Scheme, 19, 69; rules, 64, 65–66, 71–72, 228, 258n17; rural health units, 46–47, 48, 50; sanitation, 44–48, 51, 162–63, 310; Spurr, Norman F., 79–80; staff, 57, 116; TFU, 228; training schools, 186, 188; Uganda, 188; UNESCO, 61; useful cinema, 57, 149–50; Usill, H. V., 124; war and CFU, 54, 57; West Africa, 62, 117; youth, 44, 254n113, 254n114. *See also* Nigeria: Sellers, William; primitivity, theories on: Sellers, William; *individual films*
Seong, Lee Meow, 161

Seven Acres (n. d.), 131
Shaihu Umar (1976), 238, 313
Shaw, Alexander, 236–37, 294n126, 294n127
Shell Film Unit, 238
Sierra Leone, 48, 124, 131, 139, 144, 147, 154–55, 169, 240
Sight and Sound (publication), 38
Singapore, 160
Skinner, Kate, 197–98, 205
Slater, Montagu, 89–90
Slum Clearance and Town Planning (ca. 1933), 51, 53, 310
Smallpox (1950), 99–100, 101–2, 208, 214, 312
Smyth, Rosaleen, 18, 39, 115, 162, 166
Snazelle, Lionel, 82, 155*fig.*, 185, 196, 208, 217*fig.*, 218, 232
Society for the Care of Infants, 48
soil erosion, 37, 43, 122, 167, 169, 170, 192
Somaliland, 33, 122, 192
Song of Ceylon (1934), 16, 310
South Africa, 8, 25, 28, 34, 48, 132, 137, 146–47, 216, 290n73
Southern Rhodesia, 30, 123, 129
Sowande, Fela, 87
specialized techniques, 103–5; AFP, 216; African audiences, 73, 75; animation, 169; audience research, 71–72; CFU, 63–64, 71–72, 103–5, 118, 169, 184, 196; children, 74–75; *Le Cinéma Pour Africains* (pamphlet), 73; *Colonial Cinema* (1942–54), 69–70; documentaries, 16; educational films, 118; Gillan, Angus, 118; Huxley, Gervas, 113; Jamaica, 228; Lironi, H. E., 70; *Local Government* (1943), 119; Maddison, John, 73; "Mass Education in the Colonies" (memorandum), 72; MOI, 71; Morton-Williams, Peter, 103; Pearson, George, 77–78; primitivity, theories on, 118, 258n31; *Progress in Kojokrom* (1953), 203; race, 71; Raw Stock Scheme, 69; Sellers, William, 10–11, 38, 53, 65–68, 69, 72, 77–78, 98, 103–4, 108, 118, 162, 196, 258n31; *Smallpox* (1950), 208; training schools, 184; Waterfield, O., 70. *See also* film techniques; primitivity, theories on
sports, 151, 179–82, 240, 284n98, 284n99, 312
Spotlight on the Colonies (1950), 6, 179, 311
Springtime in an English Village (1944), 140–41, 311

Spurr, Norman F.: African cinema, 216; CFU, 17, 79–80, 99, 215, 218; *A Challenge to Ignorance* (1950), 167; East Africa, 166–67, 290n71; Ghana, 239; hookworm, 169–70; Johnson, Geoffrey and Mina, 281n58; local voices, 88, 90–91, 93; mobile exhibition, 83; Nigeria, 79, 83; Odunton, J. B., 82–83; *Pamba* (1950), 281n54; propaganda, 83, 93; Sellers, William, 79–80; *Smallpox* (1950), 208; Tanganyika, 215–16; training schools, 192; Uganda, 79, 83, 166, 167, 169; UNESCO, 239, 290n71; *We Benefit—We Pay* (1953), 290n71
Stenning, Thomas, 180
Stewart, J.L., 157–58
Stollery, Martin, 175, 205
Storck, Henri, 74–75
story/narrative, 78, 82–83, 199, 286n9
Strickland, C. F., 89, 275n106
Stubbs, Jonathan, 192
Sudan, 192, 194, 214, 241, 294n126
Sudan Film Unit, 241
sugar industry, 232
Sukumaland, 93, 158, 314
Sukumuland Trade and Agricultural Exhibition, The (1954), 215, 314
Sweden, 240
Swithinbank, Charles, 259n41
Swollen Shoot (1946), 163, 280n42, 311

Tallents, Stephen, 62, 247n6
Tanganyika: African audiences, 71; African cinema, 215–16; BEKE, 35, 37; Boy Scouts, 138; Densham, Denny, 294n126; film units, 154, 165, 215–16, 314; health films, 48; independence, 195, 294n126; information office/rs, 123; Kingston Davies, Robert, 275n106; mobile exhibition, 38*fig.*, 92, 240; OFTVC, 214; proposals, 33; Raw Stock Scheme, 131, 275n106; *Smallpox* (1950), 208; Spurr, Norman F., 215–16; training schools, 192
Tanganyika African National Union (TANU), 291n75
Tanzania, 83, 97
Tate and Lyle (company), 232
Taylor, Donald, 35
Taylor, John, 160
Theory of Film (Kracauer), 73
"The Royal Family" (filmstrip), 125
These Are London Firemen (1942), 137, 311

This Is a Barrage Balloon (1941), 137, 311
This Is a Special Constable (1941), 137
This Land of Ours (1962), 231, 315
This Wonderful World (1957–65), 23
Thomas, Dr., 51–52
Thomas, Hugh, 96
Thomson, Dr., 45, 254n115
Timbermen from Honduras (1943), 138, 311
Times, 23, 24, 29–30, 41, 43, 145, 172, 245n2
Together We Build (1953), 222, 314
Too Late (1957), 221, 241, 314
Touch and Go (1953), 210, 315
Tour of H. R. H., the Princess Royal (1957), 207, 313
tours, 173, 179–81, 182, 224, 231–33, 235, 240, 284n98, 284n99
To Vote Is a Great Duty (1950), 223, 314
Towards Independence (1962), 230, 314
Towards True Democracy (1947), 150, 167–68, 312
trade: *Atlantic* (1940), 55; British Empire Exhibition (Wembley, 1924–25), 20; British film, 10, 14, 15–16, 21, 24, 32, 249n35; CFU, 4, 179; *Cocoa Rehabilitation* (1951), 191; colonies, 21, 25, 27; Davson, Edward, 20; documentaries, 15; East Africa, 34–35; *Eat Jamaican* (n. d.), 227; EATUC, 172; EMB, 14, 16; geography films, 20; Grierson, John, 14; imperialism, 14, 179; mobile exhibition, 16; *Mr. English at Home* (1940), 62; Orr, James Russell, 32; Paterson, A. R., 34–35; *Portrait of Trinidad* (1957), 229; *Spotlight on the Colonies* (1950), 179
training schools, 183–93; CFU, 2, 5, 70, 90, 151, 173, 183–93, 237, 241; Colonial Office, 186; colonies, 185, 192; decolonization, 149, 151, 187; economics, 186; film units, 149, 183–84, 195; imperialism, 5; independence, 188; industries, 186–87; local voices, 186; OFTVC, 217–18; Pearson, George, 192; propaganda, 70; race, 188; Rennalls, Martin, 219; Sellers, William, 186, 188; specialized techniques, 184; Spurr, Norman F., 192. *See also* Accra training school (1948); *individual training schools*
Travel and Industrial Development Association (TIDA), 108, 116
Trinidad: *Cocoa Rehabilitation* (1951), 190–91; Commonwealth Parliamentary Conference (1969), 240; *Delay Means Death* (1951), 285n122; Dominions, India and Colonies (panel), 256n149; economics, 232; Graham, Sean, 104, 196–97, 206; independence, xvi, 229–30, 240; nationhood, 206, 232; *Portrait of Trinidad* (1957), 228–29, 314; *Road to Independence* (1962), 229–30; sugar industry, 232; *Two Royal Visits* (1966), 239–40, 315; *University in Trinidad* (1960), 229, 315; *To Vote Is a Great Duty* (1950), 223, 314; West Indies training school, 188–89
Trinidad and Tobago Government Film Unit, 229, 231, 291n181, 314–15
Trinidad Film Unit (TFU), 218, 228–30, 314
Trutor, Jonathan, 231
tuberculosis, 1–2, 90, 162–63, 191–92, 280n36, 285n122, 312
Tully, Montgomery, 206
Two Brothers, The (1940), 137, 311
Two Farmers, The (1948), 102, 312
Two Friends, The (1963), 237, 314
Two Generations (1955), 214, 312
Two Royal Visits (1966), 239–40, 315

Uganda: BEKE, 35, 37; Bell, Hesketh, 29; *Black Cotton* (1927), 30; *Boy Scouts in Uganda* (1945), 138, 311; CFU, 5, 188; *A Challenge to Ignorance* (1950), 167; Champion, Arthur, 122; disciplinary expertise, 165; filmstrips, 126; film units, 154, 165, 215, 236–37; hookworm, 169; Hyde, John, 158–59; independence, xvi, 5, 194, 236–37, 314; information office/rs, 123; mobile exhibition, 123, 240; OFTVC, 214, 237; *Pamba* (1950), 166; propaganda, 237; proposals, 33; Raw Stock Scheme, 131; Roberts, Captain, 130, 131; Sellers, William, 188; Shaw, Alexander, 294n126; Spurr, Norman F., 79, 83, 166, 169; training schools, 188
Uganda Film Unit (UFU), 215, 236–37, 294n127, 313–14
Uganda Hails Independence (1962), 236–37, 314
Uganda Police (1942), 130, 311
Underwood, Martin, 240
UNESCO: CFU, 4; educational films, 150; *Enemy in the Night* (1960), 239; *Farmer Brown Learns Good Dairying* (1951/film) (filmstrip), 273n82; Field, Mary, 14, 74–75; Gover, Victor, 214; Graham, Sean, 196–97; Grierson, John, 17,

UNESCO: CFU *(continued)*
159–60, 174*fig.*, 175; Huxley, Julian, 159; instructional films, 97, 150; Marier, Roger, 97; mobile exhibition, 87–88, 265n103; Otigba, J. A., 285n115; Sellers, William, 61; Shaw, Alexander, 294n126; *Smallpox* (1950), 208; Spurr, Norman F., 239, 290n71; Wright, Basil, 294n127
United Gold Coast Convention (UGCC), 163
United States, 115, 128, 232, 235, 240, 289n57, 292n92, 294n120. *See also* Hollywood's cultural imperialism
United We Stand (1953), 192
University College of the West Indies (1951), 150, 189–90, 229, 312
university films, 150, 189, 312
University in Trinidad (1960), 229, 315
University of the Gold Coast (1948), 150, 312
"useful" cinema, 4, 5, 12, 57, 149–50. *See also individual films; individual film types*
Usill, H. V., 124, 129–30, 275n108

Van Bever, L., 260n50
Vasili, Phil, 180
Vaughan, Megan, 50
VD films, 102, 136–37, 221, 276n119, 276n123
Vernon, Roland, 33, 35–36
Victoria, Queen, 145, 230, 246n16
Victory Parade (1946), 144–48, 311
voices. *See* local voices

Waide, C. L., 51
Wales, Prince of. *See* Edward VIII, Prince of Wales
war and CFU, 106–48; absences, 130–37, 141–42; Africa, 130–37; African audiences, 134; *Basuto Troops on Active Service* (1945), 135; BFI, 56; British Council, 116–21; British Empire, 11, 55, 106–8, 136; *The British Empire at War* (newsreel), 132, 133, 311; British film, 55, 129; colonies, 54, 106–7, 120, 129, 133, 137–44; Empire series (1925–1928), 55; England, projection of, 137–44; establishment, xv; Gold Coast, 9, 84–85; Home Guards, 138; imperialism, 106–8, 133, 144; India, 135–36; information office/rs, 121; instructional films, 55, 107; labor, 107; media, 107–8, 121–30; mobile exhibition, 55; mobilization, 2,

55, 106–7; MOI, 106–21, 274n101; *Mr. English at Home* (1940), 62–63; propaganda, 54–55, 107–8; Raw Stock Scheme, 130–37; Sellers, William, 54, 57; *Springtime in an English Village* (1944), 140; *Victory Parade* (1946), 144–48; West Indies, 56. *See also* interwar Britain; postwar; World War II
Wasson, Haidee, 5
Waterfield, O., 70, 131
Watt, Harry, 25
Weaving in Togoland (1946), 150, 162, 164, 273n77, 312
We Benefit—We Pay (1953), 215, 290n71, 314
Weigall, Alistair, 42
Welcome Home (1946), 144, 311
Welcome Home Soldiers (1949), 187, 312
welfare, 2, 7, 12, 50, 72, 114, 131, 143–44, 149, 150, 162, 211. *See also* Colonial Development and Welfare Acts (1940, 1945); Department of Social Welfare and Community Development (Ghana); *Infant Welfare Work in Nigeria* (ca. 1933)
Weller, Milton, 188–89, 219
Welsh, Trevor, 188–90, 219
West Africa: *Amenu's Child* (1950), 81; animation, 168; *Anti-Plague Operations, Lagos* (1929, 1932, 1933, 1937), 163; BEKE, 43; *Black Cotton* (1927), 20; British Empire Exhibition (Wembley, 1924–25), 20–21; British film, 94, 127; CFU, xvi, 2, 41, 56, 129–30, 132, 153*fig.*, 164; East Africa, 165–66; Feilmann, Captain, 132; *A Film School in West Africa* (1949), 184–87, 312; film units, 188, 195; Gale, Beresford, 33–34; "Handbook of Instructions for Mobile Cinema and Travelling Projector Vans," 88; industries, 152; information office/rs, 123–24; mobile exhibition, 94; Mobile Films West Africa Ltd., 213; *Mr. English at Home* (1940), 64, 258n17; Page, John, 159; race, 195; radio, 127; *Royal Review* (1939), 117; Sellers, William, 62, 117; Snazelle, Lionel, 218; sports, 181; *Victory Parade* (1946), 147; *Weaving in Togoland* (1946), 164; World War II, 114. *See also* Africa; Gold Coast; Nigeria
West Africa (journal), 20, 23, 81–82, 173, 176
West African Review (publication), 198

West African Students' Union (WASU), 141–42
West African University (1948), 150, 312
West Africa Photography Unit, 273n77, 273n78
Western Nigeria TV (WNTV), 233, 293n115
West Indians with the R. A. F. in Britain (1944), 137–38, 311
West Indies, 218–30; BBC, 274n91; BIF, 28–29; CFU, 155; Colonial Office, 56; education, 219; filmstrips, 126; film units, 218–30; GBI, 35, 42; Graham, Sean, 196–97, 206, 218; Hammond, S. A., 35; *The Heart of an Empire* (1935), 52; *Hello West Indies* (1943), 95–96, 310; nationhood, 222; *Timbermen from Honduras* (1943), 138; *University College of the West Indies* (1951), 150, 189–90, 229, 312; *University in Trinidad* (1960), 229; war and CFU, 56. *See also individual countries*
West Indies Federation, 228, 232, 293n113
West Indies training school, xvi, 82, 185, 188–92, 195
We Want Rubber (1943), 131
White, Horace, 192
Why Not You? (1950), 150, 166, 312
Wideson, Rene, 192, 285n123
Williams, Billy, 152, 155fig.
Williams, Deane, 5
Wilson, Harold, 194
Wilson, James, 127, 129
Wilson, John, 129–30, 265n119, 274n98, 274n99, 286n1
Winged Scourge, The (1943), 169, 310
Wives of Nendi (1949), 102, 312
Woolfe, Harry Bruce, 21, 31–32, 34, 42, 55
World War I, 15. *See also* interwar Britain

World War II: absences, 141–42, 146–47; Africa, 126, 130–37, 276n124; African audiences, 127, 133–34; British Council, 116–21, 270n39, 271n40; British Empire, 55, 84–85, 106–8, 114–15, 136, 173; British film, 106–8, 117, 138; *British News* (newsreel), 117; colonies, 106–8, 114, 117, 119, 128; *Crown Colonist* (publication), 114; Crown Film Unit, 63, 106–7; documentaries, 63; economics, 106, 138; filmstrips, 125–26; Gold Coast, 9, 84–85, 126–27, 132–33, 134; Grierson, John, 14; Huxely, Gervas, 114; imperialism, 106, 115, 138, 270n28; information office/rs, 121–22, 129; interwar Britain, 134; Kenya, 121, 122, 123; London, 117; media, 127, 128–29; MOI, 54, 117, 118, 270n39, 274n101; *Mr. English at Home* (1940), 63; propaganda, 54–55, 111, 119, 127, 128, 264n99; race, 106; radio, 126–27; *Springtime in an English Village* (1944), 140; *Welcome Home Soldiers* (1949), 187; West Africa, 114. *See also* war and CFU
Worry Free (1954), 210, 315
Wright, Basil, 16, 159–61, 197, 199, 204, 206, 294n127
Wynne, Donald, 216

You Can Help Your Children (1952), 228, 314
Young, H. R., 189
Young Nigeria (ca. 1937), 50–51, 310
Your Police (1962), 202, 239, 313

Zambia, 286n1. *See also* Northern Rhodesia
Zanzibar, 33, 123, 154, 165

Founded in 1893,
UNIVERSITY OF CALIFORNIA PRESS
publishes bold, progressive books and journals
on topics in the arts, humanities, social sciences,
and natural sciences—with a focus on social
justice issues—that inspire thought and action
among readers worldwide.

The UC PRESS FOUNDATION
raises funds to uphold the press's vital role
as an independent, nonprofit publisher, and
receives philanthropic support from a wide
range of individuals and institutions—and from
committed readers like you. To learn more, visit
ucpress.edu/supportus.

www.ingramcontent.com/pod-product-compliance
Lightning Source LLC
Chambersburg PA
CBHW021335230426
43666CB00006B/297